Art Rust's
Illustrated History
of the
BLACK
ATHLETE

Art Rust's Illustrated History of the BLACK ATHLETE

Edna and Art Rust Jr.

DOUBLEDAY & COMPANY, INC.

Garden City, New York

1985

DESIGNED BY MARILYN SCHULMAN

Library of Congress Cataloging in Publication Data

Rust, Art, 1927–
    Art Rust's Illustrated history of the Black athlete.

    Includes index.
    1. Sports—United States—History. 2. Afro-American
athletes. I. Rust, Edna. II. Title. III. Title:
Illustrated history of the Black athlete.
GV583.R87   796′.08996073

ISBN 0-385-15139-X
    0-385-15140-3 (pbk.)

Library of Congress Catalog Card Number: 79-6639
Copyright © 1985 by Sports Channel, Inc.

Photo Credits

(LEGEND: T=Top photo, M=Middle, B=Bottom, L=Left, R=Right, TL=Top Left, etc.)

A.P./Wide World Photos: 55, 63, 68(TL, BL, BR), 69(TR, ML), 75(TL), 77(TR, MR, BR), 90, 97(TR), 99(TL), 118, 124(TL, BR), 160(B), 161, 163, 168, 176(B), 185(B), 192, 199, 203, 207, 274, 325, 334(TR), 335(TL), 361(B); Atlanta Falcons: 287(TR); Atlanta Hawks: 333(TL, MR); Author's Collection: 5(R), 12, 13, 14, 15, 17, 18(B), 20, 22, 24, 26, 35, 41, 44(BR), 46, 51, 69(MR, BR), 74, 75(BR), 77, 79, 81, 89, 93, 105, 107, 117, 134, 136, 137, 138, 139, 140(R), 143, 146(B), 149, 154, 155(T, BR), 159, 165, 208, 211, 215(MR), 216(MR), 217(BL), 219, 277 (MR), 278(BR), 299, 300, 303, 307, 310, 311, 315, 328(TL), 329(B), 330(TL), 338, 378, 381, 387, 392, 393, 400, 401, 406, 413; Baseball Hall of Fame and Museum: 4, 5(L), 6, 16, 18(T), 52; Basketball Hall of Fame: 298; James Thomas Bell: 38; The Bettmann Archive, Inc.: 10, 57, 135, 140(L), 141, 146(T), 156(T), 157, 166, 173(T), 177, 178(T), 340; Boston Celtics: 333(BR); George Brace: 92; Buffalo Bills: 285(BL), 289(TR); Buffalo Sabres: 394; David Cantor: 286(BL); Chicago Bears: 266, 272(BR); Chicago Blitz: 287(TR); Chicago Bulls: 334(TL); Cincinnati Reds: 69(TL), 114; Cleveland Browns: 290(BL, BR); Cleveland Indians: 64; Bill Cummings: 330(R); Dallas Cowboys: 287(BR), 288(TR, BL); Detroit Pistons: 333(ML); Edmonton Oilers: 396; Alfred Fleishman: 110; Football Hall of Fame: 226, 228, 229, 230, 231, 233, 236, 245, 246, 247, 249, 250, 252, 254, 256, 258, 260, 262, 263, 265, 268, 269, 270, 272, 275, 279; George Gogkovich: 286(BR); Golden State Warriors: 334(BL); Green Bay Packers: 285(BR), 288(BR); Hartford Whalers: 397; Herbert Hawkins: 93; Houston Astros: 125(BL); Charles Isles: 301; Kansas City Royals: 125(BL); Keeneland Library: 366, 367, 368, 369, 370, 371, 372, 373, 374, 375; George T. Kruse: 270(ML); Walter F. Leonard: 32; Los Angeles Dodgers: 76(TL, ML), 98(TL); Los Angeles Lakers: 323, 333(TL); Gary Maglovkin: 287(DL); Milwaukee Bucks: 332(BL, R); Minnesota Vikings: 290(TR); New Orleans Saints: 285(TL); New York Jets: 277(TL), 289(TR, BL); New York Knicks: 328(TR), 329(T), 300(BL); New York Mets: 122(BL), 128(L), 129(TL); New York Yankees: 123(BR), 128(TR, BR); Philadelphia Eagles: 289(BR), 290(TL); Philadelphia 76ers: 331; Phoenix Suns: 334(BL); Pittsburgh Pirates: 122(BR), 123(M); Pittsburgh Steelers: 289(TL); Louis Requena: 121(TL), 122(TL); *The Ring* magazine: 145, 151, 155(BL), 169(T), 215(ML), 216(B), 217(TL); St. Louis Cardinals: 126(BL), 285(TR); San Antonio Spurs: 333(TR); San Diego Padres: 126(BR); San Francisco 49ers: 291(BL); San Francisco Giants: 85; Tampa Bay Buccaneers: 278(BL), 286(TR); U.P.I./Bettmann News Photos: 9, 27, 44(T, M, BL), 48, 59, 61, 62, 68(TR), 69(BL), 70, 75(TR, BL), 87, 97(TL, B), 98(TR, BL, BR), 99(TR, BL), 100, 121(TR, BR), 122(TR), 123(TR), 124(TR), 125(TL, TR, BR), 126(TL, TR), 127, 129(TR), 156(B), 160(T), 162, 167, 169(B), 171, 173(B), 174, 176(T), 178(B), 180, 181, 182, 183, 185(T), 186, 187, 189, 195, 197, 198, 200, 205, 206, 209, 210, 213, 214, 215(TL, TR, MR, BR), 216(TL, TR, MR), 217(TR, ML, MR), 218, 220, 221, 239, 240, 241, 242, 243, 276, 277(TR, BR), 280, 282, 283, 284, 287(TR), 291(TL, TR, BR), 318, 321, 335(TR, BR), 339, 341, 343, 344, 346, 347, 349, 350, 352, 354, 356, 357, 359, 360, 361(T), 362, 363, 364, 379, 383, 384, 388, 391, 407, 410, 414, 416; Xavier University of Louisiana: 297

Publisher's Note

Every effort has been made by the authors and editors to make certain that the facts and records listed herein are as up-to-date as possible. As sports fans are well aware, records are meant to be broken, and as America's black athletes are constantly reaching new heights in their athletic achievements, a certain amount of datedness may be encountered. However, we trust that it will be minimal and beg the reader's indulgence. Corrections, if required, will be made in future editions.

Acknowledgments

The author wishes to express his gratitude to the following individuals and organizations for their assistance, directly and indirectly, in the creation of this book:

Hank Aaron, Amherst College Archives, Ernie Banks, the Baseball Hall of Fame, the Basketball Hall of Fame, James Thomas Bell, Lou Brock, Roy Campanella, Larry Doby, the Football Hall of Fame, Monte Irwin, Buck Leonard, Willie Mays, the Professional Golfers Association, *The Ring* magazine, Frank Robinson, *The Sporting News,* University of Wisconsin Archives, Dr. Reginald Weir.

The editor wishes to thank his "team" of copy editors—Elaine Chubb, Carol Epstein, Georgiana Reiner, Scott Sack, and, especially, Mark Hurst—who so diligently and patiently checked and rechecked for accuracy the ever-changing sports statistics and events recorded herein.

To our daughter, Suzanne Beryl, with Love

Contents

Art Rust's
Illustrated History
of the
BLACK
ATHLETE

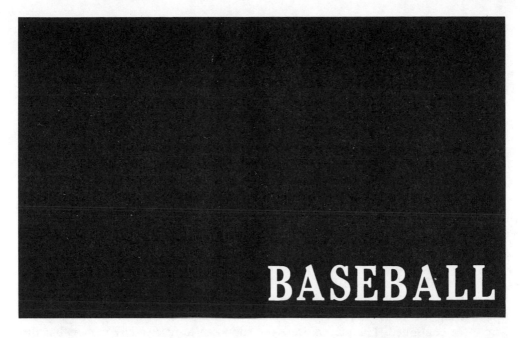

BASEBALL

part one

As American as baseball and apple pie.   **—Anonymous**

We won't delve into the intricacies of apple pie as an American institution, but we will look at baseball in that light. Baseball is an adaptation of a game played in its most primitive forms all over the world. Wherever and whenever man has had the time, space, a piece of stick, and a stone, you have had the rudiments of baseball.

The simplicity of the game has made it historically an ideal sport for children. English children played a game called "rounders," while a similar game was gaining popularity all over the American colonies, where it was called "one old cat," "two old cat," "three old cat," or "four old cat," depending on the number of children participating. The object of rounders was for the fielder to throw the ball at a runner heading for base and hit him with it. Some changes in the rules transformed rounders into a men's game called "town ball." As the name implies, town ball was played by competing teams from the various townships in England. It afforded the development of athletic skills and encouraged a great deal of pride in the participants for their particular townships.

There has been a great deal of dispute as to whether baseball is an all-American game or an importation that simply needed more details, rules, and refinements. A popular illustrated children's book printed in England in 1744 and exported to the American colonies describes a game called "baseball," and the illustrations indicate a player at the plate holding a bat, a catcher behind him, a pitcher about to throw a small ball, two bases with posts instead of bags, and a baseman standing by each post.

At first baseball was considered a common game and frowned upon by the elite of the colonies, but the popularity of the game overrode any such "aristocratic thinking." With the extension of its popularity, baseball began to define new rules and regulations. In 1845 the Knickerbocker Baseball Club established the first code of rules for baseball.

The first match game of record played under these rules occurred between the

Knickerbocker Club and a picked team which for that contest called itself the New York Club. The game was played in Hoboken, New Jersey, in 1846, and, thus, baseball was officially established as an American game. In 1858 the National Association of Base Ball Players was formed. The purpose of the association was to establish and make rules for member clubs.

During the period of the Civil War (1861–65), baseball spread into both the North and the South. It was encouraged by the military leaders of the Union and Confederate armies since it provided a good recreational outlet for the soldiers as well as for those confined in military prisons. It was probably during this period that baseball became widely known and played by the slaves and black freedmen. The appeal of the game made it contagious. In the South, with its wide fields, short winters, and the easily available ball and bat, the sport was soon propagated among the blacks.

After the Civil War, baseball, if nothing else, flourished. A baseball convention was held in New York City in 1865 and ninety-one clubs were represented. The purpose of this meeting was to see that the rules were maintained and the amateur status of the game was continued. The players were not supposed to receive any money, but the more talented did accept money for their services for a particular game on an occasional basis. This practice led to bribery and gambling, which the convention did its best to stem. The convention's efforts proved futile and it was not until 1867 that baseball evolved into a semiprofessional organization, with the clubs paying salaries to some of its players. In 1869 a team in Cincinnati was hired as an outright professional organization.

During the chaotic period of national Reconstruction, the black man fared badly. The transition from slavery to freedom was a difficult enough experience for the ex-slaves. The South was floundering with almost irreparable wounds of pride and a destroyed economy. There were men of ill will in both houses of Congress, many backed by Northern industrialists, who did not want the South to recuperate. These men did not want the Southern planters influencing problems of currency, banking, taxation, tariffs, etc., to the detriment of the North. The South viewed a great part of its problem as the loss of economic stability because of the emancipation of the slaves. Despite the sincere efforts of Senator Charles Sumner of Massachusetts and Representative Thaddeus Stevens of Pennsylvania championing the cause of newly freed black men, the Southern state legislatures established the "Black Codes," a body of laws which prohibited ex-slaves from giving testimony against whites in civil courts, among other things, and so restricted the social and economic rights of black men that they were virtually reduced to serfdom. As a result, serious race riots occurred in the South during the spring and summer of 1866.

In 1867 these incidents provided enough fodder for the nominating committee of the National Association of Base Ball Players to revise the code prohibiting the black man from participation in member clubs of the National Association. Baseball was already being touted as the "all-American" sport for "red-blooded" Americans. In no way did these phrases remotely include black America. Shattered by the Civil War and the assassination of President Abraham Lincoln in 1865, America was at last holding its wobbling head erect. It meant to show the world how young and strong it was, and baseball as a symbol was swept into this spiraling ascent of American "patriotism."

Although baseball for the most part maintained its amateur status, professional gambling made it difficult to keep the game honest and temptation tempered. The feeling was that baseball would not be such easy prey to gambling if the game were to become professional, with adequate pay for the players. Toward this end, the now ineffective National Association of Base Ball Players evolved in 1871 into the National Association of Professional Base-Ball Players. Along with strengthening and widening the scope of the now professional ballplayer, a "gentlemen's agreement" existed concerning the use, or more precisely the nonuse, of the black man in professional baseball. While the original association put its ban on blacks in writing, the new NABBP did not. Its unwritten decree just seemed to hang in the air for many years.

Particularly in the South after the Civil War and well into the twentieth century, black people had to find their own way of getting things done if they were to be done at all. If the mortician wouldn't bury the black dead or charged exorbitant prices, you opened your own funeral parlor; if you could not get proper insurance, you opened your own insurance firm; if you could not worship God in a white church, you opened your own church; thus, if you could not enter organized baseball, you organized your own teams. And like the early black undertaker, insurance firm, or church, baseball teams might appear a bit shoddy because there was little money affordable by blacks— only the dimes and occasional dollars that allowed the teams to merely exist. Nevertheless, the despondency of years of slavery and thoughts of the heaviness of survival after emancipation could be postponed in an afternoon spent on the barren field where black athletes played baseball. The games drew a big crowd and a picnic-like atmosphere pervaded the scene. The games were so colorful and the skills so great that whites began to infiltrate the crowds of cheering blacks. Often to get the money for gloves, balls, and bats, the blacks catered to their white clientele by presenting a "coon show," replete with clowning, mimicry, and exaggerated repartee between the umpire and players. The whites cheerfully paid for the reaffirmation of the "stereotypical Negro," but the gloves, balls, and bats were purchased and the game continued to grow, when possible, into a serious business.

In the North, black baseball players had a much greater degree of cohesiveness than in the South. Leagues were forming and colored "championship series" were evolving. There were even exhibition games between black teams and white teams recorded in 1867. Unfortunately, record keeping was so poor during this period that it has been almost impossible to ascertain the frequency of this type of encounter.

Cooperstown, New York, produced not only the Baseball Hall of Fame but also John W. "Bud" Fowler, the first black to be salaried in organized baseball. In 1872 he joined a white team in New Castle, Pennsylvania. He must have been awfully good. Bud Fowler could do anything on the baseball field. He could catch and pitch and play any position, but it was as second baseman that he received most of his acclaim. For the next twenty-five years he played all over the country, primarily with white teams. The economic pressures of the period, in addition to the animosity bred of prejudices by his teammates and the fans, kept him hopping from one team to another. When work with white teams was unavailable, he organized a black team, sarcastically called the All-American Black Tourists, and put on a "coon show" baseball game. The team played in top hats and tails and were preceded by a parade. Again, the instinct to survive doing what they wanted to do took precedence over making a burlesque of baseball, a game they loved: They still played a good legitimate game.

Bud Fowler was the first known black in organized baseball, but many soon were to follow in his footsteps. Before 1900 records indicate that there were more than thirty black men playing in white leagues. The reason for the letting down of the color bar

Bud Fowler **(rear center)** *with the Keokuk club of the Western League, 1885.*

has not been satisfactorily explained. However, the rapid growth and ubiquitous nature of the game and the need for good baseball players may have had a higher premium than the need to keep the game lily-white.

Outstanding in his baseball career in white baseball was Moses Fleetwood "Fleet" Walker—a man for all seasons. He was born in Mount Pleasant, Ohio, in 1857. His father, a physician, Dr. Moses Walker, moved his family to Steubenville, Ohio, where Fleet was raised. Fleet attended the integrated Oberlin College. A student of Greek, French, Latin, and German, as well as mathematics and the sciences, he also played baseball with an integrated college team. In 1884 he became the first black major leaguer when he was signed with the Toledo Blue Stockings of the American Association as a catcher.

His brother, Welday Walker, became the second major league black in July of 1884. Welday's venture into the major leagues was pure luck. Many players of the Toledo team had been badly injured, Fleet Walker included, and they needed a ballplayer immediately. Welday turned out to be a more than competent outfielder.

The appearance of the Walker brothers in the major leagues did not go unnoticed. They seemed to get along well with their teammates, perhaps because they were educated men and did not fit into the pigeonhole designated for blacks. Generally, the fans were not antagonistic and on many occasions applauded their skills. Many white

Welday Walker

Moses Fleetwood Walker with the Toledo Blue Stockings of the American Association.

fans came to boo but stayed to cheer. However, all was not sunshine and flowers. There were still the derisive cries and threats. A serious problem arose in Richmond, Virginia. A letter was received by the Toledo manager stating that if Fleet played, he would be mobbed, and there was the threat of bloodshed. Fortunately for all involved, Fleet broke a rib before the Richmond game and was unable to play.

Fleet was released from his contract the next season because of his injuries. Subsequently, he went on to play with other teams, ending his career in 1889 with Syracuse in the International League—the first black man in this previously white league. Walker eventually became involved in the movie business and invented several useful technical devices for the movie industry.

So traumatic were Fleet Walker's experiences in American life and especially in baseball that he decided to become an author, writing *Our Home Colony—A Treatise on the Past, Present and Future of the Negro Race in America*. It was his belief that the only way to deal with racial prejudice in America would be for the black man to return to Africa. Very early he voiced the opinions that were later expounded by men like Marcus Garvey in the 1920s, and some present-day militants. Baseball taught him a considerable lesson.

Welday became an agent for his brother's book and took a strong stance in efforts to persuade American blacks to migrate to Liberia.

The harassment perpetrated upon the few black men permitted to play in the early days of organized baseball did not seem to weaken their desire to play this "white man's game." But they came. They did not come expecting the camaraderie and team spirit that was supposedly inherent in the game; with talent, strength, zeal, they came just to play and be paid.

Into such a milieu came Frank Grant. He was born in Pittsfield, Massachusetts, in 1867. At seventeen he was a pitcher for the Graylocks of Pittsfield and later a catcher with a team in Plattsburg, New York. He entered organized baseball in 1886 as an infielder with the Meriden, Connecticut, team of the Eastern League. When that club disbanded in July of 1887, Grant went on to the Buffalo team of the International League as second baseman.

A first-rate player and hitter, Grant gained his celebrity by being called the "Black Dunlap." Fred "Sure Shot" Dunlap was a phenomenal white second baseman for St. Louis Maroons of the National League. This nickname was probably allowed because Grant was a good-looking light-complexioned black and was often referred to as a "Spaniard." (This ploy was later used by many black men in order to play in organized baseball.) Whatever the general public's feeling was, the players knew better. They constantly threw at his head, but missed. Then they began sliding into second base, feet-first, with sharpened spikes. After many injuries, Grant resorted to protective devices, which Bud Fowler had also used—he wore wooden leg splints to protect his legs. (Shin guards had not yet been invented.)

The treatment meted out by his white colleagues to Grant and approximately nineteen or twenty other black men in organized baseball was the result of the fanatical power brought to bear by Adrian "Cap" Anson, manager and first baseman of the Chicago White Stockings. Anson was born April 17, 1851, in Marshalltown, Iowa. He was the first white child born among the Potawatomi Indians in that area. His mother died when he was seven and he was raised by his father, who worked in the only store in the region. The Potawatomies were his early friends and he enjoyed trying to best them whenever he could. He hated school and used every subterfuge to avoid it. He grew into a bellicose, arrogant, opinionated man and one of the most exciting and remarkable players in the history of baseball. Anson was the first player to achieve 3,000 hits. A big, right-handed hitter, he smashed his drives to all fields. He was not a wild swinger, as was common in his time. He used a bat that looked as big as a telegraph pole and just met the ball, timing it with perfection. Cap Anson was easily the Babe Ruth or Joe DiMaggio of his era. Including the five years he put in with the

Adrian "Cap" Anson

National Association, he lasted in the majors twenty-seven seasons, longer than any player in the history of the game.

Anson hated blacks with an unnatural vehemence. The reason for this is not known, but the effect of it was to close the door of organized baseball to the black man for six decades.

Anson's overt attempts to get blacks out of organized baseball started in 1883. Anson threatened not to play an exhibition game with Toledo if Fleet Walker was in the game. The interesting thing is that though Toledo manager Charles Morton had no intention of playing Walker because he had a sore hand, he refused to accept that kind of intimidation and stated that Walker would play or there would be no game. Anson capitulated rather than lose his share of gate receipts.

Anson's protestations against blacks in baseball, however, did not go unheeded. He was a man of great popularity and there were many who agreed with him.

During the 1880s, the League of Colored Baseball Players was formed and included the Browns of Cincinnati, the Capital Citys of Washington, the Fall Citys of Louisville, the Keystones of Pittsburgh, the Lord Baltimores of Baltimore, the Resolutes of Boston, the Pythians of Philadelphia, and the Gothams of New York. The league proved that black baseball players had the talent and the numbers. With its wide acceptance as a legitimate organization, it was hoped that the league might become a kind of farm system for feeding blacks into organized baseball. It is not clear what happened, but the League of Colored Baseball Players dissolved after only one week.

As more blacks were entering the field of organized baseball and being paid, the white prejudice against them grew stronger. Baseball players were considered heroes, exemplifying the American way of life. The white public could not and would not condone the admiration of its children for black ballplayers. Money was not to be taken out of the hands of "red-blooded, white Americans" and given to the descendants of ex-slaves. And so it went.

On June 9, 1887, Douglas "Dug" Crothers, a white ballplayer out of St. Louis, refused to have his picture taken with the other members of the Syracuse Stars of the International League because a black pitcher, Robert Higgins, was to be included. Crothers was fined and suspended for a month (although in actuality the suspension only lasted eight days). At the time, Crothers was so enraged by the manager's suspension and fine that he shoved and struck him.

Things were now really coming to head, and on July 14, 1887, when the newly formed International League's directors held a meeting, they were bombarded with the complaints of white ballplayers over the inclusion of blacks in organized sports. Star ballplayers were threatening to leave the league because of the black situation. What with the roaring voice of Cap Anson in the background, the dissatisfaction of white players, and the resentment of the fans, the International League's board declared in writing that there were to be "no more contracts with colored men." This was the second time that the edict was put in writing.

It was all over but the shouting. The five blacks in the league were not immediately thrown out, but they knew the game was over.

On July 19, 1887, when the White Stockings, led by Cap Anson, entered the ball field of the Newark Little Giants, he shouted, "Get that nigger off the field!" He was referring to George Stovey, ace pitcher for Newark and a black man. In the fields where organized baseball was played, that cry was to resound until the blacks were no more.

In 1885 Frank P. Thompson, an enterprising black headwaiter at the Argyle Hotel in Babylon, Long Island, had been having a serious love affair with baseball. He would rather have played baseball than eat, but eat he had to. Thompson was able to secure a number of young men with baseball talent and his philosophy from among the hotel staff of busboys, waiters, and gardeners. They banded together and formed a team called the Athletics. So good were the Athletics at the game, they were invited to become part of entertainment provided for the well-to-do clientele at the Argyle who had run from the unbearable heat of New York City. To make their presence more palatable, the Athletics clowned and played the fool while playing a fine game.

When the hotel closed for the season, Frank Thompson took his group of Athletics on the road. Through hit-and-miss they built their game until they indeed became a formidable foe for any team that took them on.

Bowing to the racial pressures of the time, the Athletics changed their name to the Cuban Giants. It seemed to be better to be called anything other than blacks born in America. They spoke with what they conceived was a Spanish accent, and loud conversation on the field was conducted in made-up Spanish.

Thompson added the "Giants" tag to the team name because it was also the name of a very popular team in the majors at that time. The fans seemed to like the tag and it was used by a number of other black teams soon after, including the Lincoln Giants, the Chicago American Giants, the Bacharach Giants, and the Brooklyn Royal Giants.

Black fans proved to be highly receptive and offered enough support to allow the Cuban Giants to become the first known black baseball players to receive weekly salaries. Thus they were able to earn an adequate living doing what they loved best—a rare experience for a black man in those days.

The Cuban Giants played every team in the minor leagues and college and university teams, as well as semipros. Some games they won, some they lost; some it was expedient for them to lose. By 1895 they were a strong and independent club. They had refused to join the short-lived League of Colored Baseball Players, as well as the white Eastern League.

With the growing racial tensions, exacerbated by the activities of the Ku Klux Klan, solutions to the black problem seemed almost impossible. Then, in 1895, along came Booker T. Washington with his famous "Atlanta Compromise."

Booker T. Washington was born a slave on April 5, 1856, on a Virginia (later West Virginia) plantation. After emancipation, at the age of nine, he began working in the coal mines in West Virginia. Rising at 4 A.M., he spent all the daylight hours in the mines; at night he and his mother attempted to learn the alphabet by the candlelight. Somehow he heard about a school called Hampton, in Virginia, where blacks could go and be taught a trade. When he was fifteen, with all the black people in the little town where he lived contributing their nickels, dimes, and quarters, he was able to leave. He traveled by stage coach as long as his money lasted and then walked and worked his way to Hampton. Unable to pay all his expenses, he worked his way through as a janitor.

Washington's great admiration for his white New England teachers made him want to be a teacher. In 1881, when he was offered the job of opening a normal school for

Booker T. Washington

rural blacks in a small Alabama village, he readily accepted. There was hardly any money for his salary, and absolutely none for books, land, or building. But Washington was a man of great determination and fortitude, and he imbued his students with his own zeal. Somehow they raised funds for land and for building materials. When his students were not taking lessons in reading, writing, and arithmetic, they were laying the foundations and raising the walls for a decent school structure. Gradually, Tuskegee Institute took shape.

There was enough land at Tuskegee for a small farm and in addition to school subjects, the students learned to grow their own food and livestock. Washington's next ambition was to spread this knowledge through the whole community.

His ideas and efforts were applauded by both blacks and whites throughout the nation. At first, small contributions came from the black community in the form of food, clothing, quilts, and small amounts of money. Washington's success, and his aim "To educate the head, the heart, and the hand" (with emphasis on the hand), appealed to the great white philanthropic foundations, which made large grants to Tuskegee. United States Presidents and famous people from all over the world visited the tiny college in Alabama. Other institutions like it were established all over the South, heavily supported by white groups.

In 1893, at the Cotton States Exposition in Atlanta, Washington made his famous speech termed by his black critics as "the great Booker T. Washington compromise." In it he said: "In all things that are purely social we can be as separate as the fingers, yet one as the hand in all things essential to mutual progress." "Separate but equal" became the catchword for the black problem. Called the "Negro Moses" by the white press, Washington had provided the balm needed for the conscious-stricken whites and provided an alibi for those not so conscious-stricken.

Washington's pragmatic approach to educating the newly freed black was certainly conceived with good intent; unfortunately, he did not foresee the almost irresponsible damage he was doing by isolating the black man from the mainstream of American life. Time seems to indicate that the black man lost more than he had gained.

With the screaming of Cap Anson and the separatism seal of approval from the Black Moses, blacks in organized baseball defected to clubs like the Cuban Giants and a myriad of other black clubs that, by necessity, played in total segregation, never enjoying the same wages, working conditions, or historical record keeping of their triumphs that white organized baseball had. The die was already cast when black man Homer Plessy was thrown off of a "white" railway coach in Louisiana. He sued all the way up the line and in 1896 the United States Supreme Court "upheld the constitutionality of state laws providing 'separate but equal' accommodations for Negroes in public carriers and public places throughout the nation." It was not until 1954, in *Brown* v. *Topeka Board of Education,* that the Supreme Court revised its decision and stated in essence that separate cannot be equal.

Despite the law, unwritten and written, that barred blacks from organized baseball, there was a man—a good man—who bucked it. That man was John Joseph McGraw. He was born April 7, 1873, in Truxton, New York. One of nine children of a poor railroad section hand and his wife, McGraw grew up during the period of baseball's infancy and was to become one of the greatest managers in the game.

John McGraw

Diphtheria killed his mother, two of his brothers, and two of his sisters. He survived that and grew up a serious, seemingly humorless man. Standing only five feet seven inches and weighing 121 pounds, McGraw got his first chance in the major leagues with the Baltimore Orioles as a shortstop in 1891, when he was eighteen years old. What he lacked in size, he made up in aggressiveness. Sadie McMahon, the pitcher, told McGraw to take it easy. It was his first game. He didn't take it easy, but then, he never took anything easy. He helped the Orioles win that game, 6–5, over Columbus. In 1893 manager Ned Hanlon moved him to third base and for nine straight years McGraw hit better than .320 at the plate.

This brainy runt, with his bellicose, tough unruliness, used every trick imaginable to win the game. In those days, the Orioles played tough, close-to-the-vest baseball. They would scratch for runs, use the sacrifice bunt, discolor a baseball with tobacco juice to make it difficult for the batter to see. It was not uncommon to run direct from first to third when and if the umpire turned his back. The Orioles used—some say conceived —the hit-and-run. And they called John McGraw the father of baseball.

By the time McGraw left the Orioles, at the age of twenty-nine, he had been their manager for three years. He joined the New York Giants in 1902 and marched them to ten pennants in his first twenty-one years there. During his thirty years with the Giants, he finished in the second division only three times, and twenty-one times in that period the Giants were either first or second.

They also called him the "Little Napoleon." You either loved him or hated him, but you had to recognize him. For all his dictatorial and often contemptuous attitude to his players, off the field he was a devoted husband, soft-spoken, and an easy touch for down-and-out ex-baseball players. They say he must have contributed over $100,000 in loans and never beat a man down for repayment. He earned and deserved his place in baseball's Hall of Fame.

It would have to be a man of McGraw's caliber who would even attempt to defy the color barriers of that time. We quote veteran baseball reporter, Dan Daniel of the now-defunct New York *World-Telegram*, a longtime friend of John McGraw: "McGraw wanted to win. He played to win. He wanted the best possible ballplayers. He didn't care what they were. It was not a matter of charity or being liberal. Winning at any cost was McGraw's credo." In that spirit, McGraw watched Charlie Grant, a

Charlie Grant

bellhop at the Eastland Hotel in Hot Springs, Arkansas. At the time McGraw was the manager of the Baltimore Orioles in the brand-new American League and was in desperate need of good players. It was in March of 1901 and the Orioles were in spring training in Arkansas.

When they had free time, Charlie Grant and some of the other help would play ball on the hotel's grounds. Very impressed with Grant and aware of his major-league potential, McGraw signed him up. In his cunning, McGraw decided to pass Charlie Grant off as a Cherokee Indian (it was definitely known that Grant's father was a black horse trainer from Cincinnati and Grant himself had played second base for the Columbia Giants, a Chicago black team). McGraw dubbed Grant "Charlie Tokohama." He might have gotten away with the ruse if Charles Comiskey, president of the Chicago White Sox, and some of the other owners hadn't seen through the disguise and raised a ruckus. Grant never got to the regular-season major league and completed his ballplaying career in black baseball.

Baseball had meanwhile hit the island of Cuba full force. Ideal weather conditions had made it a year-round sport. There were two Cuban teams operating in the States on the East Coast, the Havana Stars and the Cuban Stars. In the earlier 1890s there were at least seventy-five clubs operating in Cuba. American big-league teams toured Cuba in the winter months fanning the already roaring popularity of the game.

There were no overt color lines in Cuba, and blacks and whites played together on the same teams. They were all excellent and dedicated athletes. When McGraw saw José Mendez, a right-handed pitcher of the Cuban Stars, he wanted him, but once again he couldn't beat the color bar. Mendez was a black Cuban of a very dark hue who would have gone down in the history books of baseball if his pigmentation had been several shades lighter. If it had been, McGraw would have taken him happily. Because of Mendez's great pitching skills, grace, and style, McGraw placed a value of $50,000 on him. But Mendez was restricted to playing with Cuban and black baseball teams until he retired in 1926.

John Donaldson (center)

José Mendez with the Kansas City Monarchs, 1926.

These were difficult times for John McGraw. To recognize the ability of men and be prohibited from signing them to a contract because of the color of their skin was abhorrent to him. Another case in point was John Donaldson, a superb left-handed pitcher. Donaldson was even urged to go to Cuba and legally change his name so he could pass for Cuban. Again, McGraw would have paid $50,000 to buy his contract if he could have breached the color bar. Donaldson's jug-handle curveball and general pitching ability peaked before World War I. Donaldson was a star with the All-Nations club, which was made up of men of several races. Donaldson continued to play with black teams, until many years later, when segregation loosened its hold and he became a scout for the Chicago White Sox.

For occasional short periods, there seemed to be lulls in strict adherence to segregation. It was during one of these breaks, in 1906, that McGraw hoped to sign on William Clarence Matthews. Matthews had attended Harvard University and had earned his varsity H as a shortstop/outfielder from 1902 until 1905. (He also earned a letter for football.) In 1906 Matthews was playing with Burlington in the Vermont league. Although Vermont did not have the status of organized baseball, it was nonetheless a white team. The furor caused by his entry into a white team made it impossible for McGraw to sign him. Matthews left baseball and became a lawyer.

Continuing his maverick defiance, John McGraw, when he moved from Baltimore to manage the New York Giants, brought with him Ed Mackall, a black trainer (or "rubber"), in 1902. Mackall, who stayed with the Giants for thirty years, was a colorful character who, it is said, once dispensed a laxative to all his players as well as to the local sports writers—on orders from John McGraw. Apparently McGraw wanted neither constipated ballplayers nor constipated writers.

Ed Mackall (front center) *with the New York Giants, 1920.*

Giant first baseman Bill Terry and second baseman Rogers Hornsby had protested to McGraw that they didn't want "that nigger" to touch them, but McGraw ignored them. In June 1932, when McGraw stepped down as the Giant manager, the first thing his successor, Bill Terry, did was to fire Mackall.

Continuing to defy the customs of the time before World War I, McGraw hired Andrew "Rube" Foster as a pitching coach. Foster taught a few tricks to Christy Mathewson, the great Giant right-hander. Foster was later known as the founding father of organized black baseball.

During the early years of the twentieth century, the Cuban ballplayers created a number of problems for white America. There was always the suspicion that they were black or part black. So concerned were the white racists that they offered to make special trips to Cuba to ascertain the purity of any Cuban to be signed as a major leaguer. In 1911 this was done in the cases of outfielder Armando Marsans and infielder Rafael Almeida when Garry Herrmann, owner of the Cincinnati Reds, wanted to strengthen his roster. Cuban baseball people informed his representative that both men were "pure Caucasian" and the men were signed. Almeida played through the 1913 season and Marsans through 1918. Years before, in 1882, Vincent Nava, born of Cuban parents in San Francisco in 1850, who played with the Providence Grays and the Baltimore Orioles, had not run into this problem. Nava played when Americans were unconcerned about racial and color distinctions as regards players from another country. But the growth of baseball and the tightening reins of segregation made it important for whites to keep the game as "red-blooded American" as possible. There were to be no loopholes for those who were considered less than white.

While Americans imported any number of white ballplayers, they would not countenance the use of one black man of ability of any nationality in organized baseball.

Armando Marsans

Rafael Almeida

By January 1920, when Prohibition was in full force and the United States was dry, Cuba was a favorite watering hole for Americans who could afford it. In order to provide Americans visiting Cuba with other recreational activities, McGraw and Charles A. Stoneham, owner of the Giants, bought Oriental Park, a combined ball park, racetrack, and gambling casino on the outskirts of Havana. McGraw had the idea of bringing over some ballplayers from the United States to boost the already feverish interest of the Cubans in the game. This was somewhat in defiance of the average American baseball contract, which forbade players from barnstorming ("barnstorming" in this context meant any postseason touring). In 1913 the Philadelphia Athletics had beaten the New York Giants in the World Series and had then gone barnstorming in Cuba to play against Cubans and American blacks. In 1914 Ban Johnson, American League president, stated: "We want no makeshift club calling themselves the Athletics to go to Cuba to be beaten by colored teams."

Nonetheless, in 1920 McGraw was able to snare his Yankee star Babe Ruth and some other ballplayers of note, such as Carl Mays and Fred Hofmann of the Yankees and Wally Schang of the Red Sox, to go along on his Cuban expedition. Babe Ruth was guaranteed $1,000 a game. The Cuban fans adored Ruth, but the feelings were not mutual. Ruth only hit one home run. The boundaries were farther away than in baseball parks in America. Ruth angrily referred to Cristobal Torrienti, called the "Cuban Babe Ruth," as "black as a ton and a half of coal in a dark cellar." He generally disparaged all Cuban ballplayers as inferior, mainly because many of them were black or of mixed blood.

It is ironic that Ruth, who so hated blacks, should himself be the victim of racism. Although supposedly of pure Caucasian blood, his broad nose and full lips caused many of his fellow players to call him "nigger." His reply was generally, "Call me anything you want to, but for God's sake don't call me a nigger."

When Ruth and Ty Cobb of the Detroit Tigers were invited in 1923 to a big-league hunting lodge in Brunswick, Georgia, Ty Cobb is reported as having said, "I never have slept under the same roof with a nigger, and I'm not going to start here in my own state of Georgia."

Babe Ruth

Rube Foster

Still the blacks continued to play. On September 17, 1879, in Calvert, Texas, a boy was born who was destined to become the organizer and pioneer of black baseball. The boy was Andrew Foster, son of a minister. Foster loved baseball, and his knowledge of the game was so encyclopedic that few have reached his level. While still in grammar school, Foster had organized a baseball team in Calvert. When he left school in the eighth grade, he decided to become a professional ballplayer.

A talented but unpolished right-handed pitcher, Foster joined a black team called the Waco Yellow Jackets. Then he was invited to join the Chicago Union Giants. Standing six feet four inches and weighing over 200 pounds, Foster pitched a shutout in his first game. Full of confidence, intelligence, and instinctive baseball know-how, he refined his game to the point where he took practically all comers.

It was in 1902 that Foster pitched an exhibition game for the Chicago Union Giants against the Philadelphia Athletics and their famous mound star, Rube Waddell. Foster beat Waddell, and Foster's teammates now began to call him "Rube," a significant left-handed acknowledgment that he was the premier pitcher. White or black, no one was better than he. Thereafter, he was always known as Rube Foster.

In 1905 it was reported that Foster won fifty-one games in fifty-five exhibition contests against major and minor league teams. Honus Wagner, the famous shortstop of the Pittsburgh Pirates, said he was "one of the greatest pitchers of all time. He was the smartest pitcher I have ever seen in all my years of baseball."

While Foster was with the Union Giants of Chicago, Frank C. Leland, owner of the club, was able to get only $150 for the team for a Fourth of July doubleheader. Observing the huge attendance, Foster was indignant; he worked on Leland to let him renegotiate the booking. Foster demanded a cut of 40 percent of the gate receipts from the organizers and after a long debate he was able to make over $500 for the club that day, thus adding business management to his baseball career.

In 1911 John M. Schorling, a white bar owner who also operated sandlot clubs in Chicago, approached Foster. Schorling had leased the grounds of the old White Sox park after the White Sox moved to another location. Schorling rebuilt the stadium seats, giving the park a seating capacity of nine thousand. A fifty-fifty split was verbally agreed to and the two men never discussed money again. This is the first time blacks played in a major league ball park.

When Foster retired as an active player (about 1915), he became the manager of the

Chicago American Giants. As manager he was stern and demanding but fair. He did not fraternize with his players. Although he did not drink heavily, he was tolerant of those who did—so long as it did not interfere with their game.

In August 1919 Chicago was almost torn apart by a race riot—twenty-three blacks and fifteen whites died as a result. The Giants' ball field was occupied by soldiers and the team had to travel East to play. Perhaps the rioting influenced Foster's thinking about the need for black teams to have a greater degree of organization. Also there was the fact that it was a common practice for black teams to "raid" players from each other. Foster began stressing the need for team owners to stop this cutthroat, backstabbing business.

Although skeptical, other black teams decided to go along with this concept and the Negro National Baseball League was founded in 1920. With Foster as president, the league had franchises in Kansas City (the Monarchs), Indianapolis (the ABC's), Chicago (the American Giants), Detroit (the Stars), St. Louis (the Stars), in addition to a team of traveling Cubans, the Western Cuban All-Stars.

On December 16, 1923, representatives of the Brooklyn Royal Giants, the New York Lincoln Giants, the Bacharach Giants, the Baltimore Black Sox, and the Hillsdale (a suburb of Philadelphia) club got together and formed the Mutual Association of Eastern Baseball Clubs, better known as the Eastern Colored League. While Foster's Negro National League had the Western Cuban All-Stars, the Eastern Colored League had Alex Pompez's Eastern Cuban Stars, thus making a six-team league.

The Eastern Colored League was controlled by six commissioners, one from each club. Edward H. Bolder, of Hillsdale, Pennsylvania, was the chairman, but the man who really held the strings was Nat C. Strong, a white New York City booking agent.

The Lincoln Giants, 1912

The Kansas City Monarchs, 1908

Strong, who owned the Royal Giants, arranged and controlled schedules of most of the white semipro teams, as well as most of the black ones, in and around New York.

The first season of the Eastern Colored League went fairly smoothly and successfully. Hillsdale won the pennant.

The Chicago American Giants, 1921, the club that dominated the Negro National League during its first three years. In front, Tom Williams (left) *and Bobby Williams. Seated,* (from left) *Christobel Torrienti, Tom Johnson, Otis Starks, Jimmy Lyons, Jelly Gardner, and George Dixon. Standing, Jim Brown, Dave Brown, Bingo DeMoss, Dave Malarcher, LeRoy Grant, and Jack Marshall.*

The National Negro League and the Eastern Colored League suffered from the same malady—imbalance. In the Negro National League, three teams won pennants continuously over twelve years—the Chicago American Giants, the Kansas City Monarchs, and the St. Louis Stars.

The same problem plagued the Eastern Colored League. Hillsdale and the Bacharach Giants were the only two teams to win championships during a five-year period. The Eastern Colored League reorganized in 1929 and became the Negro American League; that year the Baltimore Black Sox won the flag. Unfortunately, the league only lasted one season.

Despite the growing pains, for the first time there was more stability to black baseball than ever before, what with set schedules and the introduction of the Negro World Series. Although Foster had dreamed of the possibility that the winner of the Negro World Series would play the winner in the white major leagues, this dream never reached fruition. However, four World Series were played from 1924 through 1927 between Foster's Negro National League and Eastern Colored League. Seven other series took place in the 1940s with the second Negro National League opposing the Negro American League. Black baseball now had a sense of order, stabilized salaries, and true recognition all through the efforts of the genius of Rube Foster. Organized black baseball survived the Great Depression and flourished until the advent of black players into the major leagues in 1947.

Rube Foster retired from baseball in 1926 and died in a hospital for the mentally ill on December 9, 1930. His funeral service was attended by over three thousand people. The Negro National League floundered dangerously under the succeeding leadership of his partner, John Schorling. In 1928 Schorling sold the American Giants to William F. Trimble, a white florist. Schorling always felt that he had been pushed out because other owners wanted to keep strong clubs out of Chicago. In the early 1930s Robert A. Cole and Horace G. Hall, black Chicago businessmen, took over the team and later the leadership was passed on to Dr. J. B. Martin. Under Dr. Martin the American Giants regained some of their old glory, but never again were they the consummate power they had been with Rube Foster.

Organized black baseball in the 1930s needed a boost. The Great Depression had decimated the game for blacks. Attendance was down, salaries lowered, and leadership was nil. Blacks have always felt national financial pressure first. There was a man of power and dynamic personality to help some during this period. Cumberland Willis Posey was born in Homestead, Pennsylvania, on June 20, 1891. He had attended Pennsylvania State College and what is now Duquesne University and was well known as a basketball player. In 1911 he joined the Murdock Grays, previously called the Blue Ribbon Nines, which had been organized by a group of black steelworkers. In 1912 the Murdock Grays became the Homestead Grays.

Starting as an outfielder, Posey became the team manager in 1916. Under his leadership, the Grays became a powerhouse. On occasion, there was even a white player or two on the club.

Posey was wary about the Grays' joining a Negro league. The concept appealed to him, but he did not feel the leagues were organized well enough. Finally Posey's Grays did enter an organized league, in 1929, at which time they finished third and fourth in the split-season schedule of the American Negro League.

Posey had big ideas about how to run a league and make it a strong, cohesive unit.

The Homestead Grays, 1931, with Cumberland Posey in knickers.

He laid the groundwork for the establishment of a new East-West League. This league would include his own Homestead Grays, the Baltimore Black Stars, the Detroit Wolves, the Newark Browns, Pompez's Eastern Cuban Stars, and the Cleveland Stars. Despite all his efforts and hard work, the league could not survive—it was 1932. It was back to barnstorming for the Grays, but they survived as a strong, healthy team and a guiding light in black baseball until March 28, 1946, when Posey died.

One of the great problems of racial segregation is the unequal distribution of wealth. Those who have attained wealth seem to make every effort to thwart those who aspire to the same goals. All the ability and intelligence needed for the game of baseball that you may have will not make you rich unless you have wealthy backers who can see a club through the bad times.

The few blacks who had attained a degree of wealth—enough wealth for speculation —were those blacks in the gray areas of legitimacy. These were clever men who could see beyond the next month's rent, highly respected for their wits and money power. Such a man was W. A. "Gus" Greenlee. Greenlee was born in Marion, North Carolina, and migrated to Pittsburgh after serving overseas in World War I. He operated a bar, the Crawford Grill, and it was the focal point for his numbers business. Unquestionably, he was the numbers king of Pittsburgh. Money-rich, resourceful, he was even able to control a faction of political power. This cigar-chomping, robust man was also affectionately called "Big Red." Greenlee used surplus cash to build a boxing stable from which in 1935 a world's light-heavyweight champion, John Henry Lewis, emerged. While Greenlee had no baseball background, he did have organizational genius. In 1931 he organized the Pittsburgh Crawfords and, because he could afford it, he hired the luminaries of black baseball: Cool Papa Bell, Satchel Paige, Oscar Charleston, Josh Gibson, Jimmie Crutchfield, Ted Page, Judy Johnson, and Leroy Matlock.

Greenlee was incensed by the racism that permitted his Crawfords to use Pittsburgh's Ammon Field and sometimes Forbes Field, but would not allow any black team renting the facilities to use the locker rooms. Black teams had to shower and dress at the YMCA across town. Greenlee decided to build his own field. Although Greenlee Field accommodated only 6,000, it had major-league proportions, lockers, and showers. Greenlee had style.

After getting the Crawfords organized, Greenlee assembled the Homestead Grays, Cole's American Giants, the Indianapolis ABC's, the Detroit Stars, and the Columbia Blue Birds and formed the second Negro National League in 1933 (the first having disbanded the previous year).

Nothing went well that first season. It was a total chaos. The American Giants won out over the Crawfords in the first half of the split season, and the second half of the split season evaporated. Accused of raiding other teams, the Homestead Grays were kicked out of the league. Even with all this confusion, Greenlee's league managed to survive the Depression, make changes, and build a strong enough league to last until 1948.

One of the most important contributions Greenlee made toward the advancement of black baseball was the creation of the East-West game. All the black superstars in baseball participated in this all-star game. In Chicago in 1933 there were 20,000 fans in attendance; 51,723 attended in 1943. All games were played at Comiskey Park, home of the Chicago White Sox.

This was one time that the white press came out in full force to record these magnificent displays of black talent. In addition, it bolstered the ever-weak and fluctuating finances of black baseball. Many teams would not have been able to open the following season had it not been for their share of the receipts for the East-West game.

The second Negro National League suffered many temptations. The Dominican Republic was crying for black ballplayers to come there to play. Then Mexico exploded into baseball madness. There were many black players who left the league or took a temporary leave to go to these countries, where they were welcomed as equals. The salaries were much higher and, most importantly, players did not have to endure "separate but equal" facilities. They could eat in the best restaurants and stay in first-class hotels.

Interestingly, those who did not run off to Mexico or the Caribbean countries could demand more money in the United States with the threat of taking off for greener pastures. In addition, the advent of World War II had its influence on salaries. The scurrying to build warships, planes, and munitions brought black people into life "American-style." Well-paid jobs gave the black man money to spend on things other than just necessities. Attendance at black baseball games was phenomenal. Player salaries went up to $400 and $500 a month. Top-drawers earned as much as $1,000 a month. With Greenlee's organization and high sums of fresh money from attendance, black baseball by 1945 had reached its heights.

William "Judy" Johnson

If Judy were only white, he could name his price.   —Connie Mack

Judy was always a very smart ballplayer. He could easily pick up signals from the opposition and make the right play—an alert all-around ballplayer.   —Ted Page

Judy Johnson, circa 1933, with the Pittsburgh Crawfords.

Third baseman Judy Johnson was one of black baseball's most fabulous players. He was sure-handed on bunts, owned a strong arm, and was equally adept at fielding balls to his right and left.

William J. "Judy" Johnson was born to Annie Lane and William Henry Johnson on October 26, 1900, in Snow Hill, Maryland. He was raised and attended school in Wilmington, Delaware, and was graduated from Howard High School. As far back as he could remember, he wanted to play baseball. "Smokey Joe" Williams, Dick Redding, Louis Santop, and Phil Cockrell, stars of Negro baseball, were his idols. When he was eighteen, he played with the Bacharach Giants on Sundays and earned $5.00 a game. Then he went on to play semipro with the Madison Stars in Philadelphia. On the Stars team there was an old-time player named Judy Gans. Johnson's teammates said that Gans and Johnson looked so much alike they could be father and son. From that time on, Johnson was called "Judy." In 1922 he was sold to the Hillsdale team in Darby, Pennsylvania, for only $100; he earned $135 a month.

The Hillsdale club didn't have to travel a great deal because of the numerous other clubs nearby. The team's route encompassed Pittsburgh, Chicago, Detroit, St. Louis, and back home. In the first Negro World Series in 1924, Johnson led Hillsdale with a .341 batting average. Five years later he had the most hits of any batter in the American Negro League and was considered the best-fielding third baseman in the circuit. They called him the "black Pie Traynor," after the great Pittsburgh Pirate third baseman.

Johnson left the Hillsdale team to manage the Homestead Grays in 1930 when the Hillsdale club folded. In 1931 he returned to Darby to manage the Darby Daisies, the successor to the Hillsdale club. When the Daisies also folded, Johnson went to the Pittsburgh Crawfords, from 1932 until 1937, when he left professional Negro baseball. Without a doubt, Johnson was part of the integral potency of the Crawfords.

When Johnson reminisces about baseball, he recalls his first great thrill in 1922 when he was with Hillsdale. The club was playing an exhibition game against Earle Mack's All-Stars and he was facing Bullet Joe Bush, fresh from a twenty-six-game win season with the pennant-winning New York Yankees. Johnson says, "Man, we hit him good."

When queried about the caliber of black baseball in 1975, Johnson said he felt that on a regular day-to-day basis it may not have been of major league quality, but you could easily pick a team of black players who could "beat the hell out of the major leagues any day. Overall I would say that most of the Negro teams were of Triple-A quality. My biggest thrill playing in the Negro leagues was when we played and beat major league all-stars. It gave us confidence that our ability was equal to theirs."

After Jackie Robinson broke the color line in 1947, Johnson scouted for the Philadelphia Athletics, Milwaukee Braves, and the Philadelphia Phillies. He is now retired and resides in Wilmington, Delaware.

Judy Johnson was elected to the Baseball Hall of Fame in 1975.

John Henry "Pop" Lloyd

When queried in 1938 as to who was the best player in baseball history, a white St. Louis sportswriter replied "If you mean in organized baseball, my answer would be Babe Ruth; but if you mean in all baseball, organized or unorganized, the answer would have to be a colored man named John Henry Lloyd.

John Henry "Pop" Lloyd, with the Atlantic City Bacharach Giants.

When ten-year-old Art Rust, Jr., was busily expounding his knowledge of baseball at Camp Minisink, in Port Jervis, New York, a tall, lanky counselor with long arms and big hands approached him. He said, "Son, do you know who I am?" The young boy shook his head at the tall man who said, "Remember my name: I'm John 'Pop' Lloyd, the greatest shortstop baseball ever had."

John Henry "Pop" Lloyd was big for a shortstop, six feet two inches and about 185 pounds. He ranged all over the field. His long arms and big hands retrieved many balls that other shortstops could not reach. With reference to his talents, he was called "El Cuchara" (the scoop) by the Cubans.

Lloyd was born in Palatka, Florida, on April 25, 1884. His mother remarried after the death of Lloyd's father, and his grandmother raised him from infancy. He never finished elementary school and went directly to work as a delivery boy. In the sunlit hours of late afternoon, he played baseball with a local amateur team.

Seeking better employment opportunities, Lloyd went to Jacksonville while still a teenager. First he worked in a store and a little later became a porter for the Southern

Express Company. While in Jacksonville he began playing with the Young Receivers, a semipro club. When he was twenty-one years old, he turned professional and was the catcher for the Macon, Georgia, Acmes. After some injuries, sustained because the Acmes couldn't afford a catcher's mask, Lloyd decided to play second base. The insistent urging of his fellow porters encouraged him to try out for the Cuban X Giants in Philadelphia. In 1906 he scraped together enough money to make the trip, with nothing left over, but he made the team. Fortunately, he started the season at second. Starting off with a bang, he hit a game-winning double in the tenth inning, beating out one of the best black pitchers of that time, Charles "Kid" Carter. Also on that team was McGraw's "Indian" star, Charlie "Tokohama" Grant.

In 1907 Lloyd left the Cuban X Giants and signed on with the Philadelphia Giants as a shortstop. He remained there until he joined Leland's Union Giants in Chicago with several teammates. As a result, the Philadelphia Giants were finished. Following the money, Lloyd joined the Lincoln Giants of Harlem. The Lincoln Giants in 1913 reached their zenith when they beat great pitcher Grover "Pop" Alexander and his Philadelphia Phillies, 9–2. The next year, Rube Foster stole Lloyd, along with Smokey Joe Williams, pitcher; Billy Francis, third baseman; and Judy Gans, outfielder, for his Chicago American Giants. From 1914 until 1917 Lloyd remained with the American Giants, where he earned about $250 a month. He was the cleanup hitter with the best black club of that time.

In 1917 Lloyd was thirty-four years old. He got a job in the Army Quartermaster depot in Chicago and refused to play the winter season with the American Giants. This decision by Lloyd annoyed Foster, so by early spring they parted amicably. Older and not as fast as he had been, Lloyd became the manager of the Brooklyn Royal Giants. Although his job was with management, he often played, but at first base rather than at shortstop.

From 1918 until 1931, Lloyd managed and played for the Royal Giants; the Columbus, Ohio, Buckeyes; the Bacharach Giants; the Hillsdale Club; and the Lincoln Giants. He was forty-seven years old when he retired from top professional teams. Although he never had any of his own, he dearly loved children and the young ballplayers he managed, always giving them good advice. They responded by calling him "Pop." Lloyd was a mild-mannered man; he never drank and his cursing consisted of "Dad burn it." On the field, however, he was a tough competitor. He was compared to Honus Wagner, considered by many at the time to be the best ballplayer in the game. When Wagner heard that Lloyd was called the "Black Wagner," he said that he considered it a privilege to be compared with Lloyd.

In the middle 1930s, Lloyd became a janitor in the Atlantic City, New Jersey, school system and loved telling the children about baseball. He still continued to manage and play first base for semipro teams in Atlantic City until 1942, when he was fifty-eight years old.

In 1949 a ball park in the Atlantic City community recreation field was named for him. If he had been born forty years later, he certainly would have been in the major leagues. When asked if he felt bitter about this, Lloyd said in effect that he was proud of what he did and when he did it. It was his feeling that through his efforts and those of others like him, the road was paved for other black players to go further.

He died on March 19, 1965, of arteriosclerosis.

John Henry "Pop" Lloyd was elected to the Baseball Hall of Fame in 1977.

Martin DiHigo

His gifts afield have not been approached by any one man, black or white.

—Cum Posey

Martin DiHigo

Martin DiHigo was born in Cuba in 1908. He first played in the United States with Alex Pompez's Eastern Cuban Giants when he was fifteen years old. He pitched, and played first and second. When he reached his full growth he was six feet one inch and weighed 190 pounds. He was a right-handed thrower and hitter, but he was used at every position by the Cubans and later by the Homestead Grays and Hillsdale.

Not only could DiHigo play every position, he was a star in all of them. In the East-West game of 1935, he started in center field and batted third for the East; then he was called upon to pitch in relief in the late innings. He had a .386 batting average in the American Negro League in 1929.

After spending several seasons in Latin America, DiHigo returned, in 1945, to the Grays. During the 1950s, after Jackie Robinson broke the color bar and the subsequent collapse of the Negro National League, DiHigo played in Mexico.

DiHigo was elected to the Baseball Hall of Fame in 1977.

Leroy "Satchel" Paige

I know who's the best pitcher I ever saw and it's old Satchel Paige, that big lanky colored boy.
—Dizzy Dean

Satchel was the fastest pitcher I ever saw . . . I don't know anybody who had a ball any faster than Satchel. For a long time Satchel just had a fastball . . . didn't have a curve . . . But he finally developed a curveball, and then he was much rougher.
—Buck Leonard

Satchel Paige, 1948, with the Cleveland Indians.

Satchel Paige *was* black baseball in the 1930s and early 1940s. Paige was the majordomo. He was the Babe Ruth of the black leagues in the sense that he had the charisma, that something that filled the coffers. In many instances, he was "the franchise" for some of the Negro clubs.

This baseball phenomenon was born south of Government Street, by the bay in Mobile, Alabama. Paige says he was born July 7, 1906; others say 1899 or even earlier. Anyway, he was seventh of eleven children born to his father, John, a gardener, and his mother, Lula, a washerwoman. Paige attended the W. H. Council school as little as possible. With so many mouths to feed at home, he worked, when he was about seven or eight, at the railroad station carrying bags and satchels. He deduced that carrying one bag only brought him a dime, so he got a pole and some string and that way he could sling as many as four satchels at a time. The money he earned was doubled, but the other kids hustling bags laughed at him and called him a "satchel tree." The name stuck and everyone except his mother called him "Satchel" or "Satch."

Paige also got a job at the Eureka Gardens, which included a semipro baseball park, picking up empty bottles and sweeping. A black team, the Mobile Tigers, played there. That's when Paige became interested in the game and particularly in throwing. Unable to afford a baseball, he threw rocks. Throwing rocks as much as possible, Paige began to realize he had complete control. He became so proficient that he could throw a rock and kill a flying bird—and take his trophy home for dinner. Whatever a rifle could do with bullets, Paige could do with a rock.

On their way to school, the black children in his neighborhood in Mobile were often set upon by a gang of white kids and the rocks flew back and forth. The black kids, knowing of Paige's skill, easily got him to participate. The extent of the white gang's injuries thereafter was so great that a policeman had to be posted to stop the warfare.

When he was only ten, Paige made the school's baseball team, generally reserved for the older boys. By the time he was twelve, he was a very busy young man, working at the ball park, carrying bags at the station, playing baseball, and occasionally attending school. However, he also found time to steal a handful of cheap, gaudy, shining rings. What with his truancy and trouble with the police for throwing stones, he was sent to the Industrial School for Negro Children at Mount Meigs, Alabama.

Considering the miserable state of poverty his family lived in, Paige didn't feel that the home was that bad. In fact, he considered it a blessing. You can't play hookey in an institution, and he began to get an education, but most importantly, he learned the game of baseball. The baseball coach encouraged Paige to stick to the game, where he might be able to make something of himself.

In December 1923, Paige was released from the school. He was seventeen years old, six feet three and one-half inches tall, and 140 pounds. He tried out for the Mobile Tigers, where his brother Wilson pitched and caught. According to David Lipman, co-author of Paige's 1962 autobiography, *Maybe I'll Pitch Forever,* after the tryout the manager came over grinning and said, "Do you throw that fast consistently?" He replied, "No, sir, I do it all the time."

It was 1924 and Paige pitched for the Mobile Tigers. After playing for several semipro clubs in the Mobile area during the next two years, he joined the Chattanooga Black Lookouts in 1926, for $50 a month. In 1928 he was sold to the Negro National League's Birmingham Black Barons, where he was given a contract for $275 per month.

Paige stayed with the Barons until 1930. The club was doing poorly in attendance that year and in 1931 Paige was sold by the Barons to the Nashville Elite Giants. Thomas J. Wilson, owner of the Nashville Elites, transferred the team to Cleveland because it was not making enough money in Nashville to hold its franchise in the Negro National League. Wilson changed the name of the team to the Cleveland Cubs. The newly named club was still floundering financially, and when Gus Greenlee, who was forming the Pittsburgh Crawfords, heard about it, he sent for Paige. Paige joined the Crawfords and received $250 a month and had his foot on the stepping-stone to fame. Greenlee really got himself a prize. Paige had a brilliant pitching record of 30 and 1 in 1924, and 26 consecutive pitching victories in 1926. In 1930 he struck out 22 white major leaguers in an exhibition game.

With Paige pitching and other stars as teammates, such as Oscar Charleston, Judy Johnson, Josh Gibson, Rap Dixon, Cool Papa Bell, Jimmy Crutchfield, and others, the Crawfords won 99 games and only lost 36 in 1930.

Gus Greenlee often "rented" Paige to semipro clubs who needed a pitcher for an important game. Paige picked up as much as $500 a game, which Greenlee allowed him to keep. With all of these extras, Paige was probably the highest-paid black baseball player of his time.

He stayed with the Crawfords until 1934 and then independently pitched with semipro clubs. In 1934 he had won the East-West game, 1–0. Paige left Greenlee when he asked for a higher salary (he got married that year) and Greenlee refused. Paige quit and went on to finish the season with a white semipro club in Bismarck, North Dakota, thereby jumping his contract with Greenlee and being barred from the second Negro National League.

True to form, Paige rejoined the Crawfords in 1936. He was not penalized for jumping because of his much-needed talent and his ability to fill the stadium.

The scent of money has a strange effect upon men, and its odor drifted over Paige in 1937 when he was at spring training with the Crawfords in New Orleans. President Rafael Trujillo Molina of the Dominican Republic was having trouble keeping his dictatorship from falling apart under him and a rival for the dictatorship had imported a ball club to Santo Domingo. Trujillo wanted to prove that he could beat his rival in anything—even baseball. So it was necessary to get the best baseball team together for a showdown to accomplish this feat. Trujillo sent for the best pitcher known—Satchel Paige. That summons plus the fact that Greenlee had lost a lot of money in his numbers operation and was giving the ballplayers a rough time, decided Paige. He jumped his contract and headed for Santo Domingo. Paige called back from there to his friends in the Crawfords and rounded up nine men for the Dominican club, including Cool Papa Bell. They had a winning season, bolstered Trujillo's position, and got $30,000 for themselves.

Paige headed back to the Crawfords in the 1938 season, paid the necessary fine, and then prepared to take off again in response to an offer from Mexico. Greenlee had offered him $450 a month, but Paige refused it; Greenlee, who had had enough, sold Paige to the Newark Eagles, owned by Abraham Manley. Learning of Paige's intentions, Manley got a restraining order against the pitcher, but Paige took off anyway for Mexico.

While pitching the 1938 summer season in the Mexican League, Paige's troubles began. He developed a sore right arm that, coupled with his inability to digest the Mexican food, made his life a misery. He was even told by a doctor that he would never pitch again.

He returned to the United States and, because of his past record of unreliability, was unable to secure a job as a manager or coach. Then he got an offer to pitch and be first baseman for the Kansas City Monarchs, barnstorming. Kansas City figured that despite his injured arm, Paige still had drawing power. The Monarchs temporarily changed their name to Satchel Paige's All-Stars. Paige at first was only capable of pitching an inning or two against semipros, but then, as suddenly as the soreness appeared, it disappeared.

With Paige at the helm, the All-Stars won the recently formed Negro American League pennant from 1939 through 1942. The Negro World Series was resurrected (last game had been in 1927) and the now-renamed Monarchs of the Negro American League played the Homestead Grays, champions of the Negro National League. Paige won three of four Monarch victories.

By this time, Paige, a little older and steadier, settled in with the Monarchs for the next five years. He still hired out to pitch for the semipro games. Jackie Robinson had by then broken the color line and Paige felt that signing up with a white major league team was the only way he could go at this point in life. He looked around but found no takers. Finally, in 1948, he received a letter from Abe Saperstein, manager of the Harlem Globetrotters basketball team, who was doing some scouting for Bill Veeck, owner of the Cleveland Indians. Veeck wanted the American League pennant badly, but he needed the help of a superb pitcher. Paige was at least forty-two years old: Veeck hired him anyway.

Paige's greatest regret was that he was not admitted to organized big-league baseball when he was in his prime. The salary he made would net him about the same, but there was no need for barnstorming and playing year-round baseball—a half a year's salary for only half a year of ballplaying—$25,000.

Happy that Jackie Robinson had broken the color bar, Paige felt he was just as important by being the first black to pitch in the American League. Paige pitched in 21 games, won 6, and only lost 1, and the Indians won the 1948 pennant, which came down to a play-off game victory over the Boston Red Sox. The Indians also won the World Series, but Paige was used in only one inning.

Paige remained with the Indians for 1949. He won 4 games and lost 7 and was let go after the season. That meant back to barnstorming for anyone who had the price. In 1951 Veeck, new owner of the St. Louis Browns, signed him on again. Paige's last full season with the majors was in 1953. Released again, Paige returned to Negro baseball and barnstorming. Veeck picked him up yet again in 1956 for the Miami Marlins in the International League, where he remained until 1958. After that, he was pitching a couple of innings a game for barnstorming clubs. In 1961 he pitched for the Portland Beavers in the Pacific Coast League. In 1967 the Indianapolis Clowns paid him $1,000 a month and threw in a $250 bonus for special appearances in big-league parks. Paige was signed up by the Kansas City Athletics in 1965, but played in only one game. Paige was hired as a coach by the Atlanta Braves in 1968, his last job in baseball.

Paige had a long, exciting career. His only peers were perhaps the white pitchers Lefty Grove, Dizzy Dean, and Carl Hubbell, but then they didn't pitch every day, summer and winter, for years on end. For many of Paige's playing years his "bee" ball (a fast ball) was enough, but then he developed the curve ball—and his clowning; his singular personality was what baseball fans wanted to see. His hesitation pitch was so balklike that the baseball commissioner A. B. "Happy" Chandler outlawed it when Paige was with the Cleveland Indians.

Satchel Paige, sometimes called a hypochondriac, wrote these words of wisdom for all young baseball players:
1. Avoid fried meats, which angry up the blood.
2. If your stomach disputes you, lie down and pacify it with your cool thoughts.

3. Keep the juices flowing by jangling around gently as you move.
4. Go very light on the vices, such as carrying on in society. The social rambler ain't restful.
5. Avoid running at all times.
6. Don't look back. Something might be gaining on you.

Black baseball and white baseball each owe a debt of gratitude to Satchel Paige.

Elected to the Baseball Hall of Fame in 1971, Satchel died in Kansas City on June 8, 1982.

Walter F. "Buck" Leonard

Buck Leonard was as smooth a first baseman as I ever saw. In those days, the first baseman on a team in the Negro League often played the clown. They had a funny way of catching the ball so the fans would laugh, but Leonard was strictly baseball: a great glover, a hell of a hitter, and drove in runs. Buck Leonard was just as good as Hal Chase.

—Eddie Gottlieb

Walter "Buck" Leonard, with the Washington Grays.

Buck Leonard performed for the Brooklyn Royal Giants in 1933 and the Homestead Grays from 1934 to 1950. His best years in the Negro National League were 1941 and 1943. In 1941 he batted .392 and led the league. In 1943 he hit 42 home runs.

Born in Rocky Mount, North Carolina, in 1907, Leonard lived in a place called Little Raleigh. When he was fourteen years old, he left school and went to work in a stocking mill and later as a shoeshine boy at the Rocky Mount railway station. He became interested in baseball when they moved the municipal stadium near his home. He'd peek through the cracks in the fence and watch the games being played.

In 1922 Leonard played semipro ball around Rocky Mount and for six years also worked in the Atlantic Coast Line Railroad maintenance shop. He played on a team called the Black Swans and then with the Elks. The Elks played in Norfolk and

Newport News in Virginia and in Wilson, around Raleigh, Durham, and Winston-Salem in North Carolina. In 1933 he went to Portsmouth, Virginia, and played with a team called the Firefighters. Leonard learned how to play first base from Ben Taylor, whom he called the greatest first baseman in black baseball history.

Taylor had a team in Baltimore called the Baltimore Stars. Leonard's Firefighters played Taylor's Stars in 1933. Afterward Taylor asked him to join the Stars. Sometimes the Stars would have to pass the hat around to earn the team's expenses. Sometimes they received only enough for the meagerest board and lodging, spending sleepless nights in fourth-rate hotels infected with bedbugs. There were times when Leonard felt he almost starved to death. He quit the team before the end of the year.

The rest of the season Leonard played with the Brooklyn Royal Giants. In 1934 he joined Cum Posey's Homestead Grays, where he remained for seventeen years.

Buck Leonard:

It was tough playing in the Negro leagues. A lot of riding, a lot of playing. Some seasons we would play 210 ball games. You're riding every day, playing in different towns. No air conditioning. Meals were bad. When I first started playing, we were getting 60¢ a day on which to eat. And we stayed in rooming houses. You know we couldn't stay in the good hotels. Then they started giving us 75¢ a day to eat on. At that time—1933, 1934, 1935—you could eat for 60¢ a day, but it was tough, and then they raised it to 75¢ a day and then $1.00. When I stopped playing baseball in 1950, we were getting $2.00 a day meal money. Of course conditions then were much better. In 1943, during the Second World War, when people couldn't get gasoline to travel, our salaries went up, and from 1943 to 1950 things were much better.

When I was playing in the Negro leagues, I always thought that eventually blacks would be playing in the major leagues. But just when I didn't know. We felt that we should have been in the major leagues. Most of us knew we could have made it in the majors, but since they decided not to have us, we just made ourselves content playing in our own league. We had a Negro National League [and] a Negro American League. Six teams in each league, and in September, the end of the season, we had the Black World Series. We had a lot of fun and we enjoyed playing. We really loved the game. I played with the Homestead Grays for seventeen years. I played professional baseball for twenty-three years. I started playing sandlot baseball down home in Rocky Mount, North Carolina, until 1933. In 1933 I joined the Baltimore Stars, managed by Ben Taylor, the old first baseman. Then I came to New York and played with the Brooklyn Royal Giants. Dick Redding was the manager. Then in 1934 I went to the Homestead Grays, and I played there until 1950, the year the club broke up. Later I went to Mexico and played five years on the Mexican team. I would play in the U.S. during the summer with the Homestead Grays, then I would go to Cuba, Puerto Rico, Venezuela, and Mexico and play twenty-three summers of baseball. I was in twelve All-Star games in Chicago.

When you play for twenty-three years, you know, you have many thrills. I guess my biggest one was when my club, the Birmingham Black Barons, was in the Negro World Series in 1948. That was our greatest team. Josh Gibson wasn't with us. He was dead. We had Luke Easter and Roy Welmaker (who both went up to the Cleveland Indians), and Luis Marquez. Marquez went up to the Boston Braves.

At that time, Willie Mays was playing with the Birmingham Black Barons. He was about fifteen. He could run and he could throw. His hitting wasn't so good, because at that time he couldn't hit a curveball. In 1941 I hit .392 to lead the Negro National League in batting. In 1943 I hit 42 homers, the most I ever hit in one season. When I joined the Grays, they were a Pittsburgh-based team. We started playing in Washington in 1937. We played our games at Griffith Stadium in Washington when the Senators were on the road and in Forbes Field in Pittsburgh when the Pirates were away. For a while, we used a colored park in Pittsburgh called Greenlee Field. The stands didn't have tops on it, and you know how hot it can get in the sun.

Before I go on, I got to talk about Satchel Paige. He had my number and a whole lot of other players' numbers too. Never, never did I get a hit off him. I couldn't hit what I didn't see. Satchel called his fastball a "bee" ball—it just buzzed by you.

When the Dodgers signed Jackie Robinson, we didn't think he was that good. But you can't always tell about a ballplayer. Sometimes you can look at a guy and don't think that much of him. Then he turns into one hell of a ballplayer. But Jackie had the education, and that's what they were looking for as the first black.

There were other guys we thought were better, but they got the right man after all. When Jackie was signed, they were talking about bringing me, Willy Wells, Lennie Pearson, and Cool Papa Bell up, but they were looking for younger players, players they could depend upon for at least five years. In 1952, when I was in Mexico, Bill Veeck, who was with the St. Louis Browns—Satchel Paige was with them at the time—called me and asked me whether I would like to join the team in spring training in California. I told them no. Hell, I was forty-five years old then. My legs were gone. Who was I fooling! I knew I couldn't play baseball every day and I didn't even want to try it.

Buck Leonard was elected to the Baseball Hall of Fame in 1972.

Josh Gibson

I played on the same team with Josh for nine years. I hit third, he hit fourth. Sometimes I would hit fourth and he would hit third, according to who was doing the better batting at the time. If I was in a slump, I would move down a little and he would move up to third and that's the way we rotated. But in my opinion, Josh was one of the greatest ballplayers of all time. He wasn't the greatest catcher, so to speak, but he was one of the greatest hitters. So far as catching and handling pitchers, he wasn't so sharp at that. We had several guys who were a little better—Biz Mackey and Roy Campanella. They were better in handling pitchers and catching pop flies around home plate. But when it came to running and hitting and throwing, I don't know anybody that could beat him. Josh was the most powerful hitter we had in the Negro leagues. I saw him hit one out of Yankee Stadium. At the Polo Grounds, I saw him hit one between the upper deck and the roof. It hit an elevated train track outside the park. Josh hit 70 to 72 home runs in one year. In 1939 he hit more home runs in Griffith Stadium than all the right-handed hitters in the American League combined.

—Buck Leonard

Josh Gibson, 1945

Josh Gibson was born in Buena Vista, Georgia, on December 21, 1911. His father was a sharecropper who migrated to Pittsburgh in 1921. For three years he worked at Carnegie-Illinois steel plant until he saved enough money to have his family join him there. Josh attended Alleghany Pre-Vocational School, where he concentrated on electrical studies.

Growing up in a Northern city gave him a sense of completeness. Although chubby with thick legs, he was a fast runner and won many track ribbons. Swimming was also one of his major interests and he competed with other boys at the neighborhood pools. Although as a young child he had played baseball in Buena Vista, it really became a passion with him in Pittsburgh. Gibson was a great admirer of the Homestead Grays, never envisioning himself as possibly becoming a part of that organization. But that was the way Gibson was, easygoing, pleasant, and, in things other than sports, relatively passive.

When he was sixteen years old and had completed the ninth grade, he left school to become apprenticed to an air-brake manufacturing company and later worked in a steel mill. Gibson never lost his zest for baseball; in fact, it increased to the point where he became an outstanding sandlot ballplayer. Gibson's body and reflexes were especially attuned to the game. When he reached his full growth, he was six feet two inches and weighed 210 pounds—and he was fast. He started out with the Pleasant Valley Red Sox sandlot team and then went on to Gimbel's Athletic Club as a catcher. By 1930 he had helped to organize the Crawford Colored Giants (not to be confused with Greenlee's Pittsburgh Crawfords, which were not established until 1931). Gibson's Crawfords played other semipro teams in Pittsburgh and environs for a few dollars a game. After games they had to "pass the hat" to make those few dollars; the fans were happy to contribute for the entertainment.

The games began attracting large crowds, which were now becoming aware of Gibson's tremendous hitting. Cum Posey sent an open invitation to Gibson, stating that he would be welcome to join the Homestead Grays at any time he saw fit. Then, in July 1930, in an exhibition game between the Kansas City Monarchs and the Homestead Grays, Buck Ewing, catcher for the Grays, suffered a split finger and Gibson was sent for. He happily substituted for Ewing and from that day on he became a regular in the Grays. As an established star with the Homestead Grays, Gibson was credited with 75 home runs as the team barnstormed through New York that year.

In 1931, lured from the Grays by the flamboyant, moneyed Gus Greenlee to the Pittsburgh Crawfords, Gibson remained with that team until 1937. Satchel Paige and Josh Gibson formed one of the greatest batteries in the history of baseball.

Near the end of the 1937 season, when he could not work out contractual and financial agreements with the Crawfords, Gibson returned to the Homestead Grays. The powerful Grays were then the strongest ball club in Negro baseball. For the next two years Gibson's hitting, along with sluggers like Buck Leonard, Sam Bankhead, and Vic Harris, helped the Grays to successive championships.

Josh Gibson and Buck Leonard were such outstanding athletes that it is not surprising that Bill Benswanger, owner of the Pittsburgh Pirates, in 1939, reportedly promised these men a tryout in organized white baseball. On the other side of the coin, it is alleged that Posey asked Benswanger *not* to sign these men because it meant the demise of the Negro National League. At any rate, whatever the story might be, there was no tryout.

Later Clark Griffith, owner of the Washington Senators, talked with Gibson and Leonard about a tryout. But it was an apologetic talk because Griffith was mostly concerned about what a lot of trouble would be caused by their admission into organized white baseball and never really extended an offer.

For Griffith, the temptation must have been almost overwhelming because the Senators were in such serious trouble—a perennial last-place ball club. From his office window at Griffith Stadium, Griffith could watch the Homestead Grays when they played at the park. Griffith's first baseman was Mickey Vernon, a good ballplayer, and his catcher was Rick Ferrell, a Hall of Fame player but still no match for Gibson and Leonard. Griffith, however, was not ready to take on the challenge of this dilemma.

Sometime through this period, Gibson started drinking heavily, but he never missed a game and it apparently did not affect his hitting. On rare occasions, Cum Posey found it necessary to suspend him for a few days. Between the Homestead Grays in the summer and the Caribbean and Mexico in the winter, Gibson was averaging $7,000 to $10,000 a year. Although he had achieved fame, was aware of his abilities, and was receiving an adequate salary for a black baseball star, Gibson had bouts of depression and drank excessively. He complained of frequent headaches and suffered from hypertension.

On January 1, 1943, Gibson blacked out and went into a coma for ten days. He was diagnosed as having a tumor but refused to be operated on—fearing the consequences. His knees gave way, probably from cartilage damage, and he slowed his pace. Some days he was morose, moody, and depressed. Other days he was cheerful and pleasant. That year his knees were so bad he could not go to the Caribbean to play and instead sat on a barstool all day. His weight dropped from 210 pounds to 180.

In October 1945, Gibson, while playing in Santurce, Puerto Rico, learned that Jackie Robinson, the first American black, was signed to the Montreal Royals, a farm team of the Brooklyn Dodgers. While the obvious breakthrough brought cheers from Gibson, it also brought more depression. He learned that many other young, black ballplayers were being considered; he was not on the list. Neither were some of the other powerhouse players of black baseball—Cool Papa Bell, Satchel Paige, and Buck Leonard, among them. They were considered too old. The parade was going to pass them by.

On January 20, 1947, Josh Gibson died of a stroke, at the age of thirty-five.

Josh Gibson was elected to the Baseball Hall of Fame in 1972.

James Thomas "Cool Papa" Bell

I was only nineteen and they thought I'd be afraid of big crowds . . . I took it so cool, they began to call me "Cool." But that wasn't enough—they added "Papa" to it.
—Cool Papa Bell

Cool Papa Bell was the Willie Keeler at bat and the black Tris Speaker in center field.
—Eddie Gottlieb

Cool Papa Bell was the fastest thing I saw on a baseball field. I roomed with him for five years. When I knew Bell he was in the evening of his career, but he could still fly.
—Buck Leonard

James Thomas "Cool Papa" Bell, 1934, with the Pittsburgh Crawfords.

"Cool Papa" Bell was born May 17, 1903, in Starkville, Mississippi, and grew up on a farm. He spent twenty-one years in Negro leagues, the California winter league, the Mexican League, and in Santo Domingo. In 1933, considered his best year, Cool Papa stole 175 bases in an estimated 200-game season. He hit .480 one year. Tragically, there are no other written records of the triumphs of this great ballplayer.

Originally a right-handed batter, Bell taught himself to be a switch-hitter. He was known as the fastest runner who ever played baseball—white or black.

Cool Papa Bell:

When I played it was good, because baseball was my life at the time. I thought it was a real great thing for me to play and travel. I always wanted to travel. We were happy when we were playing. We didn't regret that the doors were not open to black players at the time, but I'm glad it's open for the black boys from now on. I didn't make a lot of money then, but you could do more with the money you were making then.

Sometimes it was tough traveling. When you first started, you had to make small towns where the trains didn't even stop, so we had to take buses. We traveled from one town to another and rested overnight. Sometimes we went 100 to 150 miles. Sometimes we would get there just in time to start the game.

I started playing Negro ball in 1922 with the St. Louis Stars. I played ten years there, from 1922 through 1931. I left there and went to the Detroit Senators in 1932. That team was owned by Cum Posey, as was the Homestead Grays. They couldn't make ends meet with both teams. They didn't want to lose the name of the Homestead Grays, so the Detroit Senators folded, but they kept about five players for the Homestead Grays. We played there a month and a half and they took us off salary. As a result, I finished the season with Kansas City Monarchs. In 1933 I went to the Pittsburgh Crawfords, where I played until 1936. In 1937 I played in Santo Domingo. I helped win the championship down there for Trujillo. We played under the name of the Trujillo All-Stars. From 1938 to 1946 I played in Mexico. In 1942 I played with the Chicago American Giants. From 1943 to 1946 I played with the Homestead Grays. From 1948 to 1950 I managed the farm team of the Monarchs, and that was my last year in baseball.

When I first started playing ball, there were two other black guys who were my idols: Oscar Charleston, a great outfielder, and Jimmy Lyons, a fine outfielder and a great base runner. Oscar Charleston was the greatest center fielder, they say. Before him, they say there was a guy named Spotswood Poles, but after him, they say, Charleston was the greatest. I started out as a pitcher in Negro baseball. Then I moved to the outfield. I also played briefly with Indianapolis in 1922, and Oscar Charleston was there. They hit baseballs to me and Charleston, and I would go farther than he could to get the ball. In Chicago they had me run against Jimmy Lyons when he was supposed to be the fastest man in the league, and I beat him.

When I became a regular outfielder, I played twenty-seven years there and two as a pitcher. I played twenty-nine summer seasons and twenty-one winter seasons of baseball. I played heads-up baseball. I never would settle for first base; I'd go to second, then third, then run home. I was an aggressive ballplayer. I tried to do a little more than most ballplayers.

In those early years of Negro baseball, only once was I approached by a major league team. In 1935 we played Connie Mack's son Earle's team in Mexico City, and they had Rogers Hornsby, Doc Cramer, Heinie Manush, Jimmie Foxx, and Max Bishop, white players, and a lot of those guys played.

There was a great big park in Mexico City, and in this particular game Hornsby, his first time up, hit a ball to deep center over my head, and I ran a long way and caught the ball. I was all over the outfield that day. Hornsby said to me, "Lefty"—that's what he called me—"how did you catch that ball?" I told him I just ran back and caught it. And he said that was the hardest ball he had ever hit in baseball, and I had to catch it. Earle Mack said to me, "I want to congratulate you. If the doors were open to black ballplayers, you'd be the first one I'd get."

He said, "I could afford to pay you $75,000 a year." I said, "Thank you," and he replied, "Maybe that time will come someday."

When I first came up, I felt a black man would never play in the majors, but as the years went by I felt that someday it would happen. We used to see scouts at the Negro league games, but those scouts used to say, "I couldn't find anyone." They would say, "If we could find one who could play major league ball, we would hire him." But they were never honest with us about why they would not allow us to play—blacks always could play if given the opportunity.

Jackie Robinson maybe did not know about this, but when we played the Kansas City Monarchs, the team Jackie was with, in Delaware in 1945, I was with the Homestead Grays. Frank Duncan, the Kansas City manager, came to me and asked me to do something for him—more specifically something for the future of the black ballplayer. He said, "This fall somehow, or in the winter when the season is over, Jackie Robinson will be signed into organized baseball. He wants to go up as a shortstop. We want him to play second, third, first, or the outfield." I was the kind of guy who could hit the ball to any field nine out of ten times, and Duncan said, "I want you to hit the ball to Jackie's right deep at shortstop. He doesn't go over there too well, and he pivots poorly." The first two times up, I hit that ball over there, and Jackie caught the ball in the hole, but he didn't backhand the ball. You're supposed to backhand the ball if you can't get in front of it. He caught the ball and had to take two steps before he threw, and I beat both of those plays out. The next two times up, I walked. I stole four bases that night, trying to confuse him. So I would go into the bag and put one foot up for him to see, he'd reach for it, I would put it back, and slide the other one over the base, reach my hand back, slide, and step over his hand. These are the kinds of tricks he did in the majors—he learned them from me. I told him, "Jackie, shortstop is not your position." So after that, he thought about it and they moved him over to second base. Jackie was satisfied, and what a great job he did.

Maury Wills was already stealing bases, but I talked to him before he broke the record. I told him when he was on the bases to tell the batters to step back in the batter's box, make the catcher back up a little bit. That would give him about two or three more steps. Wills says he didn't think about that. But he broke the record that day.

Funny, but I don't have any regrets about not playing in the majors. At that time the doors were not open, not only in baseball but other avenues that we couldn't enter. They say I was born too soon. I say the doors were opened up too late.

In 1974 Cool Papa Bell became the fifth black to be elected to the Baseball Hall of Fame.

Oscar Charleston

Oscar Charleston, 1915, in his Indianapolis ABC's uniform.

Oscar Charleston was born in Indianapolis in 1896. When he was fifteen, he ran away from home and joined the Army. Since he had previously been a batboy for the Indianapolis ABC's, he naturally gravitated toward baseball while he was serving in the Philippines. He played with the 24th Infantry, an all-black unit, and also ran on the track team, setting a record of 23 seconds for 220-yard dash. Later, he was the only black man to play with the Manila League in 1914. After he served his time in the Army, he rejoined the ABC's in 1915. Earning $325 a month, he was one of the highest-paid black ballplayers. Charleston played with the Lincoln Stars, the American Giants, the Harrisburg Giants, the St. Louis Giants, Hillsdale, the Homestead Grays, and the Pittsburgh Crawfords. During the 1940s and 1950s, he managed the Philadelphia Stars and the Brooklyn Brown Dodgers.

He was a barrel-chested, spindly-legged hero to schoolchildren as well as black adults during his prime years, 1928 and 1929, with the Hillsdale club. His tremendous speed and power at the plate, a strong arm, and an almost sixth sense about where a ball would be hit in outfield made him a subject of debate. Old-timers would say he could hold his own with Tris Speaker, Willie Mays, and Terry Moore. He was a fantastic defensive outfielder.

Oscar Charleston was elected to the Baseball Hall of Fame in 1976.

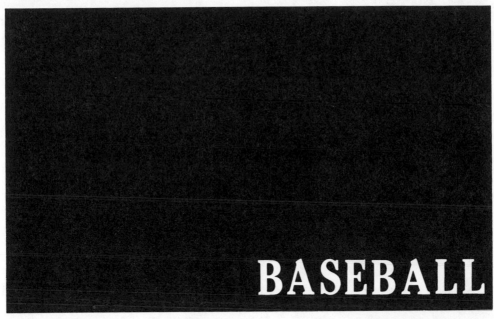

BASEBALL
part two

While there was little movement toward blacks integrating the major leagues in the 1930s and the early years of the 1940s, the invasion of the coffee-colored brigade from Cuba was escalated by Clark Griffith, owner of the Washington Senators. In 1935, under the auspices of Joe Cambria, an Italian ex-minor league owner based in Havana, Bobby Estalella from Cardenas, Cuba, was signed on as a third baseman and out-fielder for the Senators in 1935, 1936, and again in 1939. In 1941 Estalella went south with the St. Louis Browns. He returned to the Washington Senators for the 1942 season, and in 1943, 1944, 1945, and 1949 he played with the Philadelphia Athletes. Joe Cambria also imported many other promising Cubans to play in the major and minor leagues. Roberto Ortiz, an outfielder from Camaguey, Cuba, played with the Senators from 1941 through 1944 and in 1949. Pitcher Tommy de la Cruz of Marianao, Cuba, was signed with Cincinnati in 1944.

The interesting thing about all of these men is that it was suspected that they were blacks. If their names had been Bobby Smith, Robert Jones, Tommy Foster, or Hiram Johnson, they would never have made the major leagues. The need for their excellent skills and performance induced the club owners to camouflage their part-black ancestry as "Latin."

Other "Latins" in the majors at that time included Hiram Bithorn and Luis Olmo. Bithorn, the first Puerto Rican to play in the big leagues, was born in Santurce. A pitcher, he played with the Chicago Cubs in 1942, 1943, and 1946. He served in the military in 1944–45. Luis Rodriquez Olmo was an outfielder with the Brooklyn Dodgers in 1943.

The late Fred Lieb, veteran baseball writer and author of *Baseball as I Have Known It,* noted that in 1942 he had seen a performance of Katherine Dunham's Afro-Cuban dance troupe. Later Lieb was introduced to one of the dancers, who turned out to be Hiram Bithorn's first cousin. Lieb had insinuated that Bithorn might be black; a Puerto Rican baseball authority, however, denied that Bithorn had any black blood.

Bobby Estalella, 1942, with the Washington Senators.

Roberto Ortiz, 1942, with the Washington Senators.

Hiram Bithorn, 1943, with the Chicago Cubs.

Tommy de la Cruz, with Cincinnati.

But again—there was the suspicion. Apparently, the Southern baseball fans also had doubts because several of these players were booed upon their arrival on the field, though not for baseball accomplishments.

However, American blacks were still catching hell. In 1938 Jake Powell, Maryland-born Yankee outfielder, said in an interview on radio station WGN in Chicago that his favorite hobby was "cracking niggers on the head"—in the off-season, he was a policeman in Dayton, Ohio.

Despite the fact that this type of rhetoric was still being spouted by a vast majority of white ballplayers, chinks were beginning to appear in the armor of segregation. In 1940 Leo "Gabby" Hartnett, manager of the Chicago Cubs, said, "I'm not interested in the color of a player . . . just his ability . . . If managers were given permission, there'd be a mad rush to sign up Negroes." In 1941 Shirley Povich, sports writer for the Washington *Post,* said, after seeing the Washington Senators play in Florida, "There's a couple of million dollars' worth of baseball talent on the loose, ready for the big leagues yet unsigned by any major league. There are pitchers who would win twenty games a season for any big-league club that would offer them contracts, and there are outfielders that could hit .350, infielders who could win recognition as stars, and there's at least one catcher who at this writing is probably superior to Bill Dickey: Josh Gibson. One thing is keeping them out of the big leagues, the pigmentation of their skin. They happen to be colored."

On December 7, 1941, America went to war. Large numbers of big-league players were drafted. Joe Cambria even more heavily scouted Cuba and South America and was signing as many as twenty Cubans a year to play in major and minor league teams. The Cubans were given the status of nonresident aliens, permitting them to remain in the country on six-month visas but making them immune from serving in the armed forces.

The Associated Press, on July 27, 1943, reported from New York what might have been a major breakthrough: "Three Negro baseball players will make major league history on Tuesday, August 4th, by trying out for positions with the Pittsburgh Pirates. The three players to be tested by the Pirates are stars in the Negro National League, and their effort to make the club has the approval of William Benswanger, president of the Pittsburgh team. Benswanger, here with his team as they met the Brooklyn Dodgers, said he told Nat Low, sports editor of the New York *Daily Worker,* that he would be willing to have the three come to Forbes Field for inspection and Low named catcher Roy Campanella and second baseman Sam Hughes of the Baltimore Elite Giants and pitcher Dave Barnhill of the New York Cubans."

But the AP dispatch was premature. Benswanger sent a letter to Low a few days before the tryout date and informed him that he'd been the victim of pressure. The tryouts were off, and these athletes of major-league caliber were again denied their rights in the "national pastime" because of the color of their skin.

In 1943 Clarence "Pants" Rowland, owner of the Los Angeles Angels in the Pacific Coast League, announced that tryouts would be held for three black players: Nate Moreland, Howard Easterland, and Chet Brewer. Two weeks later he changed his mind, apparently succumbing to the pressure of the other owners.

Paul Robeson, in December 1943, met with baseball Commissioner Kenesaw Mountain Landis, urging him to admit blacks into major-league baseball. Landis was noncommittal, saying, "Each club is entirely free to employ Negro players to any

Judge Kenesaw Mountain Landis, 1920

extent it pleases and the matter is solely for each club's decision without any restrictions." However, Representative Vito Marcantonio of New York, the only member of the American Labor Party in the House of Representatives, requested Congress to investigate the problem. He said, "Baseball is America's greatest sport and it's silly to pretend that Negroes are not among the best players, when we have a Negro, Joe Louis, as our boxing champion, Jesse Owens was one of our greatest track stars, and Paul Robeson, stage actor, and others have been standout football players." Nothing positive came of this, other than a growing recognition of a serious malfunction of democracy.

Rumblings to integrate baseball continued to occur from time to time. When Vince Devincenzi, owner of the Oakland Oaks of the Pacific Coast League, told his manager, Johnny Vergez, to try out Chet Brewer and Olin Dial, black ballplayers, in 1943, Vergez bluntly refused.

Meanwhile, back on the East Coast in 1944, Bill Veeck, owner of the Milwaukee Brewers of the American Association, definitely wanted the inclusion of blacks in organized baseball. Veeck had a great idea. He wanted to purchase the deteriorating Philadelphia Phillies and then fill the club's roster with Satchel Paige, Roy Campanella, Luke Easter, and Monte Irvin. Jerry Nugent, owner of the Phillies, was ready to go along with the idea of selling the team but was unaware of Veeck's ultimate plan. Out of respect for Commissioner Landis, Veeck told Landis of his idea. Again, the response from Landis was noncommittal. Veeck's plan went down the drain when Jerry Nugent turned the franchise over to the National League and Ford Frick, the league president, sold it to William Cox, a lumber magnate, for half the price Veeck was willing to pay. Obviously, Landis had put the kibosh on the deal.

A state of readiness seemed to be pervading the consciousness of white Americans in the 1940s in terms of their treatment of blacks. While World War II still raged, black and white Americans were fighting and dying together. Joe Louis, the great black heavyweight boxing champ, now in the Army, was instrumental in desegregating baseball and football at the Army camp at Fort Riley, Kansas. Louis states, "There was a lot of racism in the service—Jackie [Robinson] was complaining because he couldn't get on the camp baseball or football team. That made me real mad . . . so I took myself and my influence over to Brigadier General Donald Robinson and I asked him about all this stuff about racial discrimination in ballplaying. I told him, 'Don't you know—you've got one of the outstanding players in this camp and he can't play on the team?' He asked, 'Who are you talking about?' I told him—Jackie Robinson from UCLA. . . . Then he said by all means he wanted Robinson and any other 'qualified' Negro to play on the team. First Lieutenant Jackie Robinson wound up the champion baseball and football player for Fort Riley. Not only that, it opened the door over many parts of the country for integrated ballplaying at other Army camps, even in Georgia and Virginia, and they were tough customers."

Two months after the World Series of 1944, on November 25, Commissioner Landis died of coronary thrombosis in Chicago. Landis, formerly a United States district judge, had been the commissioner since January 1921. He had been installed after the 1919 "Black Sox" scandal: eight players on the 1919 Chicago White Sox "threw" the 1919 World Series to the Cincinnati Reds. Although the players had been found not guilty by a civil court, the new commissioner said, "Regardless of the verdict of juries, no player that throws a game, no player that entertains propositions or promises to throw a game, no player that sits in a conference with a bunch of gamblers in which ways and means of throwing a game are discussed and does not promptly tell his club about it, will ever again play professional baseball." The players were barred from the game for life.

Landis was the kind of "law-and-order" man that baseball wanted and needed to survive. He was verbose, tobacco-chewing, rib jabber, an honest and egotistical man. He loved baseball, but he felt it was his duty to keep it a lily-white sport for red-blooded Americans. In short, despite his love of game, he had no intention of letting blacks, qualified or not, into organized baseball.

During the mid-1940s, under pressure from the black press, Branch Rickey, president and general manager of the Brooklyn Dodgers, was asked to look over two black baseball players at the Dodgers training camp in Bear Mountain, New York. The two men were Terris McDuffie, a pitcher for the Newark Eagles, and Dave "Showboat" Thomas, first baseman of the New York Cubans. Rickey watched but was not impressed with their performance; but the important fact was that this was the first "official" tryout since Charlie "Tokohama" Grant tried out for John McGraw in 1901.

In April 1945, Albert B. "Happy" Chandler, a senator from Kentucky, was selected baseball commissioner. Upon direct questioning, Chandler stated, "I don't believe in barring Negroes from baseball just because they're Negroes." Many historians believed that if it had not been for the death of Landis and the succession of Chandler, the "Rickey/Robinson experiment" could not have taken place at that time.

But before we get to Rickey/Robinson, it must be noted that in April 1945 Boston Red Sox manager Joe Cronin took a look at three black players—Marvin Williams of Philadelphia, Sam Jethroe (1944 batting champion of the Negro American League), and Jackie Robinson. They were sensational, but the word they got was tantamount to "Don't call us, we'll call you."

Troops were returning from World War II at this time and an overall change of attitude in black America was noticeable. The men who had fought for the United States now came home to claim their fair share in the American dream. Ironically, it was World War II that gave blacks the economic tools to begin to attack the system of rascism in America. Educational opportunities, previously economically impossible, had begun to open up. Veterans could now attend college and receive a stipend on the G.I. Bill. Political strength was widening, and blacks now had enough money for leisure activities. Economic power became social power.

Wesley Branch Rickey, who ran the Brooklyn Dodgers, assayed the race problem in terms of baseball and decided he would do something about it. To understand Rickey's manipulations, one must know the man. Rickey was born on a farm outside of Stockdale, Ohio, on December 20, 1881, to a very poor family that believed in the work and moral ethic of the Methodist Church. Rickey completed his education—the equivalent of high school—in a nearby brick schoolhouse. He immediately began teaching in another one-room schoolhouse for $35 a month. With the money he earned, he bought a bicycle, books on Latin, rhetoric, and higher mathematics, and saved $76 toward his college education.

When he received his bachelor's degree from Ohio Wesleyan, in 1904, he returned to teaching—Allegheny College and later Delaware College. Somehow he found time to play summer baseball and football in the fall. A broken leg ended any further

Branch Rickey, 1947

thoughts of football and he turned his attention to baseball. He played with a succession of baseball teams, but despite his keen, analytic mind, he did not have the ability to be productive in the field.

Rickey also refused to play ball on Sundays in accordance with his Methodist upbringing. There were many rough, tough young men playing ball in those days and they often sneered at the college boy whose strongest epithet was "Judas Priest!" Still, he persevered and even with his poor showing on the field, he was admired for his intelligence and attitude. However, his playing days were over when he succumbed to tuberculosis after the 1907 season with the New York Highlanders (as the Yankees were called then). After he recovered in a sanatorium, he attended the University of Michigan, where he got a degree in law in 1911. He practiced law for only a short period and then in 1913 was back into baseball—this time as a scout for St. Louis Browns, later becoming manager of that team.

In the winter of 1916–17, he became president—and in 1919 manager—of the St. Louis Cardinals. The club was in deep trouble financially and desperately needed new talent. Rickey's keen eye found the men he wanted in the minor leagues. But he was outfoxed in his recruiting. No sooner would he make a bid for a contract than the manager of the minor league would notify John McGraw of the Giants; McGraw in turn would offer top money and, of course, get the player. It was certainly a tribute to Rickey's judgment, but, faced with the tactics McGraw used, he was still unable to get the Cardinals off the ground. As a consequence, Rickey revived the farm system that originally had been conceived by John T. Brush, owner and president of the Cincinnati Reds from 1891 to 1902, and owner and president of the New York Giants from 1903 to 1912. Brush started the farm system when he owned the Cincinnati team. At that time, he also controlled the Indianapolis club of the Western League and he fed players from that team into the majors as needed.

Rickey's first moves in creating a farm system were to buy the Houston club from the Texas League and then to gain working control of the Fort Smith, Arkansas, club in the Western Association. By 1940 he had thirty farm clubs, some owned outright and others set up under a "working agreement." These farm clubs provided enough good fresh talent to assure the Cardinals the National League pennant six times during Rickey's reign. The system spread throughout the major leagues and Rickey was called the "Father of the Farm System"; rather, he was the first to implement the system and make it workable. Unfortunately, when Rickey left, the Cardinals plummeted. His zeal and exuberance, plus his "chalk talks" (blackboard lectures) apparently had been essential factors in the team's success.

In 1942 Rickey went over to the Brooklyn Dodgers as president (succeeding Larry MacPhail) and general manager. In view of his great success with the Cardinals, Rickey was assured of the financial support of George V. McLaughlin, president of the Brooklyn Trust Company, which had controlling interest in the Dodgers. Now dealing from strength, Rickey raised the possibility of hiring one or two black players. McLaughlin gave his consent.

It is said that when Rickey was a baseball college coach in 1910, he had one black player, Charles Thomas. Rickey saw the devastating effects of racism when he took his team out of town and Charles Thomas was refused a room at the hotel where the ballplayers were to stay. Rickey, after much ado, was able to get the hotel to put a cot in his own room so that Charles Thomas would have a place to sleep.

Another time, when Rickey was with the Cardinals, he protested the segregated seating arrangement in Sportsman's Park. Blacks could sit in the bleachers and in the right-field pavilion. Try as he might, he could not budge Sam Breadon, the Cardinal's owner, from his position of maintaining segregation. (It was only with the beginning of World War II that blacks were allowed full access to major league parks.) Rickey, a man of strong religious conviction, believed that a man should not be judged by the color of skin. Around 1940, twelve-year-old Art Rust, Jr., was wending his way to a New York Giants–St. Louis Cardinals game when he saw Branch Rickey getting out of his car in the stadium parking lot. After requesting his autograph, the boy asked Rickey if he thought Negroes would ever play in the major leagues. Putting his arm around the lad, Rickey said, "Young man, one day you'll live to see it happen!"

In 1945 Rickey surreptitiously made his plans for the breakthrough of blacks in modern organized baseball, with new Commissioner Chandler's sanction, the bank's backing, and now the approval of the Dodgers' board of directors. For ammunition, Rickey announced to the press his desire to establish a Brooklyn Brown Dodgers team. This club was to be stocked with black ballplayers who would play Ebbets Field when the regular Dodgers were on the road. To this end, he engaged the help of Gus Greenlee, who had removed his Pittsburgh Crawfords from the Negro National League in 1939, and the United States Baseball League was established in 1945. The new league included the Philadelphia Hillsdale Club, the Chicago Brown Bombers, the Detroit Motor City Giants, Greenlee's Crawfords, the newly formed Brown Dodgers managed by Oscar Charleston, and the Toledo Rays. The league never really got off the ground (it finally shut down in 1946) and did not in any way interfere with the Negro American League or the Negro National League. However, it served its purpose well. It afforded Rickey the opportunity to scout for the very special man who was going to go down in history as the first black in the major leagues. The Brooklyn Brown Dodgers provided the perfect guise for this operation—so perfect that it caused a furor in the black press. They decided that again the white man was playing his paternalistic role as regards the black man. They thought the idea of having a white man—Rickey—as the leader of a black team was abhorrent. Not only that, but Rickey would not ever countenance any questions from the press about racism in the major leagues.

Rickey then unleashed his top scouts, reportedly to secure players for the Brown Dodgers. The scouts sent him lists of names of players they felt had the special abilities that the "first" must have. Of course, the familiar names that came up were Satchel Paige, Showboat Thomas, Josh Gibson, Sam Jethroe, Luke Easter, and other black stars. But one name kept coming up over and over: Jackie Robinson.

In April 1945, Robinson, fresh out of the Army, was playing his first season in professional baseball with the Kansas City Monarchs. All season long, Rickey had received numerous and enthusiastic reports about Robinson from his scouts and he liked what he heard—so much so that Rickey went out to California to check out the young ballplayer's background. Robinson's ability was unquestioned and his personal life was exemplary. He didn't smoke or drink and he had a strong sense of pride in himself and his race. The man Rickey was looking for would have to be a man of enough pride and courage to take on "Jim Crow" abuses and derision from the fans and other clubs, as well as from his own teammates.

Rickey was euphoric about what he learned and now he wanted to meet Robinson

Jackie Robinson, 1945, with the Kansas City Monarchs.

in person. Scout Clyde Sukeforth made the arrangements and on August 28, 1945, Rickey and Robinson met. Robinson came with the expectations of being contracted for the Brown Dodgers and was completely floored when Rickey stated that he wanted him to play for the major league Brooklyn Dodgers, first starting with Montreal Royals, a Brooklyn farm team in the International League. After many hours of conversation in which Rickey used all of his skills as lawyer and lecturer to show Robinson the pitfalls, Robinson said, "Mr. Rickey, do you want a ballplayer who's

Jackie Robinson and
Branch Rickey

afraid to fight back?" Rickey replied, "I want a ballplayer with guts enough *not* to fight back."

It was finally talked through and through, and Robinson was to play with the Montreal Royals in the 1946 season. He was to receive a bonus of $3,500 and a salary of $600 per month. Robinson was sworn to secrecy and was to confide only in his mother and fiancée, whom Rickey advised him to marry as soon as possible.

To tie up further loose ends, Rickey got in touch with New York's Mayor Fiorello La Guardia. An Anti-Discrimination Committee was established by La Guardia in August 1945. Rickey and MacPhail were already at work doing their own study of the color problem as it applied to the major leagues. At this point, La Guardia formed a subcommittee on discrimination in baseball in New York and asked Rickey and Mac-Phail to be members. The subcommittee's findings were published October 31, 1945. The following are extracts from this subcommittee's report:

> We have not found a single individual who would admit that Negroes do not possess potential physical capacities which would make them worthy of major league competition.
>
> No one should be taken because of color nor be excluded because of color . . . we are merely asking that the Negro players be given their chance to compete on an equal basis and that ability to perform be the single determining factor.

Jackie Robinson

I don't know anyone who could have stood all the abuse Jackie had to take in breaking into baseball and stick it out to become the great player he was. When you know the true nature of Jackie . . . what a fighter he was and how he had to keep it inside of him . . . it's just unbelievable. Thinking back on it, I'm just glad I got to play alongside Jackie and be a part of history.   —Pee Wee Reese

Jackie was one of the most exciting ballplayers ever. He didn't impress me first with his choppy swing, but he proved to be a good hitter, really tough in the clutch. He was a good fielder, too, and a daring, upsetting base runner. A winner.

—Stan Musial

Sure, there was some grumbling when Jackie came into the league. I guess some of the Southern ballplayers didn't like the idea. But, I tell you, every day that Robinson played he made them eat every word they were saying. He took a lot, but he stuck. I heard him called some awful things by a lot of guys who didn't have the guts to back up what they were saying. Lucky for him, Jackie was playing in the right place. Those Brooklyn fans loved and appreciated him.   —Elbie Fletcher

Jack Roosevelt Robinson, the man chosen by history to change the course of baseball, was born the youngest of five children to a sharecropper and his wife in Cairo, Georgia, on January 31, 1919. When Robinson was only one year old, his father disappeared. His mother, an uneducated but intelligent, strong, religious woman, packed her brood and moved to Pasadena, California, where she was able to get work as a domestic. Since his mother worked almost continuously, the caring for Jackie fell to his sister Willie May, only two years older. When Willie May was of school age, she bundled up her little brother and left him in the sandlot outside of the school building where he played alone. The school authorities called Mrs. Robinson and demanded that she make better provisions for her son. She proudly told the authorities that she preferred working to staying at home receiving public assistance, and she pointed out that it would be far cheaper for the state of California to let her son play in a sandbox than to support a family of six. Under the inspiring leadership of the mother, this closely knit little family survived and moved forward.

Another person who affected Robinson in his youth was Carl Anderson, who organized sport teams in the neighborhood where Jackie lived. The combination of poor Mexican, black, and Japanese children often provoked trouble with the law, but after Carl Anderson came, the trouble ceased. Robinson thought then that perhaps he too would like to be a man like Anderson.

Still another great influence was Mack, Robinson's oldest brother. Mack, a track star, ran in the 1936 Olympics in Berlin and finished a close second to Jesse Owens in the 200-meter sprint.

Jackie Robinson attended Pasadena Junior College and with a partial scholarship attended UCLA, where he worked on campus to earn enough to complete his education. He became a four-sport letterman—baseball, basketball, track, and football. Not as fast as his brother, Robinson nonetheless broke the Pacific Coast Conference's long jump record. A high scorer in the basketball league and the leading ground gainer in college football in the United States, he was without question one of the best all-around athletes to enter baseball.

After college, Robinson worked with the National Youth Administration as an assistant athletic director and found time to teach Sunday school. By December 1941, he was playing professional football for the Los Angeles Bulldogs, and then the United States entered World War II. He entered Officers' Candidate School at Fort Riley, Kansas—a calvary unit—where, as noted earlier, after some resistance to his participation in the sports programs, he became the camp football and baseball champion. He was eventually honorably discharged as a first lieutenant in 1944.

Robinson coached basketball for a short period at Samuel Houston College, a black institution in Austin, Texas, and in 1945 signed to play baseball with the Kansas City Monarchs at $400 per month. However, the complete informality of the Negro leagues unnerved Robinson. For instance, one day in Baltimore, halfway through a Monarch game, the official scorer left the ball park. Teammate Satchel Paige would pitch two or three innings, travel by private car instead of by bus with the Monarchs, and work with all-star teams the rest of the week. Robinson was, therefore, ready and eager for a change on that day in August 1945 when he met with Branch Rickey and signed to play with the Montreal Royals.

John Wright, a black right-handed pitcher who previously played with the Pittsburgh Crawfords and the Homestead Grays, had also been signed by Montreal. Robinson and Wright went to spring training at Sanford, Florida. Both men were pleased that they would not be alone in their anticipated struggle. They shared the abuses of having to live in segregated living arrangements away from the team. They also shared the humiliation of being barred from an exhibition game because the local law forbade competition between blacks and whites. On the road, Syracuse, New York, proved to be the most horrendous city they faced, where the spectators' sharp, vicious tongues would have tried the patience of angels. The city of Baltimore threatened to boycott the game if Robinson and/or Wright appeared on the ball field. Mississippian Clay Hopper, manager of the Montreal Royals, asked Rickey if he thought Jackie Robinson (the implication being all blacks) was a human being. With the greatest difficulty, Robinson managed to keep his temper intact and remembered that Rickey had pleaded with him to always take out his vengeance on the field. Unfortunately, Wright could not take the pressure and after a month he was optioned to another farm team—the Three Rivers, Quebec, team in the Class C Border League—and eventually went back to the Homestead Grays. He was replaced by Roy Partlow, another black pitcher. Partlow was also optioned to the Three Rivers team.

Going along with his conviction to introduce blacks into major league baseball, Rickey next signed Roy Campanella, a catcher with the Baltimore Elite Giants, and Don Newcombe, a pitcher who had had one season with the Newark Eagles. These two young men were assigned to another Brooklyn Dodgers farm team, Nashua, in the Class B New England League.

It was April 18, 1946, opening day for the Montreal Royals—and its first black player—against the Jersey City Giants. Mayor Frank Hague of Jersey City was at Roosevelt Stadium to start the baseball season. He had declared a holiday—the

Jackie Robinson, 1946, after hitting a home run for the Montreal Royals.

crowds were coming by droves, by car, bus, and train through the Hudson Tubes. Blacks and whites wanted to see this history-making game. They saw Jackie Robinson smash a 3-run homer and 3 singles, leading the Royals to a 14 1 victory over Jersey City. To cap the day, Robinson stole 2 bases and scored 4 runs. The only blacks who didn't have tears streaming down their faces were those who were shouting with hoarse voices in a celebration of this symbolic achievement of their manhood.

Robinson moved on triumphantly through the season, through the garbage of hate and ill-will. As more and more blacks crowded the baseball stadiums, Rickey knew he had been right. The Royals won the 1946 International League pennant. Robinson led the league in hitting with .349, drove in 66 runs, stole 40 bases, scored 113 runs, and fielded a brilliant .985 at the second-base spot. The Royals played the Louisville Colonels, winners of the American Association pennant in the Little World Series. When they played in Louisville, the city slapped a quota on the number of blacks to be allowed to attend the games. But in the seventh and deciding contest in Montreal, the Royals won the Little World Series and Montreal went wild. The Canadians hugged, kissed, laughed, cried, and almost tore Jackie Robinson's uniform off; he joined with the Canadians and cried too.

In recalling that first year, Rachel Robinson, his wife, remembers:

Jackie and I got married a month before we went to spring training with the Montreal Royals in Sanford in 1946. Not only was Jackie entering a new field and very uncertain about it, but we were going South for the first time. The whole experience was compounded by our first entrance into a racially segregated area of the country. We had certainly been through racial discrimination in the North, but in the South it was blatant—we couldn't go into certain places. We were bumped off the first plane and replaced by whites. We had to use segregated facilities and that kind of thing. When we were bumped off the plane, no provisions were made for us to get to Sanford for spring training. We had to take a bus and ride in the back of the bus. These were painful things for me, but particularly painful for Jackie because he is such an assertive person and had always been and was very sure of his manhood, and so forth. To have to see him kowtow and submit to these indignities was abominable.

Despite all the problems, Jackie and I at no time wanted to give up the whole idea of his playing in the majors. We constantly supported one another. We reached the point where we joked about the horrible conditions.

When we got to Sanford, we were not permitted to live with the team. This we had been warned of by Branch Rickey. I must say that part of the cushion for us was the preparation that Mr. Rickey gave us. He really laid it out for us in terms of what he could see was in store for us. Mr. Rickey scouted out a wonderful family for us to live with near Bethune-Cookman College. We had heard rumors that certain white players were circulating petitions saying that they were not going to play with Jackie, that they were going to boycott or take some kind of action. Mr. Rickey kept us clued in to those developments. He would say, "That's what's being planned," and he would tell us what he planned to do about it, what his strategy was. When they came in to meet with him, he would tell those irate players that they could play for another club. He always indicated that he was ready to back up his experiment. Rickey was quite supportive to us. Nevertheless, Jackie didn't feel that he was performing as well as he could the first spring because the pressure was so unbearable . . . he was trying too hard . . . he couldn't sleep at night . . . he had great difficulty concentrating. It was rough. I helped Jackie by being with him constantly.

I went everywhere with him. We got up together in the morning, we had breakfast together, and I went to the ball park with him. We didn't socialize at all. We stayed isolated to some extent . . . that was one of the ways we sort of maintained ourselves. Jackie felt the pressure of the black people who were counting on him.

Those first years drew huge crowds. Take a place like West Palm Beach, where they drew a larger black crowd than white, and yet they had a very small segment of the stands set aside for blacks. It was just outrageous. It became so that they came through a hole in the fence and not through the turnstile. They literally took boards out of the fence. The black fans were so eager to come in and so excited about what was happening that they just kept pouring in. It was like seeing cattle coming through that hole in the fence. We knew that the ball clubs were profiting from their presence, and yet they would not give blacks decent accommodations. I finally got so I couldn't go into the ball park. I would sit in the car. I just couldn't stand to see my people treated like animals. The fly balls would come out into the middle of the crowd and they would scatter to let the players get in there to get the ball.

When we got to Montreal in 1946, the fans did not seem to have the same racial hang-ups that we had experienced all through the South. We found a more favorable environment. We lived in a French-Canadian neighborhood where the

Jackie Robinson, 1947, with the Montreal Royals.

people didn't even speak English and we were kind of curiosities. When they finally found out who we were, it was beautiful.

Jackie's first manager at Montreal, Clay Hopper, never really believed in this but was just doing as he was told. He first evaluated Jackie as somebody who could help him win, somebody who drew crowds, somebody whom Mr. Rickey was intent on holding. Therefore it was Hopper's job to make it work. In other words, Hopper was stuck with Jackie. Hopper never went out of his way to be abusive and he never went out of his way to be friendly. As he chewed on his tobacco, he said Jackie was doing his job. Hopper was a Mississippian. He played Jackie only as much as he had to play him. At the end of the season, Hopper came around to some extent, but you never could distinguish between whether he was feeling that Jackie was more a human and he had learned something in this experiment or whether he was just happy to have a winning ball club.

After the end of the first year, I became really worried about Jackie constantly bottling up his emotions. At least I thought he would unwind at home, but he didn't. I begged him to talk it out with me in the privacy of our house, but he just became less talkative. When I finally got him to a doctor, he warned Jackie that if he didn't stay away from baseball he might suffer a nervous breakdown. Jackie wouldn't give up. He'd relax maybe two days and he was back up again, still lugging those same problems around.

Branch Rickey looked at Jackie as a human being, I can vouch for that. Of course, I realize that Branch was a shrewd businessman. I'm sure he saw Jackie as a good business move. On the other hand, there were times he could have dropped the whole thing. Or he could have said, "I tried, but it didn't work out."

On the Dodgers [in 1947], Carl Furillo, Dixie Walker, and Kirby Higbe didn't go for Jackie at all. Pee Wee Reese initially looked at Jackie as someone competing for his job, but later he and Jackie teamed up when he saw they could work together. Carl Erskine was strongly in Jackie's corner from the start. Given the fact that the Dodgers began to win, like Montreal did the year before, people tended to forget about racial problems. Winning the pennant and getting to the World Series and becoming a championship team was uppermost. Those thoughts took over.

Jackie never let things slide by him; that is, he never let anyone get away with any slighting remarks without taking them up. He would not let them forget that he was not able to have all the privileges they had. A funny thing, in that first year, when Jackie was ridden unmercifully by the opposing teams—racial epithets and whatnot—it got so vicious that even those Dodgers who were opposed to Jackie on the club started to rally to his defense. The most vicious attacks on Jackie came from Philadelphia Phillies manager Ben Chapman and the rest of his team. Chapman claimed his bench jockeying was in the tradition, but his attacks were personal and abusive—way outside the tradition.

In the winter of 1947 Jackie said, "Okay, I've taken all the abuse and indignities, but now I've earned my place. I've demonstrated my talents, abilities, and competence. I'm going to let loose in 1948." This was Jackie's plan, whether Mr. Rickey approved or not. This was the turning point for Jackie because, as is always the case, so many liberal whites will help someone get started and want to maintain control over their behavior; then, the minute blacks want to become independent and do their own thing, their own way, they are either dumped or told they're going too fast. But Mr. Rickey went along with Jackie all the way.

Contrary to the general feeling, Jackie was not a bitter man. Jackie was the kind of person who, when he saw things going wrong, just couldn't let it happen. He had to say what he felt, even under the threat of being hurt himself. Jackie was a deeply religious person. He had a striking humility. He felt he had an obligation to do things for his people and for his family. He felt he had been chosen somehow to be the first black in the major leagues . . . that this was some kind of mission for him. He intended to carry it out at all costs.

By 1947, the year Robinson joined the Dodgers, Rickey, knowing that his choice had been correct, continued preparations for Robinson's debut in the majors. In February Rickey met a group of the leaders from Brooklyn's black community. They were advised of his plans for Robinson and he implored them not to make too big a thing of it—no big parades, welcoming committees, or speaking engagements or dinners. Rickey was remembering the catastrophic demise of the career of Andy Cohen in the 1920s. Cohen, the first Jew to play in the majors, had been signed as the second baseman for the New York Giants in 1928. He seemed to have a brilliant future, but the pride of the Jewish people in Cohen and their constant celebration of his accomplishment ruined him. His career was over in 1929. Rickey did not want Robinson to stumble into the same pitfall and he fortunately was promised the cooperation of the black community.

Early in the spring of 1947, the Dodgers and the Montreal club, including Robinson, Campanella, Newcombe, and Partlow, went to Havana for a weekend series against a squad of Caribbean All-Stars. Leo "The Lip" Durocher was the Dodger manager. He had heard rumors that Dixie Walker and Eddie Stanky were getting up a petition to say that they would never play with Robinson. Durocher was furious. In the middle of the night, he had his team awakened and assembled. According to his 1975 book, *Nice Guys Finish Last,* Durocher said, "I hear some of you fellows don't want to play with Robinson and that you have a petition drawn up that you are going to sign. Well, boys, you know what you can do with that petition. You can wipe your ass with it. . . . I'm the manager of this ball club, and I'm interested in one thing. Winning. I'll play an elephant if he can do the job. . . . He's going to win pennants for us. He's going to put money in your pockets and money in mine. . . . From everything I hear he's only the first. *Only the first, boys!* There's many more coming right behind him and they have the talent and they're gonna come to play. These fellows are hungry. They're good athletes and there's nowhere else they can make this kind of money . . . they're going to come scratching and driving. Unless you fellows look out and wake up, they're going to run you right out of the ball park."

The petition was squelched and the only player who did send a letter to Rickey was Dixie Walker. The next season Walker was traded to the Pittsburgh Pirates.

On April 4, 1947, Durocher was suspended by Commissioner Chandler for "conduct unbecoming to baseball." Actually the "conduct" was the result of an unfortunate string of events. Essentially, it involved Durocher's association with known gangsters such as Bugsy Siegel, Joe Adonis, and Memphis Engelberg; in addition, Durocher was a friend of the screen actor George Raft, thought to have underworld connections. The Catholic Youth Organization in Brooklyn under Father Vincent J. Powell protested Durocher's position as manager of the Dodgers. Along with other problems, this convinced the commissioner that in the best interests of baseball Durocher should be suspended, although charges against him were never substantiated.

In order that any possible scandal be drowned out, Rickey announced the Dodger purchase of the contract of Jackie Robinson on April 10, 1947. The news about Robinson, the first black ballplayer with the majors in modern times, overshadowed

Jackie Robinson with the Brooklyn Dodgers.

any other baseball news. It is interesting to note that Clay Hopper, the Montreal Royals' manager, who had questioned Robinson's status as a human being, was now proclaiming that he was a real ballplayer and a gentleman.

On April 15, 1947, the Dodgers played the Boston Braves at Ebbets Field—with Robinson at first base. Robinson had played second base with the Kansas City Monarchs, but Rickey had him moved to first base when he joined the Montreal club. In that first game of the season, the Dodgers won, 5–3, and Robinson's showing was not spectacular. He got no hits, but he did score the fifth run for the Dodgers. In the seventh inning of the second game against Boston, Robinson got his first major league base hit. It was a bunt down the line, which the Braves' third baseman, Bob Elliot, failed to come up with.

However, Robinson didn't feel he was playing as well as he should. The continuous racial slurs, not to mention the watermelons and shoeshine kits placed outside the opposing team's dugout, did not help Robinson's psyche. The Philadelphia Phillies were by far the worst offenders. They verbally abused his manhood and his racial heritage—they likened him to jungle animals and disparaged his family. So intense were the vituperative outpourings of the Phillies that the newspapers were beginning to comment. Ben Chapman, the Philadelphia manager, tried to pass it off as the jockeying that goes on with all players.

Then the threats started. Bob Carpenter, president of the Phillies, stated that his team would not play if Robinson remained; the St. Louis Cardinals planned a protest strike against Robinson and tried to encourage all the teams in the National League to do likewise. It was at this point that Ford Frick, president of the National League, proclaimed in writing to the Cardinal organization:

> If you do this, you will be suspended from the league. You will find that the friends you think you have in the press box will not support you, that you will be outcasts. I do not care if half the league strikes. Those who do it will encounter quick retribution. They will be suspended, and I don't care if it wrecks the National League for five years. This is the United States of America, and one citizen has as much right to play as another. The National League will go down the line with Robinson whatever the consequence.

Strong men are needed when strong measures have to be taken.

Although threats of boycotts quieted down, the abuses Robinson had to endure did not. His teammates knew that Robinson was wedded to silence and in no way could respond. Even those Dodgers who had openly expressed their discontent with having a black on the team began to form a solid block of support around Robinson. It started with Pee Wee Reese from Ekron, Kentucky. While having infield practice before a game in Boston, the Braves began taunting Reese about playing with a black. Reese did not respond; instead he walked over to Robinson and put his arm around his shoulder while they conversed.

Robinson appreciated that gesture and the others that were to follow. Anyone who knew Robinson knew that the role of the quiet martyr was not his. The physical toll this took on him would reveal itself many years later. A natural scrapper, highly vocal and articulate, Robinson made the sacrifice of his true personality during his first major league season, for the sake of the advancement of blacks in the major leagues.

Jackie and Rachel Robinson

In 1947 Robinson lived up to and surpassed the expectations of Rickey. He batted .297 and led the Dodgers in stolen bases with 29 and in runs scored with 125. He was tied for the Brooklyn home-run leadership at 12 with Pee Wee Reese. For the first time since 1941, the Dodgers won the National League pennant. Even Dixie Walker considered that Robinson had done a good job and was instrumental in bringing the flag to Brooklyn. The Yankees beat the Dodgers in the World Series that year, but Robinson was selected by the Baseball Writers Association as National League Rookie of the Year.

Robinson's athletically successful start and his stoic stance led to growing and deepening awareness and subsequent acceptance of black players during that summer of 1947. On July 5 Larry Doby, second baseman of the Newark Eagles, was signed by Bill Veeck of the Cleveland Indians and became the first black in the American League. On July 17 infielder Hank Thompson and outfielder Willard Brown of the Kansas City Monarchs were signed by Richard C. Muckerman, president of the St. Louis Browns. (Unfortunately, the latter two players were released by the Browns after a few weeks and returned to the Monarchs. Thompson, however, later signed with the New York Giants.) Joining Jackie Robinson in August 1947 at Ebbets Field was Dan Bankhead, who became the first black pitcher in major league baseball history. Also that year, sixteen black players were signed to the minor league clubs of the Brooklyn Dodgers.

In 1948 Dodger second baseman Eddie Stanky was traded, and Robinson moved to that position. He remained there until Jim Gilliam, another black player, took over in 1953; after that, Robinson was shifted between the outfield and infield for the remaining four years of his career.

Success in baseball is read in numbers and a ten-year overall hitting average of .311 meant that Robinson was successful. His best year was 1949. He led the league with a

Dan Bankhead, 1947

.342 average and 37 stolen bases, scored 122 runs, and drove in 124. That year he won the National League's Most Valuable Player Award. The Dodgers team in that period seemed to gain a sense of togetherness and a team spirit that was rooted in Robinson. Together with Robinson, the Dodgers won six pennants, lost another in a play-off, another the last day of the season, and finished third only once. After the first season, Robinson reverted to his true self, challenging his taunters with his words and with his outstanding performance on the field.

After Robinson, catcher Roy Campanella and pitcher Don Newcombe came, in 1948 and 1949 respectively, into the Dodger fold. Then other National League teams got on the bandwagon. The New York Giants signed Hank Thompson and Monte Irvin in 1948 and Willie Mays in 1950. Hank Aaron signed with the Milwaukee Braves in 1953; the Cincinnati Reds signed Frank Robinson in 1955. Much of the history of the National League's success and dominance in All-Star and World Series competition in the last three decades revolves around the signing of the high-caliber players named above and other blue chippers, such as Roberto Clemente (1954), Maury Wills (1958), Willie McCovey (1958), Bob Gibson (1958), Joe Morgan (1962), and George Foster (1968).

On the other hand, the American League did not rush to sign up black players, with the exception of the St. Louis Browns and Bill Veeck of the Cleveland Indians, who, besides signing Larry Doby in 1947, signed the fabulous Satchel Paige, who was past his prime but still a crowd pleaser, in 1948 and slugger Luke Easter in 1949. Many other teams were not so quick to take the plunge. The New York Yankees did not sign

Henry Thompson (left) *and Willard Brown, with St. Louis Browns' Manager Muddy Ruel, July 17, 1947.*

a black man (Elston Howard) until 1955, eight years after Robinson's debut. And the cautious Boston Red Sox waited even longer—twelve years—before signing Elijah "Pumpsie" Green.

Since the time when the National League teams first took the initiative and then stepped up the signing of black players, the senior circuit, in my estimation, has become the stronger of the two major leagues.

In spite of his achievements, Jackie Robinson was traded to the Giants after the 1956 season when he hit a disappointing (for him) .275. About a month after the trade, he announced his retirement in an exclusive interview with *Look* magazine. He went on to become an executive with the Chock full o' Nuts fast-food chain.

In 1962 Jackie Robinson was elected to the Baseball Hall of Fame in his first year of eligibility. At the ceremony at Cooperstown, New York, as if to make up for his introspective years, Robinson vociferously criticized baseball for not having more blacks in managerial, executive, and policy-making positions.

Soon afterward, telltale signs of the stress of Robinson's early trials in baseball began to manifest themselves. He developed a heart condition and suffered from hypertension and diabetes. He died on October 24, 1972, in Stamford, Connecticut.

Jackie Robinson was a legend in his own time. He opened the door for blacks in baseball and at the same time helped to increase major league baseball attendance. He inspired countless black youths and was a symbol all black people could look up to. His efforts have made the American experience more meaningful, enabling blacks and Hispanics to become more involved in society. A true pioneer, Robinson led by his deeds.

Larry Doby

Most of Doby's experience in baseball had been at shortstop and second base. But there was little room at either position on the Indians, what with manager-player Lou Boudreau at short and Joe Gordon, whom the club had purchased from the Yankees that winter, playing second. But Doby had the stuff; he was moved to the outfield and became a superstar.

—Bill Veeck

Larry Doby, 1947

On July 4, 1947, Bill Veeck of the Cleveland Indians announced that he had purchased from the Newark Eagles of the Negro National League the contract of a twenty-two-year-old infielder named Larry Doby, a World War II Navy veteran, who was batting .458. Since Jackie Robinson had proved to be "a real big-leaguer," Veeck declared, "I wanted to get the best available Negro while the getting was good. Why wait?"

Thus Doby became the second black to play in the major leagues and the first in the American League.

Doby, born in Camden, South Carolina, on December 13, 1923, made his debut with the Indians as a pinch hitter for Bryan Stephens, a pitcher, in the seventh inning of a game against the White Sox at Chicago on July 5. He was struck out by Earl Harrist. The following day he played a full game for the Indians at first base, replacing Eddie Robinson, and made 1 scratch hit in 5 tries.

Larry Doby's major league playing career lasted for thirteen years and he was named to the American League All-Star team six times. Doby played in two World Series and hit a career total of 253 home runs—leading the American League in 1952 and again in 1954 with 32. He stayed with the Cleveland club for his first nine years in the majors; his final four years were divided among Chicago, Cleveland, and Detroit.

He finished his professional career in 1960 with San Diego, a Triple-A club in the Pacific Coast League.

Midway through the 1978 season, Doby was named manager of the Chicago White Sox, succeeding Bob Lemon, thus becoming the second black manager in baseball history. He was dismissed at the end of the season. In recalling his days in baseball, Doby stated:

I can't say what motivated me to play baseball despite my knowing black men were not playing in the majors. I guess you have to talk about the situation of the late Jackie Robinson . . . During that time, Mr. Rickey decided that he wanted to have a black ballplayer and signed Jackie for his Montreal baseball club. I think every black youngster who was interested in baseball at that time—and we are talking about 1945 and 1946—must have thought about playing major league baseball. You had a person to identify with, and whenever you went out into the streets to play stickball or baseball, you were playing like Jackie Robinson, and I think that motivated me.

I was in the service at the time he got signed, on a little island in the Pacific. There were a couple of major league players on the island at the time also, Mickey Vernon of the Washington Senators and Billy Goodman of the Boston Red Sox, and of course during that time we would go out with each other and have batting practice, pitching to each other. They mentioned quite often that if blacks got the opportunity, I should have the opportunity to be a baseball player. I think that was the first time I thought about being in baseball.

If you ask me about my earlier life in high school baseball, there was nobody for me to identify with. You identified yourself with Joe DiMaggio if you played center field, Joe Gordon if you played second base, or Frank Crosetti if you played shortstop. This was a little odd, because you couldn't say, "I'm going to be a major league ballplayer like these people," because there were no black players involved. What we did in our neighborhood was become these people. It was a kind of fantasy, because you never thought black people would ever play baseball in the major leagues. But when Jackie got involved, it gave me some identification. Then I wanted to play major league ball.

Jackie played many positions: first, second, third, and then outfield. There were a lot of positions where a black man could identify with Jackie. Frankly, at first my thing was football. There I could identify with blacks like Buddy Young, Marion Motley, and Ozzie Simmons. I used to listen to Ohio State games broadcast by Bill Stern, and I said to myself, "I'd like to hear him call my name out one of these days." Blacks were playing and that's what I wanted to get involved in.

Truthfully, playing baseball back then with the Newark Eagles was fun. I enjoyed it. Of course, then it was called "Negro baseball." You talk about the ghetto, you talk about most blacks being born in the ghetto but enjoying life nonetheless. In the same way, if you played Negro baseball, you enjoyed doing it.

I was first approached by the Cleveland outfit around June 1946. Bill Veeck sent a fellow by the name of Louis Jones around to talk to me. He was Veeck's public relations man at the time. He told me the Indians were interested in me. They had already spoken to Mrs. Effa Manley [owner of the Newark Eagles with her husband, Abraham]. But I didn't know much about it, because she didn't discuss it with me. I told them I'd be glad to talk with them, and finally I said I'd be interested in playing. They asked me if I thought I could play major league ball. I was then a kid of twenty-two, but I know I could play baseball in any league, white or black. I was outstanding in the Negro leagues, and I knew I could be the same in the majors. A little before this, a fellow named Al Campanis told Roy Campanella that the Dodgers were interested in me. Roy called me and told me that in about a week or so I'd probably be in Montreal. This was the spring of 1946. By this time Bill Veeck had gotten in touch with Branch Rickey, and it was then decided that I would be the black player representing the American League, since Jackie was representing the National League. With Jackie already there, this was the reason, I guess, I didn't get to the Dodgers.

I'll never forget my first day with the Indians. I wasn't really scared; the toughest part for me was having to communicate with newspapermen. You were dealing with about twenty or so newspaper people, and some of the questions you answered came out a little differently in the papers.

Any time you're involved in pioneering in any field, and being black, you have the same problems any blacks would have. Just like Jackie had in Montreal, I had mine in Cleveland. Because I went straight from Newark to Cleveland, there were many people who resented me being on the club—some because I was black, some because they thought I would take their jobs. There was a Cleveland pitcher, Mel Harder: he was the guy that was always nice to me. But some of them gave me a rough time. I don't want to mention any names. When I walked into the clubhouse in Chicago, all the players were lined up against their lockers. Manager Lou Boudreau started introducing me down the line. For example, he'd say, "Larry Doby, this is Joe Gordon." And each would shake my hand. Out of the twenty-four players I was introduced to, about ten of them didn't put their hands out. The next year Bill Veeck eliminated about five of the guys who were discourteous to me.

You know, Bill Veeck was just as important to me as Branch Rickcy was to Jackie Robinson. Veeck told me to curb my temper and to turn the other cheek. The guy really motivated me. There were places my wife, my daughter, and I couldn't go into. Veeck would say, "If they can't go in, I won't go in." Veeck was quite a man, a great man. I think of Veeck as my second father.

At the beginning, I was told by some of the American League players and some of the people in the stands that I was playing in the wrong league, that I was supposed to be in the National League, where the other black son of a bitch was.

Despite all this, I had a lot of great thrills in the majors. One of my biggest was concerned with spring training when both the Indians and Giants were training in Arizona. Cleveland was in Tucson and New York was in Phoenix. After breaking camp we'd play through the South up to the North. In my first full year, the spring of 1948, we were playing a game in Houston. My first time up, I got a lot of boos from the fans, who were predominantly white. I hit a home run over the center-field fence and was told that only one other person had ever done that and that was Jimmie Foxx. The next time I came up, the stands were quiet and then I felt kind of good. The next big thing that happened to me was in 1948 also. We won the pennant, the first Indian flag since 1920. I hit a home run off Boston right-hander Johnny Sain in the fourth game of the World Series. We won the game 2 to 1. Steve Gromek was the winning pitcher, and we were hugging each other. This picture appeared on the front pages of papers across the country. This was the first time there were black and white ballplayers embracing in a picture. That was a thrill for me. In the 1954 World Series, against the Giants, Willie Mays's fantastic grab off the bat of Vic Wertz was one of the greatest catches I've ever seen. That's got to be one of my greatest thrills. Playing against those great Yankee ball clubs and being a part of the great competition made me feel good. Being able to hit a ball into the center-field bleachers at Yankee Stadium, where only two other guys, Babe Ruth and Mickey Mantle, had ever hit, was a thrill. Then there were those tape-measure shots I hit at Griffith Stadium. Those home runs really turned me on.

When I arrived in Cleveland [in 1947], Jackie Robinson called me. The first thing we discussed was the hotel and food situation. These were the two most important things. After you play a hard game of ball and you want to sit down and eat, and you have your family with you, and you can't, it really bothers you. We put up with this in the Negro leagues, but now that we were major leaguers we wanted the same treatment as the white players. This bugged us more than anything else.

Blacks have had a tremendous effect on the major leagues. People used to think the black player was dumb and just played baseball on reflex and instinct. Now they see that the black ballplayer has intelligence. I feel that baseball is far behind in hiring managers and coaches and front-office people that are black. Hell, you don't have to have a degree in psychology to handle people. Psychology has been a part of the black man for a long time.

THE FIRST BLACKS IN THE PRE-EXPANSION MAJORS

Outfielder Sam Jethroe, Boston Braves. The National League's Rookie of the Year in 1950.

Catcher Sam Hairston, 1951, Chicago White Sox

Pitcher Bob Trice, 1953, Philadelphia Athletics

Second baseman Curt Roberts, 1954, Pittsburgh Pirates

Outfielder Nino Escalera, 1954, Cincinnati Reds

First baseman Tom Alston, 1954, St. Louis Cardinals

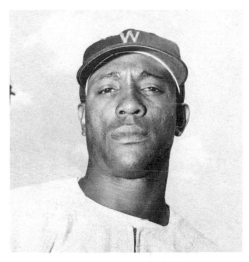

Third baseman John Kennedy, 1957, Philadelphia Phillies

Outfielder Carlos Paula, 1954, Washington Senators

Third baseman Ozzie Virgil, 1958, Detroit Tigers

Second baseman Elijah "Pumpsie" Green, 1959, Boston Red Sox

Roy Campanella

Roy Campanella, 1948

Born in Philadelphia, Pennsylvania, on November 19, 1921, Roy Campanella was a superb catcher who hit for both power and average. He was catlike behind the plate; quick and agile, with a shotgun for an arm. Roy was an expert handler of pitchers and a natural leader of the Brooklyn Dodgers from 1948 to 1957. A three-time Most Valuable Player (1951, 1953, 1955), he set a number of fielding and home run records for catchers until a tragic auto accident in 1958 ended his playing career.

Roy Campanella:

Well, I started playing the Negro leagues in 1937. I was still in school in Philadelphia, and I would just play on the weekends with the Baltimore Elite Giants of the Negro National League. When I started, we received 50¢ a day for meal money. We traveled by bus and we didn't think it was bad. I didn't think it was anything extraordinary, because I was seventeen and I just wanted to play ball. I also wanted to be an architect. That was my goal. I wanted to go to college and major in architecture, but I wanted to play sports too. I found out I couldn't do both.

In the old Negro leagues, we traveled by bus and car. Some of the stops were pretty good. The Baltimore Elite Giants was the only team I played with in the Negro National League. There was the Pittsburgh Crawfords in that league with Josh Gibson and Satchel Paige. You'd play in Baltimore one day or night and be in Pittsburgh the next day. We made this not by plane, not by train, but each team having its own personal bus. We were accustomed to traveling this way.

On the Baltimore team in 1937, we had an outfielder by the name of Bill Wright in left field, Henry Kimbro in center, and another Wright, Zolly, in right field. The two Wrights were not brothers; they just had the same name. First base, we had a fellow by the name of Jim West. Second base, Sammy T. Hughes, a tremendous second baseman, in my opinion. At shortstop we started out with a fellow by the name of Jesse Walker, and we came up with a youngster by the name of Tommy Butts, one of the greatest. And I'll go all the way to the big leagues on this: He was one of the greatest shortstops I have ever had the pleasure of playing with. At third base we had a fellow by the name of Felton Snow, later to become our manager, a tremendous player. At the time I was a third-string catcher, they had fellows by the name of Biz Mackey, Nish Williams, and myself, and being seventeen years old, it was out of this world playing with these guys. We had a tremendous pitching staff, with approximately four starting pitchers and about two reserves and that was it.

I was born and raised in Philadelphia, and I went to a mixed school. It was later, when they spoke to my mother and father and asked them to let me play on weekends in the professional Negro league, when I started to realize that blacks could not play in the major leagues. But there was a black big league. This is where I went and played when I was out of school.

Nobody ever believes me, but I didn't know blacks were not playing major league ball until the owners of the Baltimore Elite Giants came to my house and asked my parents to let me play with them on weekends. My attitude hadn't changed about wanting to play ball. But I couldn't understand why blacks couldn't play in the major leagues. Being brought up in Philadelphia and going to an integrated school all my life, and having always played with whites on the football, baseball, basketball, track, and field teams, it really never came to be an issue with me. But it did when I found out I couldn't play big league ball. Being one of the youngest players on our team, I had this explained to me by the older players and explained in such a way as to show me that none of the white players in any of the other leagues, major or minor, could play any better than we could.

In 1937 there were a lot of black ballplayers who I thought could have made it in the major leagues. Well, everyone knows this name: Josh Gibson. I played with Henry Aaron, and Willie Mays; I didn't see Babe Ruth but he had established himself as being the greatest home-run hitter in white baseball. Well, knowing Josh Gibson and playing against him, and knowing Henry Aaron and playing against him too, I think Josh Gibson was the greatest home-run hitter I have ever seen. Now it's true nobody has ever counted the home runs this man has hit, but I'll say one thing—I'll put him with anybody. Josh Gibson would have been a major league superstar.

The first contact I received from a major league team was when I was playing with the Negro All-Star team at the end of the season in 1945 and at Ruppert Stadium in Newark, New Jersey. This Negro All-Star team was playing a major league All-Star team managed by Charlie Dressen. At the time Charlie Dressen was coach for the Brooklyn Dodgers, and after the game—it was a night game on a Friday—he stopped me on his way to the third-base coach's box and told me to meet him after the game. Then he asked me to go to the Dodger office that Saturday morning around ten o'clock to talk to Mr. Rickey. I didn't know the way over to Brooklyn, but Mr. Rickey explained to me how to catch the subway and get over there, and I did and had a meeting. It was the first time I had ever met Mr. Rickey, and he told me that he would like my services but he didn't think it would be for any major league team.

I thought Mr. Rickey was interested in my services for the Brown Dodgers. I told him I was going to Venezuela to play that winter and I'd give him the address where to contact me down there. He asked me not to sign a contract with anyone. I told him I wouldn't and he said he would contact me. I told him I couldn't sign with the Brown Dodgers because at the time I was under contract with Baltimore. So when Mr. Rickey contacted Baltimore, he bought out my contract. That winter when I was playing in Venezuela he asked me to come back to New York. A few days later it was announced that Jackie Robinson had signed with Montreal. Then I started to realize that what Mr. Rickey wanted me for was a Dodger farm team, the Nashua club. So after we signed, I joined the Dodger organization.

At the beginning of the 1946 season, with the Nashua club of the New England League, our manager was Walter Alston, who later became the Los Angeles Dodger manager. He was also our first baseman at Nashua, and we had a meeting in the clubhouse, and this made me feel very much a part of the team. In this meeting, Alston told all the fellows in the club that if he ever got put out of the ball game, I was to run the team, because I had played in the Negro league for fourteen years. Alston got put out of one game in Lawrence, Massachusetts, and we were losing by one run in the late innings. I put Don Newcombe in to pinch-hit for someone. Newk came through with a run. Alston kidded me and said, "You're the manager from now on." I'll never forget that.

I'll never forget the first time when I walked through the Dodger door in the clubhouse—in 1948—and one of the Dodger white players greeted me, saying, "Oh, we're saved!" Well, this didn't hit me too good—walking in the door with my bags in my hands and I'm going in the clubhouse and that's exactly what he said to me: "We're saved!"

Well, I'm still wondering what that meant, but I didn't appreciate it anyhow. Everybody in the clubhouse heard it, including Jackie, but I didn't say anything. I just went in and Leo Durocher, the manager, came out of his office and greeted me. I doubt if Leo heard it, but Leo was a real true guy and a tremendous man. He was the first manager to accept blacks and to go along with them. That's Durocher.

The first black guy I ever played against that was traded from the Dodgers was Joe Black, and this happened in 1955 in Cincinnati. Holy gee, was I amazed when I walked in the batter's box and they called in Joe Black to pitch to me! Here's a guy I started out with in Negro leagues and I had always caught him and now I'm batting against him. What am I going to do and what am I going to look for? It was quite a problem, but I worked it out. He had to throw the ball.

It's been rumored that Jackie Robinson and I never got along. Well, we always got along, but we had two different approaches to doing things. Jackie had his way and I had my way. I think we were different individuals, but we were roommates and we were, yes, battling for the same objectives. Jackie was a politician, wanted to be a politician. I didn't. I would exercise my vote and would advise all blacks to exercise their vote, but I'd be darned if I would go out and get on a soapbox and try to preach for one party against another party, for one individual against another individual.

Now Jackie and I didn't see eye to eye on this, but other than that, I thought he was the greatest ballplayer, considering all the obstacles he had to face. I was so happy to have Jackie Robinson as a teammate, and to know him a lot better than a whole lot of other people. Jackie was a tremendous athlete, and he got better as he went along. He was someone that could take all the riding and different obstacles he had to hurdle over. Nothing could stop this man, and the more you would ride him, the better he could play. This is the kind of man he was. I lived with Jackie as an athlete and played with him. I could understand what problems he had and what problems I had coming up back then. It was quite a feat, and I only wish that youngsters could appreciate that today.

On Tuesday, January 28, 1958, Campanella was in a car accident that left him paralyzed from the chest down. After many years of running his own liquor store in Harlem, the irrepressible Campanella is now a member of the public relations staff of the Los Angeles Dodgers.

Roy was elected to the Baseball Hall of Fame in 1969.

BLACK STARS OF THE 1950s AND 1960s

Minnie Minoso, brilliant and hard-hitting outfielder from Havana, joined the Chicago White Sox in 1952.

Vic Power, a slick-fielding first baseman, had a twelve-year major league career beginning in 1954 with the Philadelphia Athletics.

Milwaukee Braves' outfielder Bill Bruton, National League base-stealing champ, 1953–55.

Jim Gilliam, switch-hitting Brooklyn Dodgers' infielder and outfielder, and National League Rookie of the Year in 1953, seen here in his Los Angeles Dodgers uniform.

Luke Easter. After leading the Birmingham Black Barons to victory in the 1948 Negro World Series, Easter was signed by the Indians' Bill Veeck. From 1949 to 1954, the power-hitting first baseman starred for Cleveland. Easter twice drove in over 100 runs, hit 31 home runs in 1952, and had a career batting average of .274. After a leg injury ended his major league career, Luke terrorized International League pitchers for a number of years as a Buffalo Bison and Rochester Red Wing, hitting shots long and far.

Richie ("Call me Dick") Allen of the Chicago White Sox in 1974. In 1964 he was the Phillies' Rookie of the Year, and in 1972 he led the American League in home runs (37) and RBIs (113) and was voted the American League's Most Valuable Player.

Tony Oliva, Minnesota Twins' outfielder, was American League Rookie of the Year in 1964, and won three American batting titles in 1964, 1965, and 1971.

Catcher Elston Howard, the first black Yankee (1955), spent twelve and a half years in New York before being traded to the Boston Red Sox.

Los Angeles Dodgers' shortstop Maury Wills, who held the stolen-base record (104) in 1962 and was six times National League stolen-base leader (1960–65), became the third black manager in major league history in 1980, with the Seattle Mariners.

Bill White, the St. Louis Cardinals' steady-fielding first baseman 1959–65, also played for the Giants in New York and San Francisco, and for the Phillies. He hit .303, drove in 102 runs, and had 191 hits in the Cardinal championship year of 1964. He is now a member of the New York Yankees' announcing crew.

Joe Black, a relief pitcher who helped the Brooklyn Dodgers win the 1952 pennant.

Gates Brown, now a Detroit Tigers' batting coach, was one of the premier pinch batters in American League history.

Sandy Amoros, the Brooklyn outfielder responsible for the seventh-game double play that stopped the New York Yankee rally and helped win the 1955 series for the Dodgers.

Don "Newk" Newcombe

He's about as fast as anybody in our league. Even Hal Newhouser, Virgil Trucks, Vic Raschi, and Bob Feller aren't any faster.   —Ted Williams, 1949

His repertoire? A hopping fastball, a low, quick-breaking curve, a couple of changeups, and adequate control. His slight wildness was in his favor: It kept the batters loose. His three-quarter overhand delivery was a thing of beauty. He could hit and field. That first year he got 22 hits, more than any other pitcher, and handled 57 chances without an error.   —Art Rust, Jr.

Don Newcombe

Big Don "Newk" Newcombe, the Brooklyn Dodger flamethrower, joined the Dodgers in 1949 and became an important factor in their pennant victory—winning 17 games against 8 losses, striking out 149 batters in 244 innings, and posting a 3.17 earned run average. During a hot stretch in the pennant fight, Newcombe hurled 32 consecutive scoreless innings. He was honored as National League Rookie of the Year. He went on to become a three-time 20-game winner. His best year was 1956, when he won 27 and lost 7 and was voted the National League Most Valuable Player.

The first game of the 1949 World Series between the Dodgers and Yankees was a classic. Don Newcombe, the Dodgers' black freshman hurler, and "Superchief" Allie Reynolds kept the capacity crowd of fans in Yankee Stadium on the edge of their seats as they dueled 0–0 through eight innings. Newcombe pitched like an old pro, just as if he had participated in many World Series before. His fastball was hopping and his curve was breaking sharply—as ballplayers would say, "He was throwing aspirin tablets"—the Yankee bats were swinging in the air. Reynolds was equally superb.

After eight innings, Newcombe had 11 strikeouts, putting him just two away from the series record of 13 strikeouts in a single game set in 1929 by Athletic right-hander Howard Ehmke. He hadn't allowed a walk and had given up only 4 hits.

In the ninth inning, Tommy Henrich led off for the Yankees. The great clutch hitter, nicknamed "Old Reliable," was facing a top fastball artist, a big man who could blaze the ball in there. Newcombe, who respected Henrich, worked him carefully, throwing two balls low and away to the Yankee pull hitter. Newk's third pitch to Henrich was a low curve. Tommy timed it perfectly and "jerked" it into the right-field stands for a heartbreaking 1–0 Yankee victory. Despite the agony and disappointment with the loss of that first game, Newcombe had established himself as one of the best major league pitchers in just one season.

Despite his size, six foot four inches and 235 pounds, at times he was accused of being against heavy work. There was a part of his personality that led many to call him lethargic.

Born in Madison, New Jersey, on June 14, 1926, Newcombe started playing baseball at an early age. When he was only nine, he pitched batting practice for a semipro team. At the age of ten, his family moved to Elizabeth, New Jersey, where Newcombe made his niche in football and baseball at LaFayette Junior High. In 1941, when Newcombe's brother Roland joined the Navy, Newcombe, although only fifteen, quit school and enlisted in the Army. His mother and father had to petition for his discharge since he was underage. When he got out of service in 1943, he had a tryout with the Newark Eagles, impressed the owners, Mr. and Mrs. Abe Manley, and was signed to a contract. That year he won 7 and lost 5. In 1945 he won 14 and lost only 4.

In October 1945, he pitched in a black-white All-Star game at Ebbets Field. One team was composed of Negro National League stars, the other major leaguers such as Whitey Kurowski, Frank McCormick, Eddie Stanky, Buddy Kerr, and Ralph Branca. He pitched impressively against the big leaguers. After the game, Brooklyn coach Clyde Sukeforth told Newcombe, "Mr. Rickey wants to talk to you." Subsequently, Newcombe signed with the Brooklyn organization and was offered to a Dodger affiliate, the Danville, Illinois, club of the Three-I League. Danville rejected the offer as they had done to Roy Campanella previously. No blacks were wanted. So Newk, with Campy, went to the Nashua club, in the New England League, where he won 14 and lost 4, duplicating his Negro National League record. The following season he won 19 and 6 for Nashua, striking out 186 batters in 223 innings. His wins and strikeouts were tops in the New England League.

In the winter of 1947, Newcombe played ball for the Caracas, Venezuela, club managed by Roy Campanella. There he won 10 and lost 3. In 1948 he was promoted by the Dodgers to Montreal, where he won 17 and lost 6, posted a 3.14 earned run average, and struck out 144 batters in 189 innings. The next year Newcombe made it to Brooklyn.

Newcombe remained with the Brooklyn club from 1949 through 1951. He was in the military in 1952 and 1953, then returned to the Brooklyn Dodgers in 1954 and remained with them until the 1958 season, when he moved to the Cincinnati Reds. His last club was the Cleveland Indians. He retired after the 1960 season.

Monte Irvin

Well, it wasn't left up to me to put him in there, but most of the black ballplayers thought Monte Irvin should have been the first black in the major leagues. Monte was our best young ballplayer at the time. . . . He could do everything. You see, we wanted men who could go in there and hit that ball over the fences, and Monte could do that. He could hit that long ball—he had a great arm; he could field, he could run. Yes, he could do everything. It's not that Jackie Robinson wasn't a good ballplayer, but we wanted Monte because we knew what he could do. But after Monte Irvin went to the Army and came back, he was sick, and they passed him up and looked for somebody else. —Cool Papa Bell

Monte Irvin, with the New York Giants.

Monford Merrill "Monte" Irvin was born in Columbia, Alabama, February 25, 1919. His family, sharecroppers, moved to New Jersey when he was about eight. The Irvins were a poor family of ten, but a hardworking and healthy family. Monte's father and brother worked at a dairy, so the children always had a lot of milk. They kept a garden which all the family worked at to provide fresh vegetables. As soon as he was old enough, Irvin was working, setting up pins in a bowling alley. By the time he was twelve, he was helping to deliver milk by horse and wagon.

He always loved sports and his first love was football. Somewhat fearful of dangerous injuries, however, Irvin decided on baseball instead. In high school he started making a name for himself. He attended Lincoln University in Pennsylvania, playing baseball on the road under an assumed name with Abe Manley's team, the Newark Eagles, in the Negro National League. Irvin had hopes of becoming a dentist but knew he would never have enough money to complete his education, so he left college after two years and in 1939 became a full-time member of the Eagles.

In 1949, when Monte Irvin was thirty years old, he entered the New York Giants organization. During the eight years he played the major leagues, he established himself as one of the National League's top right-handed hitters. He was the power hitter behind the Giants' outstanding drive to their "miracle" pennant in 1951. Irvin batted .312 and led the league in runs batted in with 121. In the World Series against the Yankees that year, Irvin led the Series with a .458 batting average, 11 hits, and 2 stolen bases.

Monte Irvin:

Playing Negro baseball wasn't as bad as a lot of people thought. In other words, we didn't make much money, but we had lots of fun. We played in the summer in the United States and then in the wintertime we would go to Puerto Rico, Venezuela, Mexico, Cuba, Santo Domingo, and Panama. You could wind up in the black with some money in your pocket, because at that time our aspirations were to buy a house and accumulate something for our families, because while we were young fellows and fun-loving and so on, we wanted security for our families. It wasn't nearly as bad as a lot of people said.

Traveling by bus was rough. It was a thrill for me because I had never done much traveling, and we used to go to Rochester, Pittsburgh, and Chicago. I had never been to any of these places and most of the fellows had never been there either. During the thirties and early forties, we were given the chance to travel extensively. So you went in anticipation of seeing something new, and most of us in the club felt that way. It wasn't tiring, even though the buses weren't that comfortable then. Later on they were, when they became air-conditioned. Any time the bus stopped, it had to be in a Negro section so that you could be accommodated, because at that time you couldn't get served on the highway. You couldn't stay at any of the hotels so, consequently we ate out of bags, so to speak. Cheese and crackers and sardines and tuna fish and milk. We got used to it because it was a way of life.

Say we played an All-Star game or an East-West game in Chicago. We got paid $50. We might have 53,000 people in the stadium, but you still got paid $50 for that game. But that was $50 more than we had. Salaries at that time averaged maybe $150 to $200 [a month], which was a lot of money at that time. Out of that you could save $100 to $150 because taxes were very low. We played good ball and had a lot of fun.

There was a great rivalry between the white semipro clubs and the black teams of the Negro National League and the Negro American League. They [the white clubs] would do almost anything to beat us. We beat them more times than they

Monte Irvin (left), Barney Brown, and Larry Doby in Puerto Rico, 1945. Pitcher Barney Brown played in the Negro National League from 1932 to 1949 with the Cuban Stars, the Philadelphia Stars, and the New York Black Yankees.

beat us, because we actually had strong teams and they would only play on weekends. We played every day. They would squeeze us—by that I mean they had their own umpires and very rarely would they be called out in a crucial situation. They had to swing to actually strike out. Some of our pitchers would throw the ball right down in there on the three-and-two count, but very often it was called ball four. What we would do before a game is get together with the umpire and ask him, "What kind of game are we going to have today?" We would tell him that we hoped he wasn't a prejudicial umpire. We would tell him that if he was competent, he would call it like he saw it. If he was prejudiced, then he would squeeze us. And we hoped he was not like that—that if he were that way, it might cause a lot of trouble and we might not play anymore. We decided to do it that way because we had no other recourse, and often it would work and he would call it the way he saw it in a crucial situation.

Another trick the white teams used to play when we were at the plate: They would substitute balls that had been put in ice boxes overnight to deaden them. When *they* were hitting, they would switch back to the regular balls. For the most part, however, it was great rivalry, and the games overall were something to watch.

In the middle thirties, more of us thought we would not get a chance to play major league ball because the feeling of the country was so anti-Negro. In other words, they wouldn't play against us. In fact, earlier there had been All-Star white teams selected to play All-Star black teams, and these All-Star major league teams were beaten most of the time. The commissioner and league presidents then said there could not be any postseason games where there were more than three major leaguers per squad to compete against a black club. They did not want to be embarrassed, because we really had some great ballplayers, like Biz Mackey, Ray Dandridge, Roy Partlow, Josh Gibson, Satch Paige, Sam Jethroe, Leon Day, Willy Wells, Joe Green, and Raymond Brown. At that time I was rated the best Negro prospect. I was the center fielder, ran like a deer, and threw with power. In fact, Josh Gibson told me that when his reign was over he thought that I came close to becoming the "King of Swat."

When I was playing black baseball, I could do it all. And I could throw like Willie Mays, Joe DiMaggio, or Carl Furillo. None of them could beat me throwing. I was a consistent hitter, a money hitter. And when the going got tough I could really hit, and everybody in major league baseball thought that if I had gotten a real chance, I would have been the first black selected to play major league baseball.

What happened was I went in the Army and lost my feel for playing and never got a chance to play. I lost my sharpness when I came out. I wasn't the same. Hell, I stayed in the Army for three years. I wasn't the same player when I came out that I was when I went in.

I was first approached by the Brooklyn Dodgers in 1945. I told Rickey at that time, "I'm trying to fight my way back to the way I used to be and when I get to that point, I'll let you know." In the meantime, they went ahead and signed Jackie Robinson. Jackie was signed in 1945 and made the majors in 1947. I just want to say they picked an excellent candidate because we know what he's done. What a great combination he made. He might not have been the greatest ballplayer starting out, but he improved and went ahead and made an excellent record. He was just a credit to us the way he handled things. He made it much easier for all of us who came afterward. Campy, if given an opportunity earlier, could have stepped right in too. Campy was a star. He was a star in 1941 and 1942. He started early, but when he polished his skills a little bit, nobody could touch him. When Josh Gibson was alive and playing, Campy knew automatically he was the second-string catcher because Josh was head and shoulders above Campy in every department. Campy was the first to admit this. They say Babe Ruth had charisma. Well, Josh had the same thing. When he talked to you, you would like him because whatever he said, he said it a bit differently than anybody else. When he hit that ball, he hit it a little bit farther than anybody else. Josh had that boyish manner about him. He knew he was the best. He had that quiet kind of confidence.

In 1948 Hank Thompson and I were playing in Cuba. We both were having great years down there. He was playing for Havana and I was playing for Alemendares. In Cuba, that's like the Brooklyn Dodgers playing the Giants. The Giants sent one of their ace scouts down there, Alex Pompez, to find out whether or not we would like to play organized baseball. This was the winter of 1948. We told them yes. The maximum salary was $5,000 [a year], so we lost money in order to sign, but we knew if we did well and came up, we could make more money in the long run. We came up, of course. Hank had been up in 1947 with the Browns. He didn't have instant success, and he was sent down, along with Willard Brown. When Hank and I signed with the Giant organization, we spent two or three months with Jersey City, then we were called up to the Polo Grounds. I was put on third base, Thompson was put on second base. Later on he played third and I played first; Leo Durocher was just experimenting to see where we'd fit. Things finally got straight when I started playing left field and Hank played third with Willie Mays in center and Whitey Lockman on first base. Then we really started to roll.*

Jackie Robinson broke the color line, but a quota system went into effect to limit the number of blacks on a team. The Giants could have won the pennant in 1950 if the team had fielded one more black man. Hank and I were already starters. The team's weakest position was third base. Ray Dandridge had been an exceptional ballplayer in the Negro leagues in his youth and although he was forty and playing third base for the Giants' Triple-A farm club in Minneapolis, he was better than anyone the Giants had at third. He could still field, he could hit well, and he was hungry. Dandridge wanted to play in the major leagues and Hank and I pleaded with Durocher to bring him up. Durocher said his hands were tied. I have to believe, at that time, nobody wanted three black men on the field.

I got a great reception from the Giants. That was two years after Robinson and Doby. Although Hank Thompson and I were the first blacks to play with the Giants and there were a lot of Southerners on the club, they treated us cordially. When I say Southerners, I'm talking about Alvin Dark, Ed Stanky, Whitey Lockman, Don Mueller, Dusty Rhodes, and Johnny Mize.

The Giants knew Hank Thompson and I had ability and all we needed was more experience and confidence. Once we started to come around, we were all right. Hank went on to become a fantastic third baseman, and I became a pretty good fielder, hitter, and base stealer and had a pretty good career. But, you see, I lost ten or twelve good years. I came up at thirty-one years of age and played until I was thirty-eight. I would like to have come up when I was eighteen or nineteen. I could have made it then. Yes, I'm a little bitter about it, but there's nothing you can do. There's no point in being uptight, because it'll only hurt you when you feel that way.

---

* On July 8, 1949, at Ebbets Field, Irvin and Thompson were added to the Giants' lineup for the first time. When Thompson stepped up in the leadoff spot in the first inning to bat against Dodger Don Newcombe, it marked the first time in major league history that a black batter faced a black pitcher. Thompson went hitless, and Irvin, used later in the game as a pinch hitter, walked as the Dodgers won, 4–3.

I think the black player has been the salvation of baseball. This is why the National League has dominated World Series and All-Star competition for the past thirty years.

Irvin finished up with the Chicago Cubs in 1956. In 1984 he retired from his post as an executive in the baseball commissioner's office.

In 1973 Monte Irvin was elected to the Baseball Hall of Fame in recognition of his outstanding play in the Negro leagues.

Willie Mays

Willie ranks with DiMaggio as the best I ever saw. He's a perfect ballplayer, too. Mays can beat a club with his bat, his glove, his arm, and his legs. Look at it either way you'd like: He's stolen more bases than any other home-run hitter who ever lived and hit more homers than any base stealer, past or present. The guy plays with a contagious enthusiasm. Why, he can run better and faster, looking over his shoulder to see where the ball is, than most players can digging for the next base with head down.
　　　　　　　　　　　　　　　　　　　　　　　　　　　　　　　　—Stan Musial

I wouldn't trade Willie even up for anybody in baseball.
　　　　　　　　　　　　　　　　　　　　　　　　　　　　　　　　—Leo Durocher

Willie Mays, 1967,
San Francisco Giants

In 1950 the Giants were desperate. They badly needed a first baseman to play for one of their Triple-A farm clubs. They received information that just the guy to fill their needs was with the Birmingham Black Barons. However, once the Giant scout arrived at the ball park, he forgot all about the first baseman. He saw Willie Mays playing center field. Before the game was over, he was on the phone to New York. "This is the greatest player I've ever seen," he told Jack Schwarz, secretary of the Giants' farm system. "I'm afraid to let this go until morning. How high can we go for him?" Almost before the phones were hung up, the Giants purchased Willie's contract from the Barons.

For twenty-two years, Willie Mays gave his all on the major league base paths, in the outfield, and at the plate.

It all started in Alabama in 1950. It started because of what Giant scout Eddie Montague thought of a nineteen-year-old outfielder with the Birmingham Black Barons. The Giants gave Birmingham $14,000 for Mays and assigned him to Trenton, a Class B team.

Mays had much success with Trenton in 1950, his first professional season. He hit .353 and was rewarded the following season with a ticket to Minneapolis. In his first 35 games, Mays hit an astounding .477; before the 1951 season progressed further, Mays was in New York.

Willie Howard Mays was born on May 6, 1931, in Westfield, Alabama. His greatest ambition when he was young was to be a singing cowboy. His parents' marriage only lasted a short time, and Willie and his father went to live with Willie's Aunt Sarah. His father was a baseball player and his mother a fine athlete herself—a track star who held a couple of women's track records in that part of the country. His mother remarried and Mays became a big brother to ten half brothers and sisters who lived nearby.

From the time Mays was two, his father had him playing ball. Mays Sr. played with semipro teams around Birmingham and because of graceful fielding he was called "Kitty Kat." With his father's competent and constant instructions, there was nothing for Willie Mays to become other than a ballplayer.

In 1951 the Giants under Leo Durocher were out to beat the Dodgers. They needed the strong hitting of a Willie Mays. But in his first twenty-two trips to the plate, Mays went hitless. He finally went to Durocher in desperation and asked to be taken out of the lineup. Durocher responded, "You're my center fielder if you don't get a hit the rest of the season." By season's end, Mays had hit 20 home runs and knocked in 68 runs. The Giants, much like Mays, made a miraculous comeback that season. They had trailed the league-leading Dodgers by thirteen and a half games during August. But the Giants caught and tied the Dodgers on the last day of the season and beat them in a three-game play-off climaxed by Bobby Thomson's home run in the bottom of the ninth inning: the so-called "Miracle of Coogan's Bluff." New York won the pennant and Mays won the National League's Rookie of the Year Award.

In 1952, after appearing in only thirty-four games, Mays went into military service. He returned in 1954 and began to tear up the league. At this point, Mays seemed to be able to do anything he wanted to do. Honus Wagner has been considered the best player in National League history, but Mays ranks right up there with Wagner in his ability as an all-around player. Both Wagner and Mays were the best defensive players at their positions and the best base runners. Mays was a powerful hitter, twice surpassing 50 home runs in a season. He led the National League in hitting with .345 in 1954 and reached his peak, .347, in 1958.

Six times Mays stole at least 20 bases and hit at least 20 home runs in a single season, including two seasons in which he stole at least 30 bases and hit at least 30 home runs.

In the 1954 World Series against the American League champion Cleveland Indians, Mays made an unbelievable catch of a drive off the bat of Vic Wertz. Mays raced to deep center field, approximately 460 feet from home plate, stuck up his glove, with his back to the diamond, and made the catch that people still talk about today.

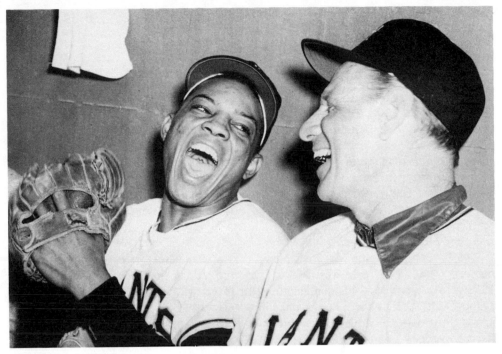

Willie Mays and Giants' manager Leo Durocher, 1954

Willie Mays:

Wertz hit the ball a long way. But it was to straightaway center in the Polo Grounds . . . and you could hit them a long way to straight center at the Polo Grounds. I turned my back and ran, looked over my shoulder once to gauge the flight of the ball, then kept running. I caught it over my shoulder . . . spun and threw . . . and Davey Williams had come out to take the relay, and on the sequence Doby managed to tag and go to third, while Rosen didn't go anywhere. I think the throw was the remarkable thing, because the ball did get back there in a hurry, and I was a good 450 feet out when I caught it. The catch wasn't that difficult. Any ball you go a long way for is exciting to the fans in the stands. They're not looking at you when you get the jump on it . . . at that moment, they're looking at the hitter. I'd gotten the good jump . . . had plenty of running room, and the ball stayed up for me. The Giants won the Series in four games.

I think the finest catch I ever made came off against Brooklyn's Bobby Morgan. I ran far to my right, into left center field. I leaped through the air so that my body was stretched full out and parallel to the ground. I caught the ball with the tip of my glove and I fell so hard that my right elbow hit me in the stomach knocking me unconscious. But somehow, as I collapsed I brought the gloved hand and the ball up under my body, tucking it against my chest, so that at no time did the ball touch the ground . . . they tell me Leo Durocher ran to the outfield and turned me over and the ball was cradled against the letters on my chest.

Mays had an electrifying quality that inspired his club, an intangible effect that cannot be reflected in batting averages or fielding records. The Giants, when he joined them in May of 1951, were in sixth place; by the end of the season they had won the pennant. Mays's contribution to the "Miracle of Coogan's Bluff" was a substantial one. He played with rare élan, many times losing his cap during mad dashes around the bases and in the outfield. He ranged far and wide to convert impossible catches into routine plays. Durocher, who sometimes spoke rather harshly to players for whom he had less regard, understood him perfectly, nursed him carefully, and let him play his own game. Mays, who had fine instincts and could remember signs, could not readily recall people's names, so he would start every conversation with "Say hey," the phrase that became his hallmark.

The Giants and Willie Mays left New York in 1958 when owner Horace Stoneham decided to move the team west to San Francisco. Along the trail, from 1951 through 1973, Mays established his qualifications for future selection for the Baseball Hall of Fame. He led the league in home runs four times, hitting his season high of 52 in 1965. He is third only to Hank Aaron and Babe Ruth in career home runs, with 660. He batted over .300 ten different seasons. He was named the National League's Most Valuable Player in 1954. He was named to the National League's All-Star team every season from 1954 to 1973. In one game he hit 4 home runs, tying the major league record.

It was perhaps fitting that Mays should end his career where it began—in New York. He joined the New York Mets in May 1972, in a trade that sent Charlie Williams to the Giants, along with $50,000. He made an auspicious debut with the Mets against his former teammates on May 14. With the score tied at 4–4, Mays sent a long drive over the wall in left center field to win the game for the Mets.

Willie Mays announced his retirement to a packed house at Shea Stadium in New York in September 1973.

I was with the Giants for twenty years, and if you would watch them and the way they played, you would see we would play sometimes seven or eight blacks on the field at the same time. To me, when you do that, you have a lot of nerve to put that together. I remember one time in Atlanta . . . we played nine black guys. When you do that in the South, you have to have a lot of nerve.

Stoneham did something else too . . . the case of Hank Thompson, the Giants' best player in the 1954 World Series. Even though me and Dusty Rhodes got all the headlines, it was Thompson who made that series move—more than anybody else. After his career with the Giants was over, Thompson got into a lot of nonbaseball trouble. Horace Stoneham helped him get clear of it.

Thompson broke into the majors with the St. Louis Browns along with Willard Brown in 1947. I don't know the motives of the Browns—what with St. Louis being a Southern city with separate rest rooms for whites and blacks in the train station and the hotels all segregated. St. Louis, however, had a good-size black population. And since the Browns were not drawing white fans, somebody told me, they got the idea they could attract black business by bringing in black ballplayers. Thompson didn't make it with them, lasting only twenty-five games. But two years later Stoneham brought him up. He was a black boy who had "failed," but he was being given a second chance. This to me was complete racial

Monte Irvin, (left), Willie Mays, and Hank Thompson: major league baseball's first all-black outfield, before game one of the 1951 New York Giants–New York Yankees World Series.

equality in baseball. Before Stoneham, a black player would have one chance to fail—white boys had many.

I almost became a Brooklyn Dodger. I was playing in Birmingham at the time, and Artie Wilson was the shortstop. He also served as sort of a Dodger scout, too. He was coming to Oakland at the time. Chuck Dressen was the manager there, and Wilson told me that next year he would try to take me to spring training in California with the club. Oakland was then a Dodger farm club. Wilson called Chuck and told him, "We have scouted Mays and we don't feel that he can hit the breaking ball right now, so we can't use him." A few months later, the Giants scouted me and I was signed immediately.

When I started with Trenton, New Jersey, in the Interstate League in 1950, I played there three months. That was something like Jackie Robinson breaking into the majors—I was there myself. It was a strange experience for me because I had to really stay apart from the ballplayers. When I say apart, I mean they would drop me off at a different hotel, then at game time they would pick me up. But I wanted to play so bad that those kinds of things didn't worry me. I felt that if I could survive that kind of treatment, I could come to the majors very quickly. Horace Stoneham to me was just as important to the black ballplayer as Branch Rickey. He didn't have a racial barrier. If you could play baseball, you could play on the Giants. He proved that over the years by having so many black players.

Running at top speed with his back to the plate, Willie Mays makes a spectacular, over-the-head catch of Cleveland Indians' first baseman Vic Wertz's 450-foot clout, in the eighth inning of the 1954 World Series opener at the Polo Grounds in New York City. The Giants went on to win 5–2.

When I joined the Giants, Hank Thompson and Monte Irvin were just like fathers to me. They took good care of me. They saw to it that I was in bed by ten or eleven o'clock at night. I admired both of them. I knew that coming to New York at an early age, if I didn't have advice from those fellows, I couldn't have made it.

Willie Mays sure could play baseball. The record tells it all: .302 lifetime batting average, 660 home runs, 2,062 runs, 1,903 runs batted in.

In 1979 Willie Mays was elected to the Baseball Hall of Fame.

Today Willie is in public relations for an Atlantic City casino.

Ernie Banks

Ernie Banks, number-one power hitter among shortstops, with the Chicago Cubs.

Ernie Banks was born January 31, 1931, in Dallas, Texas.

Do I remember my first homer for the Cubs? I certainly do. It was in old Sportsman's Park in St. Louis, off Gerry Staley, September 30, 1953. The pitch? A knuckle ball that hung inside.

A few days before that, Banks had reported to the Cubs—a thin shortstop, weighing only 150 pounds, who was purchased from the Kansas City Monarchs for a reported $25,000. He said he was frightened and really didn't get over it, didn't feel confident of himself, until about 1958 and 1959, when he won the National League's Most Valuable Player Award in successive years.

Ernie Banks played for nineteen years with the Chicago Cubs and delighted Wrigley Field fans with his long and frequent home runs. He hit 512 home runs, five times hitting over 40 in a single season. Banks hit a record five grand slams in 1955, and his 47 home runs in 1958 are the most ever hit by a shortstop.

Ernie Banks (left), *with second baseman Gene Baker.*

Ernie Banks:

I enjoyed black baseball very much. I played with some outstanding men when I was with the Kansas City Monarchs. Men like Gene Baker; Connie Johnson, who was later with the White Sox; Curt Roberts, who played for the Pittsburgh Pirates; Barney Sorrell . . . a lot of great players who were playing at that time and in the early fifties. And I remember those days extremely well—they were very important to me in my life as a baseball player. We played baseball in the Negro National League. We played good defense, had all-around good hitting . . . it was real heads-up type baseball. We had a tremendous love for the game and were happy to represent the Kansas City Monarchs. We traveled by bus. It was tough, but we had a lot of fun. We kind of enjoyed that camaraderie on the bus, in the hotels, in the ball parks. It was an all-around, well-balanced lift, a great experience.

The first major league teams to show interest in me were the Cardinals and the White Sox. I was never aware of it until I was signed by the Cubs, but at that time I didn't know the scouts who were following me. A guy by the name of Downey, who was in Chicago, followed me for the White Sox and another scout named Quincy Troupe scouted me for the Cardinals. I was just playing and enjoying it and wasn't thinking about playing in the major leagues or signing with any specific organization. But after I signed with the Cubs, I met these men and they told me they had followed me for more than a month to sign me.

When I joined the Cubs in 1953, I got great treatment. First of all, I joined the Cubs from Pittsburgh, where I played my last game with the Monarchs, and I flew into Chicago, where I was met by one of our coaches, Roy Johnson, at the airport. He took me to the hotel. That impression was a good one because it showed me they cared. It showed me they were concerned and that they really wanted me. After I arrived at the ball park the following morning, I had a chance to meet my good friend Gene Baker, who signed with the Cubs the same time I did. He kind of guided me to my locker and the players on the team and introduced me to them, because he had met them in spring training of 1953. The Cub manager at that time was Phil Cavarretta. He came out and introduced himself. Everybody was warm and candid. They let me know what I was supposed to do on that particular day: go out and take infield and batting practice, run around the bases, the usual bit you tell young players when they first arrive on a club.

Gene Baker and I worked pretty close together. We hung out together and actually did everything together on the field. I kind of followed him, because he had much more experience than I did in baseball. So it was a great warm, cordial feeling in Chicago. A lot of fine people, great people, great players like Ralph Kiner, who's now with the New York Mets broadcasting, Hank Sauer, Frankie Baumholtz, Paul Minner, Dee Fondy, and a lot of players I remember so well and still see who were nice to me. When I got out on the field, the fans' response was tremendous for Gene Baker and me.

The ballplayer, white or black, who had the greatest influence on my career was Gene Baker, because we were together in Chicago for five years. He had the experience; he played in the Pacific Coast League for five years and had great years there. He was an outstanding player, a great student of baseball with a lot of instinct for the game and for people. He had a wonderful business mind as far as contracts were concerned—what to sign and what to do. Just being with him was a tremendous influence on my baseball career. Of course, Jackie Robinson was playing when I came up. I'll always remember that he was one of the first players on the Dodgers to come over and wish me well. He told me a few things, to play hard and do the best I can. I was very appreciative of that. I'll always remember Jackie as the man who gave me great inspiration when I started with the Cubs.

As for some other highlights of my career, there have been such things as setting marks and records that created an image for us so that we can be in the Hall of Fame. The MVP award was one award that I'm truly proud of. I won it two years in a row—1958 and 1959. Then there was the fielding record for shortstops in 1959, 5 grand-slam home runs in one season, hitting more homers than any other shortstop in the majors for one season (47 in 1958). Playing in twelve All-Star games was certainly a great thrill . . . to be associated with great players like Willie Mays, Hank Aaron, and Stan "The Man" Musial, Billy Williams and Duke Snider, Jim Gilliam and Jackie Robinson, and all the other great players in the National League. Hitting a home run in the [Negro] All-Star game in Kansas City, where I started back in 1951, was certainly a great thrill.

When I was in the big leagues, there was a tremendous amount of great ball-players, but the guy who stood head and shoulders above them all was Willie Mays. He was so exciting—not only exciting to the fans, but to the teams he played with—the Giants—and against. He was just amazing. Overall, Hank Aaron had had a considerable influence on my life as far as success and balance are concerned. He's done a lot of great things in his career and is still doing a lot of things. He understands people, he accepts people. He always remembered the route he took when he came up. He has a tremendous feel for people. He has never forgotten that people are the ones that make us what we are. He is that type of player.

As far as the winning attitude is concerned in my career, Roberto Clemente was the player who gave me that winning-type feeling, that winning is the thing, winning is the only thing. To strive to win and be best—he made a great impression on me as far as winning is concerned, because I'd never been on a winner and he had. He would explain the ingredients of being a winner. "Preparation meets opportunity"—that was Roberto's basic philosophy. You've got to prepare yourself and when the opportunity comes, take command of it.

Those three fellows had the greatest influence on me. Of course, I can't leave out Jackie Robinson—withstanding all the aggravation and still being able to play outstanding baseball and being a man of history too.

I was very fortunate in the big leagues regarding treatment. I had not had any real problems, derogatory remarks, or hostility. One thing you have to understand is that everyone is not going to like you. You have to understand that in the beginning. In fact, Aaron and I used to talk about this at the beginning of our careers, that you should try to get along with the majority of the people.

A lot of fans have asked me who's the toughest pitcher I had to face in the majors. I would say Don Newcombe. He had tremendous drive. He loved competition, was a winning-type pitcher. He was the type of man who had great natural ability. He could throw a ball hard. He had great control. He could hit like hell. He was the type of man everybody would like to be like. Newk was a winner. He occasionally would talk to his competitors, but most of the time he was preparing himself mentally. Newk would visit and talk, but once he got on that mound he was a monster. Newk was tough because for two and a half hours he had the ability to concentrate on that mound. Nothing could distract him. He had complete concentration. Fans might say something; time might be called; balls might roll on the field, or hecklers from the other bench might try to get on him. He never let anything distract him from his ultimate goal, namely, getting the batter out and winning. He worked extremely hard to keep himself in tip-top shape. He ran all the time he wasn't pitching. He was completely dedicated to the game of baseball. I would come to the ball park and look out there, and here was a top pitcher like Newcombe running, running. And he's still in fine condition today. He was an amazing athlete.

Every time I faced Don Newcombe, it was always a tough day for me and the Cubs. He had explosive speed and a big jug-handle curve. We knew Newk would be right there, throwing that ball as hard as he could. He was one of the very few players that I knew of who pitched a doubleheader. That shows the strength, stamina, and determination of the man. I think that this is one thing you won't see again for a long time in big league baseball: someone pitching a doubleheader.

Fergy Jenkins is another great pitcher. Jenkins and I roomed together when he first joined the Cubs in the mid-sixties, and he knew he could pitch, despite his difficulties in Philadelphia. He was a reliever then and did a fine job in relief. One day we were playing in Atlanta and manager Leo Durocher decided to give him a chance to start. He went out there and pitched a shutout against the Braves. The Braves had a lot of "stick" on that team: Hank Aaron, Rico Carty, Orlando Cepeda, among others. Fergy went out there and pitched so beautifully and so easily, it really opened up everybody's eyes to the fact that he could start. Afterward I asked him about the game and some of the things he thought about on the mound. He said he was thinking about what they said about him in Philadelphia —that he couldn't pitch, didn't have a good enough fastball, and that he should be a relief pitcher. That stayed on his mind and gave him the drive and determination to go out there and win and prove to the people that he could win. And boy, did he do that! He had six 20-game seasons with the Cubs.

The most important thing that was gotten away from me? That's playing in the World Series. I'm sorry that eluded me during my career.

Ernie Banks was elected to the Baseball Hall of Fame in 1977.

MORE BLACK BASEBALL STARS OF THE 1960s AND 1970s

Pitcher Ferguson Jenkins, who had pitched in both leagues, had a career record of 284 games won by the end of his last full season in 1983 with the Chicago Cubs. He was the 1971 Cy Young Award-winner, and had seven seasons with 20 or more wins.

Outfielder Billy Williams, National League Rookie of the Year in 1961, his first full season with the Chicago Cubs, won the National League batting title with .333 in 1972. He played in 1,117 consecutive games, a National League record broken by Steve Garvey of the San Diego Padres in 1983 (1,207 games). Williams hit 426 career home runs. He went on to be a coach with the Oakland Athletics.

Joe Morgan, the Most Valuable Player in the National League in 1975 and 1976, with the Cincinnati Reds. Morgan was only the second National Leaguer to win back-to-back MVPs. In 1976 he hit 27 home runs, drove in 111 runs, and stole 60 bases.

Hard-hitting outfielder Tommy Davis of the Los Angeles Dodgers led the National League in batting in 1962 and 1963.

Pitcher Juan Marichal had six 20-game-winning seasons for the San Francisco Giants. He won 243 games during his sixteen-year career. He entered the Baseball Hall of Fame in 1983.

Manny Mota of the Los Angeles Dodgers, baseball's greatest pinch-hitter. He holds the major league record for most career pinch hits (150).

Willie McCovey of the San Francisco Giants was the National League's Most Valuable Player in 1969. His lifetime home run record stands at 521. He holds the National League record for most career grand slam home runs (18). He came within inches of being the hero of the 1962 World Series.

New York Mets' outfielder Cleon Jones hit .340 and drove in 75 runs in 1969, helping "the Miracle Mets" to the World Series championship.

First baseman Orlando Cepeda played in the National League with the Giants, Cardinals, and Braves from 1958 to 1972, batting over .300 nine times. He was voted Most Valuable Player in the National League in 1967 when playing with the St. Louis Cardinals. His lifetime batting average is .297, with 379 round-trippers.

Emmett Ashford, the first black umpire in major league baseball. He officiated in the Pacific Coast League from 1954 to 1965, and then in the American League from 1966 to 1970. He worked the 1967 All-Star Game and the 1970 World Series. He died March 1, 1980.

Hank Aaron

Aaron Blasts 715th Homer in Atlanta and Breaks Ruth's Record.

April 8, 1974—Los Angeles Dodgers pitcher Al Downing threw a fastball, Hank Aaron swung, the rising ball went toward the left-center alley, the ball continued up, up over the 385-foot mark. Braves pitcher Tom House caught the ball in the bullpen. The number "715" flashed on the Atlanta scoreboard. The message from the loudspeaker blasted: "You were there. You fans here at Atlanta Stadium have just witnessed the great, if not the greatest, moment in recorded sports history."

—New York *Times*

Hank Aaron

Hank Aaron, the forty-year-old Atlanta Braves outfielder, broke the major league baseball home-run record on his second swing of a noisy April evening in 1974. As the man from Mobile jogged around the bases after hitting his 715th major league home run, in a career that began twenty-five years before with the Indianapolis Clowns in the old Negro leagues, a skyrocket arched over the jammed stadium. It was seven minutes after nine o'clock, some thirty-nine years after Ruth had hit his 714th.

When Aaron ended the season in 1973 with his 713th homer, the baseball world knew it would have to wait until the 1974 season for Aaron to overtake Babe Ruth's long-standing record of 714. In February 1974, the Braves' management stated that Aaron would be kept out of the first three games of the season with the Cincinnati Reds, so he could hit his anticipated historic home run in Atlanta, home of the Braves. Controversy raged over this announcement. Many felt that the Braves should put their best foot forward in the lineup against the Reds, which meant including Aaron. Commissioner Bowie Kuhn vehemently stated that he expected the Braves to use Aaron in the opening three-game series in Cincinnati. Sports columnist Dave Anderson of the New York *Times* felt the decision about Aaron's nonparticipation in the games with Cincinnati was "in brazen defiance of baseball's integrity." Eddie Mathews, manager of the Braves, said that if necessary, Aaron would serve as pinch hitter. Aaron, who felt he was damned if he did and damned if he didn't, stuck to his concept of baseball as always: "I have never gone out on a ball field and given less than my level best." On Thursday, April 4, 1974, on his first swing of the season in Cincinnati, he hit his 714th home run. Then Mathews announced that Aaron would not play the second or third game of the series; but Commissioner Kuhn ordered Aaron to play. Mathews kept Aaron on the bench Saturday, April 6, and on Sunday, April 7, Aaron struck out. Then there was April 8, and the record breaker in Atlanta. On that very special occasion, Commissioner Kuhn was unable to attend because he had a dinner engagement in Cleveland.

Henry "Hank" Aaron was born on February 5, 1934, in Mobile, Alabama, the third of eight children born to Herbert and Estelle Aaron. In his grammar school days, Aaron was a catcher for one of the clubs in the Louisiana Recreation League. When he entered Central High School in Mobile, he could only play softball, since the school could not afford equipment for a baseball team. He played shortstop, third base, and catcher for the softball team and was an outstanding footballer as a halfback and end. After two years at Central, he transferred to Allen Institute, a private school in Mobile. It wasn't until his junior year in high school that Aaron got his first chance to play ball on a semipro level. Henry played for the Mobile Black Bears, and on the final Sunday of the season the Bears met the Indianapolis Clowns. The Clowns were so impressed with Aaron's performance that they offered him $200 a month to play for them the following year. Aaron led the Negro American League in hitting with a .467 average during his first season with the Clowns. Strangely enough, Aaron was batting cross-handed at this time, a habit he corrected long before he came up to the majors. After watching Aaron play a Negro league game in 1952, Milwaukee Braves scout Dewey Griggs recommended Aaron to the Braves' general manager, John Quinn. The Braves then purchased Aaron for $2,500 down and $7,500 later.

In 1952 Aaron played with the Braves' farm club at Eau Claire, Wisconsin, in the Northern League. In eighty-seven games, he hit .336, which was good enough to earn him Rookie of the Year in the Northern League and a place on its All-Star team.

In 1953 Aaron moved up to the Jacksonville, Florida, club, in the Class "A" South Atlantic (Sally) League. He literally tore apart the Sally League's pitching. He led the league in batting (.362), hits (208), runs (115), and runs batted in (125). He also was second in the league in triples and hit 22 home runs. He also topped the league in assists. It is not surprising he was voted the Sally League's Most Valuable Player for 1953.

Aaron was second baseman in his one year in Jacksonville, but the Milwaukee Braves had a plethora of infield prospects in the organization and put him in the outfield during the off-season while he was playing winter ball in the Puerto Rican League. During that winter of 1953–54, the Braves purchased outfielder Bobby Thomson from the Giants, so it looked like another year in the minor leagues for Aaron. But during spring training of 1954, Thomson suffered a triple fracture of his right ankle sliding into second base, and Aaron replaced him in the outfield. In the 1954 season, Aaron hit .280 and drove in 69 runs before he too suffered a broken ankle in September. He recuperated quickly, and the following season he batted .314, hit 27 homers, and batted in 106 runs. Aaron won the batting championship in 1956, with an average of .328 and had 200 hits.

The year 1957 was a great one for Aaron. With a batting average of .322, he led the league in home runs with 44 and RBIs with 132. To top it off, the Braves won the National League championship, and Aaron was voted the league's Most Valuable Player. One of the highlights of his career happened on the night of September 23. The Braves were playing the St. Louis Cardinals. With the score tied in the eleventh inning, Aaron came up with one man on. He then hit Billy Muffett's fastball over the center-field fence. His home run won the game and the pennant. At the age of twenty-three, Hank Aaron was already a superstar.

In the 1957 World Series against the Yankees, Hank had 11 hits in seven games, batted .393, and led both clubs with 3 homers and 7 runs batted in, helping the Braves beat the Yankees four games to three.

The Braves won the pennant again in 1958, but this time the Yankees beat them in the fall classic. In 1959 the Braves lost the pennant in a play-off with the Dodgers. That year Aaron won another batting title—he hit .355, the best of his career. He also led the National League with 223 hits and 400 total bases. His 39 home runs and 123 RBIs were also close to the best in the league.

After 1959 the Braves started to disintegrate, but Aaron continued to be a star. In the 1963 season, he became only the fifth man in the history of baseball to hit more than 30 home runs and steal more than 30 bases in the same year. Aaron was never a "hot dog"; he did things quickly and efficiently. After his tenth season, more and more people began to see how great he was and began to compare him to the other recognized superstars at the time, Willie Mays and Mickey Mantle.

In 1966 the Braves migrated to Atlanta. Hank hit 44 home runs his first year there, giving him the National League leadership. Subsequently, that season paid off in his receiving his first $100,000 per year contract. On April 20 that year in Philadelphia, he hit his 400th home run. In 1968 his home-run total reached 500. Shortly thereafter, he passed Mickey Mantle and started gaining on Willie Mays. People began to think he had a chance to catch Babe Ruth.

In 1969, in the National League playoffs against the Mets, Henry hit 3 home runs in a losing cause. In 1970 Henry collected his 3,000th base hit. He hit 47 home runs in 1971, batted .327, and drove in 118 runs. Before the 1972 campaign Aaron signed a new contract with Atlanta. It was for $200,000 per year, making him at that time the highest-paid player in baseball history, and deservedly so. That 1972 season saw Hank hit .265, drive in 77 runs, and swat 34 home runs. In 1973 Aaron hit 40 home runs, knocked in 96, and attained a .301 batting average. The 1974 campaign, Hank's last with Atlanta, saw him hit .268, with 69 RBIs and 20 home runs.

He finished his major league career in 1976 after two seasons with the Milwaukee Brewers as a designated hitter and outfielder. Aaron's 12 and 10 home runs in his last two major league seasons gave him a major league career record of 755.

Hank Aaron:

When I was playing in the Sally League, I never dreamed that I would break Babe Ruth's record of 714 home runs. I never thought about being in the big leagues really, so I couldn't have thought about breaking his record. I never looked beyond the Sally League while I was playing there.

When I replaced Bobby Thomson [in 1954] because he broke his ankle, many asked me my gut feelings at the time. Well, I can't recall all the details. I did feel sorry for Bobby Thomson, but it put me in the position where I could perform in the majors. It so happens I played with a manager named Charlie Grimm, who was not a robot-type manager. He told me, "Kid, the job is yours, so get out and do the best job you can." And that's what I did.

Who had the greatest influence on my baseball career? I think the one manager that I can remember was the first manager I ever played for, Ben Geraghty of the Jacksonville team. I was one of the first blacks playing in the Sally League. I was literally going through hell down there—name-calling, racial slurs, resentment for playing against whites. So many stupid things. Ben used to come over to the hotel and talk to me and just give me the inspiration and the things I needed to carry on and be a professional player.

There have been some changes for the black players since 1954, but of course we still have a long way to go, and I hope some of the changes will be made soon. We now have bigger salaries for the bigger players, but outside of that I don't think there have been any significant changes.

As to how I feel as a black man in breaking Babe Ruth's record, really I didn't look upon it as a black or white breaking a record. I thought about it as a ballplayer who had the ability to play ball for twenty years. The record was there, and I happened to be the one who was in a position to challenge it, and I wasn't going to pass it up; so I broke it. I hope some kid will come along and break mine.

Hank Aaron is now director of player personnel and vice president for the Atlanta Braves. He is the only black in an important front office job with any big league club. In a UPI release in August 1979, Aaron said:

I cannot honestly say that baseball has been absolutely fair with blacks. I cannot look myself in the mirror each day and not speak the truth, and I will continue to say it the rest of my life because I owe it to myself and everybody else . . . There is prejudice in all phases of baseball. It burns me to hell when I can pick up a *Playboy* and read Pete Rose saying that the management of the Cincinnati Reds told him to stay away from black players.

How was Joe Morgan [who was with the Reds at the time] supposed to feel? How is Joe Morgan supposed to bust his butt for an organization that thinks like that?

How am I supposed to explain to black kids that even if you play hard, you're not going to endorse pizza. Rose said, "Who would you rather have taking a bite out of your pizza, me or Dave Parker?" Hey, black people eat pizza and drink Coke too . . .

People come to Atlanta Stadium and ask me where I hit 715. Out front of the stadium is a statue of Ty Cobb, the Georgia Peach. There is not one memento of what I did. They say I hit the greatest home run of all time, but there is nothing to show it.

I'm not egotistical or anything, I'm just stating facts.

Hank Aaron was elected to the Baseball Hall of Fame in 1982.

Roberto Clemente

It is harder for a Puerto Rican or Latin ballplayer. People do not want to give them work off the field. So no one knows them. I would make a lot more money in baseball if I were a white American.
                                                              —Roberto Clemente

Roberto Clemente

For more than forty years, Latin Americans have played major league baseball, most of them coming from Cuba but more recently from Puerto Rico. Adolfo "Dolf" Luque, who for some twenty years hurled for Boston, Cincinnati, Brooklyn, and New York in the National League and Mike "Good Field, No Hit" Gonzales, Havana-born catcher for Boston, Cincinnati, St. Louis, New York, and Chicago were the only two Latins prior to 1947 who attained any success in the big leagues.

Around the time Jackie Robinson joined the Brooklyn Dodgers in 1947, major league clubs really started digging for Hispanic ballplayers from Puerto Rico, Mexico, Venezuela, Cuba, and just about every single Latin isle. The year-round opportunity to play baseball seemed to bring the Latin American players to proficiency much sooner. From Havana in 1949 came the colorful Saturnino Orestes Arrieta Armas "Minnie" Minoso, who had seventeen fine years in the majors with Cleveland, Chicago, and

Washington in the American League and St. Louis in the National League. In 1955 Roberto Clemente from Puerto Rico joined the Pittsburgh Pirates.

Clemente, for eighteen years, was modern baseball's answer to Ty Cobb and Honus Wagner. His hitting, running, and throwing were superlative. Clemente would often comment that he knew of no one in the game who could hit, run, throw, and play the outfield better than he could.

Originally, Clemente had been signed in 1954 by the Dodgers, but because of a miscalculation, the Dodger roster turned out to be filled, so Clemente was farmed out to the Montreal Royals farm team. Specific instructions were given the Royals manager to "hide" Clemente because at that time a major league rule stated that a player who was signed by a club for more than $4,000 (Clemente signed for $5,000) had to spend time with the club or be put up for grabs by another club after a year in the minors. In order to keep Clemente for the Dodgers, the manager let Clemente play only when he was in a slump, and when he was hitting well he was banished to the benches. All theoretically well and good, but Clyde Sukeforth, then a tricky old scout for the Pittsburgh Pirates, spied Clemente in practice and had the Pirates pick up his contract.

Clemente didn't set the league on fire in 1955, his first year with the Pirates. The second year, though, he began to establish his stardom, hitting .311. Looking at his completely unorthodox form, no one would suspect Clemente's hitting ability. A very introspective man, Clemente was constantly mentally planning his hitting strategies. He started as a line-drive hitter, because that was his strength in the large stadiums, but when the occasion demanded he could and would go for the long ball. No tactical lineup could be planned ahead to thwart him because he could hit all pitchers to all fields. Though not a skilled outfielder at first, he trained himself to be a good one.

His strength and accuracy were legendary. There was not one right fielder in league records who had the perfection of his right arm, which threw out many a runner and discouraged many more from taking that extra base.

Had Clemente played in New York, the communication center of the world, his name would have echoed from coast to coast, for despite his constant complaining of aches and pains, there was no one in the majors who played as hard as he did. But nationwide fame eluded him until 1971, when his performance for the Pirates in the World Series against the Baltimore Orioles was one of baseball's greatest single performances by any player in the fall classic. He won the Series almost all by himself with a .414 batting average. 7 singles, 2 doubles, 1 triple, and 2 home runs, in addition to making two impossible catches in the outfield.

At the start of the 1972 season, Clemente was 118 hits away from attaining the 3,000 hit mark. He had already led the National League in batting four times. The 3,000 mark was a frustrating goal to reach. Everything seemed to be going against him, including illness and subsequent loss of weight. The 2,999th hit came in Philadelphia in the last road game of that season. First night home against the Mets, Clemente went hitless. The second night, he hit a curveball thrown by Jon Matlack into left center field for a single. That 3,000th hit was Clemente's last one.

On December 31, 1972, he died in a plane crash while escorting relief supplies from Puerto Rico to earthquake victims in Nicaragua. In 1973 the Baseball Writers Association of America voted almost unanimously to waive a five-year waiting period and elected Roberto Clemente to the Baseball Hall of Fame.

Curt Flood

December 24, 1969

Dear Mr. Kuhn:

After twelve years in the major leagues, I do not feel that I am a piece of property to be bought and sold irrespective of my wishes. I believe that any system which produces that result violates my basic rights as a citizen and is inconsistent with the laws of the United States and of the several States.

It is my desire to play baseball in 1970, and I am capable of playing. I have received a contract offer from the Philadelphia club, but I believe I have the right to consider offers from other clubs before making any decision. I, therefore, request that you make it known to all Major League clubs my feelings in this matter, and advise them of my availability for the 1970 season.

(signed) Curt Flood

Curt Flood

Curtis Flood was born in Houston, Texas, on January 18, 1938, the youngest of six children. In search of better economic conditions, the family moved to Oakland, California. By working day and night, Curt's father and mother were just able to raise their family without public assistance. Despite his five-foot-seven-inch, 140-pound frame, Curt Flood was a strong athlete and his athletic abilities gave him a ticket out of the Oakland ghetto. When he was graduated from high school in 1956, he signed with the Cincinnati Reds. The Reds farmed him out to the High Point-Thomasville, North Carolina, club in the Class B Carolina League. Hitting .340 with 128 runs batted in and 29 homers his first year (his hitting record and RBIs lead the Carolina League), he came up to the Reds. It was near the end of the season and he only played five games.

In 1957 Flood was sent to the Savannah, Georgia, club in the Class A South Atlantic League. He had 170 hits that year, ended with a batting average of .299, and was named to the league's All-Star team. Once again he was called to Cincinnati for the final days of the season. He got his first major league hit, a home run off Moe Drabowsky of the Chicago Cubs. In 1958 Flood was traded by the Reds to the St. Louis Cardinals because, as some said at the time, Cincinnati didn't want Flood to join Frank Robinson and Vada Pinson to form an all-black outfield. Flood did very well with the Cardinals. Constantly improving, he reached a plateau in 1961, hitting better than .300 in six out of eight seasons. When the Cardinals won the pennant and the World Series in 1967, Flood hit .335.

The golden era of the Cardinals seemed for a while to have returned. They won the National League pennant in 1964, 1967, and 1968 and the Series in 1964 and 1967. But a winning team must be a cohesive one, with each man knowing how to play off the others; when good feelings abound, all's right with the world. However, if all that changes for the worse, a team can become a losing one. The Cardinals lost the World Series in 1968 and in 1969 came in fourth in their league. When that happened, the organization knew that it was time for a change; there would have to be some trading.

Flood had been a superb outfielder with the Cardinals from 1958 to 1969. In fact, he was the Cardinals' greatest ball hawk since Terry Moore, who had played with the team from 1935 to 1948. On October 8, 1969, Flood was traded to Philadelphia with Tim McCarver, Joe Hoerner, and Byron Browne for Richie Allen, Cookie Rojas, and Jerry Johnson.

Flood had known that he might be traded, yet he says, "I took it personally. I felt unjustly cast out." He was told by the Cardinal management to report to the Philadelphia Phillies and was offered a $100,000 per year contract. At that time, Flood was thirty-one years old and was established in St. Louis. Despite the ample contract (he had been making $90,000 with the Cardinals), Flood refused to go to Philadelphia. There was more involved here than just going to the Phillies: Flood was challenging the constitutionality of baseball's reserve clause.

Baseball's reserve clause was unique in professional sports. In other sports, players were signed to contracts that included an option year beyond the length of the contract. A player could thus play out his option year (at a cut in pay) and become a free agent. In baseball, though, the reserve clause bound a player to a team for life.

Flood, once he thought about legal measures, spoke with Marvin Miller, the head of the Players' Association. Miller introduced Flood to Arthur Goldberg, former associate justice of the Supreme Court. Goldberg agreed to handle the case.

Subsequently, Flood filed a suit in federal court before Judge Irving Ben Cooper in January of 1970, charging that baseball's reserve clause violated the antitrust laws. Named as defendants were baseball's commissioner, the presidents of the American and National leagues, and the twenty-four major league clubs.

At this time the baseball reserve clause reduced a player to a kind of slavery vis-àvis the club that first signed him. Regardless of his personal feelings or preferences, he was sold like a piece of property and expected to go unquestioningly to whatever other club had bought him. This was what Curt Flood refused to do. His argument was not with the Philadelphia Phillies, nor with the St. Louis Cardinals—it was with the entire concept. Such a protest had been voiced before by others but never carried to its conclusion.

On the other hand, baseball had its arguments too. If ballplayers were free to go where they wanted to, it was argued, then a single club could capture all the talent. This would lead to an imbalance and affect attendance and thus business. For baseball was not just a sport; it was big business, with its many contributing subsidiaries—a lot was at stake.

When the case came before Judge Irving Cooper in federal court in New York City, many former baseball players and owners testified. Bill Veeck, Jackie Robinson, and Hank Greenberg testified that they supported Flood's contention. A real controversy developed outside of court between the players as to who was right. Then on August 12, 1970, Judge Cooper denied Flood's bid for an injunction. He upheld the reserve clause, stating that it was needed to maintain balanced competition and fair interests, but left a door open when he suggested changes should be made between player and owner through arbitration or negotiation. Judge Cooper's decision was upheld by a court of appeals on April 7, 1971, and by the United States Supreme Court on June 19, 1971.

Flood went back to baseball with the Washington Senators at the end of 1970 for a salary of $110,000, but played only thirteen games in 1971 before retiring. But the action he started didn't end there. There was a ballplayers' strike in 1972 for thirteen days and in 1973 the threat of another players' strike was averted by the following concession from management. A player could not be traded without his consent if he had ten years' major league experience, the last five of which were with the same club. In the matter of salary disputes, the owners agreed to an outside arbitrator.

Then, in 1975, Dave McNally of the Montreal Expos and Andy Messersmith of the Los Angeles Dodgers challenged the amended reserve clause. Having each played a season without a contract, they declared they were free agents and refused to sign new contracts with their respective teams. The two men went before a three-man arbitration board comprised of Marvin Miller, the players' chief negotiator; John Gaherin, the owners' representative; and Peter Scitz, an impartial arbitrator. With Miller going along with the players and Gaherin going along with the owners, it was Peter Scitz's decision in favor of the players that struck down the reserve clause, thereby breaking a century-old tradition.

Dave Parker, Pete Rose, Rod Carew, Reggie Jackson, Dave Winfield, Don Baylor, George Foster, Mike Schmidt, Gary Carter, Rickey Henderson, Keith Hernandez, Dale Murphy, George Brett, Bruce Sutter, and their millionaire colleagues should think deeply about the enormous sums of money they are now making and celebrate Curt Flood's birthday every time they pick up a paycheck.

Curt Flood, out of baseball for a time, is, at the time of this writing, doing play-by-play on a small West Coast FM station and working with a youth program.

Bob Gibson

If he's not the greatest competitor and pitcher, he's sure amongst 'em.

—Dizzy Dean

He's tough and uncompromising.

—Bill White

I think every superior athlete has some special motivation. With Bob Gibson, it wasn't that he wanted to win so much as that he didn't want to lose. He *hated* to lose. He just wouldn't accept it.

—Mike Shannon

Bob Gibson

Bob Gibson was born in Omaha, Nebraska, on November 9, 1935, the last of seven living children. Gibson's father had died three months before he was born. This large family lived in a dilapidated four-room shack, Bob's mother supporting them on a meager income as a laundress. When times got better, the family moved into a government housing project in the ghetto area.

The deprivation of growing up without a father was mitigated by the constant presence of Bob Gibson's oldest brother Leroy. Leroy was fifteen years older than Bob and everybody called him "Josh" in honor of the great black baseball catcher Josh Gibson. Bob's brother Josh loved sports and children and worked at the YMCA coaching basketball and baseball. Josh's relationship with Bob was more like that of father and son. He pushed his little brother hard, taught him the fundamentals of sports, and gave him a moral code of ethics that stayed with him all through Bob's career. There were other athletes who came under the influence of Josh, men like basketball forward Bob Boozer of the Chicago Bulls and Gale Sayers, the great running back of the Chicago Bears.

Pitcher Bob Gibson's credo was: "Bust 'em with the hard one, break 'em with the curve, blow 'em down before they get settled." He therefore took almost as little time between pitches as his pitches took to reach the plate. In seventeen brilliant seasons—1959 to 1975—with the St. Louis Cardinals, Gibson had 251 victories, more than any other St. Louis pitcher in history; he was a 20-game winner five times, chalking up 3,117 strikeouts. He was the first pitcher since Walter Johnson to record over 3,000 lifetime strikeouts. He had an earned run average of 1.12 in 1968, the lowest ever for a National League pitcher with over 300 innings pitched in a season and a record 7 consecutive World Series wins. He was twice a Cy Young Award winner as the best pitcher in the National League (1968, 1970), and the league's Most Valuable Player in 1968.

By the time Bob Gibson entered Technical High School in Omaha, he was already a superior athlete. He tried out for the football team, but was rejected because he was too small. He turned to baseball and basketball, in which he excelled. When the football coach tried to recruit Gibson for the football squad two years later, it was his turn to do the rejecting, preferring to keep on with basketball. In addition, his brother had warned him of possible serious injuries.

At any rate, basketball was his favorite sport at the time. In 1952, in his junior year, he played for his school in the state tournament. By his senior year, Gibson had grown to 175 pounds and stood six feet tall. He went out for track and field and set a city indoor record in the high jump with 5 feet 11 inches and achieved 6 feet 1 inch outdoors. In the long jump, he made 22½ feet.

In 1953, his senior year, Gibson received an offer to sign with the Kansas City Monarchs in the Negro professional baseball league but he declined. Although he felt honored to be considered, his thoughts were of Jackie Robinson, who had broken the color line in 1947; major league baseball was what he was interested in. After an athletically outstanding senior year, he sat back and waited hopefully for the college scholarship offers. There were some from small colleges in Nebraska and a few black colleges, but Gibson was only interested in the big competitive schools. His high school basketball coach, Neal Morser, wrote Indiana University, hoping they would be interested. They replied: "Your request for an athletic scholarship for Robert Gibson has been denied because we already have filled our quota of Negroes." To the rescue of the disappointed youth appeared Duce Belford. Belford was the athletic director of Creighton University in Omaha and knew Gibson's brother Josh well. Belford arranged the basketball scholarship for Bob, who became a freshman in 1953.

Creighton University was a lot different from what Gibson had expected. He had come to work hard—work hard, that is, at playing basketball—and had not considered that the Jesuits who ran the school had a different concept of what education was about. Gibson soon learned that in order to play basketball, he'd have to maintain his grades; it took a year, but he did it. In his sophomore year, he made the varsity and was the first black to play varsity basketball and baseball at Creighton.

Gibson got his first taste of overt racial discrimination when traveling with the Creighton basketball team—he found he could not eat or sleep with his team but had to be shunted off to the other side of town.

Nonetheless, Gibson hung in and, while he preferred basketball, he constantly improved his baseball skills. He was the varsity center fielder and a switch-hitter. In 1957, at the end of his senior year, Gibson felt pleased with himself. He had broken every Creighton scoring record in basketball and was more than a competent baseball player. The Harlem Globetrotters basketball team approached him with an offer of $500 a month. Gibson had just married his childhood sweetheart, and though the St. Louis Cardinals had also made him an offer, he felt he needed more money. Negotiating with Abe Saperstein, the manager-owner of the Globetrotters, he worked out a satisfactory deal. With that he signed a contract with the Cardinals for a $1,000 bonus and $3,000 in salary to be spread over the remainder of the 1957 season. Between the two, Gibson felt he could manage to support a wife.

That first year was hard. The Cardinals sent him to the Columbus, Georgia, team in the South Atlantic League—Gibson's first time in the Deep South—and then back to Nebraska, to the Omaha team in the American Association. When the season ended, Gibson had won 6 and lost 4 with the two clubs.

With little time for rest after the close of the baseball season, he was off playing with the Harlem Globetrotters. While the experience with them was invaluable, Gibson never could play the clown successfully and knew that that was not the sports role he was searching for. Bing Devine, general manager of the St. Louis Cardinals, felt that Gibson was spreading himself too thin and agreed to make up the difference in pay if Gibson left the Globetrotters. This was entirely agreeable with Gibson.

With less than a year's experience in professional baseball, Gibson was invited in the spring of 1958 to train with the "big team" Cardinals in St. Petersburg, Florida. With hope and expectancy running high, Gibson arrived in St. Petersburg and took a cab to the Bainbridge Hotel, where he was handed a slip of paper by the desk clerk. He returned to the cab and was driven across the railroad tracks to the "Negro district." In front of the private house where he was destined, he saw several other black ballplayers including Curt Flood and Sam Jones; they, too, were denied accommodation at the Bainbridge Hotel. The entire experience was humiliating for them all. They were not able to eat with their team, had to use separate toilet facilities at gasoline stations, and were barred from the most mundane encounters outside of the ballfield.

In 1958 and 1959 Gibson went from Omaha to the Rochester, New York, team in the International League, then back to Omaha, and finally to the Cardinals in St. Louis in 1959.

Now Gibson was ready for the big stretch. He was there in the majors. So he withstood the racial slurs; he withstood being attacked by white roughnecks; he withstood being denied a room at hotels where his white teammates were staying. He withstood it all because he wanted to be at the top and when he got there, he intended to stay. And stay he did. The year 1968 was Gibson's special year of triumph: his league-leading 13 shutouts that year were more than he had recorded in any other two seasons combined; his earned run average of 1.12 also led the league; his strikeouts totaled 268 to lead the league; and his won-lost record was an excellent 22 and 9. Gibson pitched in three World Series for the Cardinals in 1964, 1967, and 1968. His total of 7 Series wins places him second only to Whitey Ford in Series victories, and his total of 92 strikeouts is second to Ford's 94. However, Gibson played in only nine Series games compared to Ford's twenty-two. In the 1967 Series, Gibson won 3 of the games with an ERA of 1.00. After retiring as a player in 1975, Gibson went on to be a pitching coach for the Mets and the Braves. His triumphs were soaring high, but he had no time for the camaraderie that baseball supposedly fosters—he is a very serious man; many consider him a deep man. Baseball to him was all business. He disdained the press and did not endear himself to reporters. He was an intimidating, unique man.

Bob Gibson was elected to the Baseball Hall of Fame in 1981, the eleventh player to enter in his first year of eligibility.

Frank Robinson

The only reason I'm the first black manager is because I was born black.
—Frank Robinson

Frank Robinson

On October 3, 1974, twenty-seven years after Jackie Robinson broke major league baseball's color ban by becoming one of the four hundred players then in the leagues, it finally happened. At a crowded news conference in Cleveland's Municipal Stadium, with the poise that characterized his career, as a slugger of 586 home runs and as a clubhouse leader, Frank Robinson was named by the Cleveland Indians as major league baseball's first black manager. He received a one-year contract. The thirty-nine-year-old Robinson was chosen to succeed Ken Aspromonte as the American League team's twenty-ninth manager and eighth player-manager.

President Gerald Ford described Robinson's selection as "welcome news for baseball fans across the nation" and a "tribute to Robinson personally, to his athletic skills and his unsurpassed leadership." Baseball Commissioner Bowie Kuhn said, "We got something done that should have been done before." Phil Seghi, the Indians' general manager, in announcing his selection, declared, "Frank Robinson has the qualities I was searching for in a manager, not because he was black or white. He has all the leadership qualities necessary to lead a major league ball club. You know what he did in Baltimore! He's a true leader."

Robinson had helped the Baltimore Orioles represent the American League in four World Series in his six seasons there. Before that, he had led the Cincinnati Reds to one National League pennant. He was the only major leaguer ever to be selected the Most Valuable Player in both leagues, winning the honor in the National League in 1961 and in the American League in 1966. Through twenty-one seasons, he had a career batting average of .294, with 2,943 hits and 1,812 runs batted in. In 1974 Robinson became the major league's first playing manager since Solly Hemus of the St. Louis Cardinals in 1959.

Starting in 1968–69, Robinson managed the Santurce Crabbers team in the Puerto Rican Winter League for five seasons. In those five seasons, his teams finished first twice, third twice, and fourth once. He was the first American black to manage an integrated team of white, black, and Latin players.

Robinson was born in Beaumont, Texas, on August 31, 1935, the youngest of ten children. A year later the family moved to California. At fourteen he played American Legion baseball.

In 1952, when he was seventeen and had graduated from high school, he was signed by the Cincinnati Reds for a $3,000 bonus. He played minor league ball for them in Ogden, Utah, in the Pioneer League in 1953; in Tulsa, Oklahoma, in the Texas League in 1954; and with Columbia, South Carolina, in the South Atlantic League in 1954 and 1955. It was while playing in Columbia, which he describes as the "dark side" of his baseball career, that he said he was first called "a dirty nigger" after striking out. It was also in Columbia that he picked up a baseball bat and went into the grandstands to threaten some fans who were cursing him. "The South," he once said, "really made me a better ballplayer. I was just determined to get out of there and the only way I could think to do it was to get all the way to Cincinnati."

He became a Red in 1956, and when the season was over he was named the National League's Rookie of the Year. His 38 home runs tied him with Wally Berger of the 1930 Boston Braves for most home runs hit by a player in his rookie season. At bat, Robinson stood very close to the plate, his bat held high and tight and unwavering. As a result, during that same 1956 season, he established a major league record for being hit by pitched balls: 20.

In 1961 Robinson was named Most Valuable Player in the National League. On December 9, 1965, Cincinnati traded him to the Baltimore Orioles in the American League. He was traded, contended the Reds' general manager, Bill DeWitt, because he was an "old thirty." Yet in 1966, his first season with the Orioles, he won the American League Triple Crown, leading the league in batting, home runs, and runs batted in. Only ten other players have ever done that.

In 1967 Robinson became the eighth player to reach the $100,000-a-year salary mark, following Joe DiMaggio, Ted Williams, Stan Musial, Willie Mays, Mickey Mantle, Sandy Koufax, and Don Drysdale.

Robinson's brilliant playing career waned in 1972, after he had been traded to the Los Angeles Dodgers. In 1973 the Dodgers traded him to the California Angels, who in turn traded him late in the 1974 season to the Cleveland Indians. On October 3, three weeks after joining the Indians and one day after the season ended, he was appointed player-manager of the Indians.

Robinson started off with a bang. On the opening day of the 1975 season at Cleveland Stadium, before 55,000 fans, he hit a home run his first time at bat in the first inning off the Yankees' Doc Medich. The Indians won, 5–3. Unfortunately, soon after that the Indians went into a slump and in June they were in last place in the American League. But they were able to get themselves together and eventually moved up to fourth place, where they finished out the season.

In 1976 the Indians again finished in fourth place. The club's fortunes did not improve the next spring and Robinson was fired in June and was replaced by Jeff Torborg, who had been a coach under Robinson.

The following month Robinson joined the coaching staff of the California Angels until the end of the 1977 season. In 1978 he went as coach to the Baltimore Orioles. In May of 1978, when Ken Boyer, the manager of the Rochester Red Wings, became manager of the St. Louis Cardinals, Robinson replaced him in Rochester. In 1979 Robinson rejoined the Orioles as coach.

Then on January 14, 1981, Robert Lurie, the owner of San Francisco Giants, announced in Candlestick Park that Frank Robinson had been named to succeed Dave Bristol as manager. Robinson became the Giants' tenth manager in the twenty-three years since they left New York. Lurie said: "I decided on Frank because I thought he knew how to manage, how to win, and how to communicate."

Robinson's credentials remain unassailable. He says, "Managing is never easy, but I feel more qualified to manage now because I've matured as a person and I've learned a little more . . . I hope people refer to me as a manager and not as a black manager."

In January 1982, Frank Robinson was elected to the Baseball Hall of Fame.

Lou Brock

I would say the turning point in my baseball career, if you could call it a turning point, was the moment that I really arrived as a big league ballplayer in Chicago, playing against Cincinnati one day. I went up in the vines at Wrigley Field and came down with a spectacular catch. The moment I made that catch and came down, it seemed as if the whole world was lifted off my shoulders—from that particular moment I knew my way around. I knew what I had to do in order to compete. Everything became clear to me at that point. Somewhere in every guy's career that happens to him.

—Lou Brock

Lou Brock

Louis Clark "Lou" Brock was born on June 18, 1939, in El Dorado, Arkansas, one of nine children in a sharecropping family. He was raised in Collinston, Louisiana. Brock was a star pitcher and outfielder when he attended Union High School in neighboring Mer Rouge. He could have sought a baseball career at that time but felt a college education would mean more. He majored in mathematics at Southern University in Baton Rouge and of course played a lot of baseball. A $30,000 bonus from the Chicago Cubs lured him away from Southern University in early 1961, at the end of his

"Brock beats ball for record." On September 9, 1974, St. Louis Cardinals' Lou Brock breaking the then-major league record of stolen bases in a single season with his 105th as he slid into second base inches in front of the ball. He went on to steal 118 that season, a record that stood until Rickey Henderson stole 130 in 1982.

junior year. Brock spent his first year in the Chicago organization with the St. Cloud, Minnesota, team in the Northern League, where he led the league in batting with .361 and in hits with 181.

In the latter part of the 1961 season he joined the Cubs for four games. Brock's first full season with Chicago was the following year, 1962, where he remained until June 1964. On the fifteenth of that month, along with pitchers Jack Spring and Paul Toth, Brock was traded to the St. Louis Cardinals for pitchers Ernie Broglio and Bobby Shantz and outfielder Doug Clemens.

In the last half of the 1964 season, Brock batted .348 and was the catalyst that led the Cardinals to the pennant and a win over the New York Yankees in the World Series.

In his first full year with the Cardinals, 1965, Brock hit .288 and was off and running, stealing 43 bases. In 1967 in the World Series against the Boston Red Sox, he hit .414 and stole 7 bases. The Cardinals were again in the Series in 1968 and Brock hit .464 and stole 7 bases. He got his 2,000th hit in 1972 and two years later . . . "ST. LOUIS, September 10, 1974, AP—Lou Brock stole second base in the seventh inning of the Cardinals' game against the Philadelphia Phillies tonight and set a major league record of 105 stolen bases for one season." Brock's steal, his second in the game, eclipsed the previous record of 104 in one season set by the Los Angeles Dodgers' Maury Wills in 1962.

His first steal had come in the opening inning following a single left before an enthusiastic Busch Stadium crowd of 27,285. Then, in the seventh inning, Brock led off with a single to left. When he stole second base—teammates and photographers poured into the field and Brock was presented with the historic base he stole.

The game was stopped and Brock, who addressed the crowd, embraced Ted Sizemore, the Cards' regular second baseman, who had been injured and who usually batted behind him. In a salute to his throng of admirers, the thirty-five-year-old outfielder said, "The left-field fans probably knew I was going to steal 105 before I did. They were behind me all the way."

Brock went on to set a record with 118 thefts that year. At one point in his career, Lou Brock led the league in stolen bases for eight out of nine consecutive years. His career total of 938 is first in major league history.

On the night of August 13, 1979, Brock got his 3,000th hit, the fourteenth major leaguer in history to reach that number. When the 1979 season was over—after nineteen major league seasons, sixteen and a half of them with the Cardinals—Brock called it quits and retired.

Lou Brock:

I always wanted to play baseball. I suppose nearly every kid, from the age of ten on, has thoughts of playing ball. You do dream about it. I think after you leave high school that dream sort of falls away and you begin to think of other interesting things you want to do in life. Of course, I went to Southern University, and at that time I was more interested in an education than a professional sports career. But things might happen in your life that turn you toward the big league.

My first introduction to baseball was somewhere around the age of nine or ten. Being one of the mischievous kids, I recall hitting my teacher with a spitball. I was punished for it. The punishment was to go to the library and then to stand before the class and give a report on five baseball players, black and white: Stan Musial, Jackie Robinson, Roy Campanella, Don Newcombe, and Joe DiMaggio. I knew nothing about these guys at the time, and after doing some research the one thing that struck me and sort of caught my attention was the fact that they got an awful lot of meal money. Money just for eating! That was one of the aspects of baseball that caught my fancy at the age of ten.

After I broke Maury Wills's record, a lot of people have asked me what was involved in base stealing. First of all, you've got to be able to hit. But the makeup of stealing bases is more than meets the eye. People generally refer to the myth that speed has a lot to do with it, but I recall at a much younger age having as much speed as anybody in baseball. Now there must be at least thirty-five guys who run much faster than I do. But one factor is experience; the other is being able to react . . . how you do react. There are a lot of mechanics that one has to go through, and a lot of time and effort have to be put into it.

People saw [U.S. champion sprinter] Bob Hayes run in 9.1. If you look at Bob Hayes getting out of the blocks, you would swear he couldn't do 9.1. There have been guys who were able to get out of the blocks much faster but could not maintain or sustain speed. The key to stealing bases is getting the jump—thrusting your body in motion—having that good breakaway. If you have that good thrust or breakaway, in my opinion, in a ninety-foot-distance span, then speed is not that important. Although it is important, it is not the key factor at that moment. Plus you've got to have that . . . positive thought about going down there to the next base. As Maury Wills always states, "You cannot be afraid of being thrown out."

You actually steal on the pitcher. It's a time element. I think that any time you can go from first base to second base using a good breakaway, reading the keys properly, if you can run down in 3.1 or 3.2, chances are you are going to be called safe. Every time you go down in 3.4 or 3.5, you are out. You're working in a time span, and this is why the breakaway means so much. This is why getting out of the blocks is important. You put each pitcher in a category and study it and take it from there.

There are certain pitchers who are tough to steal on. There are certain styles I hate. Like Don Sutton, Andy Messersmith, and Jim Barr. These pitchers decrease the margin of error because of their quickness—not their velocity on the ball, but their body movement. I've always said that each one of these guys could probably deliver a baseball, release a baseball, inside of .6 of a second, and based on that alone it doesn't give a base runner much time under that 3.2 category which I mentioned earlier. But there are guys who release a ball in about .8 of a second. That's about average, and those are the guys I can steal on.

What do I want out of baseball? I don't know what I want at this point, but I do know I love the psychological warfare of the game. And I feel that we blacks have the capacity to do anything a white player can do, including managing or working in the front office. We just don't have enough of that in baseball now. I still think there is a quota system in sports, especially in baseball.

I don't owe baseball anything and it doesn't owe me anything. We have a mutual respect for each other. I have given a lot. It has given me a lot.

Lou Brock was elected to the Baseball Hall of Fame in January 1985.

BLACK BASEBALL STARS OF THE 1980s

Reggie Jackson, with the New York Yankees in the late 1970s, and now with the California Angels, is one of the great power hitters in baseball history.

Willie Randolph, the New York Yankees' slick-fielding and clutch-hitting second baseman. Had a fine year with the Yankees in 1984.

Chris Chambliss, American League Rookie of the Year with the Cleveland Indians in 1971, later joined the New York Yankees (as seen here), and then was traded to the Atlanta Braves.

Jim Rice, power-hitting outfielder for the Boston Red Sox; the American League's Most Valuable Player in 1978. In 1983 he led the American League in home runs (39), tied Milwaukee's Cecil Cooper in most runs batted in (126). At the end of the 1983 season he had 276 career homers and 954 RBIs.

Rod Carew of the California Angels, winner of seven American League batting titles, was the league's Rookie of the Year in 1967 and Most Valuable Player in 1977.

Outfielder George Foster, who with the Cincinnati Reds became the National League's Most Valuable Player in 1977, won three consecutive RBI titles in 1976 (121), 1977 (149), and 1978 (120). He joined the New York Mets in 1982.

Willie Stargell, the Pittsburgh Pirates' career leader in home runs, RBIs, and extra base hits. He batted .400 in the 1979 World Series, including a seventh-game two-run homer that clinched the championship. He was tied in voting for MVP in 1979 with Keith Hernandez, then of the St. Louis Cardinals. After his retirement in 1982, Stargell served in the Pirates' head office and is now Pittsburgh's minor league hitting instructor.

Chet Lemon made his major league debut with the Chicago White Sox in 1975. Playing center field with Chicago in 1977 he led the league with 524 chances and 512 putouts, both records. In November 1981 he was traded to Detroit and was a strong factor in the Tigers' outstanding drive to the American League pennant and their World Series victory in 1984.

Left-hand hitter Dave Parker, as a Pittsburgh Pirate, was the National League's Most Valuable Player in 1978, and the league's leading hitter in 1977 (.338) and 1978 (.334). In 1979 he became the first million-dollar player in the history of major league baseball. He was signed as a free agent by the Cincinnati Reds in 1984.

Dave Winfield. The New York Yankees in December 1980 shocked major league baseball by signing free agent Winfield to a ten-year contract for somewhere between $13 million and $25 million. Winfield had eight great seasons with the San Diego Padres and went on to have superb years with the Yankees.

This Yankee outfielder is truly a great all-around professional athlete. He was a superstar in baseball and basketball at the University of Minnesota and was drafted by four professional teams in three sports: basketball (ABA and NBA), football (NFL), and major league baseball.

A fantastic outfielder, Winfield will go down in history as one of the New York Yankees' greatest defensive outfielders. He has "soft" hands and a powerful, accurate throwing arm. His leaping catches—with all of his six-foot-six frame fully extended, glove high —are already legendary.

Bill Madlock, third baseman of the Pittsburgh Pirates. In 1983 he won his fourth National League batting championship with a .323 average. Madlock became the tenth player in major league history to win four batting titles.

Outfielder Andre Dawson has been a pivotal member of the Montreal Expos since joining the team during the 1976 season. In his first full year with the Expos, 1977, he was named the National League's Rookie Player of the Year.

Kansas City Royals' speedy outfielder Willie Wilson led the majors in 1979 with 83 stolen bases, the third highest at that time since Ty Cobb's 96 in 1915. He won the American League batting title in 1982 with a .332 average.

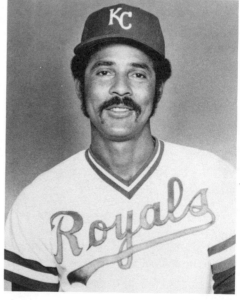

Amos Otis was for years a mainstay of the Kansas City Royals' offense and defense. He went over to the Pittsburgh Pirates for the 1984 season.

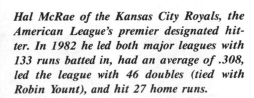

Hal McRae of the Kansas City Royals, the American League's premier designated hitter. In 1982 he led both major leagues with 133 runs batted in, had an average of .308, led the league with 46 doubles (tied with Robin Yount), and hit 27 home runs.

First baseman Cecil Cooper of the Milwaukee Brewers, a natural hitter. In 1980 he batted .352, with 219 hits, 25 home runs, and led the American League with 122 RBIs.

Outfielder Ben Oglivie of the Milwaukee Brewers. In 1980 he tied Reggie Jackson for the American League lead in home runs with 41.

Houston Astros' J. R. Richard established two consecutive modern National League records for the most strikeouts by a right-hander—303 in 1978 and 313 in 1979. Soon after these achievements, Richard was stricken with an embolism that cut short his brilliant career.

Vida Blue as a San Francisco Giant. A three-time 20-game winner with the Oakland Athletics, Blue had a 24–8 record and a 1.82 ERA in 1971, his first full year in the major leagues. He tossed eight straight shutouts that season, including a no-hitter against Minnesota, to win the Cy Young Award and earn the American League's Most Valuable Player honors. In 1983 he played with the Kansas City Royals.

Bobby Bonds, a brilliant all-around player capable of hitting 30 home runs and stealing 30 bases in a season. His high number of strikeouts moved him from club to club. Now retired, he is seen here in his Cleveland Indians uniform.

Ozzie Smith of the St. Louis Cardinals. He is the defensive shortstop of our time.

Garry Templeton of the 1984 pennant-winning San Diego Padres. Throughout his career he has consistently hit .300-plus, stole 35–40 bases, and has been a catalyst for his team's offense.

Baltimore Orioles' outfielder Ken Singleton, a powerful hitter from either side of the plate.

First baseman Eddie Murray of the Baltimore Orioles, 1977 American League Rookie of the Year. One of baseball's finest all-around players.

First baseman Al Oliver, a solid hitter formerly with the Pittsburgh Pirates, the Texas Rangers, the Montreal Expos, the San Francisco Giants, and, in 1984, with the Phillies. In 1982, with the Expos, Al won the National League batting title and tied Dale Murphy for the RBI honors with 109. He joined the Los Angeles Dodgers for the 1985 season.

Rickey Henderson, baseball's all-time base-stealing champion. In 1982 the Oakland A's speedy outfielder stole 130 bases, topping Lou Brock's record of 118. In 1983, he became the first major leaguer to steal 100 bases in three separate seasons, leading the league that year with 108 steals. He was traded to the New York Yankees prior to the 1985 season.

First baseman/outfielder Ken Griffey of the New York Yankees, formerly a catalyst of Cincinnati's "Big Red Machine" of the seventies. A consistent .300-plus hitter in his productive fifteen-plus years in the majors.

Darryl Strawberry, the National League's 1983 Rookie of the Year, had been called up from the Tidewater club in the International League in May of that year. The six-foot-six New York Mets' outfielder was the number-one draft selection in 1980 after a spectacular high school career. In 1982 he was voted MVP of the Texas League, hitting 34 home runs. With his powerhouse batting and strong throwing arm, Strawberry may be one of the great baseball stars of the future.

Don Baylor was named the American League's MVP in 1979 with the California Angels. Now with the New York Yankees, he is one of the outstanding designated hitters in the American League.

Dwight Gooden, pitcher, New York Mets. In 1984 he struck out more batters than any rookie in the history of major league baseball (276). He possesses a 95-m.p.h. fastball and an equally awesome curveball. Without question, he is a future Hall of Famer.

First baseman Alvin Davis of the Seattle Mariners was named the American League Rookie Player of the Year in 1984. He was the most productive slugger in the history of the Mariners, batting .284, with 27 homers and 116 RBIs.

BLACK MOST VALUABLE PLAYERS *NATIONAL LEAGUE*

1949	Jackie Robinson	Brooklyn	(2B)
1951	Roy Campanella	Brooklyn	(C)
1953	Roy Campanella	Brooklyn	(C)
1955	Roy Campanella	Brooklyn	(C)
1956	Don Newcombe	Brooklyn	(P)
1957	Hank Aaron	Milwaukee	(OF)
1958	Ernie Banks	Chicago	(SS)
1959	Ernie Banks	Chicago	(SS)
1961	Frank Robinson	Cincinnati	(OF)
1962	Maury Wills	Los Angeles	(SS)
1965	Willie Mays	San Francisco	(OF)
1966	Roberto Clemente	Pittsburgh	(OF)
1967	Orlando Cepeda	St. Louis	(1B)
1968	Bob Gibson	St. Louis	(P)
1969	Willie McCovey	San Francisco	(1B)
1975	Joe Morgan	Cincinnati	(2B)
1976	Joe Morgan	Cincinnati	(2B)
1977	George Foster	Cincinnati	(OF)
1978	Dave Parker	Pittsburgh	(OF)
1979	Willie Stargell*	Pittsburgh	(1B)

* Co-winner with Keith Hernandez, St. Louis (1B).

BLACK MOST VALUABLE PLAYERS *AMERICAN LEAGUE*

1963	Elston Howard	New York	(C)
1966	Frank Robinson	Baltimore	(OF)
1971	Vida Blue	Oakland	(P)
1972	Richie Allen	Chicago	(1B)
1973	Reggie Jackson	Oakland	(OF)
1977	Rod Carew	Minnesota	(1B)
1978	Jim Rice	Boston	(OF)
1979	Don Baylor	California	(DH)

BLACK BATTING CHAMPIONS *NATIONAL LEAGUE*

1949	Jackie Robinson	Brooklyn	.342
1954	Willie Mays	New York	.345
1956	Hank Aaron	Milwaukee	.328
1959	Hank Aaron	Milwaukee	.355
1961	Roberto Clemente	Pittsburgh	.351
1962	Tommy Davis	Los Angeles	.346
1963	Tommy Davis	Los Angeles	.326
1964	Roberto Clemente	Pittsburgh	.339
1965	Roberto Clemente	Pittsburgh	.329
1966	Matty Alou	Pittsburgh	.342
1967	Roberto Clemente	Pittsburgh	.357
1970	Rico Carty	Atlanta	.366
1972	Billy Williams	Chicago	.333
1974	Ralph Garr	Atlanta	.353
1975	Bill Madlock	Chicago	.354
1976	Bill Madlock	Chicago	.339
1977	David Parker	Pittsburgh	.338
1978	David Parker	Pittsburgh	.334
1981	Bill Madlock	Pittsburgh	.341
1982	Al Oliver	Montreal	.331
1983	Bill Madlock	Pittsburgh	.323

BLACK BATTING CHAMPIONS *AMERICAN LEAGUE*

1964	Tony Oliva	Minnesota	.323
1965	Tony Oliva	Minnesota	.321
1966	Frank Robinson	Baltimore	.316
1970	Alex Johnson	California	.329
1971	Tony Oliva	Minnesota	.337
1972	Rod Carew	Minnesota	.318
1973	Rod Carew	Minnesota	.350
1974	Rod Carew	Minnesota	.364
1975	Rod Carew	Minnesota	.359
1977	Rod Carew	Minnesota	.388
1978	Rod Carew	Minnesota	.333
1982	Willie Wilson	Kansas City	.332

BLACK ROOKIE OF THE YEAR *NATIONAL LEAGUE*

1947	Jackie Robinson	Brooklyn	(1B)
1949	Don Newcombe	Brooklyn	(P)
1950	Sam Jethroe	Boston	(OF)
1951	Willie Mays	New York	(OF)
1952	Joe Black	Brooklyn	(P)
1953	Jim Gilliam	Brooklyn	(2B)
1956	Frank Robinson	Cincinnati	(OF)
1958	Orlando Cepeda	San Francisco	(1B)
1959	Willie McCovey	San Francisco	(1B)
1961	Billy Williams	Chicago	(OF)
1964	Richie Allen	Philadelphia	(3B)
1971	Earl Williams	Atlanta	(C)
1973	Gary Matthews	San Francisco	(OF)
1977	Andre Dawson	Montreal	(OF)
1983	Darryl Strawberry	New York	(OF)
1984	Dwight Gooden	New York	(P)

BLACK ROOKIE OF THE YEAR *AMERICAN LEAGUE*

1964	Tony Oliva	Minnesota	(OF)
1966	Tommy Agee	Chicago	(OF)
1967	Rod Carew	Minnesota	(2B)
1971	Chris Chambliss	Cleveland	(1B)
1973	Al Bumbry	Baltimore	(OF)
1977	Eddie Murray	Baltimore	(DH)
1978	Lou Whitaker	Detroit	(2B)
1979	Alfredo Griffin*	Toronto	(SS)
1984	Alvin Davis	Seattle	(1B)

* Co-winner with John Castino, Minnesota (3B).

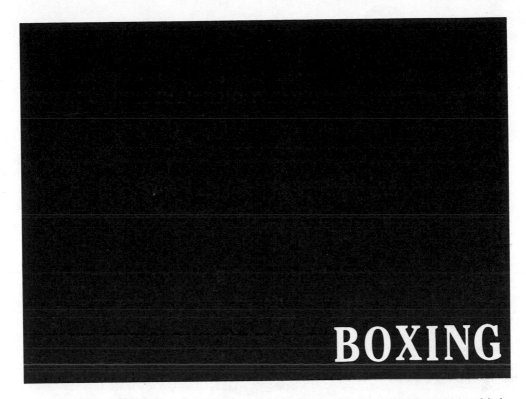

BOXING

There is evidence that the sport of boxing—hitting your opponent without being hit in return—existed in Crete as long ago as 1500 B.C., although settling disputes with the fists no doubt extends back to prehistory. By dint of geography, the Cretan culture expanded to include Greece. Greece took wrestling and boxing to a higher level, making them part of the Olympic games, which date back to 776 B.C. Rome, in its world conquests, readily adapted and encouraged the development of pugilistic skills. The Roman conquest, with its own culture and its borrowings from other cultures, spread throughout the known world and as far north as Britain, where boxing became very popular.

Despite its early favor, the sport of boxing declined in Britain for several centuries while the world became embroiled in a confusion of politics, religion, territorial claims, wars, and the emergence of nations. The development of the sport of fencing by the aristocracy in England during the seventeenth century turned it into an art. Out of fencing, which in its various stances was reminiscent of boxing, came the redevelopment of boxing, the gentler art of self-defense (as opposed to the hardness of a steel sword). With the emergence of James Figg, the first British champion, in 1719, boxing became a dominant sport and England reigned supreme as the boxing capital of the world.

Naturally, boxing became popular in England's colonies especially in America. The American aristocracy was centered in the South and, in the early days before the Revolution, it considered all things English superior. The owners of large plantations found it almost mandatory that their children be educated in England or at the very least visit England for an extended period of time so that they might acquire "culture."

When these wealthy young American colonists went to England, they were shown the "proper" way to do things and many went to professional boxing matches. These young men were trained by well-known boxing instructors in the art of self-defense. Upon their return to America, distance and lack of rapid transportation made it

Bill Richmond, boxing's "Black Terror."

impossible for them to continue practicing boxing. As a result, the young men turned to their young personal slaves and taught the skills of boxing to them. In no time, plantation slave champions were fighting other plantation slave champions. They even wore the plantation colors. Gambling followed and the boxer slave who earned enough money for his master was given special privileges, good food, comfortable sleeping quarters, and so on. As the betting became heavier, and if the master won a fortune, the boxer slave could earn his freedom, move North, and earn a living by boxing.

This situation freed many slaves and boxing spread to the North. Black freedmen and their offspring continued looking toward boxing as a career. Bill Richmond was one of these men. He was born in Staten Island, New York, and was five feet, nine inches tall and weighed 175 pounds. In 1777, when the British troops occupied New York, three British soldiers attacked Richmond in a tavern. Richmond demolished them, catching the attention of General Percy, a commander of the British troops in New York. General Percy took Richmond back to England with him, and with a number of victories under his belt, Richmond became a hero to the English working class. Over the years he faced such famous fighters as Tom Cribb, who knocked Richmond out; Jack Carter, whom he beat in 1809; and George Maddox, whom he beat in the fifty-second round. In 1818, when Richmond was fifty-six years old, he again faced Jack Carter and was the victor. He retired from the ring at that point.* He

* While Richmond was the first black American to receive such ring distinction, before him there was an African black, Joe Lashley, who was renowned for his boxing skills.

Little is known of Lashley, but his name appears in print in 1792 and 1796.

On June 13, 1796, Lashley fought Tom Treadway for thirty-five minutes and beat him senseless. This fight was reported in a volume of *Sporting Anecdotes.* It states, "During the combat, the African showed great agility, excellent bottom and a thorough knowledge of the art not to be exceeded by the most skillful among boxers."

was the first black American to achieve such acknowledgment and respect and proved an inspiration to another native-born black American—Tom Molineaux.

Molineaux was born a slave in 1784 in Georgetown, South Carolina. It is reported that his father and grandfather were both famous boxing slaves in Virginia. Molineaux earned his freedom and came to New York to the old Catherine Markets. He was triumphant over all fighters he challenged. Molineaux then went to England with a merchant ship crew where he sought to meet and emulate Bill Richmond. Molineaux was a great success in England, defeating eight English fighters. Most of his opponents were listed "Unknown," since none of them wanted their careers jeopardized by fighting and possibly losing to a black man.

The hue and cry of the British fans demanded a bout between Molineaux and the world champion, Tom Cribb. This most heralded fight took place on December 10, 1810, at Copthall Common, Essex. Molineaux weighed 196 pounds and Cribb 188, but Cribb had a two-inch height advantage. The fight was held outdoors on an especially cold, rainy, windy day at twelve noon. At the end of twenty-three rounds, it was clear that Molineaux had won, but Cribb and his handlers had a trick up their sleeves. Cribb was groggy from being knocked to the ground and would not have been able to proceed without a break. Cribb's seconds cried out that Molineaux had lead weights hidden in his fists. Time was spent looking for the supposedly thrown-away weights and arguing with Molineaux, who was claiming that he had won the championship. By this time, Cribb had become fully conscious. The fight was resumed and by the fortieth round, Molineaux could no longer fight. Without a doubt, Molineaux was robbed. His loss completely demoralized him, especially when Cribb refused a return

Tom Molineaux, the most celebrated American pugilist of the early nineteenth century.

match. Joe Rimmer, a local fight hero from Lancashire, accepted Molineaux's challenge to fight "any man in England" and was defeated. Molineaux again claimed his right to fight for the championship. This time Cribb had to meet with Molineaux. In nineteen minutes and eleven seconds at Thistleton Gap, Leicester, Cribb won the fight. Since his first "defeat" from Cribb, Molineaux had become a victim of alcohol and was an easy prey. He died August 4, 1822, at the age of thirty-four.

Many other black fighters used Molineaux's name in the early days of boxing in America. It seemed to give some credibility to the young fighter if he said he was related to Molineaux. This was not an uncommon practice. In the early 1900s, when the Irish were the kings of the boxing ring, many Jewish and Italian fighters changed their last names to Irish ones. In 1818 a young American black man named Jim Wharton arrived in England claiming to be *the* Molineaux and made a great deal of money fighting under Molineaux's name. Wharton was a superb fighter in his own right, but the use of Molineaux's name spotlighted him.

In the 1800s, there were any number of excellent black fighters. There were Bob Travers, a fighting machine who is said to have had more bouts than any fighter of his time, and Bob Smith of Washington, D.C., who also went to England and won many battles. George Godfrey of Boston, black America's first heavyweight champion, had been scheduled to fight the great John L. Sullivan. Godfrey's reputation preceded him; Sullivan refused to fight him and the match was canceled. Sullivan also refused a match with Charles Hadley of Bridgeport, Connecticut, and in fact Sullivan never did risk his title in a fight with a black man.

One of the greatest of those young black fighters, comparable to Bill Richmond, was named Peter Jackson. He was born on the island of St. Croix in 1861. Jackson traveled to Sydney, Australia, as a seaman and an amateur fighter. A professional prizefight backer, Larry Foley, observed his skills and worked with him. Jackson was twenty-two years old, six feet, one inch tall, and weighed 212 pounds. By the time he was twenty-five, he had won the championship of Australia by defeating Tom Lees in thirty rounds. He then traveled to America and fought and beat George Godfrey in San Francisco. Then Jackson beat Joe McAuliffe and his next match was with Patsy Cardiff. Cardiff was considered a formidable opponent because he had fought cham-

Heavyweight Peter Jackson

pion John L. Sullivan to a draw. It would be logical to think that after beating Cardiff, Jackson was in line to meet with other white heavyweights and with champion John L. Sullivan. But other white fighters refused to meet with Jackson, pulling the old color line. There was no place to go except England. There Jackson knocked out Jen Smith, a popular heavyweight.

A good money-making match was finally made in America for May 21, 1891, where Jackson was to fight James J. Corbett, a twenty-five-year-old go-getter with great prospects. Jackson was thirty years old, but he weighed sixteen pounds more than Corbett. Jackson, knowing he had greater power, came out looking for that one punch that would KO Corbett. However, Corbett was a master strategist and dodger who boxed and backpedaled, much to the consternation of Jackson. In round sixteen, Jackson caught Corbett and injured him, but Corbett still hung in there. By the fortieth round, both men were so exhausted that sheer instinct must have kept them on their feet. Neither man could make it to the center of the ring for the sixty-first round and the fight was called a draw.

On May 30, 1892, Jackson won the British Empire heavyweight title beating Fred Slavin. Taking to drink, he was in poor condition when he was knocked out by Jim Jeffries in 1893. From 1893 until 1897 he became a stage actor, performing in *Uncle Tom's Cabin* and other plays, and engaged in occasional boxing exhibitions. He died in Australia in 1901. He was elected to the Boxing Hall of Fame in 1956.

But even before Jackson won the British heavyweight title, another black, George Dixon, won the bantamweight title in 1890 when he beat Nunc Wallace in London. George Dixon was born in Halifax, Nova Scotia, on July 29, 1870. He was five feet, three and a half inches tall, and at the start of his career weighed 87 pounds. At the peak of his career, he weighed 122 pounds and abdicated his bantamweight crown to pursue the featherweight title, which he won from Jack Skelly in New Orleans in 1892. George Dixon was known as "Little Chocolate." He had a great deal of charisma and dressed exceedingly well. Altogether he fought about 800 times and many of the fights were undertaken on vaudeville tours where he would challenge all comers. A clever, hard-hitting boxer, Dixon had perfect timing. His popularity was boundless. Dixon was the first black champion in any division recognized in America.

George Dixon

Lightweight champ Joe Gans

Joe Gans (real name Joseph Gaines), who was born in Baltimore, Maryland, November 25, 1879, won the lightweight title from Frank Erne at Fort Erie, Ontario, in 1902 by a knockout in round one. Another very intelligent fighter, Gans was called the "Old Master." Gans did most of his fighting on the road because New York was not open to black fighters in those days. Gans weighed 133 pounds when he started his career, the limit for the lightweight class at that time, but after he put on weight, Jimmy Britt claimed the title. Gans regained his title from Britt in San Francisco on October 31, 1904.

One of the most spectacular fights Gans had won was with Battling Nelson, a Danish fighter, on September 3, 1906, at Goldfield, Nevada. For forty-two of the forty-five scheduled rounds, Gans was winning. It was then that the Dane viciously fouled Gans and the fight was stopped, with Gans retaining his title. On July 4, 1908, Gans and Battling Nelson met again in Colma, California. Gans, now thirty-four years old and his body ravaged by tuberculosis, lost by a knockout in the seventeenth round. Joe Gans died on August 10, 1910, in Baltimore. There was a statue of him in New York in the lobby of the old Madison Square Garden.

There were many other notable black fighters during the late 1800s and early 1900s. Joe Walcott, five feet, one and one half inches tall and weighing 142 pounds, was born in Barbados on April 7, 1872, and had unbelievable strength for a man his size. They called him the "Barbados Demon." He came to America on a brigantine as a cabin boy when he was fifteen years old. After settling in Boston, he started boxing and wrestling as an amateur. When he was eighteen, he won the lightweight championship of New England in both boxing and wrestling.

He could take punishment and he could mete it out, as Joe Choynski, a 200-pound heavyweight, found out. Walcott knocked out Choynski in seven rounds in 1900. On December 18, 1901, Walcott knocked out Rube Ferns in five rounds at Fort Erie, Ontario, and won the world welterweight championship. He lost the title to Dixie Kid, another black fighter, in San Francisco on April 30, 1904, on a foul.

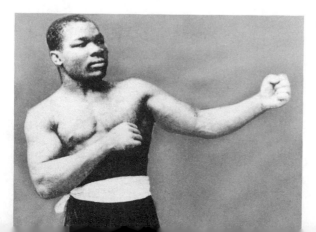

*Joe Walcott, the
"Barbados Demon"*

His professional record is one of the greatest in boxing. Arnold Raymond Cream, in memory of this great fighter, changed his name to "Jersey" Joe Walcott at the beginning of his professional career in the early '30s. Jersey Joe went on to become the heavyweight champion of the world when he knocked out Ezzard Charles in 1951.

The Versatile Sam Langford

Another great boxer was Sam Langford, the "Boston Tar Baby." He was born in Weymouth, Nova Scotia, on February 12, 1880. He stood five feet, seven and a half inches, with his weight ranging from 126 to 180 pounds. He started his career as a featherweight in 1902, and as such beat Joe Gans in 1903 and a year later drew with Jack Blackburn, who later became Joe Louis's trainer. He drew with Joe Walcott in 1904 and lost an exciting fifteen rounds to Jack Johnson in 1906. Although a rematch was clamored for, Johnson refused to meet with Langford again.

Although Langford never held a title, he was an extraordinary boxer with a remarkable record: 252 professional fights—won 37 by decision, 99 knockouts, drew 31, lost 19 decisions, knocked out by 4 opponents, 2 no contests, 59 decision bouts,* and won 1 on a foul. Langford lost his sight because of cataracts. He was elected to the Boxing Hall of Fame in 1955 and died a year later on January 12.

Other brilliant fighters of that time were the "Dixie Kid" (Aaron Brown), Joe Jeanette, and Sam McVey, who often fought Jack Johnson before he became heavyweight champion.

* A professional bout in which the governing rules state that in the absence of a knockout no decision will be rendered to determine a winner. During the 1920s, many states prohibited decisions being given in any bout.

Aaron Brown, the "Dixie Kid"

Joe Jeanette (left) and Sam Mc-Vey, two great fighters who fought Jack Johnson often—Jeanette eight times, McVey three. Jeanette met McVey in Paris in 1909 and after a total of 38 knockdowns (Jeanette 27, McVey 11) McVey quit in the forty-ninth round.

Jack Johnson

Jack Johnson

On March 31, 1878, in Galveston, Texas, a baby boy was born who many claim was
the greatest fighter who ever lived. His name was John Arthur Johnson, later to be
known as Jack Johnson and affectionately called "Little Arthur, the Galveston Giant." His father, a very pious man who was a caretaker of a public school building and
a Sunday preacher, was of pure African ancestry. He could trace his genealogy to the
Coromantees who lived on the Gold Coast in Africa. Perhaps that is why the Johnson
family was just a little different. They knew where they came from and had a kind of
assurance and pride about themselves.

When Jack Johnson was about twelve years old, he became obsessed with meeting
Steve Brodie. Brodie had become famous by leaping from the Brooklyn Bridge and
surviving. None of Johnson's family paid any attention to him when he voiced his
great desire to meet the daredevil. Since his family ignored his request and he had no
funds, Jack decided to get to New York under his own power. After several abortive
attempts by jumping a freight car, he finally stowed away on a boat that brought him
to Florida. Hungry and alone, he became a sponge fisherman in shark-infested waters.
Never swaying from attaining his goal—meeting Steve Brodie—he stowed away on a
boat heading for New York. He was discovered and worked his way to New York by
peeling potatoes en route.

When he arrived in New York, he asked everyone in sight where Steve Brodie was.
Chuck O'Conner, a picturesque character, ruler of the down and outs, and friend to

bums and politicians, who was called "the Mayor of the Bowery," took a liking to the determined young black boy and introduced Johnson to Steve Brodie. The two remained friends for a long time.

Having attained his purpose, Johnson moved on to Boston and worked as a stable boy. While exercising a horse, he fell and broke his leg, and with the help of Brodie and O'Conner he was able to get back to Galveston.

When Johnson was thirteen, he went to work on the docks. The docks were comprised of the toughest, roughest, and strongest men in Galveston. The most minor disagreement would evolve into a fight. There were bitter men who worked out their frustrations and deprivations with their fists. Even though he was the youngest, Jack fought too. He took a lot of beatings. He learned to take punishment, and then he learned to give punishment. After a while he had a reputation as a fighter. To further enhance his burgeoning skills, he took up boxing—not with the thought of becoming a professional, but to assure his survival.

Somehow, despite looking for Brodie and working on the docks, Jack finished grammar school and tired of the docks. He found a job in Dallas in a carriage-painting shop. As luck would have it, his boss, Walter Lewis, was a well-known amateur boxer. After work every evening, Johnson worked out with Lewis and other boxers. He was now fifteen and had glimmerings about becoming a professional boxer. He returned to Galveston and his first ring encounter was arranged with Joe Lee—a skillful boxer who was becoming prominent. There was a large attendance and in sixteen rounds Johnson won. Then there was a string of fights that Johnson won easily. When Bob Thompson, a proven hard fighter, came to Galveston declaring he would meet all comers and pay them $25 if they could go four rounds with him, Jack accepted the challenge. Johnson stayed the four rounds, won the $25, and spent two weeks in bed recuperating.

Although now he was a shipping clerk on the docks, Johnson decided to leave. There were few opportunities for fighting in Galveston and he had gone about as far as he would be allowed to working on the docks. He turned professional in 1897. He hopped a freight car and reached Springfield, Illinois. Here he learned that there was to be a battle royal and a boxing club was looking for fighters. There were to be five men in the ring and the bout was a winner-take-all contest. With his stomach groaning in hunger and a real need for money, Johnson volunteered. He knocked out all four opponents. Promoter Johnny Connors noted Johnson's ability and became his manager and good friend. Connors arranged a match in Chicago with a fighter called "Klondike," a white boxer who was very popular in Chicago. Johnson was knocked out in the fifth round in May 1899. Although he lost the match, he earned more money than he had ever seen at one time, and he attracted enough attention to be someone to watch. He was encouraged to go to New York. On his way, he stopped over in Pittsburgh, where a series of fights was to be held at the stockyards. He was surprised when he was recognized and a match was easily made. He fought a white man and knocked him out in five rounds. His purse was his hat spilling over with dollars, and he could hardly wait to get to New York. When he arrived he found it rough sledding; no one would give him a break and many doubted his abilities. Luckily, he found a place in the camp of Joe Walcott, "the Barbados Demon," and went with him to Boston as a sparring partner for a few months.

Johnson returned to Galveston and fought Pat Smith to a draw. In February 1901, he was knocked out by Joe Choynski in the third round. Johnson fought numerous battles that netted him little financially, but taught him much about boxing and provided excellent training.

After the Choynski knockout, Johnson began his climb to the top. Meeting and beating the outstanding fighters of that time—Joe Jeanette, Sandy Ferguson, Hank Griffin, Frank Childs, Sam McVey, and many others—firmly established him as a fighter to be reckoned with.

Jack Johnson, standing six feet and one quarter inch, weighing 195 pounds, his head shaven clean, a formidable record behind him, stood looking toward the heavyweight crown of the world, since the heavyweight division is the money-maker. No black man had ever held this title. More than forty years after the Emancipation, there was no way the white man intended to let a black have an opportunity to receive the benefits of the crown. Not only money was involved, but a kind of prestige that would allow a champion boxer to associate with kings. And that ever-present hero worship syndrome that was not meant for blacks to enjoy. Johnson had beaten every black fighter who may have been a contender for the crown, as well as formidable white opponents.

During the period of Johnson's quest for the title, Jim Jeffries, the heavyweight champion, fought Jack Munroe in a return match and KO'd him in the second round on August 26, 1904. Jeffries, claiming that opponents were scarce, decided to retire. However, Sam McVey, Sam Langford, Joe Jeanette, and Jack Johnson, the greatest black fighters of this period, outclassed all of the white fighters. The real reason Jim Jeffries retired was so that he would not be responsible for a black champion. When Jeffries retired, he persuaded Marvin Hart and Jack Root to fight for the vacated title. With Jeffries as referee, the two men fought on July 3, 1905. Hart won and Jeffries declared him the champion, thereby keeping the title for whites. Then on February 23, 1906, Tommy Burns, a French Canadian from Hanover, Canada, won the title from Hart in a twenty-round decision. Burns (real name Noah Brusso) was twenty-five years old at the time. He stood only 5 feet, 7 inches tall and weighed 179 pounds, but he had extremely long arms which he used to every advantage. Tommy Burns was, and still remains, the smallest man to ever become world heavyweight champion. Besides being a clever boxer and a powerful puncher, Burns was a keen businessman. He had acquired the most valuable of all boxing titles by sheer good fortune and proceeded to make the most of it.

Tommy Burns

Although the biggest purses to be obtained at that time were in the United States, Burns decided to go on a world tour, partly to establish his claim to the championship, but also to escape the prospect of having to defend his crown against one or more of the menacing black quartet of Johnson, Langford, McVey, and Jeanette, who regarded themselves as his foremost challengers.

Johnson was hungry for that title but was unable to get a match with Burns in the States. Johnson kept himself in condition by engaging in as many ring events as possible, hoping for a break. Finally, he set sail for England in the early part of 1908 in the company of his manager, Sam Fitzpatrick, to seek out Burns, who was already there. Johnson bided his time with fights with a few English boxers. He beat Al McNamara in four rounds at Plymouth and knocked out Ben Taylor, also in Plymouth. While not important fights, they further paved the way for Johnson to meet with Burns by removing possible contenders. The British press criticized Burns for avoiding Johnson. Burns took off for Australia.

Arrangements were finally made for Johnson to meet Burns in Sydney. At the outset Burns was the favored boxer as far as betting was concerned, but as Johnson trained he gained more and more admiration from the Australian people. Of course, there were any number of bigoted people who harassed Johnson (as well as Burns, for fighting Johnson). The two men were to fight for a purse of $35,000. Johnson was to receive $5,000. The final concession Johnson made was to allow Hugh McIntosh, Burns's manager and promoter of the fight, to act as referee. Johnson knew a win would have to be an indisputable win.

On December 26, 1908, Jack Johnson and Tommy Burns met in Sydney, Australia, for the title match. The fight was scheduled for twenty rounds. There were 40,000 spectators from all over the world. Press coverage was the most extensive ever in the history of boxing. Johnson weighed in at 192 pounds and Burns at 168. Johnson was beating Burns so badly that the police stopped the fight in the fourteenth round. Jack Johnson was declared world heavyweight champion.

Jack London reported in the New York *Herald* on December 26, 1908:
    The fight of fights it might be called, was like unto that between a Colossus and a toy automaton. It had all the seeming of a playful Ethiopian at loggerheads with a small and futile white man. . . .
    Johnson play-acted all the time, and he played with Burns from the gong of the opening round to the finish of the fight.
    "Hit here, Tommy," he would say, exposing the right side of his unprotected stomach, and when Burns struck, Johnson would neither wince nor cover up. . . . "Now here, Tommy," and while Burns hit as directed, Johnson would continue to grin and chuckle and smile his golden smile.
    . . . But one thing remains, Jeffries [Jim] must emerge from his alfalfa farm to remove that smile from Johnson's face. "Jeff, it's up to you."

The hue and cry went out for a "great white hope." It was felt by many that Johnson's "arrogance" should be wiped out by a white boxer. The search immediately went out all over Europe, and Johnson welcomed all comers.

Johnson returned triumphantly to America, where he fought a succession of no-decision bouts with Victor McLaglen, who later became an Academy Award-winning

Johnson batters Burns in the fourteenth round just before the police stepped in and ordered the bout stopped.

actor; Jack O'Brien, of Philadelphia; Tony Ross, of Pittsburgh; and Al Kaufman, of San Francisco. Stanley Ketchel, the middleweight champion, thought he could beat Johnson. Ketchel felt he was the better boxer and could win as long as no one tried to knock anybody out. Johnson could not resist the logic and the two men made a gentleman's agreement to that effect. They met in Colma, California, on October 16, 1909. It was a cat-and-mouse game all the way; Johnson was never in any trouble and was quite at ease. In the twelfth round, Ketchel saw an opening and delivered a powerful blow to Johnson's jaw and dropped the champion. Johnson saw red. He arose quickly and let go with his left and knocked Ketchel out. Ketchel remained unconscious for one hour.

After Ketchel had been defeated, there were no available white contestants for Johnson to fight. The public tried to coax Jim Jeffries into coming out of retirement. Since Jeffries had retired undefeated, it was rationalized that he was still in reality the undefeated champion and the only proper person to fight Johnson. Writer Jack London had written to Jeffries, pleading for him to challenge Johnson and bring the title

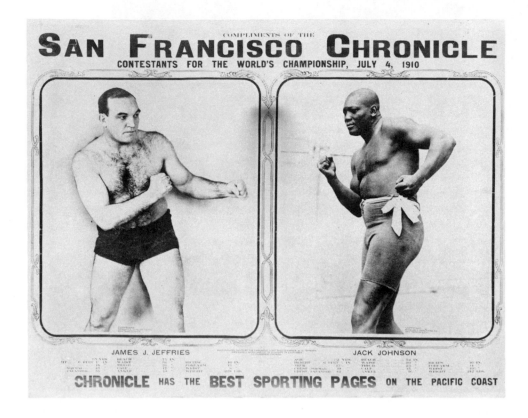

The once mighty Jeffries at the end of the trial. Battered, bleeding, and exhausted, he was stopped by Johnson in the fifteenth round.

back to the white people. The letter, public pressure, and intimates nudged Jeffries away from his alfalfa farm. Jeffries was now thirty-five years old, had been in retirement for six years, and was grossly overweight.

Tex Rickard and Jack Gleason promoted the fight and the purse was $101,000. Although the fight was originally scheduled for California, the governor would not permit it. Finally, the fight was set for Reno, Nevada, on July 4, 1910. Jeffries had trained hard and well, and had controlled his weight and was down to 227. Johnson had done likewise and was in excellent condition, weighing 208 pounds. The tremendous crowd was ready and waiting for the comeuppance of Jack Johnson. It was rumored that if by some chance Jeffries did not win the fight, Johnson would be gunned down in the ring. The tide of racial hostility was at a peak. The heat from the sun was unremitting. Jeffries was no match for Johnson. The fight was so easy that Johnson joked with those at ringside; had a running one-way conversation with Jeffries; talked at ease with the referee who was the promoter, Tex Rickard; and even took time to suggest to the telegraph operators what to say to their newspapers. In the fifteenth round, Johnson became serious and, with a left to the jaw, knocked his opponent down for the first time in Jeffries' boxing career. Jeffries got up at the count of ten and Johnson hit him again with another left to the jaw and the fight was over. Johnson had scored a knockout in two minutes and twenty seconds of the round.

New York *Times,* July 4, 1910:

Jack Johnson made the following statement after the fight:

"I won from Mr. Jeffries because I outclassed him in every department of the fighting game. Before I entered the ring, I was certain I would be the victor. I never changed my mind at any time.

"Jeffries's blows had no steam behind them. So, how could he hope to defeat me? With the exception of a slight cut on my lower lip, which was really caused by an old wound being struck, I am unmarked. I heard people at the ringside remark about body blows being inflicted upon me. I do not recall a single punch in the body that caused me any discomfort. I am in shape to battle again tomorrow if it were necessary.

"One thing I must give Jeffries credit for is the game battle he made. He came at me with the heart of a true fighter. No man can say he did not do his best. . . ."

The Daily Express in London, Wednesday, July 6, 1910, reported in the headlines:

RACE RIOTS IN AMERICA
19 DEATHS
MANY HURT AND 5,000 ARRESTED
BLACK MOBS SWEEP THROUGH TOWNS

Racial riots swept the United States last night from the Atlantic to the Pacific after Jeffries's crushing defeat by Johnson. . . . 251 persons were seriously injured. . . .

. . . Most of the casualities were Negroes who were hunted down by white mobs, mostly because of boasts by the blacks that they had demonstrated their superiority over the whites. . . .

Two Negroes were shot dead at La Providence, Louisiana, after walking down the principal street of the town and announcing that a Negro could thrash a white man if he liked. . . .

Other Negroes were killed in Cincinnati, Omaha, Little Rock, and other cities. . . .

Serious rioting occurred at Washington, Kansas City, Jacksonville, Chattanooga, Norfolk, Los Angeles, Schenectady . . . Florida and New York. . . .

Three Negro women attacked two white women . . . a mob chased the Negresses, shouting "Lynch them."

In Chattanooga, Tennessee—A Negro strutted into camp (state volunteer manoeuvers) and thrust a newspaper containing an account of Johnson's victory in the faces of the soldiers.

A soldier knocked him down and another soldier fired at him. The Negro ran away, and the soldiers formed with their rifles for an attack on the Negro quarter of the town. . . .

The result of the rioting will be to prevent the exhibition of moving pictures of the fight in a number of towns, the authorities fearing that the display will incite further bloodshed. Washington [Congress] has taken the lead in this matter. . . .

A Reuter special telegram states that three Negroes met their death at Ulvadia, Georgia, in a battle between whites and blacks at a construction camp. . . .

On the island of Jamaica in the West Indies, calypsonians made up the following ditty:

> *Hif wasn't for the referee*
> *Jack Johnson woulda kill Jim Jeffrey*
> *Right, left, and the upper cut*
> *One lick, ina Jeffrey gut†*

The repercussions of Johnson's victory over Jeffries were manifold. If he had just been an ordinary black man, it would be bad enough, but Johnson looked upon himself as a *man* first: a man who had fairly and squarely won the championship and as such was entitled to the kind of behavior and attitude that befitted his title. He wore expensive clothes and jewels, had the biggest, most costly cars, and had the audacity to marry a white woman. (His first marriage, to a black woman when he was a teenager, ended in divorce many years before.) Johnson refused to conform to the norms of the time. He was a bright and dynamic man; in fact, he acted just like a white man would have under similar circumstances. His association with white women would be his Achilles' heel. This was his one vulnerable area.

After the Jeffries fight Johnson returned home to Chicago and his wife, Etta. She was depressed over her father's death (and perhaps for other reasons which are not known). She committed suicide.

Meanwhile the National Sporting Club held a "Great White Hope Tournament" in the search for a defeater of Johnson. Johnson had no objection to fighting any great white hope. Jim Flynn had fought with Johnson previously; he exhibited above-aver-

† Remembered by Arthur Rust, Sr.

age fighting ability. Flynn had been fighting with the top fighters and had improved his boxing skills. A fight was arranged to take place in Las Vegas, New Mexico, July 4, 1912. Flynn proved to be an easy opponent and the police ordered the fight stopped in the ninth round. That was to be Johnson's last fight in the United States of America.

Johnson became involved with another white woman, Lucille Cameron. She was supposed to be his secretary and as such traveled with him. Her mother became enraged when her daughter left Chicago with Johnson; she had him arrested under the Mann Act, which forbade transportation of women across the state line for immoral purposes. Lucille Cameron married Johnson, and therefore could not be forced to testify. However, Johnson was sentenced to a year and a day on a lesser charge brought about by his association with another white woman years earlier. Johnson pleaded innocent and was freed on bail awaiting an appeal.

Now his life was completely dogged by detectives who followed him wherever he went. His house and car were watched twenty-four hours a day. He was arrested in Battle Creek, Michigan, when he and his wife were going on a vacation trip. He was taken to the police station and sent back to Chicago. He could not stand the continuous harassment and, fearful of the kind of justice that might be meted out to him, he sought to escape America.

Despite constant surveillance, Johnson made his plans. A black baseball team, Rube Foster's Chicago American Giants, was in Chicago and was going to head for New York. Johnson offered the team the use of a private railroad car with all expenses paid if he could route the direction the car was to take. Foster's team readily accepted the offer, not realizing Johnson's motivation. Most of the players were big men like Johnson and one even resembled him. Johnson gave this young man his ring and watch, which were identifiably his. Gus Rhodes, Johnson's nephew, was his only confidant. When they boarded the special train, Johnson carried bats and other baseball equipment. As the train headed across the Canadian border, the team passed the customs inspection. A car met Johnson at Hamilton, Ontario, and drove him into Toronto, where his wife was waiting. They finally boarded a steamship in Montreal and arrived in Paris on July 10, 1913.

Johnson and his second wife, Lucille Cameron, in front of his saloon, the Main Event Restaurant, in Tijuana, Mexico, March 1920.

Meanwhile the legislature had started moving. Bills were passed in several states barring interracial fights, ostensibly to protect the black population from the mayhem administered by the whites. In February 1913, the New York State Athletic Commission ruled that mixed bouts would be prohibited. California followed suit with the addition of a fine of five thousand dollars and a prison sentence of three years to offending parties. Wisconsin passed, then later rescinded, a bill prohibiting racially mixed bouts. None of these bans was constitutional, but more treacherous was the attitude of white heavyweight contenders, who declared that they would pull the color line and refuse to fight with a black man. Begun by Jack Dempsey when he won the heavyweight title from Jess Willard in 1919, this silent edict remained for many years.

When Johnson arrived in Paris, he was the toast of the town. He played short engagements at Les Folies-Bergère, and in London at music halls. He put on boxing exhibitions in Paris, Marseilles, Brussels, Berlin, Vienna, Budapest, Bucharest, St. Petersburg, Moscow, and other large cities of Europe.

On November 28, 1913, he fought a title match with Andre Sproul in Paris. Johnson knocked him out in the second round. A match was set for him to fight Jim Johnson (no relation) on October 19, 1913. Jim Johnson was an American heavyweight and a black man. This would be Johnson's first title match with a black. Previously he had refused to meet with Sam Langford, who clamored for a match in America. Johnson remembered how good Langford had been and refused to meet with him or any other black man in America, saying that that kind of fight would not draw a big enough crowd. Promoters felt that an all-black heavyweight fight would not draw and did not encourage it. Promoters are a predatory breed of psychologists. They learn to feed on the bottled hostility, fears, guilts, and prejudices of people to make money. A white man beating a black man is good business; some people want to see the abstracted clash between the races to reassure the justification of their bigotry and superiority. However, if the black man won the contest the result was often fearful. The thought of a black man beating a white reversed the concept of white superiority. Deep anger on the part of whites often caused race riots and gave license to unseemly and cruel behavior. But the clever promoters knew that a rematch would bring more money in their coffers as a result of man's quest for ethnic domination. This of course led to corruption—blacks taking a fall for a price so that the white man could again acclaim his superiority. This is an American phenomenon that had its roots in slavery. But circumstances had changed since Johnson had gone overseas. Jim Johnson was a hard fighter and it was the most serious contest that Jack Johnson had undertaken in his professional career. In the third round Jack's left arm was broken and dangled at his side. Despite the ineffectiveness of one arm, Jack Johnson fought Jim Johnson to a ten-round draw.

After Johnson's arm had fully mended, he took on Frank Moran in Paris, on June 27, 1914, and beat him in twenty rounds. Johnson finished out 1914 by venturing to Buenos Aires and knocking out Jack Murray in three rounds.

Even though Johnson was still heavyweight champion, making money, and had the adulation of Europe, he wanted to go home. He was an American and he missed his country, his family, and his friends. He had heard that his appeal from the court's judgment was successful and he was granted a new trial. However, since he had jumped bail and left the country, his status was that of a fugitive.

In the meantime, a young, white American fighter, Jess Willard, from Pottawato-
mie County, Kansas, wanted to fight Johnson for the crown and made his wishes
known. Promoter Jack Curly, who also managed heavyweight Jim Flynn, had made
arrangements for a match between Johnson and Willard in Northern Mexico, which
was controlled by the bandit king Pancho Villa, who financed the deal. Mexican
President Carranza was opposed to anything Villa fostered and declared he would
stop the fight. The only way to enter Mexico in those days was by way of Veracruz and
President Carranza declared he would imprison Johnson and have him deported to
the United States, where he would be arrested.

That plan went down the drain. Then Harry Frazee and Joe Weber, American
theatrical promoters, set up another meet in Cuba. Before the fight, it was subtlely
suggested that if Willard was permitted to win and gain the title, a lot of "trouble"
could be avoided. It would stem the tide of prejudice running against Johnson and
perhaps the charges could be dropped. It was a tempting offer and must have thrown
Johnson into a complete turmoil. He cherished that crown, but the pull of returning
home must have surpassed his prize.

Big Jess Willard was six feet six and a quarter inches tall and weighed 252 pounds.
He looked like a tough heavyweight contender, but in reality he was a lazy man who
would not train properly. His slow-moving gait and general disinterest certainly made
him poor championship material.

It was Easter Sunday, April 5, 1915, in Havana, Cuba, that Johnson and Willard

*April 5, 1915, at the Oriente Race Track on the outskirts of Havana, Cuba, Jack Johnson lost his
title to Jess Willard in the twenty-sixth round. Later Johnson claimed that he threw the fight,
offering this photo as proof that he wasn't knocked out and pointing to his use of his gloves to
"shield my eyes from the sun."*

finally had a go at it for the crown. The ring was set in the Oriente Race Track. The sun was fierce and the temperature rose to 110 degrees. Thirty thousand spectators attended. The fight was scheduled for forty-five rounds. The first twenty-five rounds were uneventful; neither man had struck a significant blow. The referee had to call Johnson from his corner in the twenty-sixth round. After Willard delivered three punches, Johnson fell and rolled over on his back and Willard became the new heavyweight champion. Did Johnson throw the fight? Fact or fiction? It reportedly was part of the "deal" for Johnson to receive $35,000, and the rights to a foreign film to be made about him. There has never been any confirmation or denial of this.

At any rate, having lost the championship and feeling that everything had been ironed out for his return to America, Johnson headed for England to await the call that never came. He traveled through Europe appearing in theatrical productions and giving exhibition fights. He finally settled down in Spain, a country he found pleasant and comfortable. He had many friends there and even took up bullfighting, successfully engaging in a number of contests. He lived in Spain for almost four years. After the First World War was over, Johnson sailed for Mexico to set up a series of ring exhibitions. He opened a small café in Tijuana that became very popular. He renewed an old acquaintanceship with Tom Carey, a Chicago politician, and told of his wish to return to America. Carey promised his full support regarding his trial. Johnson notified federal officials that he planned to cross the border and he was directed to San Diego.

In Jamaica, a soulful refrain commemorated the event:

> *God bless da man da call Jack Johnson*
> *Who da put in jail*
> *For de white folks shun his liberty*
> *While da nigger was still in jail‡*

He was sentenced to one year and a day in the Leavenworth federal prison. Although he hated the regimen of prison life, he was treated fairly and respected. He became the athletic director. He supervised the baseball fields, prison track area, gymnasium, and all aspects of athletics. He boxed some exhibitions while incarcerated.

After his release he joined vaudeville circuits demonstrating his skill with the speed bag (the small punching bag) and giving lectures on politics and race, until he finally wound up at Huberts Museum and Flea Circus in New York's Times Square.

In June 1946 he stopped in at *The Ring* magazine, boxing's bible, and talked with Nat Loubet, boxing authority and one of the owners. He was telling Loubet about the new Lincoln-Zephyr automobile he was going to purchase. He had scraped and borrowed every penny he could to buy this car. Johnson had always loved high-powered cars. As they were talking, Loubet asked Johnson how he felt about working at Huberts after all he had been and all he had had. Johnson smiled his golden smile and said, "I eat, I sleep—fuck it."

---

‡ Remembered by Art Rust, Sr.

On June 10, 1946, he was heading back to New York in his new Lincoln-Zephyr going at great speed when a truck caused Johnson to swerve. Johnson lost control of the car and crashed into a power pole. He died in the Raleigh, North Carolina, hospital in less than an hour.

The body was shipped to Chicago and most of the black population of that city came to view his remains. Over 2,500 attended the funeral; thousands more stood in the streets. He was buried in Graceland Cemetery in Chicago.

The title to the heavyweight crown remained closed to blacks from the time of Johnson's defeat in 1915 until 1937, but blacks still remained challenging and formidable foes in other divisions of boxing. One of the most colorful black fighters during the '20s was Battling Siki (his real name was Louis Phal), also called the "Singular Senegalese." Born on September 16, 1897, in St.-Louis, Senegal, he was formerly a soldier

Louis Phal, "the Battling Siki."

who had learned to box in the French Army and had won the French Croix de Guerre in World War I. He fought Georges Carpentier, a Frenchman, for the light-heavyweight championship in Paris on September 24, 1922. Siki knocked out Carpentier in the sixth round and became light-heavyweight title holder. He had the "misfortune" of fighting Mike McTigue on St. Patrick's Day in Dublin in 1923. Siki lost the fight in a twenty-round decision.

Siki died in December of 1925, at the age of twenty-eight. His body was found lying in the gutter in front of 350 West Forty-first Street in the heart of New York City's infamous "Hell's Kitchen." He had been killed by two pistol shots fired from behind. His killer was never found.

In the heavyweight division, Sam Langford still languished, never obtaining his chance at the title. The magnificent behemoth, Harry Wills, a most accomplished boxer, frequently tried to challenge the then champion, Jack Dempsey. Reflecting the pressure of the time, the New York State Athletic Commission relented its earlier position and pushed for a fight between Dempsey and Wills. Dempsey refused and was subsequently barred from fighting in New York State. In Benton Harbor, Michigan, another attempt was made to match the two, and it also failed. Tex Rickard, the promoter, was so confident that he had a bout set up between the pair in Jersey City that he even had the tickets printed with a September 6, 1924, date. Wills was an excellent contender and if by any chance he won, it was the feeling of many that another "Jack Johnson situation" would occur and shatter the complacency the white world saw as racial harmony. As a result, Wills never got his well-deserved crack at the championship.

Harry Wills

On February 26, 1926, Theodore "Tiger" Flowers fought middleweight champion Harry Greb, "the Human Windmill," and won in fifteen rounds. That made Tiger Flowers the first black man to hold the 160-pound title.

In the bantamweight division, there was Panama Al Brown, born in Panama City, July 5, 1902. Also known as the "Elongated Panamanian," he began boxing around the Canal Zone. On June 18, 1929, Al Brown outpointed Vidal Gregario as a result of an elimination tournament and was recognized as the bantamweight champion.

Most of Brown's fights took place in Panama and Europe, especially France. As a result, New York and the National Boxing Association many times claimed that the throne was vacant because Brown refused to fight in America. Nonetheless, he kept his title until he was defeated by Spaniard Baltazar Sangchilli on June 1, 1935, at Valencia, Spain, in fifteen rounds.

Tiger Flowers

Panama Al Brown

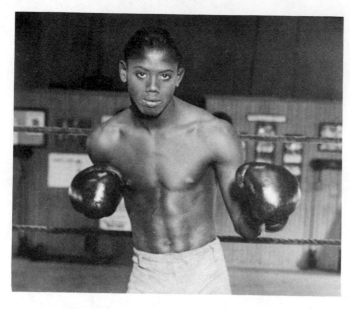

Kid Chocolate

Kid Chocolate, the "Cuban Bon Bon," was born Eligio Sardinias at Cerro, Cuba, January 6, 1910. He fought 100 amateur bouts in Cuba and scored 86 knockouts. After he turned professional and had 21 wins under his belt, he came to the United States. On July 15, 1931, he knocked out Benny Bass in Philadelphia in the seventh round and became the junior lightweight champion. Then on October 13, 1932, he won the featherweight title when he knocked out Lew Feldman in a final New York elimination. He became the New York State featherweight champion.

In 1935 John Henry Lewis, who was managed by Gus Greenlee (a black numbers man and owner of the Negro National League baseball team the Pittsburgh Crawfords), won the light-heavyweight championship from Bob Olin in a fifteen-round decision in St. Louis. John Henry was a clever boxer and a strong puncher. It has been said that he was a direct descendant of Tom Molineaux.

John Henry Lewis

Joe Louis

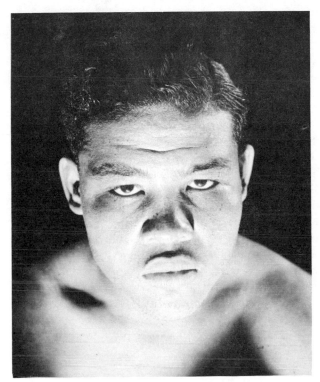

Joe Louis

Joe Louis, born May 13, 1914, was to become the greatest and most positively influential psychological force to hit black America for many years. He was the hero that black America so desperately needed, and, too, there were qualities in the man that would even transcend race. He would become the hero of the underdog. In the chaos of the Great Depression he would offer hope to all.

Joseph Louis Barrow was the seventh child born to Lily and Munrow Barrow. They were a family of sharecroppers on a poor-land farm not far from Lafayette, Alabama. When the father, Munrow Barrow, was institutionalized in the Searcy Hospital for the Negro Insane, it was reported that he died there. Louis' mother married a widower who also had eight children. They left Alabama and headed for Detroit, where they hoped to find employment in the auto industry.

Louis was a shy boy who stammered and stuttered. He did not enjoy school, but was well liked by his teachers because he was always polite and decent. As a child, Louis never fought unless provoked, but when provoked he would always win.

Louis met Thurston McKinney, winner of the 1932 Golden Gloves in Detroit for the 147-pound division, at the Bronson Vocational School. McKinney persuaded Louis to forgo his violin lessons and come to the gymnasium and learn to box. Louis fell in love with boxing. He quit school and hustled little jobs all day—selling ice and coal, working in the vegetable market—and at night he worked out in the gym. He had a string of amateur fights. His first one was with Johnny Miler, a white fighter who had been on the Olympic boxing team. Miler beat Louis so badly he almost gave up the idea of boxing. After that terrible defeat, Louis knocked out thirteen opponents consecutively and became a Golden Glover. Then he was outpointed by Max Marek in the National Amateur Championship in Boston. However, he generally continued winning his amateur bouts, only occasionally being outpointed.

In December 1933, Louis met John Roxborough, who was to have a very great influence in his life. Roxborough was a good-looking, well-dressed black man, well respected in the black community. He had a real estate office that was a front for the numbers business he controlled. Louis was nurtured by Roxborough, given an allowance, clothes, and proper gym equipment.

Louis' last amateur fight was with Joe Bauer, whom he knocked out in less than two minutes of the first round on June 12, 1934. It was then that Roxborough felt that Louis should go to Chicago to live and train with Julian Black, Roxborough's friend and fellow numbers man. Roxborough and Black became Louis' managers. Louis was very satisfied with these men; he had seen a lot of good black fighters managed by whites who did not take the time with their fighters or properly subsidize them, and these young men were burned out before they were able to reach their prime. The most important factor in the making of a champion is the training. Jack Blackburn was the right choice for trainer. In a twenty-year period, Blackburn had had over one hundred fights as a lightweight and had won most of them. In 1902 he had fought Sam Langford, who weighed 140 pounds, and it was a draw. He had been a sparring partner for Jack Johnson and later became a boxing instructor and trainer. Previous to Louis, he had trained Sammy Mandell and Bud Taylor. Blackburn knew the fight game inside out and he was a rough, tough character—just what the young Louis needed.

In his first professional fight Louis KO'd Jack Kracken in one round at Bacon Casino on the south side of Chicago. After his defeat of Kracken, Louis stormed through 1934 devastating Willie Davis, KO third round; Larry Udell, KO second round; Jack Kranz, a decision in eighth round; Buck Everett, KO in the second round; Alex Borchuk, KO fourth round; Adolph Wiater, ten-round decision; Art Sykes, KO eighth round; Jack O'Dowd, KO second round; Stanley Poreda, KO first round; Charley Massera, KO third round; and Lee Ramage, KO eighth round. Many of these men were top-drawer heavyweights.

Indeed, here was a man worth watching. Boxing had fallen on evil ways. With the death of Tex Rickard, who controlled New York boxing (New York was considered the citadel of boxing), everything was coming apart. Gambling was running rampant. Gangsters from the Prohibition days were buying fighters and their managers as well as the promoters. Taking a dive in a particular fight was almost becoming a part of the game, especially in the heavyweight division. Joe Louis played the game straight—there was no hanky-panky surrounding his fights. This was accomplished through the shrewd management of Roxborough and Black. They were powerful men with enough strength and connections in the underworld to see that their boxer was not corrupted. What with Louis' basic honesty and decency, coupled with his managers' protective aura and his natural skills sharpened by Blackburn, Joe Louis began to shine as an idealized kind of American. Blacks were proud of him and whites respected him and later many idolized him.

(Left to right) *Julian Black, Jack Blackburn, Joe Louis, and John Roxborough*

Roxborough, Black, and Blackburn started tutoring Louis on proper social behavior because they had begun to realize that he was truly championship material and they wanted to head toward that goal. (The flamboyancy and defiance of Jack Johnson still left a bitter taste in the mouths of whites; the world had not been ready for a Jack Johnson—he was way before his time.) Their primary rules for Louis were: never have his picture taken with a white woman; always carry himself with dignity; never go anywhere, particularly a nightclub, without an entourage of carefully chosen people; and anyone who approached him about fixing a fight was to be immediately reported.

In early 1935, Louis was still going great guns. His knockout punches continued and they began calling him the "Brown Bomber." Louis won a ten round decision from Patsy Perroni in Detroit on January 4; he knocked out Hans Birkie in Pittsburgh on January 11 in the tenth; February 21 he KO'd Lee Ramage in Los Angeles in the second round; on March 8 he took out "Red" Barry in San Francisco in three; Louis then fought Natie Brown on March 29, 1935, in Detroit and won a decision in ten rounds. After the Natie Brown fight Louis knocked out Roy Lazer, Biff Benton, Roscoe Toles, Willie Davis, and Gene Stanton.

It was at this time that Nat Fleischer, sportswriter and owner of *The Ring* magazine, introduced Louis to one of his best friends, Mike Jacobs. Jacobs had just organized the Twentieth Century Sporting Club to compete against the supremacy of the promoters who controlled Madison Square Garden. Roxborough and Black had previously tried to get a match at Madison Square Garden but were turned down by Jimmy Johnston, who didn't believe in black fighters. So when Jacobs came along with his sporting club and asked to promote a Louis fight, it seemed the only way to get into

Joe Louis and Mike Jacobs, 1938

New York. Thus, the forces that were to propel Joe Louis to legendary status were formed.

Jacobs set up the Joe Louis-Primo Carnera fight for June 25, 1935, at Yankee Stadium, New York. Carnera, from Sequals, Italy, one of the poorest of heavyweight titleholders, had won the championship from Jack Sharkey in 1933 and had defended his title twice before being defeated by Max Baer in 1934. Carnera was a poor fighter with few skills. Building his reputation on questionable fights, his greatest claim to fame was his six feet, five and three-quarter inches and 260½ pounds. Carnera was just an awkward cream puff and was knocked out in the sixth round. It was at this fight that Louis demanded that the black press be given the same privileges that the white press enjoyed.

Louis stands ready as Primo Carnera crouches, dazed, on the deck, after the second knockdown, in the sixth and final round of the June 25, 1935, bout at Yankee Stadium. Referee Arthur Donovan orders Louis to the neutral corner. Louis won on a technical knockout.

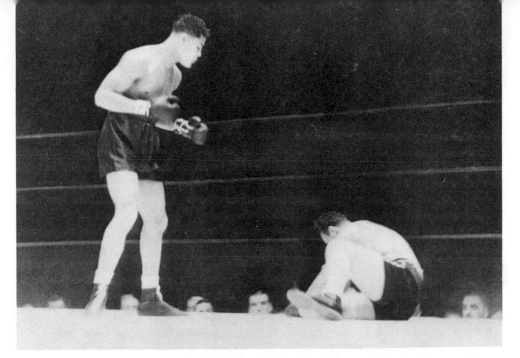

Louis stands over Kingfish Levinsky, waiting for the ex-fish peddler from Chicago to rise after his second knockdown in the first round of their scheduled ten-round bout in Chicago, August 7, 1935. The fight ended seconds later when Levinsky was once again beaten down and Louis won on a technical knockout.

On August 7 at Comiskey Park in Chicago, Louis knocked out Kingfish Levinsky in the first round. The fight ended with Levinsky sitting on the bottom strand of the ropes yelling at the referee, Arthur Donovan, "Don't let him hit me again. Don't let him hit me again."

Joe and Marva Louis, 1935

Now that Louis had a foothold in New York, the contender that he would have to go after was Max Baer. Baer was six feet, two inches and weighed 210 pounds. After Baer had won the heavyweight crown from Carnera, he lost it to James J. Braddock a year later. Baer was from Livermore, California, and they called him the "Livermore Larruper." The fight was scheduled for September 24, 1935, at Yankee Stadium. On that same date Louis was to marry Marva Trotter.

There were 95,000 people at Yankee Stadium that night. Jack Dempsey was in Baer's corner. Baer weighed 210½ pounds and Louis 199¼. After the bell rang at the end of the second round, Louis dropped his hands and Baer hit him with a left hook and a right hand to the jaw.

Steamed up in the third round, Louis banged Baer with rights and lefts. As the round was coming to the end, Louis hit Baer on the chin with a right and Baer went down for a nine count. Louis got in another right and a left hook and Baer was down again. The bell saved him at the count of four.

When they came out for the fourth round, Louis hit Baer with a hard left hook and a hard right to the head and he was down for the full count. Louis had knocked out two ex-heavyweight champions in a three-month period, first Carnera and now Baer. Louis said, "I've never had better hand speed; I felt so good I knew I could have fought for two or three days straight." It was estimated that Louis must have hooked his left to Baer's chin over 200 times. In a radio interview after the fight, Max Baer stated, "I thought all of Harlem was in the ring last night."

Joe Louis being escorted to the farthest neutral corner by referee Arthur Donovan after Louis knocked out Max Baer in four rounds on September 24, 1935, in Yankee Stadium.

In his essay, "Joe Louis Uncovers Dynamite," Richard Wright portrayed the following scene in Chicago:

"Louis! Louis! Louis!" they yelled. They snatched newspapers from the stands of astonished Greeks and tore them up, flinging the bits into the air. They wagged their heads. Lawd, they'd never seen or heard the likes of it before. They shook the hands of strangers. They clapped one another on the back. It was like a revival. Really, there was a religious feeling, but it was *something* and you could feel it. It was a feeling of unity, of oneness. . . .

. . . You see, Joe was the consciously-felt symbol. Joe was the concentrated essence of black triumph over white. And it comes so seldom, so seldom. . . . From the symbol of Joe's strength, they took strength, and in that moment all fear, all obstacles were wiped out, drowned. They stepped out of the mire of hesitation and irresolution and were free! Invincible! A merciless victor over a fallen foe! Yes, they had all felt that—for a moment.

. . . Here's that *something,* that pent-up folk consciousness. Here's a fleeting glimpse of the heart of the Negro, the heart that beats and suffers and hopes—for freedom. Here's that fluid something that's like iron. Here's the real dynamite that Joe Louis uncovered!

After the Baer fight Louis fought Paolino Uzcudun at Madison Square Garden on December 13, 1935. Uzcudun was from Spain and considered an excellent fighter. However, in July of 1935 in Berlin, Max Schmeling had beaten him in twelve rounds.

Paolino Uzcudun staggers as Louis delivers a sharp left to the jaw in the fourth round. When Joe followed with a terrific right high to the temple, Uzcudun was finished.

Max Schmeling, the former heavyweight champion (1930–32) was preparing to regain his title. The fight with Uzcudun was one step on the ladder. Since Louis had become a possible threat, Schmeling came to America to watch Louis train for the Uzcudun battle. During Louis' training session, Schmeling told reporters, "I see something. He hasn't forgotten his amateur mistakes. He drops his left after a lead and tips his head back at the same time. He can be hit with a right hand. I have a good right hand. I will beat him with my right hand."

Uzcudun fought in a crouch, his face hidden behind his gloves and arms crossed. Louis knew he would have to wait for an opening. In the fourth round Louis kept probing with the left jab and Uzcudun opened up slightly. Louis hit him with a right to the jaw. Uzcudun countered with a left hook. Louis banged a right over his left and Uzcudun was down for an eight count. When he arose, Louis hit him with a left and right to the jaw, throwing him against the ropes. His face seemed to crack open as his gold teeth fell upon the canvas. He was counted out on his feet at two minutes and thirty-two seconds. Whitey Bimstein, the trainer who worked Uzcudun's corner, came over to Louis and said he had never seen anyone hit a man as hard as Louis had hit Uzcudun that night.

At this point Louis felt he was ready for Schmeling, especially since he had knocked out Uzcudun in four rounds and it had taken Schmeling twelve rounds. If Louis were to beat Schmeling, the road would be clear to contend for the heavyweight title.

In the meantime, on January 17, 1936, Louis knocked out Charley Retzlaff in Chicago in the first round. According to Louis, up to that point it was the toughest fight he had had. Retzlaff had worked him with rights on the chin and it was the hardest Louis had ever been hit.

Mike Jacobs negotiated and set the Schmeling fight for June 18, 1936, at Yankee Stadium. Joe Jacobs, Schmeling's manager, insisted on a clause in the contract to forbid either fighter from boxing six months before the scheduled fight. (They made an exception for the Retzlaff bout because it had previously been scheduled.) There were two possibilities involved here: one, Louis had been fighting two to three times a month since he turned pro and preventing him from fighting might throw his timing off, and two, neither wanted to risk a possible defeat which would jeopardize the bout and a lucrative gate.

The problem was that Louis had a great deal of time off. And he had a good time, too good a time. He went to Hollywood and was welcomed by all. He was confident and cocksure. After all, he had won twenty-seven consecutive bouts, all except four by knockouts. Ed Sullivan had introduced him to golf and he became mesmerized by the game. He even took his clubs to training camp with him. Unfortunately, Louis' regular training camp at Pompton Lakes, where it was peaceful and quiet, had been changed to Lakewood, New Jersey, which could accommodate more visitors. Much to the consternation of Blackburn, Roxborough, and Black, Louis only half trained. The golf course was too close, and nearby Atlantic City beckoned with its overflow of pretty women.

Back in New York, Mike Jacobs was catching his own private hell. The growing animosity to Nazi Germany manifested itself in some Jewish organizations in America sending out flyers to storekeepers asking them to boycott the fight because Schmeling was representative of the Nazi decimation of German Jews. The anticipated crowd of 85,000 materialized into only 50,000. The weather was particularly bad the day the

Max Schmeling

fight was scheduled. The heavy downfall of rain made it necessary to postpone the fight, since it was being held outdoors.

Finally on June 19 they met. The first round Louis jabbed Schmeling easily, almost closing his left eye, and Louis went unscathed. Louis felt confident he could take Schmeling out any time he wanted, but he was warned by Blackburn to continue to use the left jab and not to throw a left hook until much later in the fight.

Louis did exactly what Blackburn had warned him not to do in the second round: he dropped his arm to throw a hook and Schmeling came in with a right that caught Louis on the chin. He was dazed. In the third round, Louis got in some right uppercuts but Schmeling protected with his left. Schmeling was just fending off blows and barely used his right hand in the first three rounds. Louis went down for a two count in the fourth round and never really recovered from that blow. From then on it was downhill for Louis. When he was able to get in a punch, it had no power to it.

By the ninth round Schmeling had really unveiled his right hand and pummeled Louis at will. Louis recovered his senses somewhat by the tenth round but was ineffective. In the eleventh round Louis was doing his best just holding on.

In the twelfth round, Schmeling let go with a barrage of rights that knocked Joe Louis out in two minutes and twenty-nine seconds.

The great young hero had fallen. The shockwaves ran through black America. The rationales ranged from "Schmeling had weights in his gloves" to "Some one put

Schmeling knocks out Louis in round twelve for Joe's first loss, June 19, 1936.

something in Joe's water"—how else could he beat the Brown Bomber—or to "Louis sold out"—he cares nothing for us, only for the almighty dollar. Louis, his face almost unrecognizable, was devastated and humiliated, and realized that he was a human being, not an idol. And as a human being, he had better prepare himself and prepare himself well for "the revenge."

But to get a rematch with Schmeling would prove a long and arduous trip. On August 18, 1936, Louis and Jack Sharkey were set to meet at the Yankee Stadium. Jack Sharkey had held the heavyweight crown for one year and he was on the comeback trail. If Sharkey could beat Louis he'd really be an important contender for a tug at the crown again. Sharkey was twelve years older than Louis, but otherwise they were evenly matched: Louis at 199¾ pounds and Sharkey at 197¼. This fight was important to Louis because if he lost there was a strong possibility that he'd be washed up. Louis knocked Sharkey out in the third round.

Mike Jacobs made a pitch for Schmeling but Schmeling's attitude was that he had already beaten Louis and he wanted to go on to fight Braddock for the championship. Jacobs figured they would have to squeeze Schmeling into a bout by having Louis beat all other possible contenders. On September 22, 1936, Louis KO'd Al Ettore in Philadelphia—fifth round. Jorge Brescia of Argentina was KO'd by Louis in the third round on October 9, 1936, at the Hippodrome in New York City. After a series of exhibition fights in October and November, Louis was scheduled to fight Johnny Risko, but Risko fractured his ribs in training and was replaced by Eddie Simms. The fight took place in Cleveland on December 14. In twenty-six seconds of the first round, Louis knocked Simms out, his quickest knockout ever.

Joe Louis watches as Eddie Simms hits the canvas in round one of their December 14, 1936, fight in Cleveland. The match lasted 0:26, Louis's fastest victory.

In the meantime, Jacobs had been busy trying to negotiate a no-decision, twelve-round exhibition bout for Louis with the champion Braddock. There were offers from Atlantic City and California; the idea was building but nothing had been decided or signed. Schmeling, having gotten wind of it, sailed for America to try to force a match between himself and Braddock. The Boxing Commission in conjunction with Madison Square Garden ruled out a Braddock-Louis exhibition fight in Atlantic City. When Jack Dempsey was champion, the Boxing Commission had let Dempsey fight many exhibitions, a privilege they were now denying Joe Louis. Obviously the Boxing Commission did not want a black man challenging for the heavyweight crown. They meant to keep the title lily-white even if it meant Schmeling of Nazi Germany might win. Subsequently, a match was set up between Braddock and Schmeling for June 3, 1937, and each fighter had to put up $5,000 in case there was a no-show.

In the meantime, Louis fought some more exhibition contests. Then Mike Jacobs wanted Louis to fight Bob Pastor. Pastor had won the New York State heavyweight title and had the reputation of being a clean boxer. Jacobs set up the match on the condition that he would be able to contract Pastor if he lost. This was a power play on Jacobs' part. If his Twentieth Century Sporting Club had Louis and Pastor under contract, Jacobs would have wrested control of the heavyweight division from Madison Square Garden and thus could wield more power.

The match took place on January 29, 1937, at Madison Square Garden. It was a tricky fight. Pastor would jab and run, jab and run, and Louis was having a hard time trying to catch him or trap him in a corner. Pastor never hurt Louis and spent most of the bout running. Louis won a ten-round decision, but he looked bad.

Another fight was set for February 17, 1937, in Kansas City Municipal Auditorium against Natie Brown. Louis was encouraged to make sure this was a knockout to erase all doubts about the Pastor fight. Louis breezed through the first three rounds and then in the fourth he let loose with a barrage of lefts and rights. In forty-two seconds of the fourth round he knocked Brown down. Brown attempted to pull himself up by grabbing hold of the referee's legs, pulled the referee down with him, and stretched out on the canvas; the referee counted Brown out.

With the Braddock-Schmeling encounter impending, the Anti-Nazi league sent telegrams to the state Athletic Commission and Madison Square Garden demanding that the fight be canceled. The league threatened to buy newspaper space and radio time to discourage Americans from attending because that would imply that they were supporting Nazi Germany. In addition, they threatened to picket all the box offices. They had the support of the American Federation of Labor, representatives in twenty countries, and twelve hundred women's clubs in America. Mayor Fiorello La Guardia was one of the league's vice-presidents. Joe Gould, Braddock's manager, took heed of this and decided not to honor the contract with Schmeling and lost the $5,000 guarantee fee. Finally, after a great deal of contract talk, a title bout between Braddock and Louis was scheduled for June 22, 1937, at Comiskey Park in Chicago.

Joe Louis was the first black man in twenty-seven years to be given a chance at the heavyweight championship. This opportunity was afforded him at that time because of the tumultuous forces emanating from Nazi Germany. However, Schmeling continued to pressure Braddock and offered $350,000 to fight him in Berlin that summer. Braddock was not interested in going to Germany and besides, he was getting a better deal in America for the Louis bout. He would get $500,000 or an option of 50 percent of the gate and one half of the movie and radio rights, plus a sub rosa deal wherein he would be guaranteed 10 percent of Louis's purses as long as Joe was the heavyweight champion. When questioned about this by the author, Louis rationalized this arrange-

Louis and Braddock pose at their prefight weigh-in.

ment, stating that the 10 percent didn't come from him but from promoter Mike Jacobs's end. Stubborn to the end, Schmeling said he was still going into training for the battle with Braddock in June.

Louis and his trainer became almost one person during the preparation for the Braddock fight; this was the biggest goal a black athlete had had a chance at in a long time. If Louis lost, the efforts of blacks to compete equally would be stalled for many more years.

However, Madison Square Garden was not going along with this idea of Louis fighting Braddock and wanted the Schmeling contract honored. They filed for an injunction with the United States Court of Appeals. Judge Guy T. Fake declared that the only valid contract was that between Braddock and Louis. Meantime, Schmeling was in Speculator, New York, training for what was to be called the "Phantom Fight."

At last it was June 22, 1937. Braddock came storming out of his corner, Louis stepped back and boxed him. Braddock got in a short right uppercut to Louis' chin and downed him. Louis bounced up right away. Braddock led him up against the ropes and was getting in some good right and left hands. Louis, angered by the knockdown, staggered Braddock with a left hook and a right cross at the bell.

Louis lands a right to the chin of Jimmy Braddock, knocking him out in 1:10 of round eight to win the world heavyweight title.

Referee Tommy Thomas signals Louis to the farthest neutral corner as Braddock lies dazed on the canvas.

In the second round Braddock began by jabbing away. Then Louis began getting to him with solid left hooks and right hands to the jaw. Third and fourth rounds, Louis boxed Braddock. By the fourth round, Braddock had slowed up. In the fifth round Braddock's eyes were puffy and there was a rip over the left side of his forehead. They traded jab for jab. In the sixth Louis threw a powerful right and split Braddock's lip—Braddock was reeling. Louis went all out in the seventh round and while Braddock was fending off Louis' right hand, Louis began getting in the left hook. Louis was ready to throw the haymaker when the bell rang.

When Braddock came out in the eighth round, his legs were gone and he couldn't keep his hands up. In one minute and ten seconds of the eighth round, referee Tommy Thomas counted Braddock out. Joe Louis was crowned heavyweight champion of the world. Reporters remember Louis saying, "Bring on Max Schmeling. Bring him on." Louis was twenty-three years old, the youngest heavyweight to win the crown.

Chicago's South Side Negro population celebrated Joe Louis's victory over James Braddock tonight with a party they have been preparing for twenty-two years. The new heavyweight champion is the first their race has produced since Jack Johnson.

Youngsters who should have been in bed paraded the streets in dishpan bands. Old folks who hadn't stayed up so late in years went shouting up and down the streets. They disconnected the trolleys. They clambered aboard the street cars that were still running, for free rides. And they cheered when crowds packed the streets and stopped them.

Surge Starts Suddenly

With news of the knockout, the crowds that had been waiting beneath radio loudspeakers suddenly were on the move. From all the flats poured young and old, men and women, to shout Joe Louis's fame. Taxicabs screeched down the street with tooting horns. Into them piled revelers from whom the drivers asked no fare.

Bonfires were built in the streets and around them Negroes danced. If a few windows were broken, the shopkeepers charged it up to profit and loss and joined in the celebration. Up the elevated railway structures swarmed those who wanted to go places, in numbers so great that the cashiers gave up trying to collect fares.

Chicago, June 22 (AP)

A jubilant throng of Negroes—many of them blood-kin to the new world heavy-weight champion, Joe Louis—danced in the streets tonight in celebration of his victory over James J. Braddock at Chicago. They came from tenant farms and hill cabins to listen to the broadcast of the bout, and when the knockout came in the eighth round their jubilation was unrestrained.

Approximately 1,000 Negroes—virtually the entire population of the Negro districts here—participated in the celebration.

Lafayette, Alabama, June 22 (AP)

Harlem went crazily wild Tuesday night! Within a split second after Braddock kissed his championship goodbye, thousands poured into the streets, confiscated them, and marched to the hysterical beat of staccato screams of horns and improvised drums, up Seventh Avenue and down Lenox and claimed Joe as their own. The feeling of uncertainty, doubt, and even despair gave way to joy and racial fervor.

New York, *Amsterdam News,* June 23

The essential beauty of Joe Louis' victory over Braddock was not only the inspiration and hope he offered the black man, but his public image of a clean-living, God-fearing, decent man who could conquer the incumbent forces was an inspiration to the depression-weary whites as well. Joe Louis transcended racism and became a hero to all people.

Louis did not rest on his laurels. He wanted to be a fighting champion, as opposed to one like Braddock who sat on his championship for two years. So under the urging of Roxborough and Black, Jacobs set up a match for Louis to defend his championship against Tommy Farr. Farr was born in Wales and he had started working in the coal mines at thirteen. He was the same age as Louis, weighed 208 pounds, and was six feet, one and a half inches. No one knew anything about him except that he was a tough guy. On August 30, 1937, they met at Yankee Stadium. Farr was a well-conditioned heavyweight with a lot of heart and he could take a punch as well as give one. He stayed fifteen rounds with Louis's punishing blows. It was a decision for Louis.

Tommy Farr, a tough Welshman, lost a fifteen-round decision in Louis's first defense of his crown on August 30, 1937, at New York's Yankee Stadium.

Mike Jacobs finally got Schmeling to agree to meet with Louis and that fight was scheduled for June 22, 1938. Louis had a tune-up fight with Nathan Mann on February 23, 1938, at Madison Square Garden. Louis knocked him out in the third round. On April 1, 1938, Louis met with Harry Thomas at the Chicago Stadium. Louis had a rough time but put Thomas away in the fifth round.

And now the time was drawing near for the Louis-Schmeling fight. Louis felt, for the only time in his boxing career, vengeful and impatient. In December of 1937 Louis and Blackburn had gone to Madison Square Garden to see Schmeling fight Harry Thomas. This time Louis too "saw something" and was confident he could whip Schmeling. This time Louis would know what to do about Schmeling's right hand. What Louis saw was that when Thomas used his left—he was throwing hooks, not jabs—Schmeling would step inside the hooks and bang Thomas with the right. Louis could see that Schmeling would be a sucker for straight left jabs. Schmeling, who in fact never was a Nazi, became representative of everything that was abhorrent to Americans. They wanted Schmeling really beaten good. Ironically, America began looking at Louis as the avenging angel—the destroyer of evil forces. Odd that a man whose race has been subjected to slavery and whose people continued to be repressed should be looked upon in such a light. President Franklin D. Roosevelt felt Louis's muscles and said, "Joe, we're depending on those muscles for America."

When Schmeling arrived by boat, he was picketed at the dock. When Schmeling went over to the Hippodrome to meet Mike Jacobs there were hundreds of pickets around the front of the building. Influential Jewish people threatened to boycott the fight and stated that they'd ruin Mike Jacobs's business. Jacobs promised them that he had seen Louis train and was assured he'd win and in that way Nazi Germany would see who would be the master country. Just before the fight Jacobs came to Louis' dressing room and said, "Joe, I told these folks you're gonna knock that German out. Don't make a sucker out of me, and make it a quick knockout." Louis felt the same way.

Seventy thousand people cheered as Louis walked down the aisle to his corner that June night. When the bell rang, Louis charged out of his corner and hit Schmeling with two left hooks to his face that snapped his head back and then administered a right to the jaw. Schmeling threw a right hand that Louis blocked and attempted a left to Louis's head, but it fell short. Then Louis got Schmeling to the ropes with a flurry of hooks and right hands. Schmeling covered as well as he could. Staggering, Schmeling could not lift his arms; as a consequence, his jaw was unprotected and his stomach was open. Louis hit him with five or six lefts and a right to the chin and his legs became rubbery. Sinking to the canvas, Schmeling grabbed the upper strand of the ropes and held on. Louis hit him with a right to the body. Schmeling turned and the blow hit him in the lower back. Schmeling cried out with a scream that could be heard in the press rows. Referee Arthur Donovan waved Louis to a neutral corner and gave Schmeling a count of one. Schmeling got off the ropes and Louis hit him with a right to the jaw. He went down for three. When he arose Louis tore into him with lefts and rights and he was down again for the count of two. Louis followed with two hooks and a right to the jaw and Schmeling fell to the canvas again. Max Machon, his trainer, threw a towel in the ring, but Donovan tossed it on the ropes and counted him out in two minutes and four seconds of the first round. It was reported that Louis bombarded Schmeling with about fifty blows in that short period of time. When the

Joe Louis destroys Max Schmeling in 2:04 of the first round of their June 22, 1938, match.

Germans learned how badly Louis was beating Schmeling, they cut the radio wires to Germany. Schmeling was removed to Polyclinic Hospital immediately after the fight and ten days later was carried on a stretcher aboard ship for Germany.

Louis did immeasurable good in fostering better race relations in America, and for himself he got "the revenge."

With that tremendous victory, a string of bouts was set up for Louis before he volunteered for the Army. He met "everybody" in what became known as the "Bum of the Month" campaign. Louis knocked out John Henry Lewis, Jack Roper, "Two-Ton" Tony Galento, and Bob Pastor in 1939. Galento decked Louis with a vicious left hook but suffered a severe battering.

Louis scores a technical knockout over John Henry Lewis in 2:29 of round one of their title bout in Madison Square Garden, January 25, 1939. This was Joe's first title defense against a black fighter.

In 1940 Louis started the year with a difficult fifteen round decision against Arturo Godoy of Chile, who stayed in a crouch all the time. It was almost like fighting somebody who was on the floor. Louis got even by knocking Godoy out in eight rounds in a return engagement after first stopping Johnny Paychek. A sixth round knockout of Al McCoy in Boston in December ended that year's activities.

Louis' biggest triumphs were accomplished in 1941 when Red Burman, Gus Dorazio, Abe Simon, Tony Musto, Buddy Baer, Billy Conn, and Lou Nova were dispatched. The fight with big Abe Simon in Detroit was tabbed for twenty rounds, as was the bout with Bob Pastor two years before, but neither went all the way. Simon was taken out in thirteen and Pastor in eleven.

The contest with Baer resulted in Buddy's disqualification by referee Arthur Donovan when he refused to answer the bell for the seventh round, claiming a foul. Baer said that Louis had punched him after the bell had sounded ending round six. Ironically, in the first round of the bout, Baer knocked Louis through the ropes and onto the ring apron with a left hook for the count of four.

Billy Conn, a light-heavyweight, had been clamoring for a chance at Joe Louis. Conn, a brilliant and flashy boxer, had been successful against the bigger boys, and his thirteenth round knockout of Bob Pastor had convinced him of his capacity to deal with a Joe Louis. Conn, a tough, handsome, arrogant Irishman, had all the equipment to be a heavyweight titleholder. He was young, born October 18, 1917, in Pittsburgh, Pennsylvania. He was the New York State light-heavyweight champion from 1939 to 1940.

A right-hand blow by Louis sends Billy Conn on the way down in the thirteenth and final round of their June 18, 1941, fight at New York's Polo Grounds.

Anxious to continue fighting, Louis wanted a match for June. The only possible opponent at that time was Billy Conn. They were to meet at the Polo Grounds June 18, 1941. Louis had Conn by twenty-five and one half pounds and greater height and reach, but in this fight Louis was within an inch of losing his crown. With clever boxing, superb jabbing, and ingenious maneuvering, Conn was way ahead until the thirteenth round. This was when Conn's ego got in the way of his logistics. So confident of his skills, he decided he was able to trade punches with the master and became the aggressor with the intent of knocking Louis out. In the thirteenth round Conn started a long left hook—it was just what Louis must have been praying for—and Louis zinged a right to his head. Before Conn could register this, Louis went into a series of rights and lefts until Conn was down and out.

That was the closest anyone had thus far come to taking the title from Louis. On the card of Judge Marty Monroe, one of the officials, was a score of seven to four for Conn with one round even; Referee Eddie Joseph had seven to five for Billy; another official, Judge John Healy, tallied it six to six.

In 1942 the war was well under way when Louis met Buddy Baer again on January 9, at Madison Square Garden. Baer came in weighing 250 pounds and Louis was at 205. Baer started strong and got in a couple of good left hooks that blackened Louis' left eye. After Louis hit Baer with a right to the chin he was down. When he got up at nine, his legs were so wobbly the referee stopped the fight. Louis donated all of his purse to Navy Relief, as did Mike Jacobs.

Three days after the fight, Louis volunteered for the Army. While in the service, Louis agreed to fight Abe Simon, for the Army Relief Fund, March 27, 1942, at the Garden. Before the fight Louis made his famous speech, "I'm only doing what any red-blooded American would do. We gonna do our part, and we will win, because we are on God's side." The speech was very inspiring to the nation and he received a congratulatory telegram from President Roosevelt.

Big Abe Simon, at six feet, four inches, and 255 pounds, was ready to go. Louis knocked him out in the sixth.

Louis served his country well. He gave exhibition bouts all throughout Europe. He was a morale builder, visiting veterans' hospitals and camps. He was instrumental in desegregating baseball and football in Army camps (this was instigated by his distress concerning Jackie Robinson's exclusion from the football team). In addition, under the threat of the stockade, he refused to sit in segregated camp buses, and soon after most camp facilities were desegregated. When he was discharged, he received the Legion of Merit medal for exceptionally meritorious conduct.

After his discharge he needed a fight as soon as possible to fill his dwindling coffers. Jacobs set up a real money rematch for him with Billy Conn on June 19, 1946. Ringside seats were going for an unprecedented one hundred dollars. Although Conn had gained some weight, he was not the same man Louis had fought before. It was a bad fight. Conn had lost his speed. Louis stopped him in the eighth round with a left hook and right cross.

On September 18, 1946, Louis knocked out Tami Mauriello in the first round at Yankee Stadium. Then after a series of exhibition fights in Mexico, Central America, and the United States, Louis won a controversial decision over Jersey Joe Walcott at Madison Square Garden, December 5, 1947. Louis was disgusted with his performance at that fight. He knew he had won, but it was not the way he liked to win. The judges scored it:

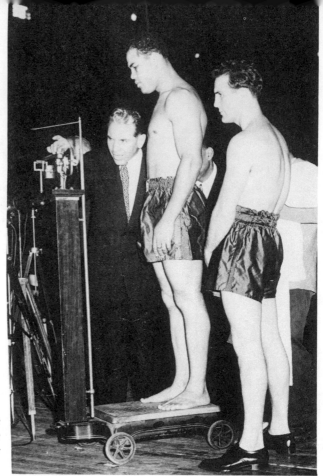

Louis and Conn weigh in before their second meeting on June 19, 1946. Boxing Commissioner Eddie Egan checks the scales.

Heavyweight Champion Joe Louis winces as he is hit with a hard right to the face by challenger Jersey Joe Walcott in the ninth round of the title match on December 5, 1947, at Madison Square Garden.

9–6 in favor of Louis—Judge Marty Monroe
8–6, 1 even, in favor of Louis—Judge Frank Forbes
7–6, 2 even, in favor of Walcott—Referee Ruby Goldstein

In a return match on June 25, 1948, Louis knocked out Jersey Joe Walcott in the eleventh round at Yankee Stadium.

Louis KO's Walcott in the eleventh round of their June 25, 1948, rematch.

After a long series of exhibitions, on March 1, 1949, Louis announced his retirement as undefeated world heavyweight champion. Louis recommended that Ezzard Charles of Cincinnati and Walcott fight for the right to succeed him. They were the outstanding heavyweight contenders at that time. On June 22, 1949, in Chicago, Charles was the winner over Walcott in fifteen rounds. The European Federation and the New York State Athletic Commission refused to acknowledge Charles as the champion but the National Boxing Association accepted this as a world title match.

Taxes proved to have the biggest knockout punch against Louis. He was constantly plagued by the Internal Revenue Service. Poor advice from incompetent lawyers and tax consultants merely multiplied his financial problems. Sound investments he had made were confiscated by the government and his generosity to one and all left him with little. He saw no alternative except a return to the ring.

He was thirty-six years old and weighed 218 pounds. Ezzard Charles, the new but

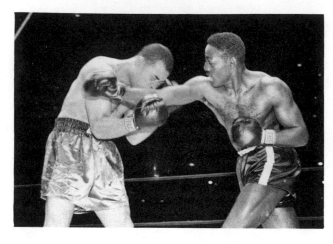

Ezzard Charles glances a right off of the shattered face of Joe Louis. The Brown Bomber was defeated by heavyweight champion Charles in their September 27, 1950, bout at Yankee Stadium.

not really accepted champion, was twenty-nine and weighed 183½ pounds. September 27, 1950, Louis climbed back in the ring at Yankee Stadium to try to beat Charles and regain his title. Charles hooked and jabbed and hit Louis with right hands at will. When Louis saw an opening he couldn't get to it fast enough. His reflexes and coordination were off. Charles's punches were telling and Louis was cut badly. By the seventh round Louis was just going through the motions. When the bell sounded for the fifteenth round, Louis practically had to be lifted off the stool by the people in his corner. Charles retained his title, and now that he had beaten Louis, he was the undisputed champion. A nation cried. There were telegrams from all over the world expressing sorrow about Louis's defeat.

So it was back to the ring. Louis fought Cesar Brion in November, won a ten-round decision, and lined up a series of fights for 1951. In 1951 he beat Freddie Beshore, Omelio Agramonte twice, Andy Walker, Lee Savold, Cesar Brion again, and Jimmy Bivins.

And then he met Rocco Marchegiano, better known as Rocky Marciano. Marciano was from Brockton, Massachusetts, and was twenty-seven years old. In thirty-seven

The end of the road for Joe Louis. After Marciano knocked him through the ropes, Louis made an attempt to counterattack his rushing opponent. But with the stakes so high, Rocky wouldn't let Louis get away from him. Referee Ruby Goldstein stopped the fight in the eighth round.

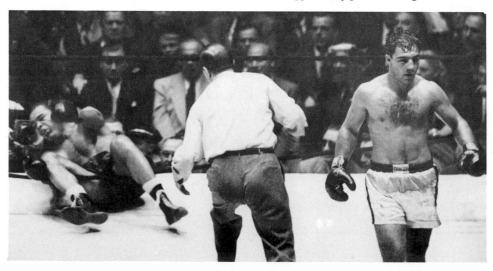

fights he had had thirty-two knockouts. Louis owed the government one million dollars and he figured Marciano little more than a street brawler. With the confidence that he would outbox Marciano, Louis was ready for the match, October 26, 1951, at Madison Square Garden. Out of the first five rounds, Louis was ahead by three. Louis was using his left jab effectively. All was going in Louis's favor until the seventh round, when his legs gave out. In the eighth round Marciano knocked Louis down with a left hook. After taking an eight count, Louis got up. Marciano caught him with a left that put him up against the ropes and followed with a looping right hand. It got Louis on the neck and he fell through the ropes. And there was the Brown Bomber with his head against the ring apron and just his legs still in the ring. Referee Ruby Goldstein stopped the fight.

Sugar Ray Robinson sobbed like an infant; Marciano was also crying when he came to Louis's dressing room. Right then and there Louis stopped fighting.

After that Louis wrestled professionally for a time until he had a serious injury. He did some public relations work for a company he helped to organize. After a bout with mental illness, he became a greeter at Caesar's Palace in Las Vegas. In October 1977, Joe Louis suffered a massive heart attack. He was flown to Houston, where he received the services of the famous heart specialist Dr. Michael DeBakey. An arterial graft was performed to correct an aneurism. While hospitalized, Louis had a cerebral hemorrhage. Singer-actor Frank Sinatra paid all the expenses for Louis's operation and extensive hospital stay.

When Louis returned to Las Vegas in a wheelchair, barely able to speak, he was not a forgotten man. All the celebrities, the staff, and the management of Caesar's Palace rallied round and gave support.

On April 12, 1981, Joe Louis collapsed in his home and was pronounced dead of a cardiac arrest shortly after he reached the hospital. His body was displayed at Caesar's Palace.

Under a special executive decree of President Ronald Reagan, Joe Louis was buried in Arlington National Cemetery. The Brown Bomber's body was carried by a horse-drawn caisson from a nondenominational memorial service in the Fort Myer chapel to the cemetery for burial with military honors, a twenty-one-gun salute, and the mournful playing of taps. President Reagan stated in a message read by Defense Secretary Caspar Weinberger that Louis's life was "an indictment of racial bigotry" and that "all Americans share in his loss."

While the coffin was being lowered, a young black man in the huge crowd of mourners began to ring a cowbell.

"Time for a low profile, brother," a soldier told the young man.

"We been low profile for a long time, brother," the man answered. "This is the bell of Liberty, rung for Joe Louis."

Joseph Louis Barrow maintained his championship from 1937 to 1949. America has always held a warm spot in its heart for the great man. He was one of the greatest heavyweight champions of all time.

Henry Armstrong

Henry Armstrong

Henry Jackson (ring name Henry Armstrong) was the first and only man in ring history ever to hold officially three world's professional championships in three weight classifications at the same time. There was no rule, as there is now, requiring a champion to give up a title if he won one in a heavier class; that rule was put into the books because of Armstrong.

Armstrong was born December 12, 1912, in St. Louis, and after some amateur fights he started his professional career in 1931. On October 29, 1937, at Madison Square Garden, Armstrong won the featherweight championship from Petey Sarron by a sixth-round knockout. Then on May 31, 1938, at the Long Island City Bowl, he captured the welterweight title by way of a fifteen round decision over Barney Ross. In his next contest on August 17, he defeated Lou Ambers in fifteen to win the lightweight crown and his third title. Armstrong finished up the year 1938 successfully defending his welterweight crown against the Filipino Ceferino Garcia in a fifteen-round decision. Then on December 5, in Cleveland, he knocked out Al Manfredo in three rounds, after which he vacated the featherweight throne.

On August 22, 1939, he lost his lightweight championship to Ambers via a fifteen round decision, but engaged in eleven successful defenses of his welterweight crown. One of those defenses was a bout with Ernie Roderick, British Empire welterweight champion, on May 25, 1939, in London, which he won by way of a fifteen-round decision. In March 1940, in Los Angeles, Armstrong again went against Ceferino Garcia, now the middleweight champion, who weighed 153 pounds to Armstrong's 139. Although most of the press covering the fight thought Armstrong had won, officials called it a draw. On October 4, 1940, Armstrong lost his welterweight crown to Fritzie Zivic in fifteen.

Armstrong's record stands alone, but mention must be made of his power of endurance. He had a fifteen-year career and within those fifteen years he is recorded as having fought 175 battles. At his peak, he fought every week. They called him at

The arm of Henry Armstrong is raised, proclaiming him the featherweight champion after his knockout of Petey Sarron in the sixth round of their October 29, 1937, fight in Madison Square Garden.

Henry Armstrong bores in on Barney Ross, whose right eye is swollen shut. Armstrong's unanimous fifteen-round decision gave him both the welterweight and featherweight crowns.

various times "Hammering Henry," "Perpetual Motion," and "Hurricane Henry." He was fast and he could take punishment and administer even more.

He was ordained a Baptist minister in 1951 and returned to St. Louis, where he is now affiliated with a Baptist church. He is also an avid worker for the Boys Clubs of America and has influenced many young men.

With his left eye nearly closed, his face puffed, his lips swollen, Henry Armstrong returns the punishment to Lou Ambers in their fifteen-round lightweight championship bout. Armstrong took the decision and his third title.

Armstrong and Ceferino Garcia at Gilmore Stadium. Although the ringside official called the contest a draw, the majority of the press covering the bout thought that Armstrong had won.

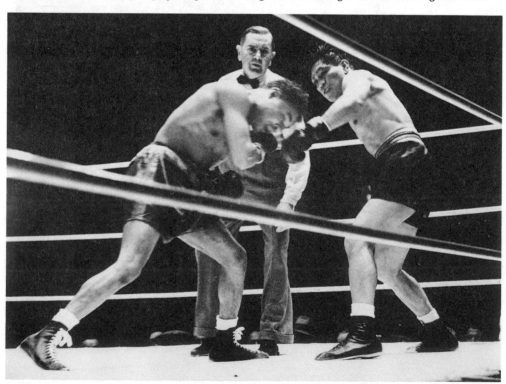

Sugar Ray Robinson

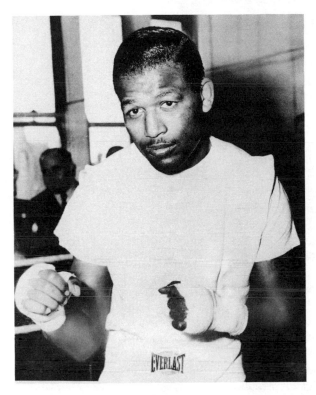

Sugar Ray Robinson

Sugar Ray Robinson, the acme of boxing perfection, has been considered by prizefight aficionados as pound for pound the greatest fighter in the world. He was born Walker Smith on May 3, 1920, in Detroit. His family was poor and could afford little to entertain little Walker and his two sisters, but Walker found his own entertainment at the Brewster Center Gymnasium, where in exchange for running errands he could watch the fighters train. His idol was an amateur heavyweight named Joe Louis. He liked Joe's slick boxing style and wondered at his knockout punch. But when his parents separated, it would be a long time before he would see Joe Louis again, because Walker's mother took the children and moved to Harlem.

When he got to New York, Walker was one of the children who hung around Bill "Bojangles" Robinson. Bill Robinson would teach the kids little dance steps and Walker was particularly adept. In fact, he probably could have made a career out of dancing. However, he just danced with other kids in midtown New York on the sidewalks for nickels and dimes.

Like a homing pigeon, Walker found his way into the Salem-Crescent Athletic Club in Harlem and had the great fortune of gaining the attention of George Gainford, a boxing coach and former professional. Walker was a natural; he enjoyed training and took instruction well. He attended an Amateur Athletic Union bout with Gainford. The promoter needed a substitute for one of the preliminary bouts, and Gainford felt

Walker could fill the bill, but because of his youth, he didn't have an AAU card. The promoter found an AAU card of a retired boxer named Ray Robinson and they used that card to show the officials. Walker fought and won and he now had a new name, Ray Robinson. The name was further appended while Robinson was on the amateur circuit in Watertown, New York. A sportswriter called out to Gainford, "You got a sweet boy there," and Gainford replied, "Yeah, sweet as sugar"; thereafter, the new young fighter's name was Sugar Ray Robinson.

Robinson engaged in eighty-five amateur bouts. He had sixty-nine knockouts and forty of those were first-round KOs. He won the Golden Gloves featherweight title in 1939 and the Golden Gloves lightweight title in 1940.

On October 4, 1940, at the age of twenty, Robinson began his professional career with a two round knockout of Joe Escheverria in New York City. In his twenty-first professional fight, on July 21, 1941, Robinson defeated Sammy Angott, the lightweight champion, in a ten-round nontitle bout. Robinson was ready for Fritzie Zivic, the welterweight champion, but before the match could be set up, Zivic lost the title to Freddie "Red" Cochrane in fifteen rounds in Newark on July 29, 1941.

Nevertheless, Robinson met with Zivic on October 31, 1941, and beat him in a ten-round decision. In a rematch on January 16, 1942, Robinson knocked out Zivic in ten. Meanwhile Cochrane joined the Navy, thereby freezing the welterweight championship during the war years.

Robinson was an outstanding gate attraction. On October 2, 1942, he fought with Jake La Motta, "the Bronx Bull," at Madison Square Garden and won a close ten-round decision. Those two men became a box office lure. They met again on February 5, 1943, in Detroit at the Olympic Arena. La Motta, tough, rugged, and durable against the brilliant boxer-puncher Ray Robinson—it was a thrilling fight. La Motta pressured and smothered Robinson, not allowing him any room to use his classic skills. In the sixth round La Motta shot a right to the body and followed with a left to the jaw and Robinson was catapulted out of the ring through the ropes. The bell saved him. After this Robinson and La Motta stood toe to toe and threw furious exchanges until the final bell. Robinson lost a ten-round decision.

Right after the fight, Robinson was inducted into the Army but given a short furlough during which time another Robinson-La Motta match was to take place, on February 26, 1943, in Detroit. This time Robinson won in ten. This daring duo were to meet on three other occasions and Robinson was triumphant in all of them.

With the end of World War II, Cochrane was discharged, and he defended his welterweight title, which had been in cold storage, against Marty Servo of Schenectady, New York, on February 1, 1946, at Madison Square Garden. Servo knocked out Cochrane in the fourth round and won the title. After that bout Servo stated he was suffering from a nose ailment and had to retire, but in truth, he didn't want to be matched against Robinson, who, in their last two ten-round bouts, had beaten him twice. One in 1941, in Philadelphia; the other in 1942, in New York's Madison Square Garden. The New York State Athletic Commission and the National Boxing Association named Ray Robinson Servo's successor because they had difficulty getting anyone to face Robinson in the elimination. Only one fighter came forth—his name was Tommy Bell, out of Youngstown, Ohio. In a tough fight at Madison Square Garden on December 20, 1946, Robinson gained a victory and the sanction of all the other boxing commissions as the world welterweight champion.

Sugar Ray knocks down Tommy Bell of Youngstown, Ohio, in Madison Square Garden. Robinson went on to win a fifteen-round decision and recognition as the world welterweight champion.

Sugar Ray and Steve Belloise square off in the first round of their nontitle bout of August 24, 1949, at Yankee Stadium. His seventh-round knockdown of Belloise made Robinson a middleweight contender.

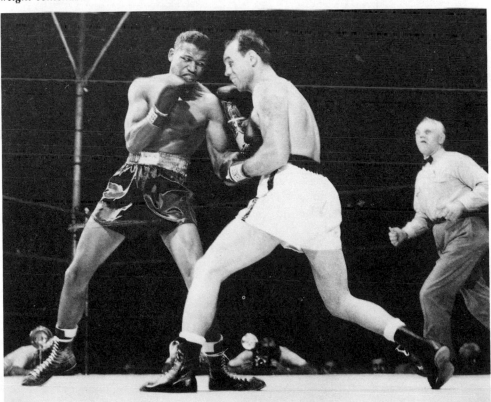

From 1947 to 1950 Robinson defended the welterweight title five times: June 24, 1947: Jimmy Doyle, Cleveland—KO 8; December 19, 1947: Chuck Taylor, Detroit—KO 6; June 28, 1948: Bernard Docusen, Chicago—W 15; July 11, 1949: Kid Gavilan, Philadelphia—W 15; August 9, 1950: Charley Fusari, Jersey City—W 15.

On February 14, 1951, in Chicago, Robinson won the middleweight championship when he stopped Jake La Motta in the thirteenth round, thus vacating the 147-pound crown.

Jake La Motta leans on the ropes, a beaten champion, after his February 14, 1951, bout with Sugar Ray Robinson in Chicago. Referee Frank Sikora halted the bout in the thirteenth round.

Robinson went to Europe on a long tour after the La Motta fight. Unfortunately, he neglected keeping fit and lost his championship to Randy Turpin, British and European middleweight crown holder. The event took place in London on July 10, 1951, and Robinson was decisioned in fifteen rounds.

The return contest was held at the Polo Grounds in New York on September 12, 1951. Robinson knocked out Turpin in the tenth round and rewon his title.

In 1952, on March 13, Robinson successfully defended his title against "Bobo" Olson by way of a fifteen-round decision. A little over a month later, on April 16, in Chicago, Robinson once again retained his world middleweight title by knocking out Rocky Graziano in the third round.

Now Robinson felt he was ready to try for the light-heavyweight crown, which was held by Joey Maxim. The fight was set for Yankee Stadium on June 25, 1952. It was an extremely hot day and under the ring lights the temperature registered 104 degrees. Robinson had just left an air-conditioned dressing room and was assaulted by the rush

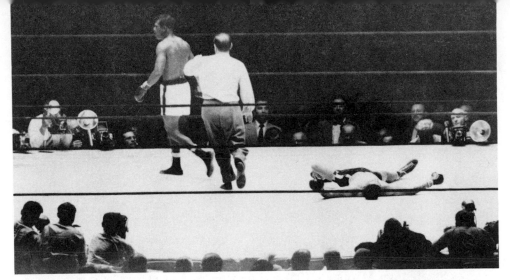

Robinson regains the middleweight crown through a tenth-round knockout of Randy Turpin on September 12, 1951, at New York's Polo Grounds. The referee is Ruby Goldstein.

of terrific heat. He was building an impressive lead, but because of heat exhaustion he was unable to answer the bell for the fourteenth round. Ruby Goldstein, the referee, also succumbed to the heat and collapsed in the tenth round and had to be replaced by Ray Miller.

Robinson announced his retirement on December 18, 1952, and set up his own stage revue in which he starred. His attempts as an actor failed and he decided to get on the boxing comeback trail. He announced his return to the ring on October 20, 1954, and on January 5, 1955, he KO'd Joe Rindone in Detroit in six rounds; January 19 in Chicago, Robinson lost to Ralph "Tiger" Jones; he won the match with Johnny Lombardo on March 29 in Cincinnati; KO'd Ted Olla on April 14 in Milwaukee in three rounds; won over Garth Panter in Detroit on May 4; and beat Rocky Castellani in San Francisco on July 22. Now he was ready for Bobo Olson, the 160-pound

Robinson floors Bobo Olson, November 11, 1955, in the second round to regain the middleweight crown in his seventh fight after a two-year retirement.

titleholder. On December 9, 1955, Robinson knocked out Olson in the second round at the Chicago Stadium to regain the middleweight throne which he had abdicated. Then he lost the crown to Gene Fullmer, a Mormon from West Jordan, Utah, on January 2, 1957, in a decision in fifteen rounds in New York. On May 1, Robinson knocked out Fullmer in a return match in the fifth round in Chicago Stadium. Robinson became the first fighter in the history of the middleweight division to win the title four times.

On September 23, 1957, in a split decision at New York's Yankee Stadium, Carmen Basilio wrested the championship from Robinson, but he lost it to him in a rematch in Chicago Stadium on March 25, 1958, giving Robinson an unparalleled fifth crown.

When the National Boxing Association vacated Robinson's title for inactivity in 1959, Gene Fullmer and Carmen Basilio met in San Francisco on August 28; Fullmer KO'd Basilio in the fourteenth to receive NBA recognition.

New York, Massachusetts, Europe, and the Oriental Foundation recognized Robinson as champion until a twenty-nine-year-old ex-firefighter from Brookline, Massachusetts, Paul Pender, won a split decision over him on January 22, 1960, in Boston. Robinson lost to Pender again in fifteen rounds in Boston on June 10.

On December 3 of 1960 Robinson went to Los Angeles and fought a fifteen round draw with NBA middleweight king Gene Fullmer. Then Fullmer beat him in Las Vegas, March 4, 1961, in fifteen.

Robinson continued to fight for five more years, having his final outing at the age of forty-five against Joey Archer on November 10, 1965, in Pittsburgh. He lost a ten rounder.

After twenty-five years in the professional ring, it was all over.

At this writing, Robinson is working with youth groups in Los Angeles.

Muhammad "The Greatest" Ali

Young Cassius Clay preparing for the 1960 Olympics.

The 1954 decision of the Supreme Court in the case of *Brown* v. *Board of Education* brought about in principle an end to the doctrine of separate-but-equal as it related to tax-supported primary and secondary public schools. At last blacks felt they would begin to obtain equal rights from the nation in which they were born. However, the white South had no intention of readily sacrificing their way of life for the "whim" of the Supreme Court and openly expressed their total dissatisfaction with this "new" concept. The failure of the whites to obey the law set the blacks into a mood of deep depression. They had waited for the heavy machinery of the system to grind out its promise of freedom, and the system now failed them again.

What other avenue could be taken at this time no one knew. But it started. On December 1, 1955, Mrs. Rosa Parks in Montgomery, Alabama, refused to give up her seat to a white passenger on a bus. She was summarily arrested and charged with violating a city segregation ordinance. A young black Baptist minister, Rev. Martin Luther King, Jr., heard about the case and with the assistance of Rev. Ralph Abernathy set about organizing a boycott of all Montgomery buses by blacks. The one-day boycott extended to 382 days until the Montgomery bus companies desegregated their vehicles.

In 1957 the turmoil continued in the effort of blacks to gain equal rights. In September nine black teenagers attempted to register at the Little Rock, Arkansas, Central High School. Governor Orval Faubus posted the Arkansas National Guard in front of the school to prohibit the black children from entering. Violence and disorder on the part of the white citizens abounded. President Dwight D. Eisenhower, in compliance with the *Brown* v. *Board of Education* decision, sent federal troops to defend black citizens seeking their constitutional rights.

Also in 1957, Ghana, the first British colony in Africa to gain its freedom, sent representatives to join the United Nations. With the emerging nation of Ghana, there came an emerging awareness among American blacks of their lost culture and a frantic commitment to absorb the early foundations of Africa into their being and become whole again. "Black" was no longer a curse word, kinky/curly hair was no longer to be plastered and tortured into a poor semblance of Caucasian hair. The watchwords were to become "Black is Beautiful."

White liberals, primarily in the North, joined with the blacks in attempting to break the back of segregation. There were the sit-in movements the black students inaugurated in Greensboro, North Carolina, and then later adopted elsewhere in other white restaurants and stores. At all times adhering to Martin Luther King's doctrine, they were nonviolent. On April 15, 1960, black and white college students organized the Student Nonviolent Coordinating Committee (SNCC) and it spread nationwide. In May of 1961 the Congress of Racial Equality (CORE) sent Freedom Riders into the South to violate segregation laws and practices. There was untold bloodshed. These courageous young people were beaten, spat upon, stomped, set upon by dogs; some were murdered.

And into this milieu there came a big, strong, beautiful, sassy young man. At that time his name was Cassius Marcellus Clay.

Cassius Clay was the older of two sons born to Odessa and Cassius Clay, Sr., on January 18, 1942, in Louisville, Kentucky. His father was a sign painter, but deep inside a frustrated artist, singer, and actor. Mrs. Clay worked as a part-time domestic to help make ends meet. While the family was not poverty-stricken in the sense that they were starving, they were poor working people, but a tight-knit family unit.

Cassius was never a serious student, preferring to daydream or clown around in class, and his life was uneventful until he reached the age of twelve. That Christmas his father bought him a new bicycle. It was a Schwinn with red lights, whitewall tires, and chrome spokes and rims, and it must have cost an exhorbitant sixty dollars. Eager to show off his bicycle, he and a friend went to a bazaar at the Columbus Gym. After eating all the free food he could, he decided to leave, and that's when he realized his bike was gone. Filled with anger and tears and worried about what his father would say, he ran back into the gym, where he was told to see Joe Elsby Martin, a policeman who was in the recreational center. His tears dried up as he watched the activities taking place—boxers sparring in the ring, jumping rope, shadow boxing, and some hitting the speed bag. He finally found Martin and reported his case. Martin wrote up the incident and advised young Cassius that they had boxing every night and on Saturday there was a TV show called "Tomorrow's Champions," an amateur boxing show in which the young men present at the gym would participate. Martin gave Cassius an application. That Saturday Cassius watched the show, filled out the application, and proclaimed, "I want to be a boxer."

His life took on another dimension. Under Martin's early direction, Cassius began to learn discipline. When he got his shot on the "Tomorrow's Champions" TV show, he won his first match against a white fighter, Ronny O'Keefe, by a split decision. His father started comparing him to Joe Louis and proclaimed he would be the heavyweight champion of the world—and he was only thirteen years old.

Cassius became the *enfant terrible* of the Columbus Gym. He was highly respected and popular, and Louisville knew it had something. In the spirit of the times and in his own ebullience, Cassius went unannounced to Angelo Dundee's gym in Miami and "directed" the famous trainer to instruct him. He even had the nerve to spar with Dundee's top fighter, Willie Pastrano, later the light-heavyweight champion, and present a good showing. It was 1960 and Clay won the National AAU light-heavyweight championship and then the national Golden Gloves heavyweight title. He promised to bring home from Rome the Olympic gold medal for light-heavyweight, and he did.

When he arrived triumphantly in New York from Rome, he was met by Joe Martin and a friend of William Reynolds, a Kentucky aluminum millionaire. He was wined and dined and given money for a spending spree and told that Bill Reynolds wanted to be his benefactor. When he arrived in Louisville Martin presented him with a managerial contract in which he would be guaranteed seventy-five dollars a week for ten years. (Prior to the Olympics, Cassius had been offered a job with Reynolds as a houseboy with the understanding that Reynolds would become his backer after he won the Olympics.) Clay, Sr., rejected the contract.

Joe Louis was Cassius' first choice as a manager, but Louis was not enthusiastic about the boy, and besides, he had enough problems of his own. Then Clay tried his best to interest Sugar Ray Robinson, but as he states in his autobiography, *The Greatest*, ". . . he brushed me off. 'Look kid, come back, maybe in a couple of years, okay.' . . . I respect Sugar in the ring as one of the greatest of all times. But he stayed out of what I call the real fighting ring, the one where freedom for black people in America takes place, and maybe if he had become my manager he might have influenced me to go his way. I'm glad he had no time."

Cassius finally signed with a group of ten Louisville millionaires who were to sponsor him. They advanced him $400 a month and a 50-50 split which they later changed to 60 for Clay, 40 for themselves. The Louisville group then turned Clay over to Angelo Dundee, an excellent trainer with all the connections necessary to "move" a fighter. Dundee had worked with three world champions: Willie Pastrano, Carmen Basilio, and Luis Rodriguez.

Cassius was justifiably proud of his Olympic medal; he even wrote a poem about it:

> *How Cassius Took Rome*
> *by Cassius Clay, Jr.*
>
> *To make America the greatest is my goal,*
> *So I beat the Russians, and I beat the Poles*
> *And for the USA won the medal of gold*
> *Italians said, "You're greater than Cassius of old."*
> *We like your name, we like your game*
> *So make Rome your home if you will.*
> *I said I appreciate kind hospitality*
> *But the USA is my country still*
> *'Cause they're waiting to welcome me in Louisville.*

(Left) *Cassius Clay in Olympic action against Z. Pietrzykowski of Poland. Clay outpointed his opponent and won the gold medal for the United States, in their light-heavyweight bout September 5, 1960.* (Right) *Clay on his arrival in New York City, September 9, 1960, bedecked with his gold medal.*

But everybody in Louisville was not waiting to welcome him. One day Cassius and a friend, Ronnie King, got caught in a downpour while out on their motorbikes. They stopped at a restaurant that was then "for whites only." The waitress, recognizing him, whispered to the owner, who replied, "I don't give a damn who he is. I don't serve niggers." In his book Clay says,

> This is supposed to be the land of the brave and the home of the free, and you're disgracing it with your actions. You all know me. I was born in General Hospital, only a block away. I was raised here. I went to Central High. And now I've brought back an Olympic Gold Medal for *all* the people of Louisville. I fought for the glory of my country and you should be ashamed of what you're doing. You serve any foreigner here, but not an American Negro citizen. You'll have to take me to jail, because I'll stay until I get my rights. You should be ashamed. . . .
>
> But I never said a word.
>
> The words wouldn't come out. Something there wouldn't let the words come out. Instead of making them feel ashamed, I felt shamed. Shamed and shocked and lonesome.

As if that were not enough, a gang of young tough white motorcycle riders jeered at him and called him "Olympic Nigger." They got it into their heads that they wanted his gold medal to give to one of their girlfriends for a souvenir. Trying to ignore them, Cassius and his friend took off on their motorbikes only later to be trapped on the Jefferson County Bridge. The leader of the gang was stopped when Clay's friend

Ronnie hurled his bike under the front wheels of the gang leader's oncoming cycle, throwing the rider into the bridge columns. Using the badly hurt and bleeding leader as hostage, they were able to halt the advance of the gang. The leader promised that if they released him he wouldn't bother them anymore. The experience was shattering to Cassius and he flung the much-prized gold medal, which he hadn't taken off since he'd won it, into the murky waters of the Ohio River.

With his new managerial setup and the outstanding trainer Angelo Dundee, Clay was brought along carefully. He made his professional debut in his hometown against a nonentity named Tunney Hunsaker on October 29, 1960. Clay decisioned him in six. Then two days after Christmas of that year he knocked out Herb Siler at Miami Beach in four.

In 1961 Clay knocked out the likes of Tony Esperti, Jim Robinson, Donnie Fleeman, Lamar Clark, Alex Miteff, and Willie Besmanoff. He decisioned Duke Sabedong and Alonzo Johnson.

Clay became hot copy: he spouted poetry; he predicted the round in which he would knock out his opponent *in rhyme;* he yelled "I'm pretty. I am the greatest." *Time* magazine with tongue in cheek proclaimed he was Galahad, Cyrano, and D'Artagnan all rolled into one. The Beatles visited him at the Fifth Street Gym in Miami Beach. And while Clay and the Beatles boyishly clowned around, no one would ever have believed that these young men of the same generation would influence the entire world.

While the public loved the outrageous young man, few took him seriously, but he was like a cool drink of water in an arid field. While Jack Johnson was indisputable in his skills, he appeared as a sinister force to white America; not only did Joe Louis have the talents to be champion, he added a picture of strength in troubled times, a gentle giant of quiet humility. Cassius Clay was an unknown quantity who was amusing, but certainly in 1962 no one to compare to Johnson or Louis.

Cassius Clay made his Madison Square Garden debut on February 10, 1962, by knocking out Sonny Banks in four rounds. On February 28 he took out Don Warner at Miami Beach in four. April 23, it was George Logan in four at Los Angeles. Then he KO'd Billy Daniels in New York on May 19 in seven. On July 20 in Los Angeles, he stopped Alejandro Lavorante in five.

The groundwork was laid out and Clay's first major test was to take place. November 1962 in Los Angeles, only two years after he triumphed in the Rome Olympics, Clay was matched up against former light-heavyweight champion Archie Moore, who even at the age of forty-six was still a crafty, cunning, and formidable opponent. And Archie Moore also had box office appeal. He was at the very least Clay's verbal counterpart. They bantered against one another, at first in a lighthearted vein. Near the time of the fight, Moore became pointed in his insults, and Clay did too; he predicted he would take "Moore out in four," and he did.

On January 24, 1963, Clay knocked out Charlie Powell in three in Pittsburgh. Still unsure of Clay's ability, the public was beginning to take him more seriously. Clay was booked to fight Doug Jones, at that time one of the outstanding heavyweight contenders, at Madison Square Garden, March 13, 1963. Jones, the underdog, had the sympathy of the crowd because of the way Clay had berated his skills. It was a close fight and it made Clay look bad. But Clay kept out of the way of Jones's punch. Clay won a controversial split decision much to the dismay of the crowd, which felt that Jones had won. It was Clay's eighteenth professional victory in a row.

Henry Cooper, Britain's top heavyweight, fought Clay on June 18 in London. Clay outboxed him, hit him with right hands, and jabbed him at will, thereby opening a cut over his left eye. But in the third round Clay was surprised to find himself on the canvas and the referee counting "four" when the bell rang. Between the third and fourth rounds, Clay gained an extra minute because it was discovered that his glove was split and it had to be replaced in compliance with boxing regulations.

Refreshed, Clay began cutting Cooper badly. He was bleeding so much the referee stopped the fight in the fifth round and Clay scored a technical knockout. Prior to the fight Clay said the fight would end in five and again his prediction came true.

1963 was a pivotal year in the black revolution. Dr. Martin Luther King felt a nonviolent movement could break the stranglehold of segregation in the South. He defied a writ of injunction and Safety Commissioner Eugene "Bull" Connor's police dogs and led a march down the main thoroughfare of Birmingham, Alabama. Dr. King and fifty demonstrators were arrested.

Then events took an ominous turn. Medgar Evers, Field Secretary of the Mississippi NAACP (National Association for the Advancement of Colored People), was killed in front of his home by whites on June 11, 1963. This triggered the union of whites and blacks in protesting this blatant murder. Citizens in every major city in America demonstrated in the streets; sit-ins were staged in the offices of Mayor Robert Wagner in New York City and Governor Nelson Rockefeller in Albany, New York. Blacks protested the unfair hiring practices and the racial imbalance in the public schools.

On August 28, 1963, almost half a million people, black and white, marched in Washington, D.C., to protest the inequality of jobs, schools, and housing for black America. President Kennedy, under pressure, put into motion legislation that would evolve into the 1964 Civil Rights Act, which outlawed discrimination and segregation in all public accommodations and public facilities that affected interstate commerce.

In September 1963, the all-black Sixteenth Street Baptist Church in Birmingham was bombed by whites: four little girls were murdered. President John F. Kennedy was assassinated on November 22, 1963. Kennedy presented a promise of a new attitude on equal rights for black people. He was considered a friend to the black people and perhaps that knight in shining armor.

Somehow during this period Cassius Clay became deeply involved with Malcolm X, the number one Black Muslim. Malcolm X had been converted to the Muslim faith during his imprisonment for burglary in 1946. He was a man of great intelligence and charisma and he rose rapidly through the ranks and was installed as minister of the Temple in Harlem. In very simplified terms, the philosophy of the Black Muslims, at that time, prohibited smoking, drinking, the eating of pork. Its members were motivated to be healthy, respectable, responsible, and manly. Women were required to be submissive and in public to be fully clothed from neck to ankle as well as to cover their heads with a scarf. It seemed a good religion that would encourage self-discipline, except it condemned to infinite hell the "white blue-eyed devils" who were the cause of all the troubles in the universe with their commitment to continue to enslave and corrupt black people. The Muslims believed in owning their own churches, stores, schools, and homes, being completely self-contained for the freedom of the black race.

They had an excellent track record; in prison they had reformed incorrigibles; they were able to heal drug and alcohol addicts; they gave a man who believed a chance he would not have elsewhere. Cassius Clay wanted to be a part of this culture.

Clay had had nineteen professional bouts and was unbeaten and he was ready for the big one—Sonny Liston, heavyweight champion. Sonny Liston was to defend his title in a return match with Floyd Patterson, the previous crown holder, on July 22, 1963, in Las Vegas. Clay made it his business to be there.

Sonny Liston

The Louisville sponsors gave Clay sufficient money to travel. Clay ran into Willie Reddish, one of Liston's trainers, and Reddish told him where Liston was gambling. Clay decided to go and stir up Liston to the point he'd be ready to fight him. He walked into the gambling casino shouting he wanted Liston and calling him a big ugly bear. He said he was a chump, not a champ. Clay went on and on berating Liston. Suddenly Liston pulled out a gun and started firing. Clay ran all the way back to his hotel with his heart pounding and perspiring profusely. That was when he found out that he had been set up for a joke by Reddish. Liston only had blanks in the gun.

Another time before the fight, Clay got a truck and went to Liston's home in the middle of the night, called the police from a nearby public phone, and announced that "Cassius Clay is getting ready to break into Liston's house." Then he began blowing the horn and beating on Liston's door. By this time the police had arrived along with reporters and Clay had run back to the truck. The police told him to get out of town but not before he yelled to the bewildered Liston, "You're a chump," and "I'm the greatest." The reporters loved it.

The night of the Patterson-Liston fight he came into the ring and shook hands with Patterson and then looked over at Liston. He feigned fear and dashed out of the ring. Clay stole the scene and the audience was in an uproar. In the first round Liston knocked out Patterson.

The bout between "the Bear" and the "Louisville Lip" had to be. The fight crowd was eager for the battle for many diverse reasons. A few felt Clay would win, others that tough, mean old Sonny would take Clay; others hoped that Clay would lose so he would stop his bragging and loud-mouthing. Forty-six boxing writers were polled and only three selected Clay to win.

By this time Clay had joined the Black Muslims. Dundee, when he found out, told Clay his career would be over. Bill McDonald, the promoter, questioned Clay about his Muslim affiliation. When Clay affirmed the fact that he was now a Muslim, McDonald pleaded with him not to associate with those "black avengers," who would ruin his life and certainly the promotion of the fight. When Clay refused to denounce the Muslims, McDonald declared that the fight was off. The Louisville sponsors also tried to no avail to get Clay to disavow his connection with the Muslims.

Clay refused to succumb to the pressures and the fight was finally on again. However, Clay stated that after the Liston fight he was changing his name to Muhammad Ali. To most Americans this name, at first, would be anathema. It was seen as a denial of his American heritage and certainly not one to cheer for. On the other hand, in the midst of the black revolution, many blacks were pleased. Quite a few were casting off their "slave names" and digging into their pre-American heritage, were using African names. Many felt cheated, degraded, and wrongfully wooed into the Judeo-Christian religion, which did nothing to alleviate their bondage to the white man.

At any rate, the Liston-Clay fight was scheduled for February 25, 1964, at Miami Beach. To build up the attendance, Clay met Liston at the airport and heckled him there and at his hotel.

The weigh-in was a memorable occasion. Clay had heard that Liston feared nothing except "crazy people" and Clay started his act at the weigh-in. Pushing through hundreds of photographers and reporters, Clay came in screaming, "Float like a butterfly. Sting like a bee." He went through the big ugly bear speech and laughed at Liston while his crew, prewarned, held him back. His tirade was of such dimensions that the doctors feared he might be experiencing a fright trauma related to the impending fight—his blood pressure was up to 200. Others present thought Clay had really snapped and were surprised the fight was not postponed. According to Clay's autobiography, Liston whispered to him, "Don't let everyone know what a fool you are."

Because of his high blood pressure, the doctors made Clay rest until it returned to normal; otherwise, the fight would have been postponed.

The night of the bout, Clay did indeed float like a butterfly, sting like a bee. As he danced away from Liston's powerhouse left hook, he jabbed with speed at Liston's head. In the third round he opened a cut under Liston's left eye but Liston seemed unaffected and the score continued to be about even. In the fifth round Clay moved away from Liston and stopped jabbing. He claimed something on Liston's glove had gotten in his eyes and he couldn't see and his eyes were burning (it was later deduced that Liston was having trouble with his shoulder and his trainer had been rubbing it with liniment and some drops had accidentally gotten into Clay's eyes), and Clay resisted coming out for the sixth round. Dundee prodded him into answering the bell and his vision, though blurred, was a little clearer. Clay gave Liston everything he had and tired him.

Just before the seventh round referee Barney Felix announced that Liston would be unable to continue due to an injury to his left shoulder and eye cuts. Clay won the heavyweight crown on a technical knockout.

But there was more. Liston's purse was held up pending the medical finding con-

Overjoyed in victory, a jubilant Cassius Clay and his handlers dance in midring. A disconsolate Sonny Liston slumps in his corner after failing to answer the seventh-round bell, thereby losing the heavyweight title to Clay in Miami Beach on February 25, 1964.

cerning his shoulder injuries. There was a question about the fight in many quarters. The officials, referee Barney Felix and judges Bill Lovitt and Gus Jacobsen, had scored the bout a draw up to that point.

The suspicions were somewhat mollified by the following statement from Dr. Alexander Robbins, chief physician of the Miami Beach Boxing Commission:

> We came to the conclusion that Sonny Liston suffered an injury in the long head to the bicep tendon of the left shoulder, with the result there is separation and tear of muscle fibers with some hemorrhage into the muscle belly. This condition would be sufficient to incapacitate him and prevent him from defending himself.

New York *Times,* February 26, 1964

Now a new twenty-two-year-old heavyweight champion with a new name, Muhammad Ali, and a new religion, Islam, was ready to take on the world. With his classic dimensions contained in a six-foot, three-inch frame, weighing 225 pounds, and with his undeniable speed of hands and feet, there was still doubt. Many reporters and sports figures refused to call him Muhammad Ali. To many, there was something frightening about his changes—he was not like most American blacks, as many thought they knew them. He was unpredictable. Despite the oppression and subjugation inflicted upon the blacks by the white majority, whites could not tolerate someone who dared to be different, who dared to have the courage of his convictions without the establishment's sanction.

It was inevitable that Ali would have to have a rematch with Liston, and that bout took place in Lewiston, Maine, on May 25, 1965. To disperse all doubts, Ali charged out of his corner and hit Liston with a right and a left to the head, followed by a twisting right to the head. Liston went down. While trying to get up, Liston fell again and an enraged Ali stood over him demanding he get up and fight. Ali would not go to the neutral corner; he just stood there badgering Liston to get up. The boxing rule states there can be no legal count over a fallen fighter as long as the standing fighter refuses to go to the farthest neutral corner. Despite this, Frank McDonough, the knockdown timekeeper, started counting from the time Liston fell on the canvas. When he reached twenty-two, Liston got to his feet and the two fighters began exchanging punches. Nat Fleischer, the editor and publisher of *The Ring* magazine, the boxing bible, yelled to the referee, Jersey Joe Walcott, that the fight was over. Walcott separated the men, accepted the timekeeper's count, and declared Ali the winner.

Although never again a major contender, Liston continued to fight. Six years later, when a Senate committee was formed to investigate the alleged criminal influence in boxing, Liston was scheduled to appear to testify. However, he could not participate; he was found dead on January 5, 1971, in his Las Vegas home. There was a hypodermic needle and heroin in his kitchen, although he was known not to take drugs.

The rumors had it that there would be questions at the hearing concerning Liston's meetings with Muhammad Ali. Allegedly in their first bout in Miami, Liston was supposed to go into the tank (throw the fight), but this was almost altered when Ali wanted to quit in his corner because of the burning and limited vision in his eyes. In

Muhammad Ali tells Sonny Liston to get up after the controversial "phantom" right-hand punch in the first round of their rematch in Lewiston, Maine.

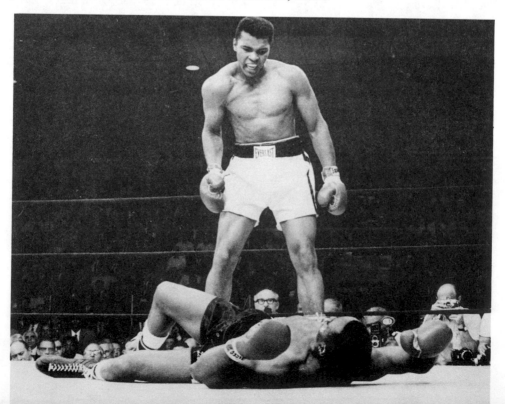

view of that, Liston was supposedly instructed that in the Lewiston, Maine joust he was to "go" fast.

The author was told by the late Joe Louis that Liston had admitted to him that both fights had been fixed, but that Ali had no knowledge of this. Two days before the Lewiston fight, Liston told Louis, "I got my money, I got my money! I ain't gonna put up a fight!"

After the second Liston fight, Ali had a series of exhibition bouts in July and August of 1965. On November 22, in Las Vegas, Ali knocked out ex-heavyweight champion Floyd Patterson in twelve rounds. On March 29, 1966, in Toronto he fought George Chuvalo and won a fifteen-round decision. Back in London on May 21, he KO'd Henry Cooper again, this time in the sixth round. Then on August 6, he KO'd Brian London, in London, in three. He stopped Karl Mildenberger in twelve in Frankfurt, Germany. Ali finished out 1966 on November 14 in Houston with Cleveland Williams. Ali decked the 210½ pound challenger three times in the second round and once in the third before referee Harry Kessler stopped the fight.

The war in Vietnam was in full swing in 1967 and while Ali was successfully defending his title, the government was weighing his request for a ministerial deferment. Earlier in 1963 Ali had failed a preinduction mental test and was classified 1-Y. Without being reexamined, he was classified 1-A in February 1966. The government had no doubt about his mental abilities. There is no way an unintelligent man could win the heavyweight title, defend it so victoriously, ad-lib poetry, and be so articulate. But now here was Ali stating that he was a minister in the Nation of Islam and that war was against his religion. Since his conversion, he was perceived as something

In what many boxing writers consider Muhammad Ali's greatest fight, he lands a stinging right to the head of Cleveland Williams in the second round of their heavyweight championship fight in the Houston Astrodome on November 14, 1966.

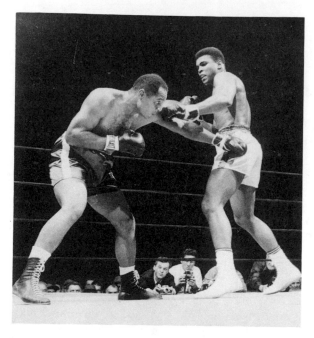

Ali's last title defense before being stripped of the championship for his refusal to enter the armed services. He knocked out Zora Folley in the seventh round of their March 22, 1967, Madison Square Garden fight.

almost foreign and un-American and he did not help matters when he made statements to the effect that he had no quarrel with the Vietcong and that the war was a personal one between the Vietnamese and the Vietcong. At that time America was very hawklike in its desire to save the Vietnamese people from communism, and Ali's request for deferment was considered unpatriotic.

While the government was reviewing his case, Ali met with Ernie Terrell in Houston, Texas, on February 6, 1967. Terrell refused to acknowledge Ali's adopted Muslim name and Ali punished him for it. With every humiliating blow that Ali administered to Terrell, he would shout, "What's my name? What's my name?" The fight went the full fifteen rounds. Referee Harry Kessler and Judges Jimmy Webb and Ernie Taylor unanimously awarded thirteen rounds to Ali.

By the time Ali went against Zora Folley on March 22, 1967, at Madison Square Garden, he was universally recognized as a brilliant fighter. Ali knocked out Folley in the seventh.

Ali was ordered to report to the Houston induction center on April 28, 1967, and he refused induction. On May 9, 1967, he was indicted by a federal grand jury for refusing to submit to the draft. On June 20 he was sentenced to five years in prison and fined $10,000. Ali's lawyer, Hayden C. Covington, filed an appeal. Ali was free on a $5,000 bond pending the court's decision. That same day the World Boxing Association stripped him of his title and the New York State Athletic Commission took his license. His passport was confiscated and he was refused permission to travel to any foreign country, thus cutting off any boxing income.

The only money Ali was able to earn during this time was from his appearances at colleges. However, he did receive largesses from the Black Muslims. Ali experienced a surprising and gratifying revelation. For the first time he was receiving support for his stand. Large numbers of students did not believe in the war and maintained that Ali, as an Islamic minister, had a right to exercise his religious beliefs. It was while visiting colleges that he learned he was on the "undesirable subversives" list compiled by the House Un-American Activities Committee.

Eager promoters sought ways to circumvent the law to permit Ali to fight. They reasoned that the law is not applicable when the event does not take place on American soil; therefore, if a fight took place thousands of feet in the air, there would be nothing anyone could do about it. So plans went ahead to secure a 747 Boeing jumbo jet with 250 seats for which fans would pay $1,000 per seat. In addition, the fight would be telecast on closed circuit TV and videotape. A pretty good dollar could be made, but the unpredictable winter weather canceled the idea.

On July 24, 1969, the Supreme Court ruled that five telephone conversations taped by the FBI were not relevant to Ali's case and directed the district court to reconsider the case. Almost a year later the district court upheld the lower court's decision.

In the meantime, on February 3, 1970, Ali, in a press conference, announced that he was retiring from the ring. He proposed that the winner of a bout of his choosing, between Joe Frazier and Jerry Quarry, be the next champion. Frazier rejected the offer. On September 10, 1970, Ali announced that he wished to pursue an active campaign to return to the ring.

In September 1970 the state of Georgia gave a license to Ali to fight an eight round exhibition against three minor heavyweights preparatory to a fight with Jerry Quarry on October 26 in Atlanta. He KO'd Quarry in three.

Federal Court Judge Walter Mansfield stated that the New York State Athletic Commission took "arbitrary and unreasonable action" when they refused to give Ali a license and he nullified their decision. As Michael Meltsner, a Columbia University professor, so aptly put it, "Freedom on bail implies the right of a defendant to pursue his normal occupation while awaiting court settlement of the case." On December 7, 1970, Ali and Oscar Bonavena from Argentina met in New York. Bonavena was knocked out in the fifteenth round. It was a hard-fought fight.

The American attitude concerning the war in Vietnam was changing. More and more resistance to the draft was being exercised. The black American protest movement was in full swing as well. Malcolm X had been killed on February 21, 1965. Disillusioned, he had left the Black Muslims and was beginning to make efforts for the unification of whites and blacks. Some say he was killed by the Muslims, some say by the CIA.

There had been riots in Watts in 1965 and in Newark and Detroit in 1967. Now the black protest troops had retrenched. The Black Panthers, for all intents and purposes, had been annihilated by the police and/or the government agencies. When Dr. Martin Luther King was preparing for a major demonstration and uniting poor whites and blacks, he too was assassinated, on April 4, 1968. As a result, there was again rioting, burning, and looting in Washington, Chicago, Baltimore, Kansas City, and many other towns. Fifty-five thousand troops were called to quell the raging protesters—forty-six people were killed.

The political events of the '60s left America stunned, despondent, and seemingly immobile.

It took until June 28, 1971, before the Supreme Court at last handed down its ruling on the Ali case. The decision was in Ali's favor.

For forty-three months he had been out of contention, his title stripped away, his freedom to travel terminated, and his ability to earn his living curtailed. He had been well punished. Ali could have taken the easy route and allowed himself to be inducted and given preferred duties—exhibition bouts, et cetera—and in no way endangered his life. But he did not believe in war, as prescribed by the edicts of his religion. He stuck by his principles at a great personal sacrifice.

And now Ali wanted his title back.

Ali's draft case had caused a great deal of confusion around the heavyweight title. The World Boxing Association, which had taken away Ali's crown, now had to find a replacement. In September of 1967 it sanctioned an eight round elimination tournament to determine which fighter should take over the championship which was open because of Ali's "vacated" position.

A monkey wrench was thrown into these plans, however, because when officials of New York's Madison Square Garden had set up a fight between Joe Frazier of Philadelphia and George Chuvalo of Canada for July 19, 1967 and Frazier stopped Chuvalo in four, he then refused to join the elimination group. In addition to Frazier, the group was to consist of Jerry Quarry, Jimmy Ellis, Floyd Patterson, Thad Spencer, Oscar Bonavena, Ernie Terrell, and Karl Mildenberger. In a retaliatory move, the World Boxing Association dropped Frazier from his top spot to number nine in its ratings, and put Leotis Martin in the number eight position as Frazier's substitute. Then the New York State Athletic Commission declared that the winner of the World Boxing Association tournament would not be recognized unless that champion triumphed over Joe Frazier.

The tournament commenced on August 5, 1967, in Atlantic City. Thad Spencer won a twelve round decision over Ernie Terrell in the first match. In bout number two, Jimmy Ellis knocked out Leotis Martin in the ninth. On September 16, 1967, in Frankfurt, Germany, Oscar Bonavena beat Karl Mildenberger in twelve rounds. The final match in the first round took place in California, which saw Jerry Quarry win a split decision over Floyd Patterson.

In the concluding round on December 2, 1967, in Louisville, Kentucky, Jimmy Ellis knocked down Oscar Bonavena twice and went from there to cop a unanimous twelve round victory. On February 3, 1968, in Oakland, California, Jerry Quarry stopped six foot, four inch Thad Spencer in the second semifinal, with three seconds left in round twelve. The final bout of the tournament took place on April 27, 1968, in Oakland, where Jimmy Ellis defeated Jerry Quarry in a fifteen round split decision.

Ellis was now the heavyweight king of the World Boxing Association, but the New York State Athletic Commission declared that it would give recognition to the winner of a Joe Frazier-Buster Mathis bout as the new champion. Five state commissions, as well as those of South America and Mexico, went along with New York's ruling. So, when Frazier knocked out Mathis in the eleventh round, New York, Pennsylvania, Massachusetts, Maine, Texas, and Illinois recognized Frazier as the champion, while all other states recognized Ellis.

On February 16, 1970, Joe Frazier knocked out Jimmy Ellis in five rounds at Madison Square Garden, and thus the title, stripped from Muhammad Ali, had at long last been filled. Frazier became the "undisputed" world champion.

Joe Frazier was born on January 12, 1944, in Laurel Bay, South Carolina, outside of Beaufort, the youngest of thirteen children. He became interested in boxing at an early age and at nine he constructed a homemade punching bag of leaves and moss. When he dropped out of school in the ninth grade, he worked on the small farm his father owned outside of Beaufort.

He married at sixteen and moved to Philadelphia. He won the Golden Gloves championship in 1962 and 1963. In 1964 he participated in the Olympics in Tokyo and won America's only gold medal in boxing that year. He turned professional in August 1965. Frazier was a hard-training and sincere man. He worked so hard and threw punches so fast that they called him "Smoking" Joe Frazier.

On March 8, 1971, at Madison Square Garden Joe Frazier, weighing 205½ pounds, and Ali, weighing 215 pounds, met for the "Fight of the Century." Frazier was intent on keeping his championship away from the taunting loudmouth, and Ali was interested in reclaiming his title to wash away the bitterness over the loss of three and one half years of his professional career—perhaps his most crucial years. The crowd eagerly paid to see two undefeated heavyweight champions.

The first nine rounds were close. Both men learned to respect one another. In the tenth round Frazier got the upper hand, and in the eleventh he almost knocked out Ali. In his autobiography Ali says, "There's something about the way he comes in, bobbing, weaving, that throws me off. He's easy to hit; then he's not easy to hit. I've never fought anyone with a will so strong." In the twelfth and thirteenth rounds, Frazier pressed on, getting in solid shots at Ali's body. Ali seemed to recoup in the fourteenth round, but too much had already been taken out of him. In the fifteenth round Ali took a left to the head and was down, but somehow he managed to get up at the count of four and stood for the mandatory eight count. Frazier was landing strong body and head punches and Ali, though he tried, could not fend them off. The fight

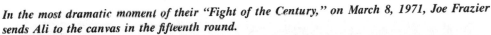

In the most dramatic moment of their "Fight of the Century," on March 8, 1971, Joe Frazier sends Ali to the canvas in the fifteenth round.

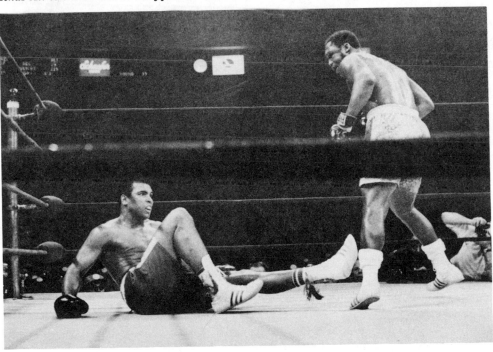

was over and Joe Frazier remained by unanimous decision undisputed world heavy-weight champion. Here's how the officials voted:

Referee Arthur Mercante: Frazier 8, Ali 6, 1 even
Judge Artie Aidala: Frazier 9, Ali 6
Judge Bill Recht: Frazier 11, Ali 4

Besides Ali, there were many who felt that Ali had won the fight—a close fight, granted, but still an Ali win. Robert Lipsyte in his book, *Sportsworld,* states:

The ring officials had a bias. . . . The Madison Square Garden press kit had declared of Frazier, "Not since the days of Joe Louis has a black man done so much for his race. Not since the days of Joe Louis and Ray Robinson and Floyd Patterson has a black man brought so much dignity to boxing."

It was a clear mandate.
It was still several months before the June decision of the Supreme Court.

After being defeated by Frazier, Ali would have to climb back to be positioned to fight the heavyweight champion again. In June and early July he had exhibition bouts. On July 26, 1971, in Houston, Ali fought and KO'd Jimmy Ellis, his former sparring partner, in the twelfth round. Again in Houston on November 17, he beat Buster Mathis in twelve. Then in Zurich he stopped Jurgen Blin in seven rounds on December 26.

April 1, 1972, in Tokyo, Ali beat Mac Foster in fifteen rounds. In Vancouver on May 1, he fought George Chuvalo and won in twelve. He met with Jerry Quarry again in Las Vegas on June 27 and KO'd him in the seventh. July 19 took him to Dublin, where he stopped Al Lewis in eleven rounds. Ex-heavyweight champion Floyd Patterson was KO'd by him in the seventh round at Madison Square Garden on September 20 for the second time. Bob Foster was knocked out in eight on November 21 in Stateline, Nevada.

Then in Kingston, Jamaica, Frazier, after two KO's in defense of his title, was stopped by George Foreman in the second round on January 22, 1973. Now Foreman carried the heavyweight title, which would make the climb back up the ladder for Ali a little longer.

Ali fought Joe Bugner, an Englishman, before he took on Ken Norton. He out-pointed Bugner in twelve in Las Vegas on February 14, 1973. On March 31, he met with Ken Norton in San Diego and lost a twelve round decision. He also sustained a broken jaw. In a rematch on September 10, Ali won a twelve round decision over Norton. October 20 found him in Jakarta, where he beat Rudi Lubbers in a twelve round decision.

By now Ali was again a big money-maker. No one publicly or in print called him Cassius Clay. He was now the underdog; he was again the champion of the people and he was the greatest. People now believed he was sincere about his dedication to the Muslim faith, and his badgering, sassy, taunting declarations were like a breath of fresh air, as they had been when he just turned professional. The fans amazingly tolerated his braggadocio, now that they knew his power was true.

Perhaps the fans also had begun to realize how unfair the system had been when they had stripped Ali of his title without legal ajudication, and made a whipping boy of the champion. The now apparent racism undoubtedly aroused a massive sense of guilt among the fans.

January 28, 1974, marked the Ali-Frazier fight number two. It was held in Madison Square Garden, and it was an unsatisfactory fight. Neither man fulfilled the expectations the previous fight had aroused. Ali was awarded an unpopular unanimous twelve round decision. Thousands who attended the fight felt Frazier had won.

In the meantime, Foreman had defended his title successfully with a knockout in the first round of Jose Roman in Tokyo on September 1, 1973. Foreman then stopped Ken Norton in a two round defense of his title in Caracas, Venezuela.

At last, on October 30, 1974, Ali was to meet George Foreman in Zaire, Africa, a new African nation and an appropriate place for two long-gone native sons. The tactic Ali employed in the fight was to use the ropes to his advantage. Fighting flat-footed with his back to the ropes and at a slanted stance, Ali was able to remove himself from Foreman's damaging blows by sliding and moving along the strands. While Foreman aimed for his head, the open target, Ali was sliding and getting in body blows. This maneuver completely threw Foreman and he punched himself out. In the first two rounds, Foreman looked overpowering. By the third round Ali had his combinations working and directed them to Foreman's head. In the fifth round, Foreman was visibly wearing down and Ali seemed stronger. At two minutes and fifty-eight seconds of the eighth round, Foreman succumbed to a knockout punch administered by Ali. For the second time, Ali was the heavyweight champion of the world.

Muhammad Ali stands over George Foreman as he falls to the canvas from a left-right combination in the eighth round. This knockdown gave Ali back the new world heavyweight championship October 30, 1974, in Kinshasa, Zaire.

In the dressing rooms following Ali's upset victory, the champion for the second time and the former ruler expressed themselves about the fight in a newspaper interview:

Ali:
I told you all I would do it, but did you listen? He was scared, he was humiliated. I told you I was the greatest heavyweight of all time.

I didn't dance. I wanted him to tire, to lose power. I decided to use the ropes. He punched like a sissy.

Foreman:
Ali was the better man tonight, give him the credit due.

Following the Ali bout, George Foreman was knocked out five consecutive times and decisioned once, after which, in the spring of 1977, he announced his retirement from the ring.

In 1975 Ali defended his newly regained title four times. On March 24 he knocked out Chuck Wepner in the fifteenth in Cleveland. May 16 in Las Vegas he took out Ron Lyle in eleven. On July 1 in Kuala Lumpur, Malaysia, he defeated Joe Bugner in a fifteen-round decision. Then on October 1 it was fight number three with Joe Frazier, in Manila. The fight was called the "Thrilla in Manila."

For their third meeting, Ali weighed 224½ pounds against Frazier's 215½ pounds.

Joe Frazier

Challenger Joe Frazier staggers (top) *after receiving a left, and then* (bottom) *a hard right to his head from champion Muhammad Ali in the fourteenth round of their fifteen-round title fight in Manila on October 1, 1975. Ali won a TKO after these punches, and retained his title.*

In the most brutal confrontation of their five-year rivalry, Ali retained the world heavyweight championship when Joe Frazier's manager, Eddie Futch, stopped the bout moments before the bell for the fifteenth round. Frazier, after winning most of the middle rounds with a furious assault, had been battered by Ali throughout the three rounds prior to Futch's surrender. Frazier, his face puffed and weary, did not appear to protest as he sat on the stool in his corner.

Ali had attempted to register the early knockout he had predicted while winning the early rounds, but Frazier, seemingly rediscovering the fury of his youth, smashed and slowed the thirty-three-year-old champion. Beginning in the twelfth round, Ali appeared desperate for a knockout that would preserve the title. Moving on weary legs, he beat Frazier constantly, staggering him in the thirteenth, although the thirty-one-year-old former champion somehow kept his feet before a crowd of 27,000 at the Philippine Coliseum.

In the fourteenth round, Ali's combinations grew sharper. He staggered Frazier again and again. Nothing but heart and legs were holding up Joe Frazier. The bell sounded. Frazier, half blinded, groped to his corner to rest for the last round. There was to be none.

In a series of lackluster performances in 1976 and 1977, Ali knocked out Jean-Pierre Coopman in five rounds in San Juan, Puerto Rico, on February 20, 1976; won a fifteen round decision over Jimmy Young in Landover, Maryland, April 30; on May 24, stopped Richard Dunn in five in Munich; September 28, won a controversial fifteen round decision over Ken Norton in New York. In 1977 on May 16 and September 29, Ali won fifteen round decisions from Alfredo Evangelista in Landover and Earnie Shavers in Madison Square Garden.

On February 15, 1978, at Las Vegas, in an unexpected turn of events, Ali lost a fifteen round split decision to Leon Spinks. Spinks, twenty-two, was the Olympic light-heavyweight gold medal winner at Montreal in 1976. This St. Louis-born young fighter had had only seven professional fights under his belt before he received a title shot. Dr. Ferdie Pacheco, Ali's doctor, had pleaded with Ali to forgo the fight because he felt "there was mounting damage that only a doctor could see." Dr. Pacheco and Ali parted company over this matter. Ali, out of condition and underestimating the inexperienced but youthful fighter, lost his title in a decision. Spinks graciously stated, "Ali's the greatest, but I'm the latest."

The event, the moment, that made Ali the top story of the 1970s occurred on September 15, 1978, in the New Orleans Superdome. There, before a near capacity crowd, Ali won the heavyweight championship of the world for the third time, beating Leon Spinks, the man to whom he had lost the title in Las Vegas seven months before.

Leon Spinks

Ali, thirty-six years old, beat Spinks in a fifteen-round decision, which seemed to surprise no one, including Spinks, who seemed psyched out from the opening bell. The rematch saw Ali dance and jab and generally befuddle the outclassed Spinks. The fight was barely a contest. Many said that Spinks was merely the vehicle Ali used to become the first man in history to win the heavyweight crown three times. After some months of speculation on the unpredictable Ali's next move, the champ retired in June

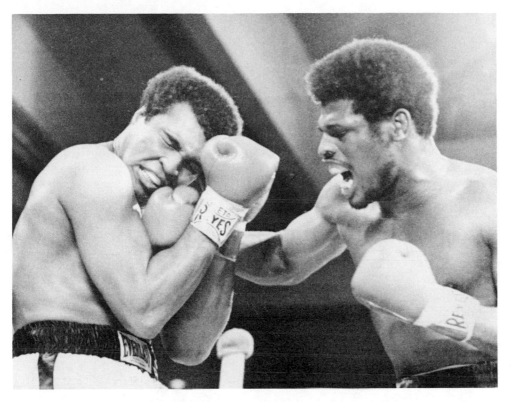

Heavyweight champion Muhammad Ali grimaces as challenger Leon Spinks gets in a stinging right cross to the jaw in the third round of their title bout. Spinks never let up the attack and took the title from Ali in a fifteen-round decision on February 15, 1978. Seven months later, Ali regained his title in a decision from Spinks in the New Orleans Superdome, September 15, 1978.

1979, leaving behind a record of fifty-six wins, three losses, and perhaps the most colorful and controversial career in sports history.

When Ali retired he vacated the World Boxing Association heavyweight title. The WBA organized an elimination tournament in its quest for a new champion. On June 2, 1979, John Tate, a black man from Knoxville, Tennessee, knocked out in eight Kallie Knoetze, a white South African, at Mmabatho, South Africa. On June 24 Gerrie Coetzee knocked out Leon Spinks in the first round at Monte Carlo. Then on October 20, 1979, John Tate met with Coetzee in Pretoria, South Africa, at the Loftus Versfeld Stadium. This was the first time Loftus Versfeld was open to blacks as well as whites. Although few blacks could afford to attend, it was a significant symbolic gesture. A black man competing with a white man in the land of apartheid for the purpose of winning the heavyweight championship is certainly to be noted. In a fifteen round decision, John Tate won the vacated WBA heavyweight title.

Early in 1980 whispers were coming from the ex-champ Ali, and on March 31, 1980, when Mike Weaver KO'd Tate in Knoxville, Tennessee, to become the WBA champion, Ali began sending out the message, "I got the title back."

Ali's battle plan had been to fight Tate, whom he thought he could beat, but Weaver upset the applecart when he KO'd Tate and became the WBA titleholder. Ali was not that interested in fighting Weaver because he felt he was easy game, whereas the big money and greater recognition would be his if he were to capture the World Boxing

Council's championship from Larry Holmes, a formidable and more worthy opponent. Ali was confident that he could beat Weaver, and if he beat Holmes, he would unite the fragmented championship as well as become the first fighter to win the heavyweight title four times.

Ali, at the age of thirty-eight, after two years of retirement, announced he would return to the ring. The question to be asked is, why? Was it sheer ego, or the boredom of retirement? Was it the need for the challenge? Did the myth, the magic man he had become, need constant perpetuation? Or did he need the money? He had earned at least $50 million in the ring. Taxes, expenses, support of a huge entourage, two former wives, one with four children, his present wife and two children, and considerable contributions to the Muslims added up to quite a bit. But Ali said, "I'm not thirty-eight like other Americans. I'm not a normal American. I'm a superman." He believed the myth.

The man Ali challenged, Larry Holmes, always said, "I want to be somebody." Holmes was born in the small town of Cuthbert, Georgia, on November 3, 1949. He was one of twelve children born to John and Flossie Holmes. The family moved to Easton, Pennsylvania, when Holmes was five. Holmes had to quit school after the seventh grade to help support the family. Earning money at different odd jobs never deterred him from his intense interest in sports. He loved to wrestle and play football

Larry Holmes

and basketball. Holmes began boxing as a way to defend himself because of the street fighting situations that always arose. Through the encouragement of an amateur trainer, Ernie Butler, Holmes went on to accumulate an impressive record: twenty-two amateur fights, winning nineteen, losing three. He won the New Jersey AAU championship and Eastern Olympic title. Turning pro in 1973, he worked as a sparring partner for both Ali and Joe Frazier.

On March 25, 1978, Holmes defeated Earnie Shavers in Las Vegas demonstrating a magnificent display of boxing skills. Then on June 9, 1978, he clearly dismissed any doubts about his talents as a fighter when he out boxed a tough Ken Norton in a fifteen round decision at Las Vegas to win the World Boxing Council heavyweight title. (And he did this with a hurt left arm.) His fistic skills are of such superb professionalism that he has maintained a firm hold on his title against all challengers for over seven years through 1985.

However, through most of his early fighting days Holmes, the "Easton Assassin," failed to receive the attention that he deserved and was often referred to as the "other champion." He stood completely dwarfed in the shadow and myth of Muhammad Ali. But with his career nearing its climax, Larry Holmes has become recognized as a great and talented champion.

Now it was time for the power broker to move into position. Don King promoted the fight. King is a phenomenon unto himself. Born in Cleveland, Ohio, about fifty years ago, King and his five brothers and sister grew up in the city's eastern ghetto. At an early age he was recognized as the "King of the Numbers" in Cleveland. He says that he became involved in the numbers business to raise money for his college tuition, but having to pay a numbers debt postponed his dream of college. In the meantime, he was arrested for manslaughter. In a fight with a distraught numbers runner, King killed the man in self-defense. King was imprisoned from 1967 to 1971. While incarcerated, he enrolled in correspondence courses at Ohio University, where he maintained a straight A average.

Promoter Don King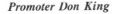

Upon his release, King, with his keen analytical mind, flamboyant style, and great talent for organization and creativity, set about making a name for himself in the boxing world. His astounding rise to prominence as a promoter extraordinaire began in 1973, and by 1974 he really stepped out on the world stage. He promoted the George Foreman-Ken Norton fight in Caracas, Venezeula, on March 3, 1974; the epic Ali-Foreman fight in Zaire on October 30, 1974; and the "Thrilla in Manila," the third meeting between Ali and Joe Frazier on October 1, 1975.

King went on to promote boxers of all weights from countries all over the world. He branched out to become a miniconglomerate dealing with recordings, talent management, athletic management, investment, management consulting, industrial development, and international relations. *Time* magazine called him ". . . the most powerful promoter in sports—and one of the most successful black businessmen in America."

He has received awards from the NAACP; the Urban Justice Awards; the Heritage Award, presented by Edwin Gould Services for Children in New York; Man of the Year, by the National Black Hall of Fame; Minority Businessman of the Year, by the Greater Washington Center; and many more. Don King is the first black man to become a boxing promoter of national and international fame. His name will go down alongside those of the other legendary fight promoters like Tex Rickard and Mike Jacobs.

King scouted the world for a suitable arena—Taiwan, Rio de Janeiro, and Cairo. Finally, after he had examined the pros and cons of various countries, the parking lot of Caesars Palace in Las Vegas was converted into a gigantic stadium and the fight was set for October 2, 1980. King had begun calling the fight "The Last Hurrah."

Then the controversy arose between fans, sportswriters, gamblers, and the disinterested man and woman. Ali, the super salesman, duped the believers. The believers wanted a magician; Ali with great profundity told them that he was the man for whom they searched. Many a wise older sports aficionado and writer wanted to believe that Ali would pull a real rabbit out of a hat. The more pragmatic looked at the facts: Ali was thirty-eight, Holmes, thirty; truly Ali's last great fight was with Joe Frazier in 1975 in Manila—that colossal battle had taken everything out of both boxers. Holmes, while not charismatic, was a skillful tactician; Ali weighed a bloated 255 pounds, Holmes was steady at 211. The increased weight consisting of mostly fat gave many cause for concern, but Ali, the wizard, shed some 37½ pounds while preparations for the fight continued, and with his new svelte figure and dancing feet, he reconvinced those who might have had doubts. Fully 24,760 seats at Caesars Palace were sold at prices ranging from $50 to $500; the odds on Holmes went from 3-to-1 to 6-to-5 in the final week.

When the bell rang for the debacle that was about to ensue, Holmes sent Ali into retreat with a left hook and it was followed by a right to the body. Ali made a vague attempt to throw a punch. Holmes pursued Ali with overhead rights, rights to the body, left jabs, and hooks to the head and body. Ali tried a right cross following a jab. The blow had no substance. The devastation continued with Ali flat-footed and doing absolutely nothing. Holmes pounded away at will, and even appeared to be holding back for ten rounds. Ali, with his eyes reddened and the telltale bruise marks under his eyes that would turn black in a few hours, and with blood trickling from his nostrils, his face lacerated, eyes blank, sat on his stool waiting for the bell for the eleventh round.

It's all over! Muhammad Ali's manager throws in the towel before the eleventh-round bell sounds. The victorious Larry Holmes parades around the ring after successfully defending his title.

Angelo Dundee looked down from the ring and caught the eye of Pat Patterson, one of Ali's bodyguards, and shouted to him to "ask Herbert", Ali's manager. Herbert Muhammad said, "Stop it, he's getting defenseless." Larry Holmes was still the WBC world heavyweight champion.

The aftermath of the fight caused a rage. The magic man had failed—he could not do it again. The public felt cheated and angry. A subdued Ali, wearing dark glasses, stated at a press conference that he had taken the drug Thyrolar. Thyrolar is known to cause weight loss, possible fatigue, weakness, sensitivity to heat, and personality changes, as well as other side effects. Ali claims to have taken more of the thyroid-controlling drug than was prescribed. Herbert Muhammad claims this was the cause of his poor showing.

Ali proclaimed, "I shall return."

True to his word, he climbed back into the ring on December 11, 1981. But success once again eluded him as he lost a ten-round decision to Trevor Berbick in Nassau. This was his final appearance as a professional.

Chalky Wright, featherweight champion 1941–42.

Ike Williams, undisputed lightweight champion, 1947–51. From 1940 to 1955 he won 124 of 153 bouts.

Colorful New York State Athletic Commission lightweight champ Beau Jack. In a 152-bout career, he won 83, KO'd 40, lost 20, drew 5, and was himself KO'd 4 times.

Bob Montgomery twice won Beau Jack's New York State lightweight crown from him.

Kid Gavilan won the world welterweight crown in a hotly disputed decision over Billy Graham, August 29, 1951.

Johnny Bratton won the National Boxing Association welterweight title by decision over Charley Fusari in fifteen rounds in 1951.

Jimmy Carter KO'd Ike Williams in the fourteenth round on May 25, 1951, to become world lightweight champ.

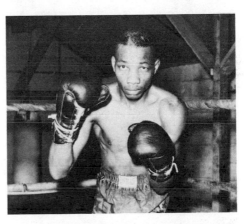

Sandy Saddler was twice world featherweight champ (1948–49, 1950–57). He KO'd 103 of 162 opponents.

Hogan "Kid" Bassey, 1957 featherweight champ

Ezzard Charles, the first heavyweight champ (1950–51) after Louis's ten-year reign.

Heavyweight Jersey Joe Walcott (Arnold Cream) KO'd Ezzard Charles in 1951, to win the world heavyweight title. He in turn lost the championship to Rocky Marciano, September 23, 1952. At the age of seventy, Walcott retired from his post as a New Jersey State athletic commissioner on January 31, 1984.

Ten-year light-heavyweight titleholder Archie Moore took on all the top heavyweights, fighting 229 times in his long career.

Harold Johnson became world light-heavyweight champ when he won a unanimous decision over Doug Jones, May 12, 1962.

Floyd Patterson was the first heavyweight champion to regain the title, KO'ing Ingemar Johansson June 20, 1960, a year after Johansson had KO'd Patterson. Patterson was an Olympic gold medalist at Helsinki, Finland, in 1952.

Jimmy Ellis, on April 27, 1968, in Oakland, California, won a fifteen-round split decision over Jerry Quarry to gain WBA recognition as the heavyweight champion. Meanwhile, the New York Boxing Commission announced that it would recognize the winner of the Joe Frazier–Buster Mathis bout as the new champion. Five state boxing commissions followed New York's decision. So when Frazier stopped Mathis in the eleventh round, New York, Maine, Pennsylvania, Texas, Massachusetts, and Illinois considered Frazier the champion, while all the others recognized Ellis.

Joe Brown successfully defended his light-weight crown ten times from 1956 to 1962.

Bob Foster became the light-heavyweight champion on May 24, 1968, when he knocked out Dick Tiger in the fourth round. He went on to defend his title fourteen times, the record for his division.

Dick Tiger at different times held the middleweight and light-heavyweight titles.

Emile Griffith. Three-time welterweight champion and twice middleweight title-holder. Griffith regained his welterweight championship on March 24, 1962, with a twelfth-round knockout of Benny Paret, a fight that had a tragic aftermath. Paret never regained consciousness and died ten days later.

Sugar Ray Leonard won the world welterweight title by a fifteen-round knockout of Wilfredo Benitez in Las Vegas, November 30, 1979. On June 20, 1980, in Montreal, Canada, he lost his championship to Roberto Duran in a fifteen-round decision. Leonard recaptured the crown from Duran in the infamous "No más" fight in New Orleans on November 25, 1980. On June 25, 1981, in Houston, Texas, Leonard won the world junior middleweight championship by knocking out Ayub Kalule in the ninth round. He successfully defended his welterweight title with victories over Tommy Hearns and Bruce Finch in that same year. Because of a detached retina in his left eye, for which he had undergone surgery, Leonard announced his retirement from boxing at the age of twenty-six on November 9, 1982. However, unable to remain inactive, Leonard attempted a comeback in 1984 before hanging up the gloves for good.

George Foreman, heavyweight champion 1973–74, shown here as he won the title from Joe Frazier in Kingston, Jamaica, January 22, 1973.

Ken Norton was proclaimed world heavyweight champion by the WBC on March 29, 1978. On June 9 of that year, he lost the crown in an epic fifteen-rounder to Larry Holmes in Las Vegas. Norton had three controversial bouts with Muhammad Ali, the last on September 28, 1976, when he lost a fifteen-round decision. Many in attendance thought it was a wrong decision.

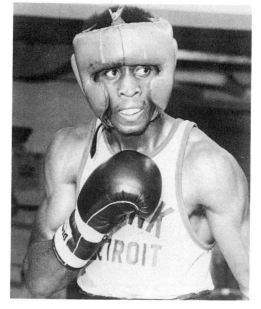

Tommy Hearns won the WBA world welterweight title by way of a second-round knockout of Pepino Cuevas. On September 16, 1981, in Las Vegas, Hearns was stopped in the fourteenth round by Sugar Ray Leonard in a battle for the world welterweight championship. The next year, on December 3, 1982, then weighing 153¾ pounds, Hearns captured the WBC middleweight crown by easily outpointing Wilfredo Benitez via a majority decision.

Mike Weaver won the WBA world heavy-weight championship on March 31, 1980, when he knocked out John Tate in the fif-teenth round in Knoxville, Tennessee.

Michael Spinks captured the WBA light-heavyweight title on July 18, 1981, with a unanimous fifteen-round decision over Eddie Mustafa Muhammad in Las Vegas. Spinks then received universal recognition by defeat-ing the WBC champion, 175-pounder Dwight Braxton, in 15 rounds on March 18, 1983, in Atlantic City, New Jersey.

Aaron Pryor of Cincinnati, Ohio, knocked out Antonio Cervantes in the fourth round of their August 2, 1980 fight, to capture the WBA junior welterweight title.

Marvelous Marvin Hagler. He captured the middleweight title by a third-round knock-out of Alan Minter in London on September 27, 1980.

Olympic Gold

In the post-World War II years, the pursuit of the Olympic gold became an important goal for black boxers who had dreams of becoming professionals. Those who succeeded in this quest include Floyd Patterson, who won the middleweight gold medal at Helsinki in 1952; Cassius Clay took the light-heavyweight honors in Rome in 1960; Joe Frazier swept the heavyweight division in Tokyo in 1964; George Foreman beat all his heavyweight opponents in Mexico City in 1968, and in the 1976 games in Montreal, Sugar Ray Leonard dominated the light-welterweights, as did Leon Spinks the light-heavyweights, and brother Michael Spinks the middleweights. After winning their gold medals, all these outstanding boxers entered the ranks of the professionals and, for the most part, had successful careers.

With such a precedent, it was no surprise when most of the members of the United States 1984 Olympic boxing team announced their intentions to become pros immediately after the closing of the games in Los Angeles. The 1984 team was the most successful group of amateur boxers that any country has ever entered in Olympic competition. Eleven of its twelve members advanced into medal rounds and nine went on to win the gold. The gold medal winners were:

Tyrell Biggs of Philadelphia, Pennsylvania—super-heavyweight
Henry Tillman of Los Angeles, California—heavyweight
Frank Tate of Detroit, Michigan—light-middleweight
Mark Breland of Brooklyn, New York—welterweight
Jerry Page of Columbus, Ohio—light-welterweight
Pernell Whitaker of Norfolk, Virginia—lightweight
Meldrick Taylor of Philadelphia, Pennsylvania—featherweight
Steve McCrory of Detroit, Michigan—flyweight
Paul Gonzales of Los Angeles, California—light-flyweight

Tyrell Biggs as he outboxed Azis Salihu of Yugoslavia at the 1984 Olympics.

Henry Tillman, right, following through on his right-hand punch at Tevita Taufoou of Tonga. The referee stopped the Olympic match in the first round, giving Tillman the victory.

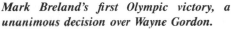

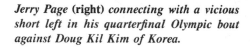

Mark Breland's first Olympic victory, a unanimous decision over Wayne Gordon.

Jerry Page (right) connecting with a vicious short left in his quarterfinal Olympic bout against Doug Kil Kim of Korea.

Pernell Whitaker stuns Farrain Comeaux in his first pro boxing debut at Madison Square Garden on November 11, 1984.

Featherweight Meldrick Taylor backs Mexico's Francisco Comacho into a corner in their Olympic bout. Taylor won on a 5–1 decision.

Capitalizing on their justly won national acclaim, sports promoter Dan Duva staged a "Night of Gold" in Madison Square Garden in New York City on November 16, 1984, where six of the Olympians made their professional boxing debuts. As was expected, all six were successful—but in varying degrees.

The most highly touted and heralded of the Olympic boxers, Mark Breland, was knocked into the ropes in 0:10 of the first round, and had a few other rough moments before he gained control in his six-round welterweight bout with Dwight Williams. One of the most exciting events of the evening was the light-heavyweight bout of bronze medalist Evander Holyfield, who pounded his tough Philadelphia opponent, Lionel Byram, with combination after combination. Tyrell Biggs, on the other hand, had easy going in his heavyweight contest with an outclassed Mike Evans.

Only two of the gold medalists scored knockouts in their bouts that night, but they were impressive performances. Featherweight Meldrick Taylor overpowered his opponent, Luke Lecce, putting him down three times in the first round, to score an automatic knockdown at 2:31. The very promising lightweight Pernell Whitaker seemed to bewilder his opponent, Farrain Comeaux, with a dazzling array of stinging punches until the referee stopped the fight at 2:50 of the second round.

Three weeks later, on December 7, 1984, the remaining two Olympic champions appeared on the same card in Houston, Texas, as they too made their pro debuts. Both Henry Tillman and Frank Tate scored knockouts in an auspicious start to their professional careers. Middleweight Frank Tate stopped his opponent, Mike Pucciarelli of Pittsburgh, at the 2:23 mark of the first round. In his match, heavyweight Henry Tillman was stunned and dropped in the first round by an overhand right from Uriah Grant, but got up at the count of eight. Tillman was less cautious in the second round and came out fighting. Toward the end of the round, he had his opponent hanging on the ropes. After an eight count, Grant tried to protect himself to last out the remaining seconds of the round, but Tillman, sensing victory, connected with an uppercut, followed by a stinging right. With Grant in obvious trouble, referee Chris Jordan wisely stopped the fight.

Is this "the dawn of a new day," as promoter Dan Duva claimed? Perhaps, but only time will tell which, if any, of these talented young boxers will continue to successfully fight their way to the top as did the other black Olympians before them. What is certain now is that they gained great honor for themselves—and their country—in the Olympics and have brought a new sense of excitement to the world of boxing.

FOOTBALL

American football as we know it today is a far cry from the ancient games played with an inflated animal bladder. Although football had been popular in England for centuries, we can trace the development of modern football there during the Industrial Revolution in the nineteenth century, when rural workers began to crowd into the cities to work in the new manufacturing areas. These concentrations of population in the cities deprived many thousands of people of the open spaces they were used to, and of the individual sports and pastimes of the country, such as fishing. In order to have some kind of recreational outlet, team games on any kind of open space became a much needed safety valve.

The early nineteenth century also saw growth in the long-established British public schools (actually private boarding schools for upper- and middle-class boys), and many youths who would have been educated at home, roaming the open fields outside class hours, now were confined within a school situation all day long. Their explosive energy found its outlet in the "kicking sport." This gave vent to boisterous and often violent behavior and was often outlawed.

In 1823 at Rugby School, an eighteen-year-old student named William Webb Ellis became frustrated when an intraschool game was almost over without a score. Ellis caught a punt and, instead of kicking it over the goal, ran through the lines of his opponents with the ball under his arm and touched the ball down in the end zone. He was severely criticized, but the act of running with the ball laid the foundation of the Rugby tradition.

The game of soccer derives its name from English Association football, "association" being transformed into "soccer." The basis of this game was that a round ball may be kicked or butted but not carried forward.

The "kicking game" had come to the American colonies with the British immigrants, often unlettered, who were seeking their fortune on American soil. As schools and colleges began to develop, the kicking sport, although disapproved of, developed too. In America the early colleges played forms of football, soccer, or a combination of the two. Football, as it generally became known, was an informal campus practice to let off steam. It evolved into a near-riot when freshmen were pitted against upper-classmen. In their competitive efforts to get the ball to the goal, pure mayhem broke out. Football day at Harvard was referred to as "Bloody Monday."

Through much trial and error, the colleges established uniform rules: An oval ball was to be used, the teams were reduced to eleven men, and a definition of touchdowns and penalties was clarified.

In 1869 Princeton and Rutgers played the first intercollegiate football game. Harvard, Columbia, Yale, Cornell, and Michigan also established teams. More specific rules were added, and essentially the game as we know it today was evolved.

Blacks participated as members of their college teams in those early days and never experienced the degree of racial hostility that abounded in other sports. The number of blacks attending colleges and universities before the turn of the century was minuscule, and the possibility of larger numbers of blacks attending white higher-educational facilities seemed remote. The threat of the black man's becoming dominant in college football was thought to be nonexistent; therefore, the use of those "qualified" blacks would not wreak havoc.

Then, too, many black colleges were being established during this period. Major religious denominations founded black schools such as Fisk University, Hampton Institute, Talladega College, Walden College, Claflin University, Howard University, Richmond Theological Seminary, Morehouse College, and Shaw University. The (black) Baptist, the African Methodist Episcopal, and the Colored Methodist Episcopal churches were also fundamental in establishing colleges and universities such as Lane College, Allen University, Paul Quinn College, and Paine College, among many others.

The Freedman's Bureau of the post–Civil War era was instrumental in aiding many of these institutions. In 1872, when the Freedman's Bureau was discontinued during the upheaval of the Reconstruction period, the survival of the schools became dependent upon philanthropists, many of them robber barons, their largesse stemming from exploitation. However, many of the funds provided by various individuals were as sincerely given as the times permitted. George F. Peabody established the Peabody Education Fund in 1867, giving $3.5 million for general aid to education in the South and Southwest. The fund did benefit many black schools, but not as much as it did white ones. (The trustees of the Peabody Fund helped to defeat the Civil Rights Bill of 1873.)

Most of the black colleges followed the principles laid down by Booker T. Washington. In order for these schools to be maintained without constituting a threat to whites, their educational policies revolved principally around agricultural and industrial skills; if they held to that course they could be underwritten by white philanthropists. While these institutions did not delve, or at most not deeply, into intellectual pursuits, they did allow the development of the black athlete. Since the concept of integrating blacks into mass education was not even considered, it was easy for all to laud these accomplishments. The black colleges and universities organized their teams, and in 1892 Biddle University and Livingstone College played against each other. Soon Howard, Lincoln, Tuskegee, Atlanta, and Shaw formed their own teams.

Walter Camp, "the father of American football," an outstanding player at Yale and a genius in developing plans for attack, was the first to name an All-America team, commonly called the Walter Camp All-America. Over the years he selected a number of black players.

William H. Lewis

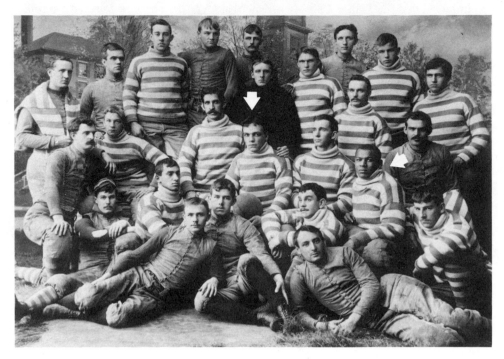

William Tecumseh Sherman Jackson and William Henry Lewis, with the 1891–92 Amherst College football team.

One of the men Walter Camp selected was center William Henry Lewis, the first black to be chosen, for the 1892 and 1893 teams. Lewis, the son of former slaves, was born in Berkeley, Virginia, in 1868. He attended Virginia Normal and Collegiate Institute and served as an errand boy in Congress. Lewis's father, Rev. Ashley Lewis, a Baptist minister, migrated to New England with his family. William Lewis was an industrious young man and, with the money he earned working in hotels and restaurants, enrolled at Amherst College in 1888.

This period was significant in terms of the development of big business, consolidations, and organized power emanating from white capital based on black labor. It was during this time that the social Darwinists, encouraged by the burgeoning capitalists, spread the belief that God as well as nature sanctified the powerful to exploit the weak. It was the old story of divine rule.

Between 1885 and 1894 approximately 1,700 blacks were lynched in America. It was a world of the survival of the fittest. William Lewis was one of those who felt strongly that he must prove the blacks were "fit," and that he had the equipment to prove it. Not only was he an outstanding scholar, selected as orator for the class of 1892, he was also an outstanding athlete. He played football for four years at Amherst and was captain of the Amherst team the entire 1891 season. Lewis became the first "roving lineman" in the game. A good-sized man for the times—five feet eleven inches, 177 pounds—he played in an era when helmets were not used, and he opposed the idea of free substitutions, allowing only unconsciousness or delirium as a reason for substitution.

Lewis entered Harvard Law School after graduating from Amherst and played football as starring center and later served as captain in 1893.

Lewis was responsible for the legislation that designated a neutral zone for linemen when the new rules, which also introduced the forward pass, were written in 1906. Lewis was also responsible for the implementation of the offside rules that exist today.

William Lewis graduated from Harvard Law School and became the first black assistant attorney general of the United States, appointed by President Taft in 1911, and the first black admitted as a member of the American Bar Association.

Walter Camp also selected William Tecumseh Sherman Jackson, halfback of Amherst as an All-American. A classmate of Lewis' at Amherst, Jackson was also a member of the track team and won first prize in many local meets. After graduating, Jackson went on to become an outstanding educator and administrator in the public high schools of Washington, D.C.

Other blacks named by Camp during this period included Bobby Marshall, end, Minnesota, who was a second-team All-American in 1905 and 1906. While playing against Chicago in 1906, he kicked a field goal that gave Minnesota a 4–2 victory, thus knocking Chicago out of contention for the conference title. It was a great moment in football history.

While football was generally considered a college sport, in Latrobe, Westmoreland County, Pennsylvania, a local YMCA sponsored a team, and on August 31, 1895, the YMCA team defeated Jeannette, another township, with a score of 12–0. The Latrobe team stayed together, became quite powerful, and for the next ten years played wherever they could find another team for whatever money they could get, and thus professional football began to take hold. Soon after, other professional teams began to appear. Pittsburgh developed the Duquesne Country Club. In 1902 Connie Mack in Philadelphia organized the Athletics. Upper New York State had teams in Buffalo, Syracuse, Watertown, Auburn, Clayton, Oswego, Alexandria Bay, and Ogdensburg. Then, in 1904, Ohio became the heart of professional football. It was here that the American Professional Football Association (which later evolved into the National Football League) was formed.

The first known black collegiate football player was Lewis of Amherst in 1892. The first black professional football player was Charles W. Follis, who on September 16, 1904, signed with the Shelby Blues in Shelby, Ohio.

Charles Follis was born in Cloverdale near Roanoke, Virginia, on February 3, 1879, one of seven children. The family migrated to Wooster, Ohio, when Follis was quite young. While in high school, Follis helped to organize the school's first varsity football team and was elected captain. That year Wooster High was unbeaten. Even in high school, Follis showed the promise of his devastating power.

Follis entered the College of Wooster in the spring of 1901. That fall he did not play football for the university, but instead for the Wooster A.A., a local amateur team. So

Charles Follis, the first black professional football player.

great were his efforts with the Wooster A.A. that he became known as the "Black Cyclone from Wooster."

As exceptional as his football skills were, his baseball skills were often considered even stronger. Follis became the talk of the Ohio college circuit. It was while playing baseball as a top catcher that he first met Branch Rickey, then playing for Ohio Wesleyan University. Follis' baseball reputation was established by his tremendous power hitting.

This handsome, multitalented young man, standing six feet tall and weighing two hundred pounds, played amateur football in the winter and baseball in the spring and summer. It was his outstanding football playing that attracted the eye of Frank C. Schiffer, manager of the Shelby Blues. In 1902 Schiffer brought Follis to Shelby, Ohio, a town without any black families. Schiffer secured a job for him at Howard Seltzer and Sons Hardware Store, where his working hours were arranged so that he could practice and play football. What a player Follis was! In the football seasons of 1902 and 1903 his superb skill gained him many admiring fans. Branch Rickey, who to earn extra money played with the Shelby Blues while attending Ohio Wesleyan, had unbounded praise for Follis, calling him a "wonder."

In 1904, when Follis finished college, he was now contracted to the Shelby Blues. While he had proved himself a superior player and had a good following, he still bore the brunt of rampant racism. In 1905 in Toledo the crowd began name-calling and urged his teammates to put him out of the game. Toledo captain Jack Tattersoll addressed the crowd, saying, "Don't call Follis a nigger. He is a gentleman and a clean player, and please don't call him that." Some of the crowd applauded and Follis was not bothered anymore that day. In another incident, at a Shelby tavern in the team's hometown, Follis, who had been invited by his teammates, was told blacks were not welcome there, and he had to leave. These are but two examples of what Follis had to constantly endure. He was known to be a man of great pride, but even on the most trying occasions he never resorted to belligerent behavior or open hostility. It has been suggested that Branch Rickey's observations of Follis' attempt to stem racism influenced him in the selection of Jackie Robinson in the major league color barrier break-through.

But the emotional strain was beginning to tell on Follis and he missed the early part of the 1906 season. When he returned to the club, his performance compensated for the time he missed and he carried his full load. On Thanksgiving Day, 1906, playing against the Franklin A.C.s of Cleveland, he suffered a severe physical injury and left football. America's first black professional football player then went into professional black baseball, ending up with Bright's Cuban Giants, where he played successfully until 1910.

Another of the black professional football pioneers was Haitian-born Henry McDonald. He was a hard running halfback, who first played at Canandaigua Academy in upstate New York. Later he joined the Rochester, New York, Jeffersons in 1912, a team in a loosely organized league that was some years later to become the American Professional Football Association, a forerunner of the National Football League.

McDonald spent seven seasons with the Jeffersons and was nicknamed "the Motor-cycle." It was while he was with the Jeffersons that he met Jim Thorpe of the Canton Bulldogs.

Henry McDonald

Jim Thorpe was another nonwhite—a pureblood American Indian. Thorpe was born near Prague, Oklahoma, on May 28, 1888, a member of the Sac and Fox Indian tribe. His tribal name translated was "Drag-his-root." He was six feet tall and 190 pounds and has been considered the finest athlete produced in these United States. In the 1912 Olympics in Stockholm, Thorpe won four out of five events in the pentathlon —the 200-meter dash, the 1,500-meter run, the long jump, and the discus. In the javelin throw he placed third. He won four events in the decathlon—the shot put, the high jump, the high hurdles, and the 1,500-meter run—and placed third in the 100-meter dash, the pole vault, the discus, and the long jump and fourth in the javelin

Jim Thorpe

throw and the 400-meter run. Out of a possible 10,000 points he scored 8,412.96. The glory that was the 1912 Olympics was Jim Thorpe's.

In 1913 a Boston newspaper discovered that Thorpe had played baseball for the Eastern Carolina League, a minor professional organization, during one summer vacation while attending college. He was charged with violating his amateur standing. The International Olympic Committee stripped him of his medals and erased his records from the official Olympic history. His amateur standing was stripped and not restored until twenty years after his death.

It is said that during a football game between the Rochester Jeffersons and the Canton Bulldogs, Henry McDonald was having a dispute with a white southern Canton player. The white player, in a boxing stance, said, "Black is black and white is white. Where I come from they don't mix." McDonald was an excellent boxer and was about to take up the challenge when Jim Thorpe said, "We're here to play football. So let's play football." The game proceeded as scheduled.

McDonald played with a variety of professional teams of the period, the Pittsburgh Colored All-Stars, the Lancaster Malleables, and the New York Colored Giants.

Jim Thorpe signed as an outfielder with the New York baseball Giants in 1913 and played for three major league teams through 1919, but his major professional achievements were in football. The Canton Bulldogs signed Thorpe in 1915 and he starred for them until 1920. In 1921 he was with the Cleveland Indians; 1922–23, the Oorang Indians and the Toledo Maroons; 1924–25, the Rock Island Independents and the New York football Giants; and 1926, back to the Bulldogs. He ended his football career in 1928 with the Chicago Cardinals at the age of nearly forty.

The professional football player was generally recruited from the colleges on the basis of ability. Football itself did not place restrictions on a player in terms of race, but, as stated before, there were relatively few blacks attending college.

Fritz Pollard

Frederick Douglas "Fritz" Pollard

One of the pioneers of collegiate and professional football was Frederick Douglas Pollard, better known as Fritz, from Brown University. Standing only five feet nine inches, weighing 160 pounds, he was "quick as a cat and twice as elusive." As one of the first black players in pro football, he led the undefeated Akron Pros to the championship of the American Professional Football Association in 1920. After the association was rechristened the National Football League, Pollard became the first black coach, in 1923. He played for and coached the Hammond, Indiana, team. His last year of pro ball was with the Province Steamroller in 1925.

Fritz Pollard (1978):
Jackie Robinson had an easy time in comparison to me. I'd run out on the field just before the whistle and they called me all the niggers in the world. At the kickoff they'd come after me even if the ball wasn't kicked to me. I learned how to "ball up" on the ground to absorb the blows.

I was born in a suburb of Chicago called Rogers Park. My father had a barber shop then. My father was a champion boxer during the Civil War days. That is the cause of my family being involved in sports. I had an older brother, Luther J., who was an outstanding athlete and football player at Lakeview High School and Northwestern University way back in the nineties. Then I had another brother named Leslie, who was a great football player at Dartmouth. Later he became coach and athletic director at Lincoln University. I had another brother named Hughes who was the reason I got a chance to play football at our high school, Lane Tech in Chicago. He was the big shot on the team and he told the coach if his kid brother couldn't play, he wouldn't play either. I weighed all of eighty-nine pounds. As years went by, I became the star of the team.

I entered Brown University in 1914. This came about after I went East to New York with Lane Tech to play a high school game. The Rockefellers (John D., in particular), who were Brown University people, took an interest in me after they saw me play ball. I talked with him and it was decided that I would go to Brown in Providence, Rhode Island. I was the first black man to live on the campus. The Rockefellers paid my tuition, so they had to let me live there.

I opened up a tailor shop on the campus and for a dollar I'd clean and press all the clothes. I wanted to get the student body behind me and I did that before I even went out for the football team because the prejudice was so great and I was so small that I knew they would set me around and what not. By now I was five foot seven and weighed one hundred fifty pounds. I became a favorite of the student body because of the tailor shop.

The captain of the Brown team was the star quarterback, Clair Purdy. We were freshmen together. He paved the way for me socially and on the football field. He fought off all the objections that came over my playing on the team. He used to say if I couldn't play, he wouldn't play. But let's not forget the Rockefeller family were great supporters of the school, so I could overcome a lot of nonsense. It made things easier.

Playing football for Brown was rough. They'd call me "nigger" from the stands. The East was accustomed to a black man playing college football, so I was the nigger out there. "Kill the nigger! Don't let him do that!" was all I heard. That was the first year. Then things started working out.

When Brown played Rutgers, I played against Paul Robeson, who soon became a dear friend of mine. I played the piano and he'd sing. Paul and I talked a lot about racial problems and what to do in a given situation. We sort of supported each other.

It was January 1, 1916, when they invited Brown out to the coast to play Washington State in the Tournament of Roses; later they called it the Rose Bowl. Nothing was said at the first game, but at the second bowl game the officials and everybody else said they didn't want the nigger to play, meaning me, of course, but our team and our manager refused to play unless I played, so everything was all right.

I graduated from Brown in 1917. Then I attended the University of Pennsylvania Dental School, but also during that time I was the coach of the football team of Lincoln University in Chester, Pennsylvania. Paul Robeson came down to help me.

In 1919 a friend of mine approached me to play pro football in Akron, Ohio. I couldn't find a place to stay because of prejudice and almost didn't sign up. Anyway, I finally got an apartment and Paul Robeson joined me in 1920. I was a halfback and Robeson was an end. Had a hard time at first, but then the team warmed up to me. We went through the 1920 season undefeated. We beat the Canton Bulldogs before 6,000 fans in Canton on Thanksgiving Day.

Paul Robeson

Paul Robeson

Born April 9, 1898, to William Drew Robeson and Maria Louise Bustill, Paul Robeson, another great collegiate/professional football star, came out of this era, a man for all seasons. His father was a runaway slave who became the Reverend W. D. Robeson, pastor of the St. Thomas A.M.E. Zion Church in Somerville, New Jersey, where Paul and his brothers and sister were raised. Robeson sang in the church choir and gave every indication of being a gifted singer. When in high school he competed in an oratorical contest, with professors from Rutgers University acting as judges. Dr. Charles S. Whitman, head of the English Department of Rutgers, was so taken with Robeson that he became instrumental in securing a scholarship at that university for the young man.

In his junior year at college, Robeson was elected to the Phi Beta Kappa academic honor society; however, he was not permitted to live on campus. Although he dearly wanted to, he was not welcome to join the choir and glee club, although he would go on to become the world's leading concert singer in the late thirties and forties. Robeson was the valedictorian of his graduating class and a champion debater.

Weighing over 200 pounds and standing six feet three inches, he alternately played linebacker and end for the Rutgers football team and became one of the greatest football players of all time.

When the thirty-man squad heard that Robeson might join, there was an uproar. Half the players swore that they would "go home" before they would play with a black. When the Rutgers team was badly beaten by Princeton, there was some reconsideration. Though they needed Robeson desperately, they were determined that he would have to "keep in his place." Robeson suffered his trial by fire on his first day of scrimmage; he suffered a broken nose, a dislocated shoulder, a split eye, two swollen eyes, and many cuts and bruises. Instead of being discouraged, Robeson was all the more determined to make the team. The brutality continued until one day, as Ralph Edwards reports Robeson in *Paul Robeson: His Political Legacy to the Twentieth Century Gladiator,*

> The next play again came right at my defensive end position; the whole backfield came at me. In rage, I swept out my arms . . . [and the] interference just seemed to fall down. Then there was only the ball carrier; I wanted to kill him. . . . I actually had him up above my head . . . I was going to smash him so hard to the ground that . . . he'd break right in two.

It was that moment that Paul Robeson made the first-team varsity at Rutgers. The same coach who had stood silent as Robeson was being physically brutalized by his white teammates yelled, "Robey, you're on the varsity."

Despite his large proportions he was very fast, a great pass receiver, a tremendous offensive blocker, and the best middle linebacker of his time. He won thirteen varsity letters in four sports. Walter Camp named him for the All-American team honors in 1917 and 1918, the first black Rutgers player to win All-American honors. He led the Rutgers football team to a record of 20 wins and 4 losses during his college playing days.

Years later, because of political persecution, he was denied a place in the College Football Hall of Fame, although he is the *only* two-time Walter Camp All-American who is not so placed and although the Hall of Fame is located at Rutgers University.

This verse appeared in the *Scarlet Letter* Rutgers yearbook in 1919.

> *All hats off to Robey, men,*
> *All honors to his name.*
> *On the diamond, court, or football field*
> *He's brought old Rutgers fame.*

After graduation, Robeson turned professional and played with the Hammond Pros in 1920. He joined Akron in 1921 and then in 1922 he went with the Milwaukee Badgers—a team that had three black players, an unheard-of occurrence in professional football.

He left football to study law, but after he earned his degree the stage beckoned. He went on to become a stage actor, a concert singer, and a movie actor, his career flourishing both in the United States and abroad. He became disillusioned with America in view of its oppressive stand in regard to blacks. He voiced his opinions loudly, visited the Soviet Union, and was labeled a Communist. His passport was confiscated by the State Department in 1950, at the height of the cold war, or in what is known as "the McCarthy era."

In his testimony before the House Un-American Activities Committee in 1956, in response to a question from a committee member who wanted to know why he did not remain in Russia, Robeson responded, "Because my father was a slave, and my people died to build this country, and I am going to stay here and have a part of it just like you. And no fascist-minded people will drive me from it. Is that clear . . . ?"

Under worldwide pressure, Robeson's passport was returned in 1958, and he embarked on a European concert tour. In 1961 he retired from public life. In 1972 the Paul Robeson Campus Center, Rutgers University, was dedicated to him.

Paul Robeson died January 23, 1976.

The First Blacks in Pro Football

The "vintage" years for blacks in pro football also produced Charles "Doc" Baker, part of the backfield of the Akron Indians, 1906–8 and 1911; John Shelburne, half-back, Dartmouth, who played with the Hammond Pros in 1922; James Turner, back, with the Milwaukee Badgers in 1923; end Jay Mayo "Inky" Williams from Brown University, a teammate of Fritz Pollard with the Hammond Pros, 1923–24; Edward "Sol" Butler, back, 1923 Rock Island and 1923–24 and 1926 Hammond, 1924 Akron, 1926 Canton; tackle Fred "Duke" Slater from the University of Iowa, Rock Island Independents, 1922–25, Milwaukee Badgers, 1926, and Chicago Cardinals, 1927–31; Joe Lillard, University of Oregon, tailback and defensive back on the Chicago Cardinals, 1932–33; and tackle Ray Kemp of the 1933 Pittsburgh Pirates.

Charles "Doc" Baker

Fred "Duke" Slater

James Turner

Ray Kemp

The American Professional Football Association, formed in 1920, and then its off-shoot, the National Football League, formed in 1922, had since their inception been struggling along for years with limited support from the fans and less from the press, found itself in a state of chaos; new teams joining and then dropping out or moving to other cities. The players hopped around from team to team looking for the largest paychecks. Football could in no way come near the fevered pitch of acceptance that baseball had accomplished. Then in 1925 Harold "Red" Grange of the University of Illinois caught the imagination and spirit of American sports fans. The fabled redhead from Wheaton, Illinois, finished his collegiate football career and, with a scrapbook full of headline-blazing newspaper articles, signed with the Chicago Bears. At his debut in Wrigley Field against the Chicago Cardinals, 36,300 fans turned out. A week later, 68,000 watched him play against the New York Giants in the Polo Grounds. Big league football was up and away.

By 1933 football increased in popularity and, despite the throes of the Great Depression, the game was becoming big business—with the subsequent big dollars. That year, 1933, was a big year: the league formed two divisions—Eastern and Western—and established a championship game between divisional winners.

While President Franklin Delano Roosevelt was pushing his New Deal legislation through Congress, even the football itself had taken on a new shape, slimming down to its modern form—easier to pass but almost impossible to drop-kick. Changes in the playing rules saw the goalposts moved from the back of the end zones up to the goal lines. This permitted passing from any point behind the line of scrimmage, instead of at least five yards beyond the scrimmage line, as had been the case. The year 1933 suddenly saw more field goals, more passes, more points scored, and the beginning of the "wide open" play in professional football.

The end of 1933 also saw the disappearance of the black man in professional football. What happened?

George Preston Marshall, owner of the Boston Redskins franchise, George Halas, owner of the Chicago Bears franchise, and Art Rooney, who owned the Pittsburgh Pirates, had a "gentlemen's agreement" concerning the exclusion of black football players. Joseph F. Carr, league president, sanctioned the ban. Marshall publicly declared that his team was "the team of the South," and he did not mean southern blacks. Football was seen as a soon-to-be rival of baseball. Millions of dollars were to be made, and historically when vast sums of money are involved, blacks are either placed at the end of the line or taken off the line altogether. In the midst of the Depression, it was considered unseemly for a black man to earn more money than a white man, whatever the field of operation; thus tailback Joe Lillard of the Chicago Cardinals and tackle Ray Kemp of the Pittsburgh Pirates were dropped after the 1933 season. It would not be until 1946 that the unofficial color bar in professional football would be lifted.

Although blacks were totally excluded from baseball and now recently disenfranchised from pro football, black sports continued to develop and flourish. One of the first black basketball teams, the Renaissance Big Five, an independent club from New York, was organized in 1922. From 1932 to 1940 they toured the nation, taking on all comers, and proving themselves the best basketball squad in the country. John Henry Lewis became the light heavyweight champion in 1935. Jessie Owens won four gold medals at the 1936 Olympics in Berlin. In 1936 Dr. Ralph Waldo Emerson Jones set the groundwork for the beginning of Grambling College in Louisiana; Grambling would many years later be a major feeder of black players into professional football. Joe Louis won the heavyweight title in 1937. Henry Armstrong held three world championship boxing crowns simultaneously, in 1938.

On the college level the opposition was sharp. Many blacks continued to play collegiate football and had to go along with the new mores of the game. Ohio State's Bill Bell was not allowed to compete against Navy (the next year, however, Ohio State backed him up and he was "allowed" to play). Wilmeth Sidat-Singh of Syracuse was purposely benched when his school competed against the University of Maryland. When Georgia protested, New York University's Dave Meyer was prohibited from playing. When running back Leonard Bates of New York University in 1940 was denied the right to play against Missouri, it caused quite an upset. Fellow students held a rally, and passed out buttons reading BATES MUST PLAY, but Missouri maintained its position and Bates did not play.

The formation of the Congress of Industrial Organizations under the leadership of John L. Lewis gave blacks almost equal opportunities. They formed the Committee to Abolish Racial Discrimination and a Political Action Committee.

Through the auspices of President Roosevelt's New Deal, blacks were able to organize any number of groups (Southern Negro Youth Congress, Joint Committee on National Recovery, National Negro Conference) to strive for equal citizenship. Although these fledgling groups and committees accomplished very little, they set the stage for innovating and developing techniques that would be useful in later years.

Still within this very difficult period, Homer Harris of the University of Iowa was selected team captain in 1938—the first black to be accorded that honor in the Big Ten. Archie Harris (no relation) proved to be a great end at Indiana. Then there was Willis Ward at the University of Michigan; Horace Bell, guard, Minnesota Gophers; and Fritz Pollard, Jr., at the University of North Dakota; Jerome "Brud" Holland, end, of Cornell's Big Red football team, who won All-American. Jackie Robinson and Woodrow Wilson "Woody" Strode of University of California at Los Angeles, were also well known. Bernie Jefferson of Northwestern was known to play sixty minutes straight. These were all good men who should have gone into the mainstream but for the color of their skins.

It is very difficult to survive a society that has denied you the full potential of your brain power and substituted physical power. But when the physical power reaches unexpected levels and the rewards for these accomplishments are also denied you, it is, to say the very least, discouraging.

One unfortunate event became a blessing in this schizoid culture, helping the black man bridge the gap that has separated the races. This bloody bridge was World War II.

The G.I. Bill of Rights gave blacks a chance to attend college that they never would have without the war. Large numbers of blacks flooded the schools and the college football teams. The long years of war had depleted the football fields, and as a sign of normalcy new players were encouraged. Very slowly, the color bar began to descend. But before this could happen, the South tried a few last-stand attempts to stop integration. In November of 1946 the University of Nevada called off a game against Mississippi State when it learned that "Ole Miss" objected to Horace Gillom and Bill Bass,

Homer Harris

Jerome "Brud" Holland

Bernie Jefferson

both black, in the Nevada lineup. For the same reason Penn State canceled a game with the University of Miami.

On the other side of the coin, Charles Pierce, Harvard, became the first black to play against a Southern college—the University of Virginia at Charlottesville in 1947. Penn State's Wallace Triplett and Dennis Hoggard played in the Cotton Bowl in Dallas against Southern Methodist University. Taylor University of Indiana, with an all-white team, played at Kentucky State College—an all-black school. On November 23, 1947, the third annual Piedmont Tobacco Bowl game at Durham, North Carolina, played an all-white team against an all-black team with a nonsegregated audience. The game was a 6–6 tie. In 1948 the University of Nevada, with its participating black players, went against Tulsa in Oklahoma. Nevada beat Tulsa 65–15, aided by the outstanding plays of blacks Sherman Howard and Alva Tabor in two touchdowns. Levi Jackson became the first black grid captain at Yale in 1949. On September 30, 1950, Flint Greene, of the University of Pittsburgh, was the first black in a Southern Conference game, in North Carolina.

Levi Jackson

In 1954 the Supreme Court decision barring racial discrimination in public schools caused the South to react vehemently. The Ku Klux Klan reared its hooded head, and a cry for the return of the "old ways" was heard throughout the Southland. Georgia Tech and the University of Pittsburgh, which had a black fullback, Bobby Grier, were slated to play the 1956 Sugar Bowl game. A Georgia states' rights group protested that Grier's participation would be in violation of the "laws, customs and traditions of racial segregation." Governor Griffin of Georgia sent a telegram to Bobby Dodd, coach of Georgia Tech's football team, suggesting he join with the states' rights group. The students at Georgia Tech protested and hung Governor Griffin in effigy. Meanwhile, the University of Pittsburgh refused to back down and drop Grier from the game.

Bobby Grier

The Georgia Tech students, 2,000 strong, picketed outside the governor's mansion in Atlanta. Police patrol cars and state patrolmen armed with tear gas were ready to disperse the crowd should it become unruly. The Board of Regents of Georgia's university system refused to back Griffin's position and the game was played on January 2, 1956, with an attendance of 80,000. Bobby Grier started at fullback.

There were many college football players who, because of their abilities, will always remain well known. Some of these men are Lennie Ford and Bob Mann of Michigan; Emlen Tunnell of Iowa; Bill Willis of Ohio State; Ike Owens and Claude "Buddy" Young of Illinois; George Taliaferro of Indiana; Linwood Sexton of Wichita. The man who broke the total yardage record set by Red Grange was J. C. Caroline of Illinois. Then there was Eddie Bell of Penn State; Bob Boyd of Loyola at Los Angeles; Lamar Lundy of Purdue; Raleigh Owens of Idaho College; Ollie Matson of the University of San Francisco; and Joe "the Jet" Perry of Compton Junior College in California.

Professional football had been going through its own upheaval. During World War II, 638 National Football League players entered the service. Every team was weakened by this massive departure. Then in 1946 the postwar boom in the American economy provided more than enough money to be spent on leisure activities. Toward that end, the All-America Football Conference, a league organized by Arch Ward, sports editor of the Chicago *Tribune,* sought wealthy men to become owners of almost every franchise. The NFL felt the pinch. The new league lured 100 players away from the NFL, and for those remaining the salaries reached top levels. Jim Crowley, ex–Notre Dame star, became commissioner of the new AAFC and was able to bring quality football to New York, Brooklyn, Buffalo, Cleveland, Chicago, Miami, San Francisco, and Los Angeles.

To counteract this challenge, Bert Bell, part-owner of the Pittsburgh Steelers, was made Commissioner of the NFL. Bell would lead the NFL to unconceived levels of wealth.

The financial battle between the AAFC and the NFL placed most clubs in serious and sometimes irreparable debt. However, the Cleveland Browns of the AAFC prospered under the leadership of Paul Brown. The NFL Cleveland Rams had deserted that city for Los Angeles, but the Browns drew and had an average of 57,000 fans at each of their home games.

With the Rams' move to the West Coast, the AAFC followed suit and established the Los Angeles Dons and the San Francisco 49ers; thus football became the first major league sport to venture West.

Woody Strode

Kenny Washington

Black players were signed by both leagues for the first time since their departure in 1933. The times had changed, and the war had caused a maturing of the American people. Perhaps, too, the attitude of the Californians was somewhat different from that of the rest of the country. Californians set great store in UCLA and remembered the remarkable performances of two black players—end Woody Strode and halfback Kenny Washington—when they were undergraduates. In compliance with the wishes of the fans, these California football giants were contracted by the NFL Rams. The AAFC Browns signed Marion Motley and guard Bill Willis.

The signing of the black players in pro football almost coincided with the signing of Jackie Robinson with the Brooklyn Dodgers. With this double-barreled breakthrough, every team went all out to find long-untapped power and talent that was right before their eyes. These early football players suffered the same hostility that Robinson had, but football had yet to become the All-American game that baseball was.

Bobby Mitchell

George Marshall, owner of the Washington Redskins, refused to admit blacks to his teams, and without the infusion of fresh blood, the Redskins were weakened and ineffective. Marshall's vehement refusal to admit black players fostered picketing at Yankee Stadium by various black groups under the leadership of Jimmy Young, one of Harlem Congressman Adam Clayton Powell's disciples, when the Redskins visited New York. In 1962 Marshall wanted a new stadium built and needed federal funds to do so. His exclusion of blacks would have made him ineligible, so he made a deal for Bobby Mitchell of the Cleveland Browns. Mitchell led the NFL in catching passes that year, and Marshall was able to get his stadium built. The Redskins soon hired other blacks.

Thus the march of the Greats began.

Five-foot-four-and-one-half-inch, 160-pound Claude "Buddy" Young in 1947, with the New York Yankees, rushed for 1,275 yards and caught passes for an additional 703 yards. He later became the NFL's Director of Public Relations. Buddy was killed in an automobile accident in Terrell, Texas, on September 4, 1983, enroute to Dallas after representing the league at the memorial services for the late Kansas City Chiefs' running back Joe Delaney, who drowned while trying to save three young boys from a rain-swollen lake.

Marion Motley

I think that Motley was the best fullback I ever saw. He was a better all-around player than Jim Brown, perhaps not as good a runner but certainly a much better blocker, particularly a great pass-blocker. Nobody ever ran over him and rarely did they get around him. He was a great team player too. —Otto Graham

He was one helluva unselfish player. Marion Motley never thought about Marion Motley—only the team! —Tony Adamle

Marion Motley

Marion Motley was born in Leesburg, Georgia, on June 5, 1920, and when the family migrated to Canton, Ohio, he began to play football at McKinley High School.

In the 1930s the Massilon, Ohio, High School was coached by Paul Brown. Although McKinley High was highly successful, with nearly all-winning seasons, they lost to Brown's Massilon team each year.

After high school Motley worked in the steel mills for two years before he entered the University of Nevada where he became the star of the Nevada Wolfpack in 1941–43. During the war Motley was in the Navy and played for the powerful Great Lakes Navy squad, coached by Paul Brown, in 1944 and 1945.

In 1946 the new All-America Football Conference was established and Paul Brown was one of the major founders. The Cleveland Browns were organized as a charter member of the AAFC.

When Motley got out of the Navy, he wrote his old coach Paul Brown for a tryout. When the Cleveland team opened its training camp in Bowling Green, Ohio, Motley was there. Bill Willis, a guard, was the first black man on the team and it is said that Motley had the idea he would not have been called so soon if Willis did not need a black roommate. Now there were two blacks in the AAFC in 1946.

Motley played both on offense as a fullback and on defense as a linebacker in 1946 and 1947 before he reached his full capacity as the greatest all-around fullback in football history.

During the AAFC's four-year existence, the Cleveland Browns won all four cham-

pionships and completed an astounding regular season record. Motley was the
AAFC's all-time leading rusher with 3,024 yards. Then, due to severe financial difficulties, several of the AAFC teams, including the Browns, were absorbed into the
NFL in 1950. Motley played in the NFL for five seasons, gaining 1,696 yards lifetime,
and he led the NFL in rushing in 1950.

The 240-pound, six-foot-one-inch Motley proved an awesome power—he moved
with a speed and crunching force that perhaps no other man ever possessed. Not only
did he have speed but he also had tremendous acceleration, which made him impossible to stop on quick shots into the line or while suckering opponents with the "Motley
trap." The trap was a perfect complement to Otto Graham's explosive passing attack,
forcing the defenses to bunch up in the middle and leave the deep passing zones
undermanned.

Marion Motley is the genuine yardstick for measuring greatness. In 1968 he was
enshrined in the Pro Football Hall of Fame in Canton, Ohio.

Bill Willis

The Browns' press passbook once boasted that photographers had shot Bill at 1/500th of a second to stop the action. But at least they could stop him. That's something no opponent really ever did successfully.

—From the archives of the
Pro Football Hall of Fame

Bill Willis

Bill Willis, born in Columbus, Ohio, on October 5, 1921, and a graduate of Ohio State, came to the Cleveland Browns for a tryout. His former coach, Paul Brown, was so overwhelmed by his performance that he signed Willis to a pro contract. Brown at first thought that Willis was constantly offsides in his defensive charge, but after looking more closely he found the young ballplayer really to be extraordinarily fast and fluid. Willis played both ways—offense and defense—for the Cleveland Browns in both the AAFC and the NFL but it was as a middle guard that he received most of his kudos. He was extremely agile and was a devastating tackler, in spite of his small (by pro football standards) size—six feet, two inches and 215 pounds. His touchdown-saving tackle in the championship game against the New York Giants in 1950 helped the Browns win their first NFL title in their initial season in the league. In seven out of his eight years as a pro (1946–53), Bill Willis was an All-Pro selection.

He is now the director of the Ohio Youth Commission.

Willis was inducted into the Pro Football Hall of Fame in 1977.

Emlen Tunnell

There was rarely a game in which I wasn't amazed by Em's "reading" of plays and his catlike reactions. At first I thought he was lucky, then I realized he was just great. He was gifted with the physical quickness that a defensive safety must have and yet his biggest assets were his perception of the overall picture and his knowledge of each individual opponent.
—Frank Gifford

Tunnell was a genius for setting up the offense for a mistake. I remember once I thought for sure I had Em set up. But as soon as I threw the ball, I knew I'd been suckered. Like a flash, Tunnell was in front of the receiver and touchdown-bound for the Giants.
—Bobby Layne

Emlen Tunnell

Emlen Tunnell, who was born in Bryn Mawr, Pennsylvania, on March 29, 1925, came a long way to receive this kind of praise. As a freshman gridder at Toledo University, he suffered a broken neck and was told he would never play football again. The Army and Navy rejected him after considering him a physical risk. Finally he was accepted by the U.S. Coast Guard. After three years of active service, during which his ship was torpedoed twice, Tunnel must have thought a broken neck the least of his worries!

After the war Tunnell attended the University of Iowa and made the varsity. Tunnell had been the offensive star, but when the coach wanted to use him on defense he quit. He felt he deserved better.

Without being drafted and without an agent, the six-foot-one-inch, 200-pound Tunnell asked Tim Mara, the owner of the Giants, for a job. Mara was quite taken with the personable young man and checked his records at Iowa State. Mara offered Tunnell a $5,000 contract, plus $500 for signing and another $500 when he reached camp —a cheap investment that would pay untold dividends.

Tunnell would be the first black to play for the Giants and Mara's concern was the reception he would get from the Southern players who comprised a third of the team. With his bubbling personality, Tunnell was easily accepted and proved to be very popular.

Tunnell's rookie year in 1948 was dismal. But in 1949 he was brilliant. He intercepted 10 passes for 251 yards and 2 touchdowns and ran back 26 punts for 315 yards, finishing third in the league in both departments. Then coach Steve Owen put his "umbrella defense" into effect in 1950 to defense the Browns' passing attack. The "umbrella defense" was essentially a 4–1–6 alignment, with two defensive ends dropping back to team with the four defensive backs on passing situations. Tunnell, a safety, played the top—or back—of the umbrella-shaped alignment to perfection for years.

During Tunnell's tenure with the Giants (1948–58), the team won two Eastern divisional titles and in 1956 they beat the Chicago Bears 47–7 for the NFL title. Emlen Tunnell got his release when he found himself unable to fit into the more controlled style of play introduced by defensive coach Tom Landry. Tunnell joined the Green Bay Packers in 1959, along with new coach Vince Lombardi. In 1963 with the Giants, he became professional football's first black coach.

Today Tunnell is second in lifetime interceptions (79), first in career interception yardage (1,282), and first in punts returned (258). He held the record for lifetime punt return yardage (2,209) until it was eclipsed by Rick Upchurch of the Denver Broncos in 1979. During his brilliant career, Tunnell played in nine Pro Bowls and was named All-Pro four times.

In 1967 he became the first black and the first purely defensive specialist to be inducted in the Pro Football Hall of Fame. Emlen Tunnell died on July 23, 1975.

Len Ford

He can become the greatest all-around end in history. He has everything—great size, speed, strength, sure hands.
—Jimmy Phelan

Len Ford

Len Ford, who was born on February 18, 1926, in the nation's capital, began his athletic career at Armstrong High School in Washington, D.C. He captained the football, basketball, and baseball teams in his senior year and won All-City honors in each sport in 1942–43. While attending Morgan State in Baltimore in 1944, he achieved All-CIAA honors in his freshman year.

After a tour of naval duty, Ford entered Michigan in 1945. In 1946 and 1947 he was chosen All-American and was the driving force on Michigan's Rose Bowl squad of 1947 when they trounced the University of Southern California 49–0 on January 1, 1948.

The six-foot-five-inch, 260-pound Ford signed with the Los Angeles Dons in the AAFC as a two-way end in 1948 and caught 67 passes in 1948–49. When the Dons went out of business after the 1949 season, Paul Brown seized upon the chance to sign Ford in a special draft in 1950, even though the Cleveland Browns were well staffed with ends.

Brown used Ford as a full-time defensive end and shifted defenses to take advantage of his exuberant pass-rushing skills. After overcoming a serious facial injury in 1950, he went on to earn All-Pro honors five times, from 1951 to 1955. He finished his career with the Green Bay Packers. Ford played in four Pro Bowls and recovered 20 opponents' fumbles in his career.

Len Ford died on March 14, 1972, at the age of forty-six.

He was enshrined in the Pro Football Hall of Fame in 1976.

Joe "the Jet" Perry

When we need a touchdown, we just hand him the ball, point him in the right direction, and watch him go!
—John Woudenberg

I'm telling you, when that guy comes by to take a handoff, his slipstream darn near knocks you over. He's strictly jet-propelled.
—Frankie Albert

Joe "the Jet" Perry

Joe Perry, who was born in Stevens, Arkansas, on January 27, 1927, could have been a musician, but he wanted to study engineering. While attending David Starr Jordan High School in Los Angeles, he ran the 100-yard dash in 9.7 seconds and the 220 in 21.9. Then he put the shot 55 feet, broad-jumped 23 feet, 6 inches, and high-jumped 6 feet, 3 inches. He excelled in basketball and baseball—and broke his ankle in his first practice football scrimmage.

After graduation, his ankle healed, Perry entered Compton Junior College, where in one season he scored 22 touchdowns. Then it was time for him to serve in the military. John Woudenberg, coach of the Alameda, California, Naval Training Station football team, saw something special in the six-foot, 200-pound ace fullback, and he introduced him to Tony Morabito, owner of the San Francisco 49ers. Begrudgingly, Morabito promised to look at Perry in action. Morabito knew about Perry's track skills but was not too sure about his football talents. In the game Morabito watched, Perry carried the ball four times and scored 4 touchdowns. In the next game Perry scored 2 touchdowns in six minutes.

Now Morabito was impressed and invited Perry to a 49ers' practice session and to talk about a contract. Perry, though, was in a bind. He wanted to complete his education but now, halfway through his naval service, he wondered if he would have enough money to pursue his career. By this time the Rams had approached him and offered more money than the 49ers, but Perry liked Tony Morabito and decided to go with the San Francisco team. Morabito was bitterly criticized for hiring a black in 1948, but on Perry's first play he jetted 63 yards for a touchdown and dispelled further talk about "the hiring of blacks."

He rapidly became an established star and in 1949 he won the All-America Football Conference's rushing title. His two-year totals in the AAFC were impressive: 1,345 yards rushing, 108 points scored, and 20 receptions for 215 yards.

In 1950 the 49ers entered the NFL and Perry became the first NFL back to rush for 1,000 yards in consecutive years (1953–54). In his fourteen NFL seasons, Perry gained 8,378 yards rushing, caught 241 passes for another 1,796 yards, and scored 375 points.

Joe "the Jet" Perry was inducted into the Pro Football Hall of Fame in 1969.

Dick "Night Train" Lane

Don't throw anywhere near him. He's the best there is.

—Vince Lombardi

People go broke throwing into Lane's zone.

—Red Hickey

Dick "Night Train" Lane

Dick Lane was born in Austin, Texas, on April 16, 1928. He was raised by foster parents in Austin and attended Anderson High School. He tried out for the football and basketball varsity teams and earned letters twice.

Upon completion of high school, Lane was reunited with his natural mother in Scottsbluff, Nebraska. He enrolled at Scottsbluff Junior College, where he played one season of football and basketball before going into the Army for four years. He joined the Fort Ord team and, in 1951, playing as an offensive end, caught eighteen touchdown passes.

After his discharge, Lane worked for a while in an aircraft factory. Then, in 1952, armed with a sparse scrapbook testifying to his football feats in high school, junior college, and the Army, he went over to the Los Angeles Rams' office to ask for a tryout. Joe Stydahar, the coach, gave him that chance. Lane was offered a $4,500 contract, which he happily accepted.

He was posted on the roster as an offensive end, but, with Tom Fears and Crazylegs Hirsch holding starting spots, his offensive stay was brief. This worried Lane a great deal and he would often go to Fears's room to discuss his situation. Fears frequently played the record "Night Train" on his phonograph and when Lane entered the room a teammate would cry out, "Here comes Night Train!" The nickname stuck.

Coach Stydahar was not pleased with Lane's performance on offense and decided to try out the six-foot-two-inch, 210-pound player on defense. That was it! Lane, with his supercharged reflex action, great speed, agility, and with the nose of a winner, tore up the NFL in his rookie season. That first year's record still stands—he intercepted 14 passes in a twelve-game schedule and two of his steals were returned for touchdowns.

And like a night train bearing down, Lane became known for his almost violent open-field tackling. Lane detested the idea that he was sometimes thought to be a "dirty" player. When reporters talked about his "necktie" tackles, Lane vehemently stated that he never deliberately attempted to grab a man by the face mask. For his time and for his day, many coaches and the public defend Lane, praising his intercepting skills. Some declare him the finest cornerback ever.

In 1954 Lane moved to the Chicago Cardinals and for the second time won the league interception title. He won All-Pro acclaim for the first time in 1956.

Lane joined the Detroit Lions in 1960 and in the next four years his career would reach its zenith. He was an All-Pro cornerback from 1960 through 1963, and made six Pro Bowl appearances. As a result of injuries, he retired in 1965. He stands third on the all-time interception list with 68.

Lane was enshrined in the Pro Football Hall of Fame in 1974.

Oliver "Ollie" Matson

I've never seen anything like him. I think he's faster than George McAfee and he has lots more power. He can run over people!
—Hampton Pool

Ollie Matson

Ollie Matson fulfilled his promise of greatness, but he never had a good enough team behind him to achieve his ultimate goal: to play in an NFL championship game.

Matson was born on May 1, 1930, in Trinity, Texas. He attended George Washington High School in San Francisco and excelled in both football and track. While attending high school he clocked his fastest 100-yard dash time at 9.6 officially (and 9.5 unofficially).

Matson chose to attend the University of San Francisco, mainly because of Joe Kuharich, the football coach. In his senior season he was unanimously declared All-American and deservedly so; he had scored 21 touchdowns and gained 1,566 yards.

Although he was the first-round draft choice of the Cardinals in 1952, he decided to go out for the United States Olympic track team before turning pro. Since USF had no track program, there were many who felt that Matson couldn't make the American team after not participating in the sport for such a long time. Characteristically, Matson said, "I'll be on the boat" and he was. In the Helsinki Olympics of 1952, he ran the 400-meter race, winning a bronze medal, and was a member of the American silver medal 1,600-meter relay team.

In the meantime, Matson's USF coach, Kuharich, turned pro and became the Cardinals' coach. It was a happy union. Kuharich played Matson on defense and offense and he shared Rookie of the Year honors with Hugh McElhenny, another future Hall of Famer.

The next year Matson was in the Army and, with his six-foot-two-inch height and 220-pound weight, played for the Fort Ord Army team. In a preseason game against the Rams, Matson scored on a 91-yard pass play and a 74-yard sprint around end.

His individual and spectacular success with the Cardinals led the Los Angeles Rams to trade *nine* players for Matson in 1959. He was called "the Messiah" and he was supposed to lead Rams to the promised land of the NFL Championship. Unfortunately, Matson was unable to accomplish this, but that still takes nothing away from his abilities as a football player. He played with Los Angeles until 1962 and went on to the Detroit Lions for the 1963 season. Then, in a Detroit-Philadelphia swap in 1964, he was reunited with Kuharich.

In 1966, the Philadelphia Eagles were 5–5 for the year when they met the 49ers in Kezar Stadium. The score was 20–7, in favor of the 49ers, when Tim Brown was injured. Matson replaced Brown and responded with a bone-crushing effort and then capped off the Eagles' comeback with a leaping catch for the winning touchdown. The Eagles won the rest of their games that year and finished second in the NFL eastern division.

Never having played for a championship team, and despite the fact that he was the one that was always zeroed in on by the opponent's defenses, Matson maintained an imposing record. Throughout his career, he gained 12,844 yards on rushing, receptions, and returns. He rushed for 5,173 yards and caught 222 passes for another 3,285 yards. He scored 438 points on 73 touchdowns: 39 by running, 23 on pass receptions, 9 on kick returns, and 1 on a fumble recovery. Matson had four continuous years of All-Pro honors as a Cardinal, and Pro Bowl appearances after his first five seasons.

He was elected to the Pro Football Hall of Fame in 1972 in the first year he was eligible after the obligatory five-year retirement period.

Roosevelt "Rosey" Brown

Rosey Brown

Drafted on the twenty-seventh round by the New York Giants in 1953, in what is generally regarded as one of the greatest "sleeper" picks of all time, Rosey Brown did not seem to be a typical football player. Even with his six-foot-three-inch height and 255 pounds and twenty-nine-inch waistline, he did not look the part. Maybe it was the horn-rimmed glasses and the conservative dark suits he wore. Other than his size and speed, his inexperience and youth were the only obvious things you saw. When he joined the Giants for his first summer training camp in 1953, coach Steve Owen, though, saw something he liked and Brown not only made the team but became a starter in his first season.

Brown was born on October 20, 1932, in Charlottesville, Virginia. He attended Morgan State College in Baltimore, Maryland. There he made quite a name for himself. Brown was a two-time member of the Negro All-American eleven and co-captained the Morgan State team for two years. In the 1951 Negro Grid Classic, he played in the Polo Grounds against Wilberforce University. Overall, he won three football letters, two in wrestling (he was the heavyweight champion of the Central I.A.A.), and one in baseball.

Brown began his professional career as an offensive tackle. With his powerful arms and great strength, he was the classic pass-blocker. He also made blocks that left gaps in opponents' ranks. Utilizing his great speed and mobility to get upfield on long gainers or to protect a scrambling quarterback, Brown did everything he was supposed to do and did it superbly. Still he had a few extras: He had the special ability to pull and lead on wide ground plays, such as a pitchout to the halfback, and was the first tackle in the NFL with the speed to get out in front. Then, although he was an offensive tackle, Brown was placed in the Giants' defensive line on goal-line stands.

During Brown's tenure with the Giants, they achieved six divisional crowns and one NFL title in an eight-year stretch—surely Brown deserves a good share of the credit for the Giants' success. For eight consecutive years he was a unanimous All-Pro selection. Named to ten straight Pro Bowls, he played in nine of them. In the 1956 NFL championship game, the Giants beat the Chicago Bears 47–7. Brown handled defenses so well in that contest that he won lineman of the game honors.

Phlebitis forced his retirement after the 1965 season. He was then named assistant line coach with the offense and worked in that capacity until 1969. When Jim Trimble switched over to defense, Brown was moved up to head line coach. His work there prompted head coach Alex Webster to state, "Our offensive line has been our most consistent unit over the past two years."

In 1975 Roosevelt Brown became the second offensive lineman to be named to the Pro Football Hall of Fame on the basis of his line play alone.

Lenny Moore

Go tell Weeb Ewbank not to miss this guy because if he does, it will be the greatest mistake he could ever make.   —Joe Paterno

Lenny is so good he gives backs like me an inferiority complex.   —Alex Hawkins

He was so good that when you told people how good he was they thought you were lying.   —Andy Stopper

Lenny Moore

Lenny Moore, who was born on November 25, 1933, in Reading, Pennsylvania, was a superb running back and flanker. Moore was the number-one draft pick of the Baltimore Colts in 1956 after gaining All-American honors at Penn State. His six-foot-one-inch, 198-pound frame caused some concern. The Colts wondered if this long, thin football player could withstand the pounding of the gigantic defensive linemen that played in the NFL. Moore rapidly allayed their fears when he won Rookie of the Year honors.

Although he was assigned the combination role of flanker and running back, his main responsibility was to catch passes thrown by Colt quarterback Johnny Unitas. This deadly duo devastated the opposition's defenses.

Moore enjoyed great success when he was used outside rather than in the middle. Moore played a leading role when the Colts won the NFL Championship in 1958. He contributed 1,633 combined net yards—938 of those on receptions—and 14 touchdowns, and for the first time he won All-Pro honors. Again in 1959 Moore won All-

Pro glory and the Colts won their second straight championship. In all, Moore made All-Pro five times and played in seven Pro Bowls.

Moore went along successfully for the first five years of his career, averaging around 500 yards rushing and 40 to 50 pass receptions. Then in 1961 the Colts acquired Jimmy Orr in a trade.

Since Orr was such a superlative receiver, coach Ewbank felt he could improve his team's ground attack by placing speedy Moore inside and leaving Orr on the flank. This was a poor position for Moore; he was best outside in the open pass-catching lanes. His yardage dropped and his rushing average plummeted. Trying to get through the big men, he suffered a number of injuries. He missed his first NFL game in 1961 as a result of head injuries. A cracked kneecap caused him to miss six games in 1962. Then in 1963 an appendectomy resulted in his missing the first two games and he missed the last five games because of head injuries.

The Colts tried to trade him, but there were no takers and Moore was placed on second-team duty. In 1964 the Colts had lost the opening game to the Minnesota Vikings and in their second game with the Packers the going was rough. Moore was placed in the first quarter lineup. Unitas hit him on a 58-yard pass play for the go-ahead touchdown. Later on in the game, Moore scored the winning touchdown and Baltimore won 21–20. When the teams met again, Moore scored two game-breaking touchdowns, leading the Colts to a 24–21 victory. Those two victories broke the Green Bay Packers' three-year reign in the West and gave the divisional title to the Baltimore club.

Moore was selected the Comeback Player of the Year and the Most Valuable Player in 1964, when he scored 20 touchdowns and gained over 1,000 yards rushing and receiving after many thought his career had ended.

Moore retired in 1967 with 11,213 combined net yards in a twelve-year career, including 5,174 rushing and 363 pass receptions for 6,039 yards. Overall Moore scored 678 points on 113 touchdowns (second only to Jim Brown, who scored 126 touchdowns in his career), with stretches of eighteen straight games scoring at least 1 touchdown and eleven straight scoring at least 1 touchdown rushing, both NFL records.

Lenny Moore was elected to the Pro Football Hall of Fame in 1975.

Jim Brown

That Brown! He says he isn't Superman. What he really means is that Superman isn't Jimmy Brown!
—An admirer

Jim Brown

Jim Brown was magnificent. He was the greatest runner football has ever seen. Eight times in nine years, he led NFL in rushing and he carried the ball for a career total of 12,312 yards (a record for many years), averaging 5.2 yards (another record) every time he ran. He scored 126 touchdowns (a record that still stands), 106 by rushing (another record). Three times he was voted the Most Valuable Player in the NFL.

This man, who many consider the best football player in history, was born on February 17, 1936, in St. Simons, Georgia. Jimmy's parents separated when he was a baby and he was raised by his grandmother until he was seven, when he went to live with his mother, who was employed as a sleep-in domestic in the wealthy town of Manhasset, Long Island, New York. Life for young Jim was lonely; his mother's job made it difficult for her to spend much private time with him. As a result, his boredom and increasing restlessness found an outlet in sports. At Manhasset High School he studied just enough to be eligible to play ball. And play ball he did. He won thirteen letters. Over forty colleges offered him athletic scholarships, but on the advice of his friend Ken Molloy, a Manhasset lawyer who had previously attended Syracuse University, he elected to go to Syracuse without a scholarship. It was Molloy's feeling that Syracuse would give him a scholarship on the basis of his performance. The lawyer and a group of friends paid Brown's first-year expenses.

Brown was the only black on the football squad and was virtually ignored by the coach in his freshman year. He was so discouraged he wanted to quit, but Molloy talked him into trying again. Brown made up his mind and went all-out and became outstanding in lacrosse, basketball, and track.

The coach finally took proper notice and Brown went on to become a football hero. In his senior year as a halfback, he scored 106 points and set a Syracuse rushing record of 986 yards.

Upon graduation the Cleveland Browns drafted and signed him in 1957. Brown's first-year salary was $12,000, plus a $3,000 bonus. On his way to becoming a legend, he won Rookie of the Year honors and was named an All-Pro. The six-foot-one, 232-pound Brown was a regular and a star from his first pro game on.

For nine seasons with Cleveland, Brown's assignment was to run with the ball, and he did this better than anyone else ever did, winning the league rushing title in eight out of his nine seasons. This young fullback played in 118 NFL regular season games, averaging 20 carries every game and 104 yards rushing. In 1963 he became the only football player to ever rush for more than a mile in one season. That year Brown's 1,863-yard total placed him 845 yards ahead of second-place finisher Jim Taylor.

Brown also caught 262 passes for an additional 2,499 yards receiving in his career and scored a total of 756 points, the highest NFL total by a nonkicker. In addition, he was named an All-Pro eight times and played in nine straight Pro Bowls. Jim Brown played in three NFL championship games—1957, 1964, and 1965. The Browns lost to Detroit in 1957, won over Baltimore in 1964, and lost to Green Bay in 1965.

Having done all there was to do in football, Brown decided to retire prior to the 1966 season at the age of thirty to become a movie star.

His record is so immense that it would be difficult to list everything here. Suffice it to say he won the Hickock Award as the outstanding pro athlete in 1964 and three times—in 1958, in 1963 (a co-winner with Y. A. Tittle), and in his final 1965 season—he was awarded the Jim Thorpe Trophy as the NFL's Most Valuable Player. The durable Brown never missed a game in his nine-season career.

Jim Brown was elected to the Pro Football Hall of Fame in 1971.

Jim Parker

I used to think I could outmaneuver any big tackle, but that Parker can stay with anybody. He sure could move with me. The only way you can beat him is to make him move his head. But he is too strong and too good and too smart to do that.

—Andy Robustelli

Jim Parker

Jim Parker was one of the best of those unsung heroes who spend their entire professional careers clearing the way for the backfield stars who capture the headlines. We know a great deal more about Parker because it was his job to protect the Colts' legendary passer, Johnny Unitas. The fantastic success of the Baltimore team was in part the unprecedented passing feats of Unitas, and Unitas could not have achieved his acclaim without the foresightedness, strength, and speed of Jim Parker.

Parker excelled on defense at Ohio State, was a two-time All-American, and won the 1956 Outland Trophy as the nation's outstanding college lineman. Parker, who was born in Macon, Georgia, on April 3, 1934, attended Ohio State because of the astute eye of coach Woody Hayes, who had seen him at Scott High School in Toledo, Ohio. Hayes was so impressed he even had the six-foot-three-inch, 273-pound youngster stay at his home during Parker's freshman year at Ohio State. Upon graduation, Parker was the number-one draft choice of the Baltimore Colts in 1957.

For eleven seasons he was an extraordinary star for the Colts. During his first five and a half years as a professional, Parker played left tackle; then in 1962 he was switched to left guard. As a tackle, Parker drew the defensive end as his primary blocking assignment; as a guard, he drew the defensive tackles and could be relied upon to make gaping holes in the defense for the Colts' running backs. Parker was endowed with many admirable nicknames: "the Mother Hen," "the Guardian," "the Den Mother," "Johnny Unitas's Bodyguard." Strictly a team man, Parker refused to participate in the 1967 campaign because he felt his knee injury would damage the chances of his teammates. He was an All-Pro for eight consecutive seasons—the first four as a tackle and the last four as a guard—and played in eight Pro Bowls.

Immediately after the mandatory five-year retirement period, Jim Parker was enshrined in the Pro Football Hall of Fame in 1973, the first offensive lineman to be inducted.

Herb Adderley

He's just a class football player. He'd strengthen any team in the league.
—Fran Tarkenton

I'm just thankful he's playing for the Packers. He's the best cornerback I've ever seen.
—Bart Starr

Adderley is the most difficult man in the NFL against a passing attack for three reasons. First is his all-around ability. Second is the great help he gets from the rest of his defensive unit. Third is that Adderley himself is the best team player of any cornerback I know.
—An anonymous opponent

Herb Adderley

An All Big Ten running back at Michigan State, Herb Adderley was the number-one draft pick of the Green Bay Packers in 1961.

Slowed down by a training camp injury and unable to move incumbents Paul Hornung and Jim Taylor out of the running back jobs, Adderley was mired on the Packers' special teams until late into the year.

After regular cornerback Hank Gremminger sustained an injury on Thanksgiving Day, coach Vince Lombardi selected Adderley as Gremminger's replacement. As things turned out, he recorded his first career interception as Green Bay whipped Detroit.

Adderley became a full-time starter in 1962 and for more than ten years was the starting left cornerback for the Packers and then for the Dallas Cowboys. Until he was replaced halfway through the 1972 season, the six-foot-one-inch, 200-pound speedster missed only three games.

As a Packer, Adderley was named an All-Pro five times (1962, 1963, 1965, 1966, and 1969), played in five consecutive Pro Bowls (1963–67), and appeared in Super Bowls I and II. With the Cowboys, Adderley teamed with Mel Renfro to give Dallas a brilliant cornerback combination, a tandem that helped the team to advance to Super Bowls V and VI.

Born on June 8, 1939, in Philadelphia, Adderley played on offense exclusively at Northeast High School. At Michigan State he played defense only briefly as a middle safety in a three-man deep alignment. In the 1961 College All-Star Game against the Philadelphia Eagles, coach Otto Graham put him in on defense in an attempt to neutralize Tommy McDonald and Pete Retzlaff, the Eagles' outstanding pass receiving duo.

After winning All-Pro honors in his first two seasons on defense, Adderley quickly became totally committed to the idea of being a cornerback. He had a perfect attitude for the position. Adderley was a gambler on the field and he knew that if his guess was wrong, he would end up looking very bad: "You have to recognize that you are going to get beat once in a while. You just can't dwell on it. You just have to concentrate on not letting the same man beat you again."

Adderley was inducted into the Pro Football Hall of Fame in 1980.

David "Deacon" Jones

He can humble you.   —John Brodie

He was a real inspiration out there. I never saw him quit on a play. . . . He set a great example for the younger players.   —George Allen

When John Sanders, the scout who discovered him, said, "You know, Deacon, you're the best bargain the Rams ever drafted." Deacon replied, "You know, Johnny, you sure are one smart man."

Deacon Jones

Born in Evanston, Illinois, on December 9, 1938, David "Deacon" Jones of the Los Angeles Rams was one of the most awesome defensive ends in the history of professional football. But Jones had even more—he had charisma, style, flair. He made everything seem exciting and important. He even changed his name. Reasoning that David Jones was a name no one would remember, he dropped "David" and substituted "Deacon" because it had a religious ring to it and would be noticed.

Jones also gave football the word "sack." The word is now commonly used for the tackling of a quarterback behind the line of scrimmage. In the 1967 season, Deacon recorded twenty-six unassisted sacks.

When John Sanders was looking for a defensive back at Mississippi Vocational College and saw Jones catch a tackle-eligible pass and outrun the defensive back for a touchdown, he forgot all about the defensive back and concentrated on the speedy tackle. Jones, a six-foot-five-inch, 272-pound player, was the fourteenth-round draft pick of the Rams in 1961. He was named an All-Pro five times and played in eight Pro Bowls. Jones' great talent for tackling opponents set a record of 53 in a single season. Sportswriters began calling him "the Secretary of Defense."

Along with Lamar Lundy at the other defensive end and Merlin Olsen and Roosevelt Grier at the tackles, the Rams developed the best defensive line in football. The group was called "the Fearsome Foursome."

Jones played with the Rams from 1961 to 1971 and was with the San Diego Chargers in 1972 and 1973. He completed his football career with the Washington Redskins in 1974.

David "Deacon" Jones was inducted into Pro Football Hall of Fame in 1980.

Gale Sayers

I hit him so hard, I thought my shoulder must have busted him in two. I heard a roar from the crowd and figured he had fumbled. Then there he was, fifteen yards away and going on in for the score.
—Rosey Grier

There never was another to compare with him. What else is there to say!
—Pro Football Hall of Fame Selection Committee

Gale Sayers

Gale Sayers was born on May 30, 1943, in Wichita, Kansas. While he was still very young, his family moved to Omaha, Nebraska. At Omaha Central High School he became an all-state football and track star.

Many colleges clamored for him and he selected Kansas, where he established a memorable record. He rushed for 2,675 yards, caught passes for 408 yards, and added 835 yards on kick returns.

One of three first-round draft picks of the Chicago Bears in 1965, Sayers became the NFL Rookie of the Year. He scored 22 touchdowns and led the NFL in scoring with 132 points. (He scored 6 touchdowns in a game against the San Francisco 49ers on December 12, 1965.) In 1966 Sayers led the NFL in rushing with 1,231 yards.

Sayers dazzled the football world with his flashing feet, speedball running, and graceful ball-carrying thrusts, and earned himself the title "the Kansas Comet." Like a comet he had the brilliant burst, the defying speed, the destructive forces that could devastate every opposition defense that stood in his way.

During the ninth game of the 1968 season against the 49ers, Sayers' right knee buckled as Kermit Alexander applied a crushing tackle. Massive ligament damage demanded an immediate operation. Under the compulsion to run as he had, Sayers undertook a strenuous leg-building program. In 1969 he was slowed up, but he finished the season with a bang and attained his second NFL rushing title with a 1,032-yard total. Although not the same player, Sayers still had a remarkable season.

Then, in a summer season game against the St. Louis Cardinals in 1970, he was hit hard by a Cardinal rookie. Again he suffered severe ligament damage, but this time in his left knee. In October 1970 and in February 1971, he underwent surgery but could only play in two games. Desperately, he tried for a 1972 comeback, but by now foot and ankle problems, along with injured knees, made it impossible to continue and he played in only two games that year before he retired.

In his seven seasons (five healthy), Sayers totaled 9,435 combined net yards (4,956 yards rushing) and he scored 336 points. He was named an All-Pro for five straight years (1965–69) and he played in four Pro Bowls, winning offensive player of the game honors in three of them.

Gale Sayers was elected to the Pro Football Hall of Fame in 1977. At the age of thirty-four, Sayers was the youngest player to ever receive this honor and his effective playing time was also the shortest, but the quality of his play attests to his greatness.

Bobby Bell

Bobby Bell

Bobby Bell was an overpowering defender for the Kansas City Chiefs of the American Football League and AFC for twelve years. Born in Shelby, North Carolina, on June 17, 1940, he attended the University of Minnesota, where as an outstanding tackle he won the Outland Trophy in 1963. Bell was drafted by the Minnesota Vikings, but chose to sign with Kansas City, where he was converted into a starting linebacker by Chiefs' coach Hank Stram.

Out of Hank Stram's triple-stack defense came Bell, a six-foot-four-inch, 228-pounder, who was strong enough to handle pulling guards on sweeps, quick enough to get away from pass-blocking tackles, and fast enough to cover speedy running backs and wide receivers in pass coverage. Bell was versatility personified. He earned All-Pro honors at linebacker for eight straight years, during which time he played in two Super Bowls, six AFL All-Star games, and seven Pro Bowls. A member of the American Football League's All-Time team, Bell scored eight touchdowns, six of them coming on returns of his twenty-six interceptions (and one each on an onside kick return and a fumble recovery).

According to Hank Stram, Bell "could have played any position on the football field, and your team would have won. How many players can you say that about? At various times he was a running back, tight end, quarterback, defensive tackle, defensive end, linebacker, and he snapped for us. Most people don't know that during his entire career with the Chiefs, he snapped on every punt and placekick we had. He never missed one."

Bell was selected to the Pro Football Hall of Fame in 1983.

Bobby Mitchell

If you asked me who would be the toughest player to stop, it would be Bobby Mitchell. I don't think anybody in the history of professional football has left one team as a star (Cleveland), then gone to another team (Washington), integrated it, was switched to another position (from running back to wide receiver), and then led the league in receptions. Bobby Mitchell was the most unsung hero that I've ever known. There's never been anybody who could do more with a football. His character, his ability . . . all those things are important. If he doesn't deserve to be in the Hall of Fame, then, I guess, I don't belong there either. —Jim Brown

Bobby Mitchell

Born in Hot Springs, Arkansas, on June 6, 1935, Bobby Mitchell was a pioneer. On December 14, 1961, he was dealt by the Cleveland Browns to the Washington Redskins in the historic trade that gave the Browns the draft rights to the late Ernie Davis. Just as it is with any pioneer, there were some painful moments as Mitchell became the first black player on the Washington roster. Secretary of the Interior Stewart Udall had threatened to throw the Redskins out of D.C. Stadium, the original name of the park, unless they integrated.

Mitchell went on to do it all with Washington. Twice he led the NFL in receiving yardage, caught a league-high 72 passes in 1962, was selected to the Pro Bowl three times, and scored 53 touchdowns in seven years. Prior to playing in Washington, Mitchell was a running and receiving star for the Browns from 1958 until 1961. His 743 yards rushing in 1959 placed him fifth in the league. His total of 91 career touchdowns still ranks sixth in the NFL, behind only Jim Brown, Lenny Moore, Don Hutson, Jim Taylor, and Franco Harris.

Mitchell was voted into the Pro Football Hall of Fame in 1983.

Paul Warfield

Paul Warfield

In 1964 the Cleveland Browns drafted Paul Warfield in the first round as a defensive back. At Ohio State, Warfield had been used primarily at that position and at running back, playing wideout only sparingly in his junior and senior years. The late Blanton Collier, the Browns' coach at the time, decided to conduct an experiment with Warfield: to try him as a wide receiver during training camp. The experiment was an unqualified success. In his first season in the NFL, the fleet Warfield caught 52 passes for 920 yards and 9 touchdowns to help lead the Browns to the 1964 NFL Championship.

Warfield, who was born on November 28, 1942, in Warren, Ohio, went on to set many standards for the wideout position. In addition to his amazing quickness, he exhibited a great leaping ability and specialized in the spectacular—or "circus"—catch. And catching the ball was just the beginning for Warfield; he'd then throw a few fakes at defenders and speed on by them down the field. Opposing defenses employed many different strategies to try to stop the man, but few teams were successful.

In Warfield's thirteen seasons with the Browns and the Miami Dolphins, he caught 427 passes for 8,565 yards and 85 touchdowns. He averaged 20.1 yards per catch for his career and had seven consecutive seasons with an average of 20 yards or more per catch, both NFL records. Warfield was selected for seven Pro Bowls, but only played in six due to an injury one year. In addition, he was named to All-NFL teams as a Brown in 1968 and 1969 and as a Dolphin in 1971, 1972, and 1973. He appeared in Super Bowls VI, VII, and VIII with Miami.

Paul Warfield also has the distinction of having a President call his number in a Super Bowl. After the Dolphins defeated Baltimore to qualify for Super Bowl VI against the Dallas Cowboys, President Richard M. Nixon phoned coach Don Shula to congratulate the team. During the conversation, President Nixon, an avid football fan, said, "The Cowboys are a good defensive team, but I think you can hit Paul Warfield on that down-and-out pattern." The President's words of advice were widely reported in the papers, however, and coach Tom Landry of the Cowboys was ready. Although Shula ran the play during the game, the Cowboys, who won the Super Bowl, double-teamed Warfield and he couldn't get open. Coach Landry later commented, "We made sure they didn't complete that pass on us." The Dolphins, undaunted, went on to win the next two Super Bowls and Paul Warfield was a major contributor to the team's success.

Paul Warfield was elected to the Pro Football Hall of Fame in 1983.

Willie Davis

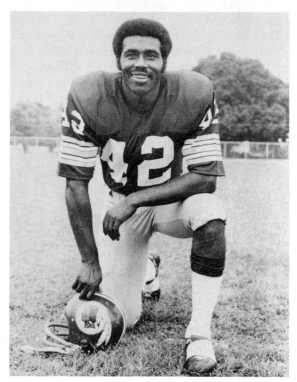

Willie Davis

A defensive lineman, Willie Davis was blessed with the three attributes—speed, agility, and size—that Coach Vince Lombardi considered most important for a successful football lineman. Davis, a dynamic six-foot-three-inch, 245-pound athlete, also had such intangible assets as dedication, intelligence, and leadership that enabled him to climb above almost every other player. In his ten seasons with the powerful Green Bay Packers, he became widely recognized as one of the very best defensive ends ever to play in the NFL.

The Grambling graduate was an all-star NFL selection five times in six years, spanning 1962 through 1967. He participated in six NFL championship games and the first two Super Bowls. He was a Pro Bowl choice five years in a row. He played twelve seasons, the first two with the Cleveland Browns in 1958 and 1959, and the balance with Green Bay, and didn't miss one of the 162 games played in that period. By the time of his retirement in 1969, Willie had recovered 21 opponent's fumbles; just 1 shy of the all-time record.

Born in Lisbon, Louisiana, on July 24, 1934, Willie was one of three children who his mother, Nodie, raised by herself. Willie grew up in Texarkana, Arkansas, where he starred in football, basketball, and baseball at Booker T. Washington High School. His athletic skills earned him a scholarship to Grambling, where he became a team captain for two years.

Willie was a seventeenth-round draft pick of the 1956 Browns, but an Army call cut short his first Cleveland training camp. While in the service, he played football and won All-Army and All-Service awards. After his return to the 1958 Browns, he was shifted from position to position on both offensive and defensive squads until coach Paul Brown ticketed him for the regular offensive tackle position. In the spring of 1960, however, he was traded to the Green Bay Packers for an offensive end, A. D. Williams. Since Brown had often used the threat of a trade to Green Bay (then considered an equivalent of Siberia) to spur on his players, Willie was not only hurt and very upset but considered quitting. Once he arrived in Green Bay, Coach Lombardi quickly assured him that he, not Brown, had engineered the trade because he needed a top-flight defensive end and that he thought Davis fit the bill. The rest is history.

Davis was elected to the Pro Football Hall of Fame in 1981.

Willie Brown

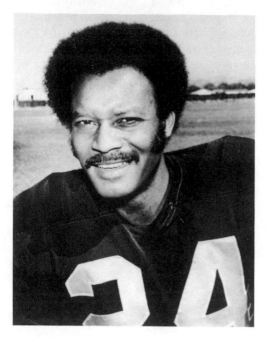

Willie Brown

A defensive back, Willie Brown joined the Denver Broncos in 1963 as an unheralded and untried free agent who just happened to possess all the natural tools of the perfect cornerback: speed, size, mobility, aggressiveness, determination, and a keen football sense. As it turned out, all the youngster from Grambling needed was a little time and playing experience.

The six-foot-one-inch, 210-pound rookie became a starter six games into his inaugural campaign, and won All-AFL acclaim in his second season in 1964. By the time the Broncos traded him to the Raiders in 1967, he was a much coveted standout.

It probably is not pure coincidence that during Brown's tenure in Oakland from 1967 through 1978 the Raiders' won-lost mark was the best in pro football and the Oakland club appeared in three AFL and six AFC title games and Super Bowls II and XI.

As a leader, Brown inspired his teammates with his willingness to play hurt. He played with his arm in a cast, a pulled groin muscle, and a broken thumb throughout the 1971 season, yet permitted only 10 pass receptions in his area. Despite other severe injuries, Willie missed only nineteen games in sixteen seasons.

Willie Brown, born on December 2, 1940, in Yazoo City, Mississippi, was enshrined in the Pro Football Hall of Fame in 1984.

Charley Taylor

Charley Taylor

Born in Grand Prairie, Texas, on September 28, 1941, and educated at Arizona State, Charley Taylor, the great Redskins' wide receiver, played for Washington from 1964 until 1977. Big and fast, he provided the Redskins with their greatest offensive threat in years. Combining blazing speed with instinct and agility, he was one of the most feared pass receivers in the NFL. Taylor established an NFL career receiving record with 649 receptions, which was broken by Charlie Joiner in 1984. He is presently the Redskins' receivers coach. Taylor was selected into the Pro Football Hall of Fame in 1984.

Black Pro Quarterbacks

One of the great barriers to the black football player has been his inability to get the opportunity to play the quarterback position.

> I feel many times the problem is that many black quarterbacks are switched to other positions. In high school, the quarterback is the best athlete. I don't know why there aren't more black quarterbacks in the league. Maybe the answer is that there are no black coaches, and very few black general managers.
>
> —James Harris

Until recently the only place a black player could be a quarterback would be on his college team. When it was time to go pro, the black quarterback learned to switch positions. It was an unwritten law that is now being tested. There were a few black players who had a fling at it: Joe Gilliam with the Pittsburgh Steelers and later with the Washington Federals of the United States Football League; Marlin Briscoe with the Denver Broncos; Freddie Solomon of the San Francisco 49ers and Miami Dolphins; Johnnie Walton for the Philadelphia Eagles and then with the Boston Breakers in the United States Football League; John "J. J." Jones of the New York Jets; Sandy Stephens with the New York Titans of the American Football League, who later fled to Canada; James Harris, who quarterbacked for the Buffalo Bills, Los Angeles Rams, and the San Diego Chargers; Vince Evans with the Chicago Bears; Doug Williams with the Tampa Bay Buccaneers, who in August of 1983 signed a five-year pact with the Oklahoma Outlaws of the fledgling United States Football League; and Reggie Collier with the Birmingham Stallions of the United States Football League.

Joe Gilliam

Marlin Briscoe

John "J. J." Jones

Sandy Stephens

Freddie Solomon

Johnnie Walton

Vince Evans

James Harris

The first time in pro football that two black quarterbacks played against each other was in October 1979: Doug Williams, Tampa Bay, against Vince Evans, Chicago Bears.

In January of 1980, Doug Williams brought Tampa Bay to the championship game of the National Football Conference. James Harris says of Doug Williams, "As a pro, I think everyone realizes he has great talent. What people don't realize is that he's a student of the game. For a quarterback to make it in this league, whether he's white or black, it depends on three things—it depends on the individual, the people around him, and the coach. Doug Williams was lucky; he had all the components."

As of 1985 there were four starting black quarterbacks in American professional football. In the United States Football League Doug Williams calls the signals for the Arizona Outlaws, Walter Lewis for the Memphis Showboats, and Vince Evans for the Denver Gold. While in the NFL Warren Moon returned from the Canadian Football League in 1984 to take on the quarterbacking chores for the Houston Oilers.

Doug Williams

Reggie Collier

Grambling State University

It is impossible to conclude this chronicle of America's black football stars without paying proper homage to the role played by the legendary all-black Grambling State University. Now coached by the equally legendary Eddie Robinson, the school was established back in 1936 by Dr. Ralph Waldo Emerson Jones. The school is located some three hundred miles northwest of New Orleans. The remarkable success of this college has been its ability to continually churn out scholar-athletes who have gone on to star in professional sports.

From the time Paul "Tank" Younger came out of Grambling in 1948, the Tigers have been well known for their steady production of players into the professional ranks. Every National Football League franchise has had at least one Grambling player on its official regular-season roster. Numerous Grambling graduates have also starred for Canadian Football League teams, the now-defunct World Football League, and the USFL.

Paul "Tank" Younger, the first prominent NFL player from an all-black college, is now the highest-ranking black executive in pro football.

Eddie Robinson

Eddie Robinson

Coach Eddie Robinson, son of a laborer, was born in Baton Rouge, Louisiana, in 1919. He was the first in his family to graduate from college. At Leland College he was a single-wing tailback.

Dr. Ralph Waldo Emerson Jones hired Robinson to coach football in 1940 when the school was known as the Louisiana Negro Normal and Industrial Institute. Robinson has established auspicious career credentials: 305 victories, twenty straight winning seasons, and 8 or more triumphs per year in the last ten years; his teams have produced over 160 pro players, the most ever produced by one coach, as well as attracting over 2.7 million to football games since 1969.

Without a doubt, Eddie Robinson is cut from another cloth. He is a nondrinker and nonsmoker and is very firm in his religious beliefs. There was a time when Robinson compelled all of his athletes to attend the New Rocky Valley Southern Baptist Church on Sunday morning by distributing their weekly $10 laundry allowance there. "They should believe in the Deity," he said. The only known vice that can be attributed to Robinson is that he sometimes diagrams plays during the sermon.

Robinson will not condone racially motivated behavior or Black Power statements —or the raised fist unless it has a degree or money in it. Exaggerated Afro-styled hair, beards, and touchdown "boogies" in the end zone are forbidden. Of course, he has been accused of being an Uncle Tom, but Robinson's replies are "If you think you have two strikes on you because you're black and you aren't allowed to do anything, then you'll strike out" or "I don't care what they [black militants of the sixties] call me. They are not going to relay their message through me. What I say, the youth is going to read. If a man doesn't stand up for what he believes, he's not worth a damn."

Whatever is said about Robinson, his success is undeniable. His students revere him. They exhibit discipline, unity, and a sense of fairness and pride born of deserved labor. Mike Moore, one of his students, explained, "Around here education comes first. . . . We're taught never to count on just one thing. That time in pro ball may be short if it comes at all. Then we're taught to be proud Americans." Others have called him "the Wizard," "the Godfather," "the Legend," "Mr. Football," "the Mastermind," and "Mr. Inventor."

Despite his legend, Eddie Robinson was given his only interview by the NFL in 1978 for the Los Angeles Rams' coaching job. The job went to George Allen. There was an outcry of racism but, philosophically, Robinson said, "When Mr. Rosenbloom talked to me, he also talked to Dan Reeves, offensive coordinator of the Dallas Cowboys. He didn't hire Reeves. It wasn't because he was white. He didn't hire me either, and it wasn't because I was black."

For over forty years now, Robinson has been turning out superior football players, as well as a number of fine citizens. His aim remains the same—to be the finest coach in the United States. However, he remarks, "But then there are people like Bear Bryant and Woody Hayes who have made it hard for me to be the best."

Even though the NFL stands to be a great loser in not hiring Eddie Robinson, he is not an anguished, unhappy man. He says, "You know when they call the roll, I would like to feel I have made some positive contribution to society, some little something. Coaching for coaching's sake is fine, but there are other things—like teaching boys to compete in society—and I don't know if I could have done some things I've done anywhere else than Grambling."

BLACK HEISMAN TROPHY WINNERS

Ernie Davis, Syracuse, a big, rugged six-foot-two-inch, 212-pounder, played left halfback and was his team's leading ground gainer for three seasons. In 1961 he became the twenty-seventh recipient of the Heisman Trophy and the first black athlete to be so honored. After graduating from college, Davis was signed by the Cleveland Browns for the then-astronomical sum of $80,000. Shortly after signing his contract and before he had suited up for his first game, he was struck down by leukemia. He died on May 18, 1963, after a sixteen-month battle for survival. Davis was elected posthumously to the Pro Football Hall of Fame in 1979.

Mike Garrett. In three years with USC, he gained 4,876 net yards in rushing, passing, receiving, punt returns, and kickoff returns. He won the Heisman Trophy in 1965. From college Garrett went on to play five years with the Kansas City Chiefs and four years with the San Diego Chargers.

O. J. Simpson. He piled up a monumental record in his two seasons at USC. In eighteen games he gained 3,187 yards. Simpson scored 13 touchdowns in 1967 and 21 in 1968. His 40 carries in the UCLA game his senior year gave him an NCAA record of 334 for one season. In 1968 he became the second Heisman Trophy winner from USC. His NFL record for most yards gained in a season (2,003 in 1973 with the Buffalo Bills) was broken in 1984 by Eric Dickerson of the Los Angeles Rams.

Johnny Rodgers of Nebraska. He won the Heisman Trophy in 1972. Operating as a punt returner, pass receiver, and running back, he broke offensive records by the dozens. In his three-year career, he racked up 5,586 all-purpose yards for an NCAA record. Rodgers had an outstanding career in the Canadian Football League and with the San Diego Chargers.

Tony Dorsett, Pittsburgh, 1976. Now the star running back of the Dallas Cowboys, he finished the 1982 season with a scorching 99-yard touchdown run against the Minnesota Vikings, the longest run from scrimmage in NFL history. He climaxed 1984 with his seventh 1,000 yard season.

Earl Campbell, Texas, 1977. For several years the focal point of the Houston Oilers' running attack, he now plays for the New Orleans Saints.

Charles White of USC. He was the Heisman Trophy winner in 1979 who, from his running back position, led the nation with an average of 194.1 yards per game in his senior year. Drafted by the Cleveland Browns, he is now helping them in their quest to win the NFL Championship.

Billy Sims, Oklahoma, 1978. He is now the Detroit Lions' number-one running back. He gained 1,303 and 1,437 yards in his first two pro seasons, 1979 and 1980, scoring 13 touchdowns each year.

Marcus Allen, the brilliant, versatile running back of the Los Angeles Raiders, was the Heisman Trophy winner of 1981. While at Southern Cal he set an all-time single season rushing record of 2,342 yards. He was named Rookie of the Year and All-Pro in his first season with the Raiders. He capped the 1983 season by being named MVP of Super Bowl XVIII, where he rushed for a record 191 yards and scored two touchdowns, one of them for a record 74 yards. He was tied in 1984 with Mark Clayton of the Dolphins for most touchdowns scored (18), while rushing for 1,168 yards and catching passes for 758 yards. He's not only a superlative runner and receiver, but he can pass as well—a triple threat man par excellence!

Herschel Walker. As a junior, he won the Heisman Trophy at the University of Georgia in 1982. The six-foot-one-inch, 222-pound running back amassed an unbelievable 5,097 yards rushing (an NCAA record for yards rushing in three seasons). He left Georgia with a year left of eligibility to sign a contract with the New Jersey Generals of the United States Football League for $1.5 million per annum and led the league in rushing yardage in his first year of play.

George Rogers, South Carolina, 1980. Now a star running back with the New Orleans Saints, in his initial 1981 pro season he set an NFL rookie rushing record (1,674 yards) and scored 13 touchdowns.

Mike Rozier, Nebraska, 1983. In his last year, he became the second collegiate star to rush for more than 2,000 yards in a season, averaging nearly eight yards per carry. As first choice in the USFL draft, he was selected by the Pittsburgh Maulers, who signed him to a multimillion-dollar contract.

BLACK FOOTBALL STARS OF TODAY

Wes Chandler, the former New Orleans Saints' wide receiver, caught 65 passes in 1980 for an outstanding 15.0 yards per catch average. He has now brought his finesse to the San Diego Chargers' lightning offensive squad.

Ottis "OJ" Anderson, St. Louis Cardinals' running back, holds the club all-time rushing records, including the five times in which he has rushed for over 1,000 yards in a season.

Running back Joe Cribbs who played for the Buffalo Bills before joining the USFL. His 1982 90-yard per game ground-gaining average led the NFL.

John Jefferson

Walter Payton, the Bears' running back par excellence. His 1984 season was the eighth in which he gained more than 1,000 yards rushing (1,684) for a career total to date of 13,309 yards, topping the great Jim Brown's all-time rushing record.

Hugh Green of the Tampa Bay Buccaneers, a premier linebacker.

Lawrence "LT" Taylor of the New York Giants, a 1983 Pro Bowler, the most respected linebacker in the league today.

Kelvin Bryant. Outstanding running back with the Philadelphia Stars of the USFL.

Wide receiver Trumaine Johnson of the Chicago Blitz of the USFL. He had 32 touchdown receptions in four seasons at Grambling and scouts rated him the best receiver in the draft. He led the USFL in 1983 with 81 receptions for 1,322 yards and 10 touchdowns.

Running back William Andrews of the Atlanta Falcons. In 1982 he led the NFC in total yardage (1,076), rushing for 573 yards and amassing 503 more on forty-two catches.

John Corker, six-foot-six-inch, 235-pound linebacker for the Michigan Panthers of the USFL, led the league in its initial 1983 season with 28 sacks, twice as many as his nearest competitor.

Ed "Too Tall" Jones of the Dallas Cowboys, one of the finest defensive ends in the game. He took the year of 1979 off to pursue an ill-fated wrestling career.

Drew Pearson, the Dallas Cowboys' premier receiver, retired at the end of the 1983 season. In his eleven years with Dallas he averaged 13.4 yards per pass reception. He played in eight NFC and NFL championship games.

Brilliant wide receiver Jerry Butler of the Buffalo Bills. He set a team record by catching 4 touchdown passes in a single game.

Dallas Cowboy tight end Billy Joe DuPree, one of the most respected pass targets in pro football.

James Lofton and his Green Bay Packers' teammate John Jefferson may just be the best pair of wide receivers in the NFL.

Wide receiver John Stallworth of the Pitts-burgh Steelers. An outstanding athlete, he suffered by playing in the shadow of Lynn Swann. With Swann's retirement, Stallworth has received the recognition he deserves.

Wide receiver Wesley Walker of the New York Jets, one of the fastest receivers in the game. He caught 6 touchdown passes in 1982, which gave him a 5.3 touchdowns per year average for his six seasons of play.

Freeman McNeil, the New York Jets' superb running back. He led the NFL with 786 yards rushing and a 5.2 yards per rush aver-age in the 1982 season. Beset by injuries in 1983, and again in 1984, he nevertheless was leading his conference in yards rushing (1,070—a team record) when a broken rib forced him to miss the last games of the sea-son.

Wilbert Montgomery, Philadelphia Eagles' running back by way of Abilene Christian College. At this point in his career, he seems destined to break the marks of the famed Steve Van Buren, the team's record holder for rushing yards and attempts.

Six-foot-eight-inch tall wide receiver Harold Carmichael of the Philadelphia Eagles was one of the truly dominating players in the recent years. He is one of the top ten all-time pass receivers. In his thirteen pro years, he caught 589 passes, for 8,978 yards. He established an NFL record for most consecutive games in which he caught a pass—127.

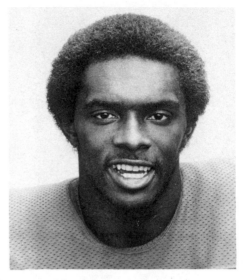

Sammy White of the Minnesota Vikings is as good a wide receiver as there is in the NFL.

Running back Greg Pruitt was the leading rusher for the Cleveland Browns from 1973 to 1981. He was traded to the Los Angeles Raiders in 1982, and in the following season, 1983, established an NFL record for punt return yards in one season, 666.

Tight end Ozzie Newsome of the Cleveland Browns. His coach at Alabama, the late Bear Bryant, called him the finest receiver he had ever seen.

Art Monk, wide receiver of the Washington Redskins, set an all-time season high with 106 receptions in 1984 and gained 1,372.

San Diego Chargers' wide receiver Charlie Joiner set a new league career reception record (650) in 1984, his sixteenth pro season, and is closing in on Don Maynard's career pass catching record of 11,834 yards. No wonder he's called "Mr. Reliable" and "Old Man River."

Earl Cooper, San Francisco 49ers' fine running back.

Eric Dickerson running back of the Los Angeles Rams, set a rushing record for rookies (1,808 yards) in 1983, while leading the league in carries (390). But this was only the beginning. In his second pro season, he set two new records: 2,150 yards in rushing and the highest-ever combined rushing and receiving yardage in a season. And the best is yet to come!

Despite the prestigious list of black Hall of Famers and the acknowledgment of present-day black football greats, it is not a time to be deceived into thinking that blacks have it made—in football or anywhere else. America is now going through a difficult period in history. A recession bordering on major depression has decimated many a dream. A conflict with the oil barons of the Persian Gulf has minimized an American way of life. The threats of war and nuclear destruction have sent the American people scurrying for a safe harbor. That safe harbor has always been a definite swing to the right and that swing of conservatism could affect the progress of black people in competing for their rightful share in America.

The time stop in football has been superbly represented by Ed Garvey, Executive Director, NFL Players Association. The NFLPA is the result of the merger between the NFL and the AFL in 1970. The NFLPA was formed so that football players could establish benefits, pensions, hospitalization, etc. Ed Garvey took a giant step with the NFL in the following memorandum in November 1979:

Proposed Press Release

The following is a proposed press release sent to each NFL team's player representative by Ed Garvey, Executive Director, NFL Players Association:

I am today speaking on behalf of the Board of Representatives of the NFLPA on an issue that we deem to be of extreme importance. That issue is racism in the National Football League and the NFL as a racist institution.

First, we must review some of the facts. Blacks were first allowed into the NFL in limited numbers in the forties and fifties. White quotas were obviously in effect and certain positions, such as quarterback, middle linebacker, center, and guard, were reserved to whites. Blacks started coming into the NFL as players in large numbers in the sixties and seventies. Yet it is incredible that the first time in the NFL's sixty-nine-year history that two teams with black quarterbacks faced each other was in 1979.

Blacks have been denied entry into all other phases of the NFL. Apologists for the NFL point to a few front-office positions but always fail to go beyond the surface.

1. There are not now and never have been any black general managers;
2. There are not now and never have been any black head coaches;
3. There are now no black offensive or defensive coordinators;
4. Of 290 coaches in the NFL, fewer than 10 are black, when nearly half of the players are black;
5. There are no black owners and probably will be none in the foreseeable future;
6. There are no blacks in positions of importance in the NFL office. Buddy Young's role as Director of Personnel is strictly [sic] ceremonial. He has never visited the Union offices to discuss policy, nor does he work with the players. The other black in the NFL office lectures players on drugs, women, and booze and his performance is a standing joke among our players.

We believe it is time to ask—no, demand—that Pete Rozelle get in step with the realities of the times. He is responsible for a consistent pattern of racism in the league. He tells us that he is urging owners to hire "qualified" blacks as coaches but can't explain why so few are hired. Can he be telling us that there are only nine qualified black former players who could coach in the National Football League? Are there no qualified blacks to become general managers? Public relations directors? Head coaches?

His normal response to problems is to suggest that it is a matter between the Union and the Management Council. As head of the NFL, he cannot duck this issue by pushing it off on someone else.

Pete Rozelle decided that the NFL should establish a journalism scholarship for black sportswriters. The act belongs in the Chutzpah Hall of Fame. Buddy Young went to Howard University to announce the award. How about a scholarship program for blacks as administrators? How about blacks in policy-making decisions in the twenty-eight clubs?

We, the Union, believe it is time to stop the hypocrisy. We think it is time that Pete Rozelle comes forward to discuss this vital issue. Affirmative action is needed now in the National Football League. We are tired of trying to explain to black players that their association with the NFL will terminate with the end of their playing career. While the record in other sports is bad, the NFL is a monument to racism in professional team sports.

- ☐ I ENDORSE THE ABOVE STATEMENT.
- ☐ I FEEL IT IS TOO STRONG AND SHOULD BE TONED DOWN.
- ☐ I FEEL IT IS NOT STRONG ENOUGH.
- ☐ WE SHOULD AVOID THE ISSUE.

DATE
SIGNATURE _____

Whether Garvey's press release succeeded or not, it was not half as important as the fact that it was written and dispersed to players, managers, and the press. It was a step toward the recognition of a wrong and a statement of awareness.

BASKETBALL

Basketball is truly the only major sport that originated in the United States. Its inventor, Dr. James A. Naismith, a Canadian, was born on November 6, 1861. He was an outstanding athlete at McGill University and later entered Presbyterian Theological College to study for the ministry. In 1890 he transferred to the International Young Men's Christian Association Training School in Springfield, Massachusetts (later called Springfield College).

During the long, cold New England months, Dr. Luther S. Gulick, head of the school's physical education department, became concerned about the disruptive, undisciplined behavior of the young men in his charge. It was too late in the year for them to play football and too early for baseball. He charged Dr. Naismith with devising a game that would occupy the time and energy of these future YMCA training instructors. Considering the limits of indoor space, and through trial and error, Dr. Naismith, using two half-bushel peach baskets on poles and a soccer ball, invented basketball in 1891.

While the sport was played with enthusiasm at the YMCA Training School, its popularity did not spread immediately. The training school graduates took the game with them as they were sent to various YMCAs across the country. At first many considered basketball to be merely a YMCA exercise. But interest in the sport persisted—the children who learned the game took it to high school and then to college. By the late 1890s, such schools as Iowa, Yale, Geneva, Nebraska, Trinity, Kansas, Wesleyan, and Penn had varsity teams. Then, too, the rules of basketball were such that women could play. Women's colleges such as Smith, Vassar, Wellesley, and Bryn Mawr soon adopted the game.

An intercollegiate league was established in 1899, but because of its YMCA origins basketball was still considered a church game by many. Then in the early 1900s, the United States Navy, which also suffered from a limitation of space and a need to occupy the sailors' time, made basketball a mandatory sport. With the sanction of the Navy, basketball really became competitive. It is said that some college basketball coaches even waited outside of naval bases for basketball-playing sailors to receive their discharges.

The YMCA dropped basketball from its program for a while because the sport, while drawing big crowds, also attracted fans who were often rowdy. The game continued, however, in armories and dance halls. The rental costs of these buildings made it almost impossible to pay the players a prescribed amount of money, but admission was charged and any money left over after the rent was paid was divided among the players. The date of the first professional game is uncertain, but the evidence points to a game played in Trenton, New Jersey, in 1896.

Logistically, basketball was an indoor sport that required large arenas. These were not available outside of large metropolitan areas, so cities such as New York, Brooklyn, and Pittsburgh were essential to the game's early growth. The first black team to gain a reputation between 1900 and 1915 was the Smart Set of Brooklyn, soon followed by the St. Christophers, the Alpha Big Five, and the Spartans of New York City; the Leondis Five of Pittsburgh; the Jersey City Athletic Club; and the Williamsburg Colored Men's Association.

With the advent of World War I, basketball went on a decline. Many of the players were drafted and the armories were not available. As a result, there were very few basketball games played. However, an exception to this hiatus on the sport's development were two teams in Pittsburgh—a white team called the Coffey Club, in honor of Rabbi Jake Coffey, and the all-black Leondis Five—both of them having strong reputations. They played against each other frequently over a six-year span, exchanging victories in close games.

On the college level, few blacks were involved at first because of the unwritten decree that blacks and whites could not play on the same team. In addition, it was difficult for a coach to make separate accommodations for blacks, particularly in the South. Nevertheless, several black players excelled in the postwar years: Wilbur Woods played for the University of Nebraska; Reverend John Johnson was the first black to play basketball for Columbia University; Paul Robeson played at Rutgers; Maynard Garner of Hamilton College was captain and played center; John and Samuel Barnes played at Oberlin. Dr. Ralph J. Bunche (later a Nobel Peace Prize winner) played outstanding ball for UCLA. More recent black all-time collegiate stars include Maurice Stokes of St. Francis, Bill Russell of the University of San Francisco, Oscar Robertson of Cincinnati, Elgin Baylor of Seattle University, Wilt Chamberlain of the University of Kansas, Jimmy Walker of Providence, Cazzie Russell of the University of Michigan, Lew Alcindor (now Kareem Abdul-Jabbar) of UCLA, David Thompson of North Carolina State, Adrian Dantley of Notre Dame, Marques Johnson of UCLA, Earvin "Magic" Johnson of Michigan State, Phil Ford of North Carolina, and Ralph Sampson of the University of Virginia.

Perhaps the greatest all-black southern college team was the club that represented Xavier College of New Orleans in the mid-1930s. The Xavier Ambassadors won 67 games and lost 2 in four seasons. The teamwork and ball-handling skills that made Xavier so potent were due not only to ability but to an extended period of togetherness. The entire lineup—Bray, Rhodes, Colege, Gant, and McQuitter—had played together at Wendell Phillips High School in Chicago and all of them went on to Xavier

The Xavier Ambassadors

College. After a total of eight years together, they knew each other well and what could be expected of each of them. Their outstanding record supports this.

Basketball on the professional side for blacks was limited entirely to traveling teams. Very few blacks managed to go to college and play with collegiate teams in the North, and the majority who did play competed for segregated black colleges in the South. And so, in order to play, you had to go on the road—very much reminiscent of the early baseball players.

One of the first great black basketball teams was the Renaissance Big Five, an independent team from New York City that was organized in 1922 by Bob Douglas and that was undeniably the best team in the country from 1932 to 1935.

Robert Douglas

Bob Douglas

I saw my first basketball game at 52nd Street on Tenth Avenue in 1903. I was then working at 312 Manhattan Avenue near 114th Street as a doorboy for $22 a month. I roomed downstairs in the basement, where I paid the superintendent $3 a month for the room.

I came from St. Kitts, British West Indies, three years before, and soccer was the game played there. But when I saw that basketball game, I thought it was the most remarkable game ever.

Around that time George Abbott, J. Foster Phillips, and I formed the Spartan Field Club, which took part in all types of games. We played soccer, cricket, basketball, and track. The basketball team was known as the Spartan Braves and we were very successful.

We played in an amateur league called the Metropolitan Basketball Association. It consisted of three teams in the New York area; they were the Alpha Big Five, the Puritans, and the St. Christophers. We played games as far away as Pittsburgh to meet the Leondis Five and Chicago to go against the Forty Club. We played our home games at Young's Casino at 131st Street and Park Avenue.

Members of the Spartan Braves were Frank Forbes (who later played in the Negro National League and became a prominent boxing official with the New York Athletic Commission), Leon Monde, George Capers, Hilton Slocum, Richie Wallace, Hobey Johnson, Jimmy Ross, J. Foster Phillips, Charles Robinson, and me. Despite being the coach and owner, upon occasion I also took the floor.

Near the end of 1921, the Metropolitan Basketball Association, who protected against professionalism in amateur basketball, directed us to release Frank Forbes and Leon Monde because they'd played sports for money during the summer months. We ignored the association and, by doing this, they accused the Spartans of threatening to wreck the organization.

But you know, I loved the professional game so much and needed a real home court, so in October of 1923 I approached William Roach, owner of the Renaissance Ballroom on 137th Street and Seventh Avenue. I asked him about having a basketball team playing there and he said, "Definitely not. You guys will play rough basketball and those rough crowds will break up my place." But I guaranteed him we wouldn't do any damage to his ballroom. Since it was a new place, first opening in 1920, I told him the team would give the place publicity and I'd name the team the Renaissance, although I didn't like the name. I wanted to call the team the Spartans after my old club. I told Roach he'd make money with the percentage of the gates he'd receive. He finally said yes.

So on November 30, 1923, the Renaissance Big Five played their first professional game at the ballroom against the Collegiate Big Five. We won 28–22.

On that first team we had Harold Slocum, who was the captain until 1932, the year he left the squad. We also had Frank Forbes, Harold Mayers, Zack Anderson, Hy Monte, and Leon Monde.

The following year Clarence "Fats" Jenkins, George Fiall, James "Pappy" Ricks, and "Clix" Garcia joined the team. Monde, Harold Jankins, Anderson, Forbes, and Wardell left. The substituting of Walter Saunders for Garcia in 1925 and the addition in 1926 of Eyre "Bruiser" Saitch were the only changes in the club until 1930, when Fiall was replaced by Bill Yancey, who also played shortstop with the New York Black Yankees of the Negro National League. In 1932 Johnny "Casey" Holt made the grade and replaced Harold Mayers. I'd say that the team I had from 1932 to 1935 was the greatest that ever played any kind of basketball.

That team had Charles "Tarzan" Cooper, Wee Willie Smith, Holt, Saitch, Yancey, Ricks, and Jenkins. We won eighty-eight consecutive games. That team used to beat the hell out of the famous Celtics [white team].

Pappy Ricks left the Rens after the 1935 season. John Isaac replaced Jackie Bethards in 1936 and then Al Johnson replaced Yancey.

John Isaac

In 1939 we had William "Pop" Gates, who was a standout at Benjamin Franklin High School; Clarence "Puggy" Bell, a great player from the Harlem YMCA, and Zack Clayton, a beautiful defensive ballplayer from Central High School in Philadelphia. In addition to these three, Jenkins, Cooper, Smith, Isaac, and Saitch made up the team.

You know, every October we'd try out dozens of young players who hoped to make the team. I'd pay the fare and all the living expenses while each youngster was making his bid. If they didn't make it, I would pay his fare to go home.

I paid all the living expenses of the members of the team while they were on the road. Guys like Fats Jenkins and Tarzan Cooper were getting $250 a month, plus expenses, plus $3 a day for meals—which was big money at that time.

In later years, the highest-paid player on the team was Pop Gates, who got $1,000 per month. Funny thing . . . when we broke up, he went with the Harlem Globetrotters and only got $600 a month.

The team would cover about thirty-eight thousand miles each season and they'd travel in the team bus. The club would appear at places like Iowa, Wyoming, New Orleans, and other faraway sections of the country. I'd never travel with the team; I would stay in New York and arrange the bookings and map out the itinerary. We had a club secretary, Eric Illidge; a trainer, Doc Bryant; and my assistant, Frank Richards, who handled the publicity. He got out releases, posters, and whatnot.

For all the years that the team was in existence, we treated the fans to some of the classiest basketball in the world. At the end of the 1939 season, we'd won 112 games and lost 7. In the years after that, we never failed to win at least 100 games every season. In Chicago in 1939, we went through the toughest clubs in the country to win the first world professional basketball championship tournament on record. The victory in Chicago was one of the team's greatest achievements. The Rens had brought full realization to the world that they were the best.

The 1939 world champions

WILLIAM SMITH × TARZE COOPER × JOHN ISAAC × WILLIAM GATES × PUGGY BELL × EYRE SAITCH × ZACK CLAYTON × FATS JENKINS

In 1948 Mike Duffey, president of the white National Basketball League [he also had a club in the league, the Anderson Duffey Packers], asked us to replace the Detroit Vagabond Kings' franchise, which lasted until mid-December and then folded. We came into the league representing Dayton, Ohio, and called ourselves the Dayton Rens. The team was led by our player-coach Pop Gates, Hank DeZonie, William "Dolly" King, and George Crowe, who later played major league baseball.

Forward William "Dolly" King from Long Island University played pro ball with Dayton Rens.

We really didn't want Dayton, Ohio, as our home court, but the league insisted. The people in Dayton just refused to attend the games. They would not accept an all-black club.

Despite a lack of size, a lot of our players being over the hill, a thin bench, and DeZonie's illness, which caused him to miss the last eight games, our club—the only all-black franchise in the history of major league sports—built a competitive 14–26 record over the rest of the season. That season proved to be the last for the Rens.

Bob Douglas was elected to the Naismith Memorial Basketball Hall of Fame in 1971. The Renaissance Big Five were named to the Naismith Memorial Basketball Hall of Fame in 1963.

Bob Douglas died on July 16, 1979.

Clarence "Puggy" Bell

I started playing basketball at the YMCA on 135th Street in Harlem. At that time it was the ambition of everyone to play for the Rens someday. That was everybody's dream. Around 1936 I was playing with a team in Passaic, New Jersey. The team had John Isaac, Charlie Isles, and Frank Caffey. We played the Rens and almost beat them. The next day they took Isaac on their team. After that, the rest of us tried out for the Rens. I finally made it in 1938.

The only black professional team in the East at that time was the Rens. In the West you had the Globetrotters. The strength of the Rens was togetherness . . . scoring and defense. We had a nice big bus with reclining seats. It was a lot of fun. Sometimes we'd get out of the bus and have footraces to settle arguments. We didn't make a lot of money, but we had a lot of fun.

The team was so good we'd spot clubs ten points, with the racists officiating being taken into account. At that time we had a policy not to beat a team by more than ten points. In other words, hold the score down so we could come back and play them again. Don't show the other team up. After all, we had to make money.

The only time we didn't spot any team ten points was when we played the Celtics, or some of the other good clubs like Fort Wayne, Sheboygan, Oshkosh, or the Brooklyn Visitations.

William "Pop" Gates

William "Pop" Gates

Playing for the Rens was the greatest thing in the world for a player at that time —be he black or white. The Rens were the premier ball club in the country. We played the best and beat the best.

We played anywhere from 140 to 150 ball games a year, many times only losing 12 to 18 games per season. In my first professional year with the New York Renaissance in 1938, we won the world's first recognized professional basketball championship in the Tournament of Roses in Chicago. That year we won 68 straight before we were beaten by the New York Celtics. The Rens of 1922–23 won 88 straight.

I went to Benjamin Franklin High School in New York City. Then I went to Clark University in Atlanta, Georgia, on a basketball scholarship. Instead of playing basketball there, I played left end on their football team. I only stayed at Clark for about six months because I couldn't take the discrimination in Atlanta —riding in the back of the bus or trolley. I just couldn't adjust to that kind of life.

Then I contacted a fellow we used to call "Owner" [Arthur] Josephs. He had the Harlem Yankees basketball team in New York. I told him about my problem and he sent me bus fare to come back to New York. So I began to work out with the Harlem Yankees at the Harlem Bathhouse on 134th Street and Fifth Avenue. The Yankees had Charlie Isles, Lou Badger, Lou Henderson, Benny Garrett, and a host of other people. Subsequently, Bob Douglas saw me and told Owner Josephs he'd like to have me on the team. So they worked out something and I joined the Rens.

The Rens played every day; sometimes we'd play twice on Saturdays and three times on Sunday. Many times we'd have to ride 250 to 300 miles to get to a ball game, especially when traveling in the Midwest and the South. We had to eat in the bus because we weren't allowed to eat in the restaurants. We'd stop in grocery stores along the way to buy sandwiches and whatnot. We'd call it grocery bag lunches. Even changed uniforms in the bus because we weren't allowed in white dressing rooms. A lot of times we'd have to drive another 150 miles to find a place to sleep.

All the rookies on the Rens used to have to ride in the back of the bus. Tarzan Cooper used to give all the young guys a hard time—taking food and drinks from them. He felt he was a veteran and was entitled to do that.

Many times when we played in the South, we'd have to fight our way in and out of the arenas. Sometimes we'd have to have a police escort in and out of gymnasiums. One time in Marion, Ohio, Puggy Bell went into the crowd scrambling for a ball and a woman kicked him in the behind. One time in Cicero, Illinois, where we were playing, a fight broke out. The lights went out and when they came back on, twelve of us were in the middle of the floor with chairs in our hands. Then another time in Indianapolis, Indiana, some white guy kept yelling "nigger" this and "nigger" that. After we picked out who was yelling, I conveniently missed a Puggy Bell pass and the basketball knocked the guy right off his chair. We had to do that a lot of times.

The Harlem Globetrotters

While the Renaissance Big Five were thriving on the East Coast, Chicago was brewing up another championship black basketball team—the Harlem Globetrotters. Abe Saperstein, a white man, was the catalyst. Saperstein was born in London and moved to Chicago when he was eight years old. He became a social worker on Chicago's North Side. Seeing the skills of the youth in the ghetto areas and recognizing their potential, Saperstein in 1926 gathered together five basketball players and called them the Savoy Big Five in honor of their home court, the Savoy Ballroom in Chicago. When the ballroom was converted into a roller skating rink, Saperstein decided to take his team on the road and renamed them the Harlem Globetrotters. He wanted people to know his team was black and the word "Globetrotters," he felt, would give the impression that his team was widely traveled, although most of his players had never been to Harlem, much less outside of the United States. The name was prophetic: the Globetrotters have traveled over five million miles to almost one hundred countries and have played before over sixty million spectators.

When they first started out, Saperstein drove the car; coached the team; was manager, trainer, and physician; and served as the team's only substitute. They played some memorable games and had some memorable experiences. In Shelby, Montana, the local gamblers threatened to shoot them if they won and the local sheriff threatened to shoot them if they lost. The Globetrotters played the game fast and easy and won; then they had to sneak out of town with their street clothes rolled up under their arms.

The Trotters became so good that—with their reputation preceding them—they had difficulty finding teams to play. Everyone knew the Globetrotters would win. Even fans began to stay away. With the team's energy drained from daily travel and uncomfortable sleeping quarters, Saperstein suggested that they only play hard during the first ten minutes of each game and then slow things down with a little clowning around. This way the score could be kept within respectable bounds for the opposing team and would provide the fans with a little amusement while the Trotters rested from their arduous traveling conditions.

The team began by running less and passing more. Al "Run" Pullins and Inman Jackson were born comedians anyway and they had fun with the razzle-dazzle style of passing the ball, shooting the ball behind their backs, spinning the ball on their fingers, and totally confusing the opposition. The fans loved it and began to talk about it and the crowds grew.

Their first major breakthrough came in 1940. The promoters of the world professional basketball championship tournament invited the Globetrotters to play—just to fill out the opening round. They thought it would be an amusing bit of fluff for the fans. The surprise came when the Globetrotters walked off with the championship—and then the team was up and away.

Saperstein proved himself to be an excellent promoter and the Globetrotters became international favorites. They played before a white-tie audience in London's Wimbledon Stadium, in the cowpastures of Morocco, and before Pope Pius XII.

Reese "Goose" Tatum, a six-foot-three-inch basketball genius, was their top attraction from 1942 to 1955. His lean, awkward appearance and comedic timing made him a natural and his antics gained Tatum the nickname "the Clown Prince of Basketball," but he was an extraordinary player as well. He always scored—whether on a long hook shot or hanging from the rim—and never seemed to look at the basket before launching his shots.

From 1946 until 1952, the Trotters' act was enlivened by Marques Haynes, who was billed as "the World's Greatest Dribbler." Haynes had unbelievable fingertip control of the ball and could dribble from every conceivable position—on his back, on his stomach, on his knees, and so on. One of his favorite bits was to have the Trotters stand around talking to each other, some reading the newspapers, while Haynes dribbled around, through, and under the opposing team.

Haynes left the Globetrotters to organize his own team—the Fabulous Harlem Magicians—and was joined by Goose Tatum in 1955.

Meadowlark Lemon took over as top comedian and pivot man after the departure of Haynes and Tatum and contributed an even zanier brand of offense to the team, including the "bounce basket"—made by bouncing the ball off the court and through the net.

Tatum died in 1967.

Abe Saperstein died in 1966 and his heirs sold the team for more than $3 million.

The Globetrotters who went on to successfully play in pro basketball were Nat "Sweetwater" Clifton, Wilt "the Stilt" Chamberlain, and Connie Hawkins.

To this day, the Globetrotters still enjoy great acclaim and play to capacity audiences all over the world.

Marques Haynes

Marques Haynes

I started playing basketball at Langston University in Langston, Oklahoma, under Zip Gayles, who I consider the greatest coach of all time. It was under him
that I felt I learned most of my basketball—the real fundamentals of the game.

Langston played in the Southwestern Conference. In that conference we had
teams like Bishop College [Texas], Wiley College [Texas], Texas College, Southern out of Louisiana, and Arkansas State out of Pine Bluff. All of this was
between 1942 and 1946. We also played against Xavier, Grambling, Tilliton, and
Sam Houston.

While I was attending Langston, we played against the Harlem Globetrotters
in Oklahoma City. The Globetrotters had asked our coach to have Langston
substitute for a team that had canceled. We played them at the Municipal Auditorium in Oklahoma City and beat them 74–70. Langston and Lee Blair [uncle of
baseballer Paul Blair]; Lawrence and Lance, the Cudjol twins; Willie Malone out
of Seminole, Oklahoma; Clarence Hawkins; Ivory Moore; and Frank Luster. We
all had such a terrific game that shortly after that we got invitations to join the
Harlem Globetrotters, who at that time were en route to Dallas, Texas. Since it
was my senior year and I was so close to getting my degree, I decided to turn the
offer down. In May of 1946, I received my degree from Langston and planned a
career in coaching or teaching.

That summer I ran into Ted Strong, who played on the Harlem Globetrotters' team when we beat them. Ted was playing baseball with the Kansas City Monarchs of the Negro National League. I talked with Ted and he gave me the Trotters' address. I wrote a letter to Abe Saperstein in Chicago and he offered me an invitation to try out for the team.

So Willie Malone, John Smith [who played with Langston before Haynes got there], and myself all went to Chicago for the Trotters' tryout. That was in 1946. Fortunately, all three of us made some branch of the team. I got a spot on their farm club, the Kansas City Stars, coached by Sam Wheeler out of St. Louis, who later played with the Trotters. This was a team Jesse Owens traveled with. He was an announcer and he put on demonstrations of track stars, signed autographs, and so forth.

I played with the Stars for three months. During that time, I created somewhat of an uproar with my dribbling and ball-handling. My deft ball-handling came about through my oldest brother Wendall, who was quite a dribbler and passer, and then too my other brother was a fantastic passer. I guess this just rubbed off on me. My brothers used to call this "Showtime Basketball."

The Globetrotters did not have a fancy dribbler and the type of ball-handler and passer that I was. So after three months with the Stars, I joined the Trotters.

After a seven-year period with the team, Abe Saperstein and I had a contractual disagreement. I decided to field a team of my own—the Fabulous Harlem Magicians—in December 1953 in Elk City, Oklahoma. I had NBA offers from the Minneapolis Lakers in 1955, and the Philly Warriors. I turned the offers down because I had my own thing going and Tatum was with me then.

I wouldn't trade my ball-playing days for anything in the world. I met great people and friends like Sam Wheeler; Clarence Wilson; Chuck Cooper, who played with the Trotters, Magicians, and the Boston Celtics; Eldridge Webb; and more.

I operated the Magicians for eighteen years through 1971, at which time I rejoined the Harlem Globetrotters in a player-coach capacity.

After World War II many ex-servicemen took advantage of the G.I. Bill of Rights and set about to obtain a college education. As more blacks appeared on white college and university courts, it was obvious that it would be impossible to segregate the best black players into a single group.

Although overt discrimination and segregation were on the way out, twilight battles still had to be fought. On December 23, 1946, Duquesne University met with the University of Tennessee for a scheduled game. Coach John Mauer of Tennessee's Vols refused to allow his team to play unless assured that Charles "Chuck" Cooper, a black freshman at Duquesne, would not play. Coach Chuck Davies of Duquesne made a conditional promise. Dissatisfied with the quibbling, Mauer stalked off before twenty-six hundred fans and stated his team would not play if there were even the remotest possibility that Cooper would participate. On January 15, 1947, the University of Miami announced that an outdoor game scheduled in the Orange Bowl against Duquesne was to be canceled, announcing that a city ordinance prohibited competition between blacks and whites in the same athletic event.

Nothing was immediately done about the Cooper situation, but in 1948 some colleges began to take action. Kansas City was the host for the 1948 National Intercollegiate Basketball Tournament. A contract was to be signed by all participating teams prohibiting blacks from playing. Manhattan College, although they had no blacks on their team, announced its intention to resign from the tournament unless the ban on blacks was lifted. Following suit, Long Island University and Siena College turned down their invitations. It was then that the NAIB executive committee reversed its decision and the tournament was opened to blacks.

By no means was this the end of racism in basketball, but it was one significant step forward.

Chuck Cooper

The Boston Celtics stunned the 1950 draft meeting of the National Basketball Association when they began the second round of selections.

"Boston takes Charles Cooper of Duquesne," announced Walter Brown, the Celtics' founder.

The closed-door meeting in a Chicago hotel fell mute.

Another owner finally broke the silence by asking, "Walter, don't you know he's a colored boy?"

"I don't give a damn if he's striped, plaid, or polka dot!" Brown roared. "Boston takes Charles Cooper of Duquesne."   —George Sullivan, New York *Times*.

Chuck Cooper

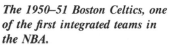

The 1950–51 Boston Celtics, one of the first integrated teams in the NBA.

On April 25, 1950, Chuck Cooper, an All-American forward, became the first black player ever to be drafted by a team in the National Basketball Association. The Boston Celtics, in selecting Cooper, broke the color line, opening the door for future black players. The 1950–51 NBA season featured two other black players: Earl Lloyd (drafted by the Washington Capitols in the ninth round after his collegiate career at West Virginia State) and Nat "Sweetwater" Clifton (whose contract was purchased from the Harlem Globetrotters by the New York Knickerbockers). Although Chuck Cooper was the first black selected by the NBA, by a trick of scheduling Earl Lloyd played one day before Cooper.

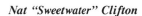

Earl Lloyd

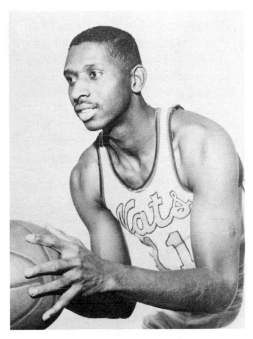

Nat "Sweetwater" Clifton

Charles Cooper:

As a youngster, I was a pretty good athlete, but I really had no intention of going out for the high school team. Apparently, the coach at Westchester High had seen me play in the schoolyard and chased after me to come out for basketball. When I joined in the ninth grade, it was the first time I'd played any organized sport.

One of the people who inspired me to seek a future in basketball was Dolly King, who was a star at Long Island University during the 1940s. He had been the subject of several national magazine articles and LIU was a national basketball power at that time. I had wanted to go there after I graduated from high school, but instead attended West Virginia State before being drafted into the Navy.

After a year-and-a-half stint there, I was released just after the school year had started. My desire to go to LIU was still there and the coach, Clair Bee, had even offered me a scholarship before I went into the Navy. Being a little naïve about the way things worked, I went over to Duquesne University, where Chuck Davies was coach. I knew he was friendly with Clair Bee and I hoped he'd put me in contact with him. See how naïve I was?

Well, with the help of the black trainer at Duquesne, Brue Jackson, who incidentally was a longtime trainer of the Steelers also, I ended up attending Duquesne and, as a "walk-on," made the team. It was unusual for a freshman to do that.

Duquesne had a tradition of blacks in athletics. One of the first blacks in the National Football League went there and there was another black basketball player in the early 1930s, but I was the first black starter they had.

Only in my freshman year did we have any real racial incidents. We had a game scheduled against the University of Tennessee at home and they refused to play against me. I never met them face-to-face, but from what I understand they were not aware of my presence until the last minute. We were already dressed when it was called off. There is the possibility that somebody told them I would be held out of the game. But to the credit of the school officials, they didn't back down. It didn't cause me any kind of emotional anguish. If that was what they wanted to do, let them go back to Tennessee. As long as nobody called me "nigger," it was all right. "Nigger" automatically meant a fight! There was another game canceled at the University of Miami. These incidents put the school on notice that they could run into situations like this and I think they tried to anticipate them. I remember a period when every time we played the game below the Mason-Dixon line, our team would be setting a precedent for a "mixed" contest. Games in some states were out of the question. Alabama, Mississippi, and those other Deep South states were prime examples.

Racism wasn't limited to the South. We were playing the University of Cincinnati out in the Midwest. There was an out-of-bounds play and they were lining up to guard us. One guy shouted, "I got the nigger!" I walked over to him and said, "And I got your mother in my jockstrap." He was shocked. After the game, which as I remember they won, he came over to apologize. I thought I had already said what needed to be said and I told him that. I also said, "If you can take what I said, then I can take a thousand 'niggers.' "

That was the only time during my college career that I was called "nigger" to my face.

When the Celtics drafted me in the second round in 1950, I wasn't surprised. A scout for Boston named Art Spector had already talked to me about the possibility before the draft. At the time of draft, I was on a three-week tour with the Globetrotters, so I was pretty confident about my ability to continue as a ballplayer. When I joined the Celtics, the players' attitude toward me was pretty good. Coach Auerbach and the owner, Walter Brown, made me feel at home.

The major thing I had to adjust to upon entering the pros was the stationary pivot. In college, with my size and agility, I liked to go down low and utilize that space, but in the pros a big man in the middle would clog that area up.

There is one area of my Celtic career that I would like to clarify. Over the years, a number of the men I played with have claimed some distinction for helping to shepherd over me. Well, I had only one fight in the NBA that was clearly over race—not several as one of these men, Ed Macauley, has stated. In fact, during that one incident, Macauley was nowhere in sight. That one fight was against the Tri-Cities Blackhawks. After fighting, for a loose ball, a player said, "You black bastard." Not looking for a fight, I gave him a chance to back down, by asking him not to say that again. He looked me dead in the eye and said it again. So I took my open hand and shoved it as hard as I could into his face. Since there was some hostility between players on both teams, but especially between Auerbach and the opposing coach, other fights suddenly broke out. I was fined for what happened, but after the commissioner heard the whole story he rescinded it. I never thought about myself as black pioneer in basketball. When Jackie Robinson broke the color line, he's the one who shouldered the burden that helped blacks in other sports. He was the pioneer!

Traveling around the league, I encountered all the problems any black man of that period—be he a diplomat, a porter, or a basketball player. I had to sleep in different hotels than the team in Washington and Baltimore. My teammates and the management acquiesced to this like everybody else at the time. Only later when things had changed somewhat and players with stature—like Bill Russell and Elgin Baylor—came along did conditions change. Being superstars and working in a better environment, they could boycott games if they felt things were unfair.

What really disturbed me was how the Globetrotters were treated by Saperstein. When I was with the Trotters, they were playing a series of games against the College All-Stars, who were almost all white. While we all traveled in the same chartered bus, the hotel accommodations were very different. Saperstein had one of the few solid moneymakers in the game at that time. The NBA was even on thin ice at that time, yet Saperstein had his black players staying in dirty, roach-infested holes in the wall. I used to point this out to the Globetrotter players. Not only were the living conditions bad, but there was a big pay difference between the NBA players and themselves. For doing that I got the reputation as a troublemaker.

After four years with the Celtics and two with the Hawks, I spent another year with a team called the Harlem Magicians, sort of an offshoot of the Globetrotters. I could have stayed with them—the money was pretty good—but I was beginning to get tired of it. I also had a serious automobile accident and that helped me make the decision to stop playing.

As I look back on my career, I can't help but feel dissatisfied about a lot of things. There were things I had to adapt to throughout my career that I wouldn't have had to if I were white. I was expected to play good, sound intensified defense and really get under the boards for the heavy dirty work. Yet I never received the frills or the extra pay of white players.

I remember Sweetwater Clifton, the first black on the Knicks, was told to play less of his game. Men like Bobby King, who played like Cousy, and Kenny McBride were hurt by prejudice. They said that King was erratic and that he didn't know where he was passing. McBride's biggest crime was that he might have dated a white girl once or twice. Can't prove that was the cause of his troubles, but it makes you wonder.

Injuries were a problem too. If I was hurt, they got suspicious. Auerbach, in fact, had me labeled a hypochondriac. In my four years in Boston, I never had an X ray—lots of stitches, but never an X ray. There were one or two white players on the Celtics that if they jammed a finger it was a cause of great concern. But then you know how strong black skin is. We don't get hurt. Ha!

Another thing I'm somewhat resentful about is that at the time I would have liked to get into coaching. I felt I knew the game and how to handle young men. But there were no opportunities for black coaches then. I got one offer from a school in Piney Woods, Mississippi, but they were still killing black people down there then. So I declined. When my alma mater was looking for a coach, they approached me in a very roundabout way, but it was only for a position as an assistant coach. If I was white, they would have offered the top spot. So when I see Lenny Wilkens win an NBA title, I feel a bit of resentment that I didn't get a chance and also an overwhelming sense of pride in what he accomplished.

Wilt Chamberlain

Wilt Chamberlain

When Celtic owner Walter Brown signed Chuck Cooper, his franchise was $460,000 in debt. The fledgling NBA was in deep trouble—six teams had gone under that spring and more were expected to go that winter. Something had to be done—and fast—if the NBA was to remain in business.

Now also, for the first time, Saperstein's autocracy over black players was challenged. Saperstein responded by announcing that he would not take his team into Boston or Washington. This boycott seriously hurt the NBA because teams depended on doubleheaders with the Globetrotters for heavy gates. But to Walter Brown, it was a do-or-die situation.

The inclusion of black players revived the flagging interest and gate receipts of professional basketball. Wilt Chamberlain, the greatest offensive threat of his era, is a case in point. Born in Philadelphia on August 21, 1936, Chamberlain was an outstanding athlete at Philadelphia's Overbrook High School. He ran the 100-yard dash and the 440 with speed that was unusual for a seven-foot-one-inch tall, 275-pound man.

While still in high school, boxing trainers and promoters and pro football scouts approached him. It was not only his formidable size that enticed the scouts and promoters; it was also his speed and coordination that made him a man who could play virtually any professional sport. His outstanding abilities at the University of Kansas produced a change in college basketball's out-of-bounds procedures. At Kansas, the inbounds toss would be looped over the basket and Wilt Chamberlain would catch it as soon as it cleared the top of the backboard and put it through the hoop. This was beyond the ken of other teams and the rules committee barred the play.

After two celebrated seasons at Kansas, Chamberlain passed up his senior year to travel with the Harlem Globetrotters. Wilt Chamberlain then signed with the rather wealthy Philadelphia Warriors in 1959. He reportedly received a contract for $65,000 a year—an unheard-of amount in basketball at that time. In his first National Basketball Association season, 1959–60, Chamberlain lived up to and beyond the public's expectation. He averaged a record of 37.6 points per game and offensive rebounds were his forte. With surprising accuracy, he sank fall-away jumpers and he made the dunk shot famous. With his great height, he would soar above the basket and slam the ball through the hoop, leaving the backboard zinging in response.

You could not stop Wilt "the Stilt" Chamberlain anywhere near the basket. His fantastic offensive power was demonstrated against the New York Knicks on March 2, 1962, in Hershey, Pennsylvania. It was a wild night for basketball, as Chamberlain scored 100 points—the first and only player to ever do so—in a 169–147 Philadelphia victory. He connected on 36 of 63 field goal attempts and 28 of 32 foul tries. Chamberlain had previously scored 78 points for the Warriors in a triple-overtime game against the Los Angeles Lakers on December 8, 1961. He also scored 73 twice and 72 once during his career. To give you an idea of Chamberlain's offensive superiority, the only other pro players to *ever* score 70 points in a game are David Thompson of the Denver Nuggets (73) and Elgin Baylor of the Lakers (71). During that record-setting season (1961–62), Wilt Chamberlain *averaged* 50.4 points a game (an all-time record). He was the NBA's top scorer for seven straight seasons until Rick Barry won the scoring title in 1966–67. Chamberlain also led the league in rebounding ten times and on November 24, 1960, in a game against the Celtics, his 55 rebounds set an NBA record. In addition, Chamberlain also won seven field goal percentage titles (the dunk shot *is* a high-percentage shot), was consistently among league leaders in total minutes played, and was the first center to ever lead the league in assists, averaging 8.6 a game in 1967–68. Wilt Chamberlain was clearly the dominant offensive center of his era.

Despite Chamberlain's superior record, the Philadelphia Warriors failed to become a winning team. Even their move to San Francisco for the 1963–64 season failed to revive them. Granted, the team—with the notable exception of Chamberlain—was lacking in overall talent. Even so, Wilt the Stilt's tendency to sparkle individually while his team faltered prompted critics to brand him a "loser" and "selfish." But what must be primarily considered is that during Chamberlain's NBA career with the Philadelphia and San Francisco Warriors he was not surrounded by championship-type players.

Wilt Chamberlain was then traded to the Philadelphia 76ers (formerly the Syracuse Nationals). Now—with players of the caliber of Hal Greer, Chet Walker, and Lucius Jackson—Chamberlain was with a talent-rich club. Together these men formed an imposing team. The 76ers emphasized Wilt the Stilt's defense and rebounding more than his scoring and that strategy was the start of a string of Eastern Division titles. At last Chamberlain got to play with his first NBA championship team in the 1966–67 season, leading the 76ers to victory over the powerful Boston Celtics.

In 1968, in accordance with his wishes, Chamberlain was traded to the Los Angeles Lakers, a team already boasting two superstars, Jerry West and Elgin Baylor. Even with these three future Hall of Famers, the Lakers failed in several championship appearances against the Celtics and the New York Knicks, but Chamberlain's hulking presence in the middle made their defense tough. Chamberlain's—and L.A.'s—patience was finally rewarded when the Lakers won the 1971–72 championship, beating the Knicks 4 games to 1.

Wilt Chamberlain held the NBA all-time scoring record (13,419 points) for over ten years until it was surpassed in 1983–84 by Kareem Abdul-Jabbar. Named the league's Most Valuable Player four times, Chamberlain was selected first-team All-NBA seven times and second-team All-NBA three times. He still holds many game, season, and career records.

Wilt the Stilt left the NBA to sign as a player-coach with the San Diego Conquistadors of the American Basketball Association in 1973. He was forbidden to play by court order because he had not fully completed his option with the Los Angeles Lakers. He spent one year as a coach and then resigned.

Wilt Chamberlain was enshrined in the Naismith Memorial Basketball Hall of Fame in 1978.

Bill Russell

Bill Russell

Perhaps the most dominant figure in the history of professional basketball—certainly the best defensive player the game has ever seen—was Bill Russell. He combined the ultimate in achievement—leading the Boston Celtics to eleven NBA championships in thirteen seasons—with clear, articulate, conscience-baring recognition of the black man in sports in America. He was a true champion in every sense of the word.

Russell's sense of self, of dignity, mixed with self-assertion based upon a true knowledge of his worth, inspired many black athletes to defy the old taboos and demand their fair share. The goal of the present-day black athlete—to be accepted as a *citizen,* a citizen who happens to be black—has its roots in Bill Russell's determination to lead the way for blacks in basketball and in public life.

There is an old story told about Russell when he was with the Boston Celtics. A Boston social club called the Celtics' business office to obtain the services of Bob Cousy as a guest speaker at the club's annual sports night. They were offering Cousy $1,500 for that night. Since Cousy was unavailable, the Celtics offered to substitute Bill Russell, the league's Most Valuable Player. The chairman of entertainment called Russell and offered him $500. Russell replied, "I love and respect Bob Cousy. In fact,

I love and respect Bob Cousy so much that I would not work for one penny less than he would work for."

Bill Russell's phenomenal rise to the top had a very inauspicious beginning. He was born on February 12, 1934, in Monroe, Louisiana, later moving with his family to Oakland, California. As a sophomore, he failed to make the high school team. Even as a senior, in his best game he only scored 14 points. Perhaps it was his size—six feet ten inches tall and 220 pounds—but Hal De Julio, alumnus of the University of San Francisco, avowed basketball fan, and unofficial scout, saw something no one else had ever seen in Russell and referred him to USF for a basketball scholarship. Russell made fantastic progress during his freshman year and taught himself the fundamentals of playing defense. He became the leader of the team in his junior and senior years (1954–55 and 1955–56), guiding USF to two national championships and a streak of 60 consecutive wins to establish a national collegiate record.

Upon graduation, Bill Russell opted to try for the 1956 Olympic team rather than turn professional at that moment. He led the United States basketball team to a rousing 89–55 victory over the U.S.S.R. in the final and brought home a gold medal.

When he returned, Russell was drafted by the St. Louis Hawks, but Arnold "Red" Auerbach, Celtics coach and general manager, wanted Russell so badly that he convinced Walter Brown to trade two established pros—Ed Macauley and Cliff Hagen—for the young Olympic star.

With Russell as the starting center, the 1956–57 Celtics won the NBA championship. The next year Russell injured his ankle and the Celtics made it to the championship series but lost to the Hawks. After that, though, it was all pure gravy as Russell led Boston to eleven championships in thirteen years, including a stretch of seven straight—an extraordinary feat, since no other NBA team has ever managed to win two championships in a row.

Bill Russell revolutionized the game of basketball with his emphasis on defense. The strategy of his defensive play was that it worked as an offensive weapon. Auerbach's theories about an organized fast break did not become reality until he obtained Russell. Players certainly had blocked shots with skill before Russell arrived, but very few were able to block shots and control the direction of the ball afterward, a skill that Russell perfected. He was also an excellent rebounder, leading the league four times and finishing second (to Chamberlain) five times.

With a lifetime average of only 15 points per game, Russell was no razzle-dazzle on the court. Although an excellent foul shooter, his offense consisted of an awkward left-handed jumper and a maladroit-appearing hook. What he did do was to make sure his team won, primarily through disrupting the other team's offense. On offense, he occupied the low post, setting up picks for Celtic players who whirred around him and passing off when he got the ball. In effect, he became the inert hub of a merry-go-round.

While Wilt Chamberlain starred on offense, Bill Russell starred on defense. Their rivalry through the years was spectacular. While Chamberlain won the scoring titles, Russell's Celtics won the NBA championships. Chamberlain's comment on their brilliant competition says it all: "I've been in seven playoffs with Boston where it came down to the final game and Boston won six."

Largely in recognition of his defensive skills and overall team play, Bill Russell was selected first-team All-NBA three times and second-team All-NBA seven times and was the league's Most Valuable Player five times.

Upon Red Auerbach's recommendation, Russell, while continuing as a player, took over the Boston coaching job in 1966–67, thus becoming the first black head coach of a major league franchise in the United States. It was not an easy chore to undertake, since Bob Cousy had retired and many of the other Celtics were older. Russell led his team to the semifinals, but they were defeated by Wilt Chamberlain and the 76ers, who went on to win the championship, thus ending the most phenomenal string of consecutive titles in the history of professional sports. In 1967–68, Russell closed out his playing career as a winner when Boston regained the NBA championship by defeating the Los Angeles Lakers in the title series.

Bill Russell was enshrined in the Naismith Memorial Basketball Hall of Fame in 1974, much against his wishes. He says, "Aside from racism or my own feelings about cheers and boos in sports, I don't respect it as an institution. Its standards are not high enough. It's too political, too self-serving. I'm not trying to take it away from the people who run it . . . I'm just saying the Hall of Fame is separate from me." There were people inducted who he felt he did not wish to be associated with, for instance, Abe Saperstein, who, Russell states, "worked against the aspirations of an entire race just to keep his little franchises."*

Russell can best be summed up in his following quotation:

There was a sense of self-degradation. We believed what the white man told us, that we were inferior. When I look at the struggle of the American black, I can't help but be very proud. With what we've been given to work with—and we've been given damn little—we've done a magnificent job of surviving. We still have a long way to go and we have to believe we can do it. Egotism is important. When somebody asks me if I think I'm a real good basketball player, I tell him, "Hell no, I'm the greatest basketball player." The black man has to beat his chest as hard as he can beat it.

---

* *Second Wind: The Memoirs of an Opinionated Man* by Bill Russell and Taylor Branch, New York: Random House, 1979.

Oscar Robertson

Oscar Robertson

Oscar Robertson, the "Big O," was a complete ballpayer who combined more skills than any NBA player in history. He could thread a needle with his passes, his outside shooting was deadly, his ball-handling was deft, and he could rebound as well as many forwards. Standing only six-foot-five and weighing 205 pounds, the Big O's physical control, intelligence, and imagination enabled him to do just about anything he wanted on the basketball court.

Born in 1938 on his grandfather's farm near Charlotte, Tennessee, Robertson moved to Indianapolis with his family in 1942. This move was a fortunate one because Indiana is known for its high-quality basketball program and statewide enthusiasm for the sport, having produced some of the most outstanding teams, players, and coaches in basketball's history. When Robertson led the all-black Crispus Attucks High School team to consecutive state championships in the 1954–55 and 1955–56 seasons, he received national attention. College scholarship offers poured in from all over the country, but Robertson elected to attend the University of Cincinnati because of George Smith, UC's outstanding basketball coach.

During his three varsity seasons with UC, Robertson led the Bearcats to three Missouri Conference titles and NCAA berths, advancing as far as the NCAA semifinals in 1959. The Big O led the nation in scoring three times and scored more points—2,973—than any prior major college player. A three-time All-American, Robertson was named Player of the Year all three seasons, leading UC to 79 wins and only 9 losses. Robertson was so impressive that Coach Phog Allen of Kansas once commented, "Oscar Robertson is the greatest player of all time for his size."

As the first black basketball player at the University of Cincinnati, Robertson was subjected to racial discrimination, even though he never considered himself a crusader for civil rights. On one road trip, he was barred from the Shamrock Hotel in Houston. Enraged, the Big O threatened to quit the team and return home. After that the

University of Cincinnati made sure that eating and sleeping accommodations were provided on every campus the team visited. On another occasion, at the Dixie Classic in Raleigh, fan abuse incited a wrestling match on the court between Robertson and a player from Wake Forest. But none of this intimidated the Big O. His overall excellence and dazzling moves continued to draw record crowds for the remainder of his collegiate career.

After graduation from UC in 1960, Robertson joined the Olympic basketball squad —possibly the finest U.S. team ever assembled. The Big O led the team to the gold with eight consecutive victories, including a 90–63 drubbing of Brazil in the final.

The number-one draft selection of the Cincinnati Royals, Oscar Robertson turned pro for the 1960–61 campaign. In his first year, the Big O scored at a 30.5 points per game clip, was selected Rookie of the Year, and was named first-team All-NBA. He led the Royals to the playoffs for six straight seasons, a streak broken in 1967–68 when Robertson was hurt and out of the lineup much of the time. But the Royals—even with the Big O—never won the NBA championship.

When Bob Cousy, former Celtic great, took over as the Cincinnati coach in 1969–70, he wanted to change the Royals' offense into a Celtics'-type running offense. Robertson felt more at home with the Royals' pattern offense. When Cousy tried to trade the Big O to Baltimore for Gus Johnson, Robertson vetoed the deal. At the end of the season, he and Cousy were still at odds, so Robertson okayed a trade to the Milwaukee Bucks. The Bucks at that time featured a heralded young center named Lew Alcindor. As "Mr. Outside" and "Mr. Inside," Robertson and Alcindor terrorized the league and the Bucks won the NBA championship in 1970–71, finally realizing one of the Big O's most cherished dreams.

Throughout his outstanding career, Robertson was the consummate playmaker, leading the NBA in assists six times. He still holds the NBA record for career assists —9,887—and has the second-highest per game average for a season—11.5 in 1964–65. The Big O is the highest-scoring guard in the history of the NBA, averaging 27 points per game, and is the third-highest scorer (after Abdul-Jabbar and Chamberlain) in NBA history. He also holds the NBA record for foul tries made with 7,694. The NBA's Most Valuable Player in 1962–63, Robertson was named first-team All-NBA for nine straight years and second-team All-NBA twice. The NBA All-Star Game seemed to be the Big O's personal showcase; he was chosen the game's MVP three times.

Robertson retired in 1974, but his influence on the game of professional basketball was to extend beyond his prowess as a player. In 1970 Robertson filed a class-action suit on behalf of all NBA players. When Lawrence O'Brien took over as league commissioner in 1975, he negotiated a settlement of the Robertson case, effective in 1976. Thus the option clause was eliminated, the college draft was revised so that teams would no longer hold a player's lifetime rights, and a compensation clause for free agents who had signed with new teams was created. With this change in the college draft rules, players became freer to move from team to team. And without Oscar Robertson, this new freedom for all players—black *and* white—would not exist.

The Big O was elected to the Naismith Memorial Basketball Hall of Fame in 1979.

Elgin Baylor

Elgin Baylor

Elgin Baylor, considered by many to be the greatest forward in NBA history, was a study in motion. Blessed with both physical size (six feet five, 225 pounds) and natural agility, Baylor had tremendous body control, dynamite inside moves, and the ability to seemingly hang suspended in midair on his drives to the basket. A prolific scorer, Baylor was also a rugged and tenacious rebounder.

After leading Seattle University to the runner-up spot in the 1958 NCAA tournament with a season-long average of 31.5 points per game and a total of 590 rebounds, Elgin Baylor was drafted by the Minneapolis Lakers and may just have saved this faltering franchise. Laker president Bob Short has said, "If he had turned me down then, I'd have gone out of business. The club would have gone bankrupt." Baylor's presence helped transform the Lakers, who moved to Los Angeles before the 1960–61 season, into one of the wealthiest franchises in professional sports.

In his initial season in the NBA, 1958–59, Elgin Baylor averaged 24.9 points and 15 rebounds per game, was named Rookie of the Year, MVP of the All-Star Game, and first-team All-NBA, fulfilling all of the promise he had shown as an All-American at Seattle. The scoring records were yet to come. On November 8, 1959, Baylor set a single game scoring record with 64 points against the Boston Celtics. On November 15, 1960, Baylor scored 71 points against the New York Knicks at Madison Square Garden, an NBA record until Wilt Chamberlain scored 100 in 1962. During his fourteen-year professional career, Elgin Baylor scored 23,149 points in only 846 NBA regular season games, totaled 3,623 points in 134 playoff games, and averaged 27.4 points per game, the second-highest lifetime scoring average among retired players.

In recognition of his tremendous talents, Baylor was named first-team All-NBA ten times. He still holds the single-game scoring record in the playoffs with 61 points in a 1962 game. In career rebounding, Baylor is seventh on the all-time regular season list with 11,463. In addition, he is the third-leading career rebounder in the playoffs and the fifth-leading all-time rebounder in All-Star games.

But Elgin Baylor's career was not without disappointments. For one thing, Baylor never played on a championship team. Although the Lakers made it to the finals seven times with Elgin Baylor in the lineup, they never came away a winner, losing six times to the legendary Celtics and once to the New York Knicks. Ironically, the year that Baylor retired was the year the Lakers went on to win it all. Another disappointment was the injured kneecap that Baylor sustained while coming down with a rebound in the 1964–65 playoffs. Many said he would never play again. But with a strength born of determination, Baylor exercised daily and returned to action five months later. He went slowly at first, but a 46-point, 17-rebound performance against the Knicks signaled his complete recovery. Then, on October 28, 1966, in another game against the Knicks, Baylor injured his knee again in a scramble for a loose ball. Again he came back, leading the Lakers into the playoff finals in 1967–68, but the championship eluded his team once again.

Elgin Baylor, one of the most remarkable basketball players of all time, was inducted into the Naismith Memorial Basketball Hall of Fame in 1976.

Kareem Abdul-Jabbar

Kareem Abdul-Jabbar

During the telecast of a game in the 1972 NBA playoffs, Hall of Famer Bill Russell was asked whether he or Wilt Chamberlain was the greatest pro player of all time. "Kareem Abdul-Jabbar," Russell replied, "is the greatest player to play this game." Jabbar justified this claim on April 5, 1984, when the slim superstar center surpassed Chamberlain's career scoring mark, reaching a total of 31,421 lifetime points to become the most prolific scorer in NBA history.

After a standout high school career at Power Memorial in New York City, including a record 2,067 points, 2,002 rebounds, and 71 consecutive victories, Jabbar—then known as Lew Alcindor—was heavily recruited by colleges across the country. He chose UCLA and spearheaded the freshman team to an undefeated season. In his three years on the varsity squad, Alcindor was nothing short of phenomenal, leading the Bruins to three consecutive NCAA championships and being named Most Valuable Player of the tournament three times. With Lew Alcindor in the lineup, UCLA's record was 88 wins against only 2 losses. His three-year scoring average was 26.4 points per game and his 62.4 shooting percentage set an NCAA record.

Drafted by the Milwaukee Bucks, an expansion club, Alcindor signed a five-year, $1.2 million contract and proceeded to lead the team out of the doldrums and into respectability. In his first year, 1969–70, Alcindor finished second to Jerry West in scoring with a 28.8 average and third in rebounding with 1,190. He was named Rookie of the Year and second-team All-NBA.

The next season, 1970–71, Alcindor teamed with Oscar Robertson to take the Bucks to the NBA crown. He was named Most Valuable Player of the Year after leading the league in scoring (2,596 points, 31.7 average) and finishing fourth in rebounds (1,311). Alcindor was also named first-team All-NBA.

During the 1971–72 season, Kareem Abdul-Jabbar (he changed his name for religious reasons in 1971) again won the MVP award, led the league in scoring (2,822 points, 34.8 average), finished third in rebounds (1,346 for a 16.6 average), and was named first-team All-NBA.

In the 1972–73 campaign, Jabbar finished second in scoring (2,292 points, 30.2 average), fourth in rebounds (1,224 and a 16.1 average), and was again named first-team All-NBA.

In 1973–74, Jabbar led the Bucks into the playoffs for the fourth straight season, but Milwaukee lost to the Celtics in the finals, 4 games to 3. Winning the MVP award for the third time, Jabbar finished third in scoring (2,191 points, 27.0 average), fourth in rebounds (1,178 for a 14.5 average), and was named first-team All-NBA.

Despite leading the Bucks to 60 or more wins on three separate occasions, Jabbar became disenchanted with the coaching philosophy of Coach Larry Costello and asked for a trade when his contract expired in 1975. Jabbar's request was granted and he moved to the West Coast, joining the Los Angeles Lakers for the 1975–76 season. Kareem led the league in rebounds for the first time (1,383 and a 16.9 average), but his supporting cast was inadequate and the Lakers failed to make the playoffs. Jabbar, however, was named first-team All-NBA and won his fourth MVP award.

In 1976–77, Jabbar led the Lakers to the best regular season record in the NBA, but Los Angeles lost to the Portland Trail Blazers in the playoff semifinals. Again Kareem Abdul-Jabbar was named MVP, finished among the league leaders in scoring and rebounding, and was named first-team All-NBA.

The Lakers failed to qualify for the playoffs in 1978–79, largely due to an incident that occurred in the first game of the season. Kent Benson, Milwaukee's top draft selection, elbowed Kareem while going for a rebound. Jabbar retaliated by punching the rookie, a costly move because Jabbar fractured his wrist, was fined $5,000 by the league, and had to miss 20 games. When he returned to the lineup, Jabbar was not his usual self and even considered quitting until Coach Jerry West talked him out of it. Jabbar soon regained his form, averaging 25.8 points per game, fourth best in the NBA.

In 1978–79, the Lakers finished third in the Pacific Division and lost to Seattle in the first round of the playoffs. Jabbar had a respectable year, amassing 1,025 rebounds for a 12.8 average. For the second straight year, Kareem was named second-team All-NBA.

The next season, 1979–80, the acquisition of Earvin "Magic" Johnson solidified the Los Angeles Lakers. The team developed an awesome running attack and went on to win the NBA championship. Kareem Abdul-Jabbar won the Most Valuable Player Award for an unprecedented sixth time. The Lakers, again a league powerhouse, won the NBA crown again in 1981–82 and lost in the finals to the Philadelphia 76ers in 1982–83.

There are many ways that the graceful Jabbar can beat you. His scoring and rebounding abilities are brilliant. "Mr. Inside's" offensive moves feature a unique hook shot—the "sky hook"—that is virtually unstoppable because of Jabbar's seven-foot-plus height. But Kareem is also a master on defense. He has led the NBA in blocked shots several times and is a perennial member of the All-NBA defensive squad. In many ways, having Kareem Abdul-Jabbar on your team is like having the skills of Bill Russell on defense and the power of Wilt Chamberlain on offense.

Jabbar broke two new records in 1984. He became the first "$2 Million Man" in NBA history and surpassed Wilt Chamberlain's 13,419 career points to become the league's all-time leading scorer. Every point Kareem scores establishes a new NBA career scoring plateau.

Willis Reed

Walter "Clyde" Frazier

It was seven years after Chuck Cooper, Sweetwater Clifton, and Earl Lloyd success-fully integrated the NBA that the full impact of the black in professional basketball would take hold. That was the year that Bill Russell—intimidating shot blocker and rebounder deluxe—joined the NBA. After that, players such as Wilt Chamberlain, Oscar Robertson, Elgin Baylor, and Kareem Abdul-Jabbar would begin their tremen-dous careers. Each brought new talents and pizzazz to the game.

People often talk about the New York Knicks in "the good old days," the days of Willis Reed, Walt Frazier, Earl Monroe, Dave DeBusschere, and Bill Bradley—an integrated five. Those five men represented the power and success of a winning team. They weren't judged as blacks or whites—just as winners.

The New York Knicks of 1979–80 became the first all-black NBA team, proving that people will pay to see quality basketball—regardless of the color of the players on the team. Professional basketball has come a long way since the days when Chuck Cooper heard those taunts from opposing players and the acceptance of blacks as basketball players has contributed to acceptance of blacks in general.

Marques Haynes claims that the black athlete brought more than physical talents to basketball. "He also brought his competitiveness to the game," he says. "It's now more intense, a harder-played game."

Many athletes feel that there is no other sport where the creativeness of the black athlete is more apparent than in basketball. "It was—and is—a very simple game," says Julius Erving of the Philadelphia 76ers. "But what the black athlete did was to enhance the game with an expression all his own, taking the basics to another dimen-sion. Soon the white player began to emulate these thoughts and moves and eventually the game became what it is today—a stage where a unique combination of the team concept and individual expression are presented in pure form."

Earl "the Pearl" Monroe

*Wes Unseld of the Washington
Bullets, the only player besides
Wilt Chamberlain to win both
MVP and Rookie of the Year in
the same season.*

GREAT BLACK BASKETBALL STARS OF TODAY

Forward Buck Williams of the New Jersey Nets. He's the first player since Dave Cowens to grab more than 1,000 rebounds in his first two seasons of pro ball (1980–81 and 1981–82).

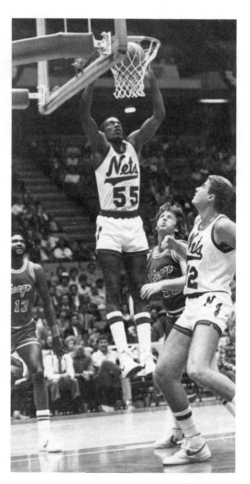

Forward Albert King (number 55) of the New Jersey Nets. He is a top outside forward.

Forward Bernard King of the New York Knickerbockers. He is undoubtedly one of the premier small forwards in NBA, and without question the best player on his team.

Center Moses Malone of the Philadelphia 76ers. He is the most dominating offensive rebounder at his position since Wilt Chamberlain. At the end of the 1982–83 season, Malone had won the NBA MVP award for three of the last four seasons.

Guard Andrew Toney of the Philadelphia 76ers is one of the league's most feared scorers.

Guard Maurice Cheeks of the Philadelphia 76ers. He may be the NBA's most effective penetrator; he shoots well from the outside and always seems to score better in the playoffs.

Forward Julius "Doctor J" Erving of the Philadelphia 76ers. He is undoubtedly one of the best ever to play the game. In the 1982–83 season, he averaged 18.4 points per game and 7.6 rebounds per game in the playoffs. He began the 1983–84 season with 24,393 points in his combined ABA-NBA career, the ninth best total in pro basketball history. His magical moves and soaring ability around the hoop have dazzled teammates and opponents for years.

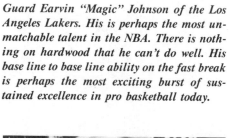

Guard Earvin "Magic" Johnson of the Los Angeles Lakers. His is perhaps the most unmatchable talent in the NBA. There is nothing on hardwood that he can't do well. His base line to base line ability on the fast break is perhaps the most exciting burst of sustained excellence in pro basketball today.

Forward Marques Johnson of the San Diego Clippers, one of the best small forwards in the NBA. In the 1981–82 season, with the Milwaukee Bucks, he averaged 21.4 points per game, led the team in assists (363), and was the second in rebounds (7 per game).

Guard Sidney Moncrief of the Milwaukee Bucks is one of the top all-around players in the league.

Dan Roundfield, former Atlanta Hawks star, now with the Detroit Pistons, is one of the top power forwards in the game.

Guard George "Iceman" Gervin of the San Antonio Spurs is the best pure shooter in the NBA.

An All-Star in each of his three pro seasons in the NBA, point guard Isaiah Thomas spearheads the Detroit Piston attack.

Forward Dominique Wilkens of the Atlanta Hawks is an exciting open court player with an exciting assortment of dunks.

Robert Parish of the Boston Celtics was one of the few centers in the NBA able to generate any consistency against Moses Malone in the 1981–82 season.

Guard Reggie Theus of the Kansas City Kings. During the 1982–83 season, he led the Chicago Bulls in scoring (23.8 points per game), steals (143), assists (484), free throw percentage (.801), and minutes played (2,856). Traded to the Kings in mid-1983–84 season, he helped lead them to the playoffs.

Forward Clark Kellogg of the Indiana Pacers is a great offensive rebounder and a creative point-getter.

Lloyd "World B." Free of the Cleveland Cavaliers is one of the most prolific scorers in the NBA.

Guard Walter Davis of the Phoenix Suns, one of the most fluid and elegant offensive players in the game today.

Akeem Olajuwan, the 7-foot center from Nigeria, was the NBA's number one draft choice in 1984, and was teamed with 7-foot, 4-inch Ralph Sampson to become the Houston Rockets awesome "Twin Towers."

Center Ralph Sampson of the Houston Rockets. He is one of the great college basketball stars of all time. He missed out on that elusive NCAA title, but did taste victory when his Virginia team won the NIT championship in 1980. Was named Rookie of the Year for the 1983–84 season.

Michael Jordan was the experts' choice to be named Rookie of the Year in 1985, and this prolific and acrobatic guard of the Chicago Bulls did not disappoint.

TRACK

In 490 B.C., an Athenian general, Miltiades, led his troops against a Persian invasion. The Athenians were far outnumbered, but the clever and relentless attack of Miltiades forced the Persians back to their ships, leaving over six thousand invaders dead. Miltiades requested that Pheidippides, a champion Olympic runner, carry news of the victory more than twenty-six miles to Athens, where city fathers anxiously awaited the outcome. A battle-weary Pheidippides threw down his shield, removed his armor, and set off from Marathon. Hours later, Pheidippides, with bloodied feet and sore lungs, reached the marketplace in Athens and called out, "Rejoice! We conquer!"—whereupon he collapsed and died. The modern race known as the marathon was named in honor of Pheidippides' historic run.

Before the advent of modern communications, the act of running to carry a message to distant places was common to all races everywhere. The joy of competing in races dates back to man's earliest beginnings. The ultimate goal of track enthusiasts is to compete in the Olympic Games and Olympic stars gain worldwide recognition of their abilities.

The Olympic Games began in Greece in 776 B.C., but they were banned in A.D. 393 by Roman emperor Theodosius I, who considered them a public nuisance. French educator-sportsman Baron de Coubertin was responsible for the revitalization of the Olympics after a fifteen-hundred-year lapse. It was Baron de Coubertin's conviction that nations would understand each other better if the games were reborn. The first modern Olympic Games took place in Athens in 1896.

At that time, there was no Olympic Committee in the United States and there was no funding to send Americans to the games. However, Robert S. Garrett, captain of the Princeton University track and field team, and three fellow students decided to participate. Paying his own expenses, James B. Connolly, a Harvard freshman, joined the group. Then the Boston Athletic Association raised a fund for others to participate and five more Americans joined the team. With very little time to prepare for the

Olympics, the Americans arrived just as the games commenced and proceeded to win nine out of the ten events they entered, a remarkable record.

Blacks did not participate in the 1896 games. However, in 1904, George Poage, an outstanding hurdler and quarter-miler who had established a college record for the 440-yard dash and for the low hurdles while attending the University of Wisconsin, became the first black runner in the Olympics. In the third modern Olympiad, held in St. Louis, Poage finished fourth in the 400-meter dash and third in the 400-meter hurdles, thus becoming the first black to capture a medal in the games.

Howard P. Drew, another great black sprinter, won the national title in the 100-yard dash in 1912 and 1913 and won the national title in the 220-yard dash in 1913.

Howard P. Drew

During the next few years, blacks began to participate in national track and field competition to a greater extent. Sol Butler of Dubuque, Iowa, won the AAU title in the broad jump in 1920. Black broad jumpers soon began to dominate the event, winning twenty-six national championships in a thirty-six-year span. DeHart Hubbard of Cincinnati won for six consecutive years (1922–27).

In the Olympics of 1932, held in Los Angeles, Eddie Tolan of Michigan and Ralph Metcalfe of Marquette both performed in an outstanding manner, winning gold and silver medals for America in the sprints. Tolan, a stubby, diminutive man, won the 100-meter dash—all the while chewing gum and with his horn-rimmed glasses held in place with adhesive tape—in a controversial photo finish over Metcalfe, who had been considered the favorite. The following day, Tolan beat Metcalfe again, this time in the 200-meter dash, to earn his second gold medal of the 1932 Olympiad. Tolan went on to compile a remarkable streak of triumphs in amateur racing. In more than three hundred races, he was beaten only seven times. Big Ralph Metcalfe went on to win another silver medal in the 1936 Berlin games, finishing second to Jesse Owens in the

Ralph Metcalfe (left) *and Eddie Tolan at the 1932 Olympics.*

100-meter dash. He and Owens also ran on the 400-meter relay team, taking home a gold medal and setting a new world record in the process.

The first broad jumper to surpass 26 feet was Sylvio P. Cator, a Haitian. On May 25, 1935, at Ann Arbor, Michigan, the amazing Jesse Owens jumped 26 feet, 8¼ inches, setting a world record that would stand for nearly thirty years.

By the time the 1936 Berlin Olympics commenced, the world was beginning to respond to the tyranny of Adolf Hitler. Rumors of the inhuman treatment of the German Jewish population were spreading far and wide. Hitler's incredibly cruel persecution of the Jews—and other peoples—would soon be regarded as preparation for his planned conquest of Europe and the world. The "troubles" in Germany were minimized by Americans, who focused on economic rehabilitation after the Great Depression and the New Deal policies of President Franklin Delano Roosevelt.

In the meantime, Hitler was spreading his doctrine of Aryan supremacy—the concept of the "pure" German people who, in Hitler's terms, comprised "the master race."

Yet, while Hitler was amassing his armies and spreading his poisonous propaganda, he felt he needed the tacit approval—or at least the passivity—of the world's other nations to pursue his goals. And what better way to assure the world of Germany's respectability than through the Olympic Games? As a result of Hitler's desires, the 1936 Berlin Olympics were supercharged with politics and an undercurrent of racism. Hitler was confident that his Aryan supermen would completely smash the American team, largely because the American team had blacks on it. Dr. Julius Streicher, one of Hitler's propagandists, considered blacks to be "little more than trained baboons." Hitler's theory was demolished by the performance of Jesse Owens, grandson of an American slave.

Jesse Owens

Jesse Owens

Born in Danville, Alabama, in 1913, James Cleveland "Jesse" Owens was the seventh child of a poverty-stricken sharecropper. When Jesse was six years old, he was already working in the cotton fields. His family called him "J.C.," which was later changed to "Jesse" by his classmates and teachers. He was a sickly child who was pampered a great deal by his mother. As he grew older and met other children in school, he expressed an interest in going to college. His mother, tiring of the constant "dirt poor" existence they suffered in Danville, persuaded her husband to migrate North—they certainly could do no worse and perhaps little Jesse would somehow get a chance to go to college.

They moved to Cleveland, Ohio, where Jesse's father was intermittently employed as a laborer. However, Jesse's older brothers, who could read, were able to find steady menial employment. His mother and sister were conscientious domestics. The combined family income meant that they could often eat meat twice a week.

Two momentous things happened to Jesse Owens when he went to school in Cleveland; in the fourth grade he fell in love with his classmate Ruth (whom he later married), and in the fifth grade he met Charles Riley, coach of the high school track team. The integrated elementary school Owens attended did not have a gym, so they went to the high school for all sports activities. Charles Riley noted something special in Jesse and encouraged the scrawny little kid to prepare himself for the high school track team when he graduated. So Jesse did his running exercises every morning before school under the tutelage of Riley.

By the time Jesse was thirteen, he entered his first formal competition and lost, but soon he was the star at East Technical High School, setting his world scholastic record there. Owens had a year of an unbroken string of victories and record breaking performances and was a natural for all the scholarships offered to him. When Jesse asked Riley which scholarship to take, Riley, who knew the young man well, said, "None of them. I think you should pay your own way."

Already married, Owens enrolled at Ohio State University with no scholarship. He was in class from 8 A.M. until 3 P.M. and then would work out on the track for two hours. Then he went to work as a night elevator operator earning $150 a month. He was home by 1:30 A.M. and would get a few hours of sleep before the deadly routine started again. He studied while in transit from field to job and from job to home.

Larry Snyder, an outstanding coach at Ohio State, worked with Owens, honing Jesse's starts and forms to augment his natural talent.

Just before that memorable Big Ten track and field meet on May 25, 1935, at Ann Arbor, Michigan, Owens injured his spine when he fell down a flight of stairs. His sore back made it impossible for Jesse to bend over. After applications of heat and hours in a hot tub, Jesse recovered. He then proceeded to make track history. From 3:15 to 4 P.M. . . . he jumped 26 feet, 8¼ inches—a world record; he sprinted 100 yards in 9.4 seconds—tying his own world record; he ran the 200-yard dash in 20.3 seconds—

Jesse Owens winning the 100-yard dash at Ann Arbor.

another world record; he skimmed over the 220-yard low hurdles in 22.6 seconds—another world record. No one has matched that magnificent record in one day . . . or, to be more specific, in less than an hour.

Next stop: the Olympics. Larry Snyder was determined that Owens not burn himself out. The winter before the Olympics, Owens's activities were cut and heavy concentration was placed on grooming him to be a star. In the final American tryouts, Owens won the 100-meter and 200-meter races and the broad jump.

Germany was awarded the honor of holding the Olympic Games of 1936. Amidst the rumors and press reports of book burning and the opening of concentration camps, Germany sought to symbolize the cultural superiority of the Third Reich. The symbolic German eagle appeared everywhere: above the five Olympic rings, attached to all signposts on the Olympic grounds, and fastened to every streetlight.

Some Americans protested that participation by the United States in the Olympics would suggest approval of Hitler's policies. Avery Brundage, president of the United States Olympic Committee, insisted that the games were international—not national—in scope and it was sports—not politics—in question. He refused to discuss anti-Semitism, religion, or racial problems. But when the pre-Olympic pamphlets read, "Among inferior races, Jews have done nothing in the athletic sphere. They are surpassed even by the lowest Negro tribes," Brundage was forced into action. He was able to secure a promise that the Germans would not discriminate against Jewish athletes or spectators. Thus Brundage was able to override protests concerning American participation in the games.

The Germans then placed Rudi Ball, a Jew, on their winter hockey team, and fencer Helene Mayer, another Jew, on their summer team. Without a doubt, Rudi Ball was the best hockey player in Germany and Helene Mayer was formerly an Olympic champion, so the German selections were not suspect.

Before the games, anti-Semitic signs were taken down in Berlin and all the homes facing the athletic fields were freshened with paint and planted with an abundance of flowers. A replica of the shrine of Zeus was built and a torch was lit by young Greek girls. A relay of three thousand men brought the Olympic flame across seven countries to Berlin. Germany had indeed captured the spirit of the Olympics and presented a beautiful showcase for the "new Germany" of Nazism.

Despite Hitler's anti-black propaganda, Jesse Owens was a heavy favorite of the German people. The Nazis conceded this point when they featured his picture on the official flyers.

After the crowd sang "Deutschland Uber Alles," the Olympics were ready to begin. One of the most exciting events was the 100-meter dash. Owens hit the finish line one yard in front of Ralph Metcalfe and tied the world record at 10.3 seconds.

The next day was the broad jump. The broad jump trials gives each participant three tries to make a qualifying distance of 23 feet, 5½ inches. Owens fouled. He was not worried; he had fouled many times before. The next jump he fouled by overstepping the take-off and he was in a panic. So many had put so much faith in him and he had worked so hard. For the world's greatest broad jumper to fail in the trials was totally unthinkable. Just before his third attempt, Lutz Long, the German champion, came over to introduce himself. Lutz Long, who looked like the ideal Aryan, was also competing for the broad jump record. Long placed his hand on Owens's shoulder and told him, "You are 100 percent when you jump. I'm the same. You cannot do halfway,

Jesse Owens winning the Olympic 100-meter dash.

but you are afraid you will foul again." Long calmed Owens and encouraged him to recount his measurements. Owens took off, soared through the air, and came down, setting an Olympic record that day of 26 feet, 5¼ inches. Lutz Long, who had jumped nearly 26 feet himself, warmly congratulated Owens and the two men from such different worlds became close friends.

The 200-meter dash was Owens's third event. He set another Olympic record by clocking 20.7 seconds. And then he ran the first leg on the American 400-meter relay team with Metcalfe, Foy Draper, and Frank Wykoff following. Owens received a record-setting four gold medals and the American 400-meter relay team set a world record.

Jesse Owens's Olympic record-breaking broad jump.

"The Black Auxiliaries," as they were called by a German newspaper, carried their share in that 1936 Olympics. Ralph Metcalfe, former 1932 winner, won a silver medal in the 100-meter dash and a gold medal in the 400-meter relay. John Woodruff, a University of Pittsburgh freshman, became the first American in twenty-four years to win the 800-meter run. Fritz Pollard, Jr., from the University of North Dakota, son of the All-American football player at Brown, led for half the race in the 100-meter high hurdles, then fell to third. David Albritton, from Ohio State, won a silver medal in the high jump. Archie Williams and James LuValle came in first and third in the 400-meter run. Mack Robinson, brother of baseball's Jackie Robinson, placed second to Owens in the 200-meter dash.

John Woodruff, a University of Pittsburgh freshman who had absolutely no notion of running style, stormed from last place to become the first American in twenty-four years to win the 800-meter run at the 1932 Olympics in Los Angeles.

Cornelius Johnson, a strong favorite in the running high jump, had set a new Olympic record when he soared 6 feet, 7 15/16 inches on the opening day of the Olympics. While Johnson, the first black champion of the 1936 games, was receiving his medal, he looked up into the stands and saw Hitler leaving the stadium. Johnson just smiled. Several German winners had been led to Hitler's box and personally congratulated by Herr Hitler. By the time Cornelius Johnson won his medal, Hitler had been reportedly advised by Count Henri Baillet-Latour, president of the International

Olympic Committee, that as guest of honor he had no right to publicly acknowledge the winning of any person. Thereafter, Hitler congratulated no one in public.

When Owens arrived in New York after the Olympics, there was a ticker tape parade for him and a reception at the Waldorf-Astoria in his honor. However, in keeping with the racial policies of the hotel at that time, Jesse had to take the freight elevator to the reception room.

The riches—wealth and prominence—that the Olympics seemed to promise were never received by Owens. The only job that was available to him was that of a school coach. With his young family growing, he needed money desperately. He tried to open a string of dry cleaning establishments but was embezzled by some slick promoters and left with an enormous debt. It was then that he agreed to race in competition with horses and motorcycles at athletic events. No longer able to endure the humiliation, Owens tried public relations and eventually became secretary of the Illinois Athletic Commission.

When his oldest daughter, Gloria, was the first black to be chosen as homecoming queen at Ohio State, Owens returned to his alma mater for the ceremonies, which were held at a football game. The roar of the crowd when he entered the stadium acknowledged the glory of the man.

Jessie Owens died on March 31, 1980 but he has not been forgotten. In his honor, his granddaughter, Gina Hemphill, carried the Olympic torch into the Los Angeles Colisium for the internationally televised opening ceremony of the 1984 Olympics.

Harrison "Bones" Dillard

Harrison Dillard hits the high hurdles as Milt Campbell (right) *tries in vain to catch him.*

World War II and its aftermath precluded any Olympic competition for twelve years, but when the games were resumed again in 1948, England was selected to be the host country. Lord David Burghley, former hurdles champion and chairman of the British Olympics Committee, managed to organize and prepare for the long-awaited contest, even though England was still in the process of rebuilding after the war.

Some six thousand athletes from fifty-nine countries participated (excluding the Germans and Japanese) and, despite a heat wave, continuing rains, and muddy fields, the Olympics went on as scheduled. The times demanded dramatic heroes and America had one—Harrison Dillard.

Dillard was born in Cleveland, Ohio, in 1924. He grew up so poverty-ridden and malnourished that his friends called him "Bones." Dillard had a hero, though: Jesse Owens. He wanted to do everything Jesse Owens had done. Starting out in junior high school as a sprinter, his coach urged Dillard to switch to hurdle races because he seemed too frail to endure the rigors of sprinting. When Dillard attended Baldwin Wallace College, he was five feet, ten inches tall and weighed 152 pounds. They thought he was too small for the hurdles, a tall man's event. Harrison went on to become without question the finest high hurdler in the world. In one stretch spanning 1947 and 1948, he won 82 consecutive races. He was unbeaten and more than ready for the 1948 Olympics.

In the final trials for the Olympic team, Dillard fell in his qualifying race and failed to make the U.S. hurdles squad. In an attempt to salvage his Olympic dreams, Dillard went over to the area where the sprints were starting and entered the trial runs. By barely beating Ed Conwell for third place, he made the team for the 100-meter dash.

Mel Patton, a Californian, was the favored United States contender. He had run 100 yards in 9.3 seconds on May 15, 1948—a world record. Patton's most formidable opponents were Lloyd La Beach, a Panamanian, and Barney Ewell, a fellow American. La Beach had set the previous record for 100 yards, which Patton had broken. Ewell had defeated Patton in the U.S. Olympic trials. The rivalry between these three men was so intense that they took very little note of Alistair McCorguodale and MacDonald Bailey, the two Englishmen in the event, or Harrison Dillard.

Patton, Ewell, and La Beach drew lanes one, two, and three. Then came the Englishmen, thereby placing Dillard in the outside lane. Ewell surged ahead of Patton and La Beach and was so confident he had won the race that he did a little dance. Much to Ewell's dismay, Bones Dillard, the man he had been least concerned about, had crossed the finish line first, thus producing the biggest upset of the 1948 games. And Dillard had tied his hero Jesse Owens's Olympic record of 10.3 seconds for the

Barney Ewell

race, truly the stuff of which dreams are made. Later Dillard said, "When I stood there listening to 'The Star-Spangled Banner' and seeing the American flag fluttering and watching my name hoisted on the high scoreboard, I felt that this was the end— the absolute climax to everything for me."

But in Helsinki, in the 1952 Olympic Games, Dillard won another gold medal in his specialty, the 110-meter high hurdles, proving that his performance in 1948 was no fluke.

Harrison Dillard:

I was born in Cleveland in 1924, where I attended East Tech High School, which happened to be the same high school that Jesse Owens attended. Jesse, of course, was a few years ahead of me. Dave Albritton, the Olympic high jumper, was also a student at that school. They had a great tradition in track and field, one of the best reputations of any high school in the country. I was city champion and state of Ohio champion.

Ivan Greene, my coach at East Tech, taught me the basics in hurdling. I was supposed to go to Ohio State because Jesse Owens went there and because the school was big in sports, but it was 140 miles from Cleveland. That was awfully far away. So I went to Baldwin-Wallace, where my coach Eddie Finnigan had always dreamed of being the coach of a national champion. He thought that I had the potential to become that champion. Finnigan told me quite frankly that he didn't know a lot about hurdling, but he said we could learn together.

The track cage at the college was much too small for hurdles, so when the weather was bad we worked in the women's gym. Having only one hurdle to work with, I learned how to start fast and get there ahead of the big guys so their elbows wouldn't knock me on my behind.

Blacks at one time didn't excel in distance running, simply because we didn't go out for distance running. Then we found out in the fifties, sixties, and seventies, in particular, that the Africans were once accustomed to running distances— those who tended farmlands and ran after sheep and goats and other animals ran fifteen, twenty, thirty miles a day. We found out distance running is just a matter of acclimation—having the willingness to run the distances. If you are willing, you can do it.

The first black to really dispel that myth about the inability of blacks to run the distance was Frank Dixon at NYU. Frank ran the mile and won it in the Millrose Games and other places to help break down that mythical nonsense.

Frank Dixon winning the Millrose Mile.

Ralph Boston

Ralph Boston breaking the Olympic broad jump record in 1960.

During the 1960 Olympic Games in Rome, Ralph Boston consulted with Jesse Owens. Boston told Owens that he wanted that gold medal and to win it he would have to beat Owens's record and, therefore, this gave him a feeling of sadness. Owens smiled and told Boston that records were made to be broken, that he had had his time and now it was Boston's time. Although he was competing with the world's best jumpers (three of whom had bested 26 feet), on his third try Ralph hyperventilated, pumped his legs nearly chest-high, accelerated his speed, and flew 26 feet, 7¾ inches, erasing the Olympic record of 26 feet, 5¼ inches, that Owens had set in Berlin in 1936.

In Mississippi, Mrs. Eulalia Boston watched the television and began to cry when her son, Ralph Boston, held up his gold medal and said for all the world to hear, "Mom, this is for you."

Boston was born in Laurel, Mississippi, on May 9, 1939. There were ten children and Ralph was the youngest. His mother raised the children alone and supported them with the money she earned as a domestic. Boston was a quiet, introspective boy and no one paid much attention to him until he reached high school and made the track team. In 1954, at the age of fifteen, he broad jumped 20 feet, 10 inches. Ralph proved to be a multitalented athlete and once took eight first places in a school meet.

When he attended Tennessee A&I, he proved to be exceptional in the high jump, the hop-step-and-jump, and in low and high hurdles. In one meet, he took first place in all of these events, in addition to his specialty, the broad jump.

In Moscow, in 1961, he jumped 27 feet, 1¾ inches, breaking his own record and establishing a new world's record. In the 1964 Olympics in Tokyo, he finished second to a British jumper. Later, in a Modesto, California, meet, he set a new mark of 27 feet, 4¾ inches, which was broken by Bob Beamon's unbelievable jump of 29 feet, 2½ inches, at the "Rare Air Olympics" at Mexico City in 1968.

Wilma Rudolph

Wilma Rudolph winning her second gold medal in the 200-meter dash at the 1960 Rome Olympics.

Wilma Glodean Rudolph was born on June 23, 1940, in Saint Bethlehem, Tennessee. She was the seventeenth of nineteen children. At birth she weighed barely more than four pounds and seemed a most unlikely candidate for the Olympics. Her parents and older siblings worked in the tobacco fields and just barely survived. As if life was not hard enough, Rudolph contracted double pneumonia, scarlet fever, and later polio—which paralyzed her legs.

With a fierce determination, Wilma's mother traveled ninety miles once a week to a free hospital clinic. The entire family was trained to massage and exercise little Wilma's legs. Finally, after years of medical treatment, she was able to walk, with the aid of corrective shoes and a leg brace, at the age of eight.

From there on in, it was up to Wilma. She began running in elementary school and in high school Wilma won every race she entered. Her recovery was more than complete. Competing within the state of Tennessee, she won every dash from 50 to 220 yards for five consecutive years. Not only that but she became an outstanding basketball player and was named to the All-State squad. When she was only sixteen, Wilma scored 803 points in 25 games for her school.

She entered Tennessee State College in 1958 and immediately was tutored by famous track team coach Ed Temple. With a great deal of confidence, Wilma said she intended to become the most famous woman runner in America. The Olympic trials confirmed Wilma Rudolph's status as the most outstanding American woman runner.

The 1960 Olympics started off as a disappointment to the many Americans in attendance. The great John Thomas, who had previously set a world record of 7 feet, 3¾ inches, lost to two Russians in the high jump and the American team lost the 100-meter dash to the Germans.

But there was a lot of excitement centered around a pretty, long-legged, twenty-year-old black woman, who the French were beginning to call "La Gazelle" and who the Italians dubbed "The Black Pearl." Her clockings at preliminary heats were drawing enormous crowds. And then it was time for the 100-meter dash. As soon as the starting gun sounded, Rudolph surged out in front. With every stride, she lengthened her lead until she had outdistanced the pack by at least three yards. Cutting half a second off the Olympic record, she ran the 100 meters in 11 seconds flat and won her first gold medal.

In the 200-meter dash, she set an Olympic record of 23.2 seconds and won again by three yards. Then, in the 400-meter relay, she came from behind on the anchor leg to lead the United States to another victory.

Wilma Rudolph thus became the first American woman to win three gold medals in Olympic track and field competition. She was voted Female Athlete of the Year by the Associated Press. In 1961, Wilma won the James E. Sullivan Memorial Trophy, which honors the athlete who has best advanced the cause of sportsmanship during the year. America welcomed her return and honored her everywhere she went.

She declined to participate in the 1964 Olympics, saying, "The best I could do if I went back is win three gold medals again. If I won two, there would be something lacking. I'll stick with the glory won—like Jesse Owens did in 1936."

Rafer Johnson

Rafer Johnson in the shot-put event in the 1960 Olympic decathlon.

Rafer Johnson was born in Dallas, Texas, on August 18, 1934, one of six children. Hoping to better their living conditions, the family moved to Kingsburg, in California's San Joaquin Valley, when Johnson was a young boy. The family lived in a railroad boxcar which they redesigned into a home.

When Johnson attended Kingsburg High School, he was the star halfback on the football team, leading his school to three football championships. He was also an outstanding basketball player. During his junior year, he played center field on the baseball team and batted .512. His talent in football earned him a scholarship to UCLA, but his real love was track. Fearful that football injuries might harm his track career, he decided not to continue playing football.

Even before he attended college, Johnson dreamed about qualifying for the Olympics and becoming the decathlon champion of the world. He excelled in the 100-meter and 400-meter runs, the shot put, and the discus. The high jump, pole vault, and broad jump were more difficult for him, but he had the ability, the determination, and the size. In his zeal to prepare himself for the 1956 Olympics at Melbourne, Australia, Johnson aggravated an old football injury, but he still managed to place second to Milt Campbell in the decathlon and won a silver medal.

Knowing he had four years before he could try again, Johnson trained strenuously for the 1960 Olympics. In the 1958 "Little Olympics" in Moscow, he set a world decathlon record of 8,302 points, defeating Vasily Kuznetsov, Russia's "Man of Steel," by 505 points.

Johnson is an extraordinary man. While at UCLA, he maintained an almost A average, was president of the student body, was the first black to pledge a white fraternity, and headed three campus honorary societies. Under the auspices of the State Department, he toured Africa, Australia, and Europe. He was also a baritone in two church choirs and served on California's State Recreation Committee.

A year before the 1960 Olympics in Rome, Johnson was in an automobile accident and injured his back severely. After several weeks in the hospital, he recovered enough to win the Olympic trials. In the grueling twenty-six-hour, ten-event decathlon contest in Rome, Johnson finished with a fantastic 8,392 points, setting a new world record. Rafer Johnson's dream came true—he proved himself to be the greatest overall athlete in the world.

Twenty-four years later, Rafer Johnson participated in another Olympics, when he took the Olympic torch from Jessie Owens's granddaughter and ran up the giant stairway at the Los Angeles Coliseum to light the flame that symbolized the opening of the 1984 Olympic Games. It was a moment that honored not only Rafer Johnson but all the black athletes who have competed in the Olympic Games.

BLACK TRACK AND FIELD STARS OF YESTERDAY

Eulace Peacock of Temple University, one of the truly outstanding dash men of the 1930s.

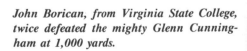

John Borican, from Virginia State College, twice defeated the mighty Glenn Cunningham at 1,000 yards.

Mal Whitfield, a United States Army Air Force sergeant. At the 1948 Olympic Games in London, in perhaps the greatest individual performance since that of Jesse Owens in the 1936 Games, Whitfield set a new Olympic record in the 800-meter race by clocking in at 1 minute and 49.2 seconds; ran anchor on the winning 1,600-meter relay team; and took third in the 400-meter race. Whitfield's combined points were the highest individual scores of the 1948 games.

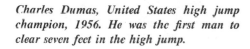

Charles Dumas, United States high jump champion, 1956. He was the first man to clear seven feet in the high jump.

Milt Campbell of Indiana University. He won the decathlon gold medal at the 1956 Olympics in Melbourne, Australia.

In terms of racial equality, the tumultuous sixties was a decade of sit-ins, freedom rides, confrontation riots, and assassinations. It was a time when blacks demanded equal rights and put their lives on the line for them. It seemed natural that these protests and sacrifices would somehow extend to the International Olympics.

In 1964, Dick Gregory, black human rights activist and comedian/humorist, proposed a boycott of the Olympic Games in Tokyo as a protest against unequal treatment of blacks. Gregory was unable to gain any substantial support, but the seeds of the concept were planted and black athletes soon began to weigh the pros and cons of a boycott.

Early in 1965, black athletes selected to play in the American Football League's East-West All-Star classic threatened to boycott the New Orleans game because some of them had been refused admission to the city's social clubs. Joe Foss, the commissioner of the league, reassigned the game to another city. Thus, the unity of these black athletes produced tangible results.

When he was in Japan, Tommie Smith, a black student athlete at San Jose State College in California, was asked by Japanese sports reporters about the possibility of American blacks boycotting the 1968 Olympics. Smith replied that it was a possibility in light of the racial injustices in America. This went over the wire services.

It was approximately at this point that Harry Edwards, a black sociology professor and former athlete, became involved. Edwards evaluated the situation at San Jose and determined that racism was evident in every area of campus life and in the poor treatment received by black athletes. As a result of his findings, a boycott of the opening football game was planned as a protest. As a result, the college was forced to make some concessions to the demands of the students.

As a further result, Professor Edwards organized and became chairman of the Olympic Committee for Human Rights. Dr. Louis Lomax, civil rights activist, was a consultant, as were Dr. Martin Luther King, and Floyd McKissick, director of the Congress of Racial Equality. Kenneth Noll, at that time a master's degree candidate at San Jose State, was the chief organizer.

The goals of the proposed Olympic boycott were:

1. Restoration of Muhammad Ali's title and license to box in this country;
2. Removal from the International Olympics Committee of the anti-Semitic and anti-black personality Avery Brundage;
3. Curtailment of participation by all-white teams from South Africa and Southern Rhodesia in the United States and the Olympic Games;
4. Two black Olympic coaches;
5. Two black people on the Olympics Committee;
6. Desegregation of the New York Athletic Club.

While Edwards received a great deal of support from some prominent black athletes and from black leaders in general, the participants in the Olympics were fragmented. Many black athletes had trained hard for years to reach the Olympics; some were afraid of being labeled troublemakers and losing out on potentially high-paying jobs in professional sports; others were afraid of losing their scholarships. At any rate, the boycott was called off.

The year 1968 was a bad one for the Olympics in general. Not only were black boycotts imminent but there were objections to the Olympics being held in Mexico because of the high altitude. There was scandal concerning the alleged embezzlement of Olympic funds. Then, after the exclusion of South Africa, it was decided that the country should be readmitted. There were many questions concerning the use of drugs and stimulants. Genetic tests were run on all women athletes to ascertain that they were of the proper sex. And all of this happened before the games even started!

Tommie Smith and John Carlos, followers of Professor Harry Edwards, won the gold and bronze medals in the 200-meter dash. Smith's time of 19.83 was an Olympic record. While on the victory stand, Smith and Carlos were presented with their medals and as "The Star-Spangled Banner" was played, the two men raised black-gloved fists in a Black Power salute and lowered their heads. The crowd was shocked. Its silence turned to anger. Smith and Carlos were suspended from the Olympic team, and the International Olympic Committee ordered them out of Olympic Village and gave them forty-eight hours to get out of Mexico.

Tommie Smith (center) *and John Carlos* (right) *at the 1968 Mexico City Olympics.*

Bob Beamon breaking the world Olympic broad jump record in Mexico City, 1968.

The next day Bob Beamon from Texas-El Paso University, by way of Jamaica, New York, and under great pressure, startled the crowd by soaring 29 feet, 2½ inches in the broad jump final. Beamon's extra-long leap bettered the world record by almost two feet and won him the gold medal; a record that has not yet been surpassed, and will not be challenged until the 1988 Olympics in Seoul, Korea.

Lee Evans, a friend of Tommie Smith's, won the 400-meter race in the world record time of 43.8 seconds. Evans wore a pair of black socks as a silent sign of protest against the ousting of Smith and Carlos. Evans said, "A lot of things were on my mind. But I had to push them out of my mind and concentrate on winning the gold medal just like a friend of mine did. Further, I feel I won this gold medal for black people in the United States and black people all over the world.

"I learned a lot about people being in the boycott movement. If I had it to do over again, I'd support the movement. I never knew people until I supported something people were against."

Evans teamed up with Ronald Freeman, Larry James and Vincent Mathews to break another Olympic record in the 400-meter relay in 2:56.1. The 100-meter relay squad of Charles Greene, James Hines, Melvin Pender, and Ronnie Ray Smith also made Olympic history when they established a new speed record of 38.19. Teammate Hines had already won the gold medal for a record-breaking 100-meter dash in 9.95.

On the distaff side in this record-breaking year, Wyomia Tyus repeated her gold medal performance in the 1964 games by winning the 100-meter dash, and in doing so became the first athlete—man or woman—to win back-to-back Olympic gold medal victories. Wyomia then, along with Barbara Ferrell (who had taken the silver medal in the 100-meter event), Margaret Bailes and Mildrette Netter banded together to take another gold medal in the 100-meter relay. So, despite the bad start and the dramatic boycott protest, America's black athletes did themselves proud in the track and field events of 1968.

The next games in Munich in 1972 were overshadowed by the terrorist attack on the Israeli team that took the lives of eleven athletes, sending a wave of horror and revulsion through the Olympic village, and the world-at-large. Despite the tragedy and the turmoil, the games continued. In the 100-meter relay event, Larry Black,

Wyomia Tyus winning her first Olympic gold medal in 1964.

Eddie Hart, Robert Taylor, and Gerald Tinker matched the Olympic record set by Evans, Freeman, James, and Mathews in 1968. Vincent Mathews, while not a member of this year's relay team, scored individual honors by capturing the gold in the 400-meter race. The other black track and field gold medalist of this year was Rod Milburne, who set a new Olympic record of 13:24 in the 110-meter hurdles.

The Montreal games in 1976, also troubled with political overtones, saw the beginning of the remarkable reign of Edwin Moses in the 400-meter hurdles. A superbly trained and dedicated athlete, Moses set a new Olympic record of 47.64, which has yet to be surpassed.

America's athletes were all primed to go to Moscow in 1980 when, a few months before the opening of Olympics, the Soviets invaded neighboring Afghanistan and, in protest, President Jimmy Carter called for a boycott of the games. A political gesture that was supported by fifty-eight other nations. The Americans had a strong track and field team and their inability to compete was a bitter blow to all concerned.

Ed Moses, unquestionably the greatest hurdler in the history of track and field, as he breezes here to an easy victory in the 400 meter hurdles at the 1976 Olympic trials in Eugene, Oregon. Later that year, he won a gold medal for the event at the Olympics in Montreal. Moses repeated his victory in the 1984 Olympics, being only one of two men to have won gold medals at both the Montreal and Los Angeles Games. Moses was named 1985's Sportsman of the Year.

In Pursuit of Jesse's Record

Carl Lewis celebrating his second gold medal for the long jump at the Los Angeles Games, August 6, 1984.

It had been fifty-two years since the summer Olympic Games had been held in the United States, in Los Angeles. Once again this colorful metropolis on the Pacific was a host city, in 1984. The spirit of the games had been somewhat dampened by another boycott, the Soviet bloc this time, but the sponsors were determined to make the occasion a gala event in true movieland style. As both stadium and TV viewers all over the world will attest, the opening and closing ceremonies were indeed a Hollywood spectacular. But for drama and excitement nothing could surpass the individual athletic competitions that took place on the field, especially as many Olympic and world records began to fall.

In the track and field events, names and memories of past Olympics kept surfacing. There was Rafer Johnson and Jesse Owens's granddaughter in the opening day ceremonies. Edwin Moses was back hoping to repeat his 1976 Olympic gold medal performance. Carl Lewis had publicly announced his intent to repeat Jesse Owens's 1936 record win of four gold medals. And Wilma Rudolph, of the 1960 games, was remembered when Valerie Brisco-Hooks became the second woman in Olympic history to win three gold medals.

Because of the pregame media buildup, there was much interest in the performances

The victorious United States 400-meter relay team. **(Left to right)** *Sam Graddy, Calvin Smith, Ron Brown, and Carl Lewis (who won his fourth gold medal of the meet, equaling Jesse Owens's incredible feat).*

of Carl Lewis and Edwin Moses, and the stadium audiences focused their full attention on both athletes. Lewis was successful in duplicating Jesse Owens's feat, the only man to do so, with a long jump of 28 feet, 1/4 inch; a 100-meter dash in 9.99; a record-breaking 200-meters in 19.80; and he was the anchorman in the 400-meter relay that established another world record of 37.83. Although bothered by a sore left leg during the meet, Lewis nevertheless ran his anchor lap in a sparkling 8.94. His victorious teammates were Sam Graddy, Ron Brown, and Calvin Smith.

With his pretty wife Myrella in the stands, Edwin Moses won his second gold medal for the 400-meter hurdles (in 47.75), eight long years after the first. That win was his 105th straight victory without a defeat; a remarkable feat.

With their strong performances in recent world competition and in the Olympic trials, a great deal was expected of the women's track and field team, and our athletes did not disappoint. They swept eight out of the 18 scheduled events, breaking four Olympic records as they did so. They won 13 Gold, 5 Bronze, and 2 Silver medals.

The comely Valerie Brisco-Hooks became the only 200- and 400-meter double winner of any sex in all Olympic history, and her times of 21.81 and 48.83 set new Olympic records. She won her third gold medal with the record-breaking 3:18.29 victory of the 400-meter relay team.

Another Gold medal winner was the beautiful Evelyn Ashford. In 1983 at the world games in Helsinki, Finland, Evelyn set the world record for the 100-meter dash (10.79). Her Olympic gold medal triumph was but a slim margin slower (less than one fifth of a second) but at 10.97 it was the first sub-11-second race by a woman in the history of the Olympic Games.

Evelyn, Valerie, and their medal-winning teammates, Benita Fitzgerald-Brown (gold—100-meter hurdles), Alice Brown (silver—100 meters), Florence Griffeth (silver—200 meters), Chandra Cheeseborough (silver—400 meters), Kim Gallagher (silver—800 meters), Judi Brown (silver—400 meter hurdles), along with marathon gold medalist Joan Benoit, constituted the strongest female track and field team America has ever assembled.

Evelyn Ashford (center)

Valerie Brisco-Hooks

Chandra Cheeseborough

Benita Fitzgerald-Brown

HORSE RACING

Around 1500 B.C., Libya occupied almost all of the northern coast of Africa, with the exception of the Delta of the Nile. The Libyans had horses which were quite small by today's comparison. Their average height was 42 inches. Although there were many wild horses in various parts of the world, these were the first known in that part of Africa. When the neighboring Egyptians attacked and conquered Libya, they sought booty to take back to their Pharaoh. Besides the usual prizes of gold, jewels, and precious stones, they took along this strange animal. The Libyan horse was different from any other known relative to the horse. It was not like the zebra or the ass. How it became the distinctive breed that it is has not been discovered, but the horses that came out of Libya into Egypt were the ancestors of today's Thoroughbred. The Egyptians used the horses to haul carts and carry war supplies and they practically drained Libya of its horse population.

Around 500 B.C., a ruler in Persia named Darius sought to breed the Egyptian horses larger and stronger, hoping they would be suitable to carry soldiers. Darius never succeeded, but other men slowly were able to breed the horse to a height of 62 to 65 inches and increase its weight from 500 or 600 pounds to 1,050 pounds. When this was accomplished, around the third century A.D., men began riding bareback.

Horseback riding was popularized by Mohammed around A.D. 590. With the founding of his new religion, he was anxious to have his message carried all over the known world. He gained many converts when his disciples—aboard horseback—thundered into some small countries whose populace had never seen a horse.

When the Moors drove the Goths from Spain, they brought with them the Arabian horse of the Middle East and breeding farms were established. King Henry I of England heard about the value of these specially bred Arabian horses and he purchased a stallion in Spain in A.D. 1110. He bred the Arabian steed with the strong, powerful mares that were abundant in England. The results were so fulfilling that King Henry I bought even more stallions from Morocco.

The owners of the new purebreeds took great pride in their horses and would make wagers as to who had the fastest horse and who was the better rider. This concept grew to a point that in around A.D. 1174 the first public racecourse was built outside the gates of London at Smithfield.

At first, horse racing, the sport of kings, was done for sheer pleasure, but later promoters of fairs throughout London gave prizes to winners and encouraged more audience participation. Wagers were made and gambling abounded.

In 1644, Colonel Richard Nicolls of England invaded the Dutch territory called New Amsterdam. After conquering the Dutch, Nicolls became the first English Royal Governor of New York. Governor Nicolls was a great horse racing enthusiast and in 1665 he laid out a two-mile horse racing course near Hempstead, Long Island, and called it the Newmarket, honoring a place in England. (This course was just a few miles from the present Belmont Park track.)

The imported English Thoroughbreds were bred with heavy mares. The concept of horse racing spread to the Colonial South and, eager to emulate the British, the plantation owners of Virginia, Maryland, and Kentucky undertook the importation and breeding of the aristocratic Thoroughbred. The job of grooming, feeding, breaking, exercising, and training horses was turned over to the slaves. And when it came time to race these magnificent steeds, it was the black slaves who brought them to victory or defeat. Although official records were kept, the names of the black jockeys and trainers did not appear in the racing programs.

At the first Jerome Handicap at Belmont Park in 1866, a black rider named Abe won with a horse called Watson. Abe went on to win the third Travers Stakes at Saratoga Springs in 1866 with a horse called Merrill.

In May 1875, the first Kentucky Derby was held at Churchill Downs in Louisville. Of the fifteen jockeys in the first Derby, fourteen were black. Oliver Lewis, one of the black jockeys, won that race with a horse called Arisitides in 2:373/4, over a mile-and-a-half track. Today the Derby distance has been shortened to a mile-and-a-quarter. Black jockeys won fifteen of the first twenty-eight runnings of the Derby.

Oliver Lewis

The jockey with the best winning average in Kentucky Derby history—two victories, one second, and one third in four starts—is Jimmy Winkfield . . . a rider who was somewhat unknown to the American public at that time.

Had Winkfield not gone abroad in 1905 and spent the next twenty-five years winning races such as the Moscow Derby, Prix du President de la République, and Grosser Prix Von Baden, he might today share a fame comparable to that of Isaac Murphy, considered one of the greatest riders in American history. Murphy was the first man to ride three Derby winners and, according to his records, he rode in 1,412 races from 1875 to 1895, winning 628, or 44 percent. No other rider yet has approached that mark.

Isaac Murphy

Isaac Burns Murphy was born Isaac Burns on January 1, 1861, right in the heart of horse country—Lexington, Kentucky. His father, James Burns, was a freedman and a bricklayer who joined the Union forces and died as a prisoner of war. His mother was a laundress in the employ of Richard Owings of the Owings and Williams Racing Stable. In 1874, the seventy-pound Isaac started galloping horses for the Owings and Williams Stable, then trained by Eli Jordan, a black.

Isaac's mother changed his name to Murphy, in honor of her father with whom she lived after her husband's death.

In 1875, at the age of fourteen, he brought home his first winner. By the 1880s, he was so well regarded that Lucky Baldwin, noted gambler and horse owner, paid Murphy $10,000 just to have first call on his services.

Murphy rode Buchanan to victory in the 1884 Derby, Riley in 1890, and Kingman in 1891.

His record of three Kentucky Derby wins was not equaled until 1930, when Earle Sande came home with Gallant Fox, and was not surpassed until 1948, when Eddie Arcaro won the fourth of his five, on Citation.

Murphy had style and flair and, besides being a superb jockey, he was a pleasure to watch. His specialty was the whirlwind finish. He never worked himself into a frenzy as many jockeys did, but remained cool, upright at all times, and dramatic. Murphy had an uncanny sense of pace. He rode with long stirrups and tried not to take more out of a horse than was needed to get the job done. He frightened many owners with his come-from-behind style, which led to hairbreadth finishes.

The 1890s were the greatest times of Murphy's career.

Though he is remembered today for his Kentucky Derby record, Murphy won other races that were more important at that time than the Louisville classic. He won five Latonia Derbys and four of the first five American Derbys at Washington Park near Chicago. He won the Swift, the Travers, and the Saratoga Cup. In some celebrated match races, Murphy led a mount called Salvator to three victories over a horse called Tenny, which was ridden by a white jockey, Ed "Snapper" Garrison. Snapper was a great jockey in his own right and the term "Garrison finish"—a stirring, last-minute, come-from-behind victory—is attributed to him. Garrison, with his neck-hugging style and wild whipping, got a lot of attention, but it was Murphy, who gently pressed his knees against Salvator's side and whispered something in the horse's ear, that won the race.

On February 13, 1896, Isaac Murphy died of pneumonia at the age of thirty.

In 1956, he was elected to horse racing's Hall of Fame.

William Simms

In the year that Isaac Murphy died, 1896, Willie Simms won the Kentucky Derby. Simms was born in Augusta, Georgia, on January 16, 1870. He rode five winners at Sheepshead Bay in New York in 1893 and he did the same thing again at New York's Jerome Park in 1894. After he won the Derby aboard Ben Brush in 1896, he won again in 1898 with Plaudit.

Simms became a turf hero. Richard Croker and Michael F. Dwyer hired him to ride their horses in England. There he became the first American jockey to win an event on an English course with an American horse, owner, trainer, and equipment—a first all-American victory—and he was catapulted to international fame. He stayed in England for a long period and continued to ride with success.

Jimmy Winkfield

Winkfield was born in Chilesburg, not far from Lexington, Kentucky, on April 12, 1882. He went to work at Latonia for eight dollars a month when he was fifteen and made a spectacular debut as a jockey sometime later in a race in Chicago. Breaking fourth from the rail, he cut straight across the path of the three inside horses as he drove for the rail and all four horses fell down. The stewards put Winkfield down, too —for a year. When the suspension was over, Winkfield won his first race. Brainy and tough, he was on his way, a natural rider.

In 1901, he captured the Derby on His Eminence and in 1902 followed up with another victory on Alan-a-Dale. In the 1903 Derby, he was on a colt named Early. He was well ahead and about to go into the stretch when he decided to let Early coast home. It was a costly mistake. A horse named Judge Himes, a fast finisher, nipped Early at the wire. The 1902 Derby, which Winkfield won, was the last won by a black jockey.

Winkfield left the United States to compete in France, where he was a leading jockey for twenty years. In 1923, he won the Prix du President de la République at St. Cloud on a horse named Bahadur.

Winkfield retired in the mid-twenties from horseracing but remained in France as a highly successful trainer. His mounts were sent out all over Europe.

Alonzo "Lonnie" Clayton

Clayton was born in Kansas City, Missouri, in 1876, and like many boys had a fondness for riding horses. His ambition to become a jockey soon asserted itself and he prevailed upon his parents to allow him to join the E. J. Baldwin Stable. He remained with the stable for one year and then went East, where he was employed by the D. A. Stable in Clifton, New Jersey. It was at this track that he had his first mount, Redstone.

In an era where records were poorly kept, Clayton's name appears many times in the record books as a winning jockey. Among his important victories in 1894 are the Brooklyn Handicap and the Futurity, and in 1895 the Cotton Stakes at Memphis and the Saratoga Stakes. His brilliant win on Tillo in the Suburban of 1898 had the turf world buzzing for many years.

James "Soup" Perkins

Being a native of Lexington, Kentucky, that home of racing and Thoroughbreds, Perkins naturally absorbed the intimate knowledge of horses that is part of the childhood training of many Kentucky youngsters.

His first race was for an owner named Peter Wimmer on a horse called Ordrain and he finished second. His performance made an impression on the racing world and he was soon in demand as a jockey. His first winning mount was on a mare named Caroline Kinney.

His appearance at Morris Park in the spring of 1897, where he tied the 4½ furlong record of George Keene, brought him worldwide attention. Soup, as he was best known, was considered one of the best middleweight jockeys of his day and his mounts were always of championship class.

George B. "Spider" Anderson

Spider Anderson quickly gained a reputation as a winning jockey. He was a native of Maryland, having been born in Baltimore in 1871. He rode for some of the most exacting owners of the times, including August Belmont, Sr.; D. D. Withers; William L. Scott; and Byron McClelland. While in the employ of August Belmont and William L. Scott, Anderson won some of the most important stakes events of the American turf.

Anderson went on to become a noted steeplechase rider.

John H. Jackson

Jackson was born in Lexington, Kentucky, in 1879 and began racing for the Lee Christy Stable in 1894. He was an exercise boy for about six months until Christy recognized his riding skills. Good mounts were readily offered to him and in the next six months that he stayed with the Christy Stables he rode in seventy-five races, winning eighteen of them.

In 1895, Jackson joined the stable of Samuel C. Wagner and had even better success than the year before. He rode in about one hundred and fifty races and won forty of them. The horses that he rode included Umbrella, Alice W., and other top mounts.

In his time, Jackson was looked upon as a firm, strong rider, capable of holding his own against any and all competition.

Jimmy Lee

Few details are known of the early days of Jimmy Lee, except that he was on the racing scene at the turn of the twentieth century, racing mostly in the South. His claim to fame in the racing annals came from such notable achievements as riding six winners in one day at Latonia in 1909 and in riding five winners twice in one week.

Although he had amassed a small fortune during his racing career, Lee was penniless when he passed away at his home in Raceland, Louisiana, in May 1915.

Robert "Tiny" Williams

Williams, better known by his nickname "Tiny," was born in Chillicothe, Ohio, on December 10, 1868. His racing experiences began in 1879 with prominent owners of the times, such as J. E. Seagram, from Canada, and William L. Scott and E. J. Baldwin. He rode in his first race in 1883 and had his first win shortly after on a horse named Lillie Dale at New Orleans.

Williams had the reputation of being a good, serviceable rider, hard working and reliable.

Anthony Hamilton

Born in Columbus, South Carolina, in 1866, Hamilton's racing career began in the stables of William Lakeland, for whom he rode until 1886. In his time, he rode a winner in every important event on the American turf calendar. He had exciting victories in the Brooklyn Handicap, which he won with Exile in 1889, and with Hornpipe in 1895; and the 1895 Suburban on Lazzarone, as well as the 1896 Metropolitan on Counter Tenor.

Henry J. Harris

Born in Richmond, Virginia, on September 9, 1876, Harris was among the lightest jockeys of his era. He started riding in 1891 and was soon up on some of the better horses of the time, such as Pamway, Eastertide, Concord, Decide, Brightton, Hornpipe, and Winged Foot. To his prime weight advantage he added the admirable qualities of a clear head, steady hands, and good judgment.

Bud Haggins

A native of Kentucky, Haggins was born in July 1870 and started to become familiar with the world of horse racing in 1881. He started with the West Stables and worked for one year as an exercise boy. He quickly demonstrated his riding ability and his employer gave him a number of mounts before the end of that first year. Haggins won two races on a colt named Major Lee. He was then offered a position to ride for Henry Colston, who at that time had several good horses in his stable. Haggins allied himself to the fortunes of that owner and was successful in winning a number of races. He was not only outstanding on the flat but was also an excellent steeplechase rider.

William Porter

A native of Lexington, Kentucky, Porter was born on July 11, 1877. Porter's first stable connection was in 1891 with Edward Brown, with whom he went first to Chicago, then to Saratoga, and back to Kentucky. This first year of varied racing experiences was invaluable to the young rider's career, especially since it provided him with the opportunity to ride some excellent mounts. Two years later he was engaged to ride for E. J. Baldwin at Latonia. His first mount for his new stable was El Reno and he finished third. His next ride on the same horse was more successful—he finished first.

In subsequent years, Porter rode for W. Showwalter, William M. Wallace, and Albert Cox. He was the first to win a race on the famed Commoner, at three quarters of a mile in 1:14.

Some of the other great old black jockeys were Linc Jones, Tommy Knight, Johnny Hudgins, Clarence Reed, Charlie Gregg, James Irving, John Donnelly, Asher Waller, and C. Dishmon.

Jesse Conley, who finished third in the Kentucky Derby in 1911 on a horse called Colston, was the last black jockey to have a mount in the Derby. And then the black jockeys just "disappeared." Disappeared is a euphemism for exclusion when speaking in terms of a number of blacks. There were two significant events that happened prior to Jesse Conley's participation in the 1911 Derby. Governor Charles Evans Hughes saw to it that the New York Legislature passed his bill outlawing all racetrack betting. Without gambling, horse racing no longer had the appeal and every track in New York closed down. The repercussions were inestimable. Over forty thousand persons earned a legitimate living as a result of horse racing, breeding farms, stable hands and trainers, licensed bookmakers, farmers who supplied grain, etc. The result almost killed the sport overall in New York.

The other event that preceded the demise of the black jockey took place July 4, 1910, in Reno, Nevada. Heavyweight champion Jack Johnson defeated America's legendary Jim Jeffries, former heavyweight champion. Jim Jeffries had been dragged from retirement to fight and defeat the upstart, arrogant Jack Johnson, who had taken the crown from Tommy Burns in Australia in 1908. When Johnson defeated Jeffries, there were immediate and violent repercussions—race riots throughout America. The backlash against Johnson most assuredly affected the fate of the black jockey as well as all black athletes. With the vast moneymaking potential of horse racing, blacks were blocked out of the possibility of receiving any share. By the time horse racing was reestablished in New York, there were no more black jockeys "available."

However, in the 1960s, with the increase of civil rights activities, there have been a few black jockeys seen on the tracks. Alfred Johnson and Ronnie Tanner rode during the sixties and James Long had a first-place finish at Saratoga Springs in 1974. Today's black jockeys speak another language.

GOLF

The game of golf was invented in Scotland. Of course there are historians who argue that it might have been created in pre-Christian times by lonely shepherds who used their hooked staffs to hit small rocks to a point of destination. Another historian will proclaim that the game was invented in Holland on the basis of some ancient drawings depicting an ice skater with a slim stick with a knob on the end. Whatever the actual origin, golf is an integral part of the history of Scotland. By 1440, the game enjoyed a great deal of popularity. In 1457, James II, ruler of Scotland, had Parliament rule the game unlawful because it took away too much time from the practice of the bow and arrow, which were the major weapons of warfare.

But James IV of Scotland loved the game and played it as well as his granddaughter, Mary Queen of Scots. With the encouragement of the Queen, the game grew and the world's most famous golf course—St. Andrews—came into being during her reign around 1552. Golfing flourished as a game for those who were members of a club, which would of course restrict membership to the elite. The first tournament took place in 1860 at the Prestwick course in Scotland and later became known as the British Open.

In America there were "golf clubs" in South Carolina and Georgia in the eighteenth century, but golf seemed to be a very minor function of these clubs; they seemed to have been simply private country clubs.

Golf really got its start as a game in America in 1885. Joseph Mickle Fox from Philadelphia took a trip to Scotland and became completely fascinated by the game. He founded the Foxburg Golf Club near Philadelphia in 1887. This club, the oldest in America, is still in existence. Then in Yonkers, New York, a Scotsman named John G. Reid introduced the game to some friends in 1888. Their enthusiasm for the game helped to spread the popularity of golf in the United States.

By 1894, there were golf clubs with primitive links throughout New Jersey, New York, and Connecticut. The United States Golf Association was established to maintain rules and conduct annual tournaments—the amateur championship and the United States Open (i.e., open to the world).

American blacks became involved with golf at this time. Many of the caddies who worked on private courses were black. The very nature of the game precluded black participation at that time: the expense of owning and maintaining golf courses was prohibitive and certainly no black man would utilize valuable pasture or agricultural land for the purpose of playing golf. However, the caddies became great golfers because they could practice the game on club grounds during their off periods. In fact, they became so proficient that some of the private clubs would hold "caddies' matches."

Golf remained an elitist sport and, as such, blacks were not even considered for the game; that is, except for one—John Shippen. At the turn of the century, Shippen was probably the only American-born golf pro at that time; most pros came from Scotland and England. In 1900, Shippen and his brother Cyrus were instructors at exclusive clubs in the East and on many occasions played exhibition matches with celebrated golfers.

In 1896, when he was only eighteen, Shippen entered the United States Open. It was only the third year of the Open and objections ran rampant, but Theodore Haverman, president of the USGA, stated he would call the tournament off if Shippen were not allowed to participate. Shippen defeated Charles Macdonald, a big name in golf and the first winner of the United States amateur title the year before. At the end of the

John Shippen

tournament, Shippen had placed fifth overall. Having made a name for himself, Shippen continued to teach golf until he retired.

The 1920s were prosperous times and a number of golf clubs were organized by blacks throughout the metropolitan areas of the nation under the auspices of the United Golf Association—the black PGA. A national black tournament was established in 1926. John Shippen won that first year; Robert "Pat" Ball of Chicago was the titleholder in 1927, 1929, 1934, and 1941. Howard Wheeler of Georgia was champion in 1933, 1938, 1946, and 1947. John Dendy of Asheville, North Carolina, held the title in 1936 and 1937.

The black golf clubs in no way were commensurate with the private white clubs. Most of the courses were only nine holes and were difficult to maintain because of the exorbitant cost to properly care for them. Many blacks had to wait for "Caddy Day," which was generally on a Monday, to play on decent greens at the white clubs. The fine courses were given to white members during the week, except for Monday. There were segregated public courses, but they too were inferior to the all-white public courses.

Black colleges attempted to encourage black participation in golf and Tuskegee sponsored the first black college competition in 1938. Despite the poor condition of the courses and the lack of time to concentrate on the game, there were a number of excellent black players. Bill Spiller and Ted Rhodes qualified in the Los Angeles Open in 1947, but were barred from the Richmond, California, Open by Horton Smith, president of the PGA. Rhodes was Joe Louis's instructor and Horton Smith sent a message to Joe Louis advising him not to show up for the tournament either.

Bill Spiller

Ted Rhodes

By now World War II was over and blacks were making fierce civil rights challenges. In 1948 in Baltimore, blacks could only play on a nine-hole course that did not compare to the white courses at Mount Pleasant, Clifton, and Forest Park. John F. Law, a black Baltimorian, instituted a suit protesting the exclusion of blacks. He won the case on July 13, 1948, and all municipal links were desegregated.

In January 1952, Louisville opened its courses to blacks and a pattern was formed. The *Brown* v. *Board of Education* decision in 1954 culminated in the desegregation of the schools and in its aftermath affected the progress of blacks who wanted to play golf. Blacks began to show up on restricted golf courses demanding to play. The Supreme Court ruled that separate golf courses were not equal and that segregation of the races on public golf courses, which were often federally subsidized, was illegal.

The wall came down and it was now possible for blacks to enjoy, practice, and easily participate in the United States Open and in April 1961 Charles Sifford became the first black to play in the Professional Golfers Association tournament in the South.

Charles Sifford

Charles Sifford

Sifford began his career as a golfer caddying on a public course in Charlotte, North Carolina. Young Sifford liked the game and soon began swinging the clubs. Clayton Heafner, a professional, and Sutton Alexander, the manager of the course, were impressed by what they saw. Alexander saw to it that Sifford was allowed to practice every chance that was available. As a result, he was shooting in the seventies when he was only thirteen. By the time he was fifteen, he broke seventy.

Shortly after that, he moved to Philadelphia and got a job as a golf instructor. His first pupil was the popular singer/bandleader Billy Eckstein. Sifford still had time to sharpen his own game and occasionally won money in the black tournaments, but he made most of his money hustling in pickup matches. In 1952, when he was twenty-eight, Sifford started on the professional tour. By 1957, he took the Long Beach, California, Open and, later that year, he finished second in the Pomona, California, Open. He earned $18,000 in 1957. There is always the question: "What would he have earned if more professional golf tours were open to blacks at that time?"

As the color ban eased, Sifford's career broadened. In April 1961, Charles Sifford became the first black to play in a PGA tournament when he entered the Greater Greensboro, North Carolina, Open. He won the Greater Hartford, Connecticut, tournament with a 272 in 1967 and earned $47,025 that year. In 1975 he won the World Seniors Championship in Florida. Sifford was also the first black golfer to endorse particular brands of golf clubs, golf balls, and related products—another great breakthrough.

Lee Elder

Lee Elder

Golfdom's most prestigious event is the Masters Tournament, which takes place yearly in Augusta, Georgia. No black golfer had ever played in the tournament until 1975 when Lee Elder entered. A lot of "firsts" are attached to Elder's name: first black to play in the Masters Tournament; first black golfer to earn more than $100,000 in a single season; first black golfer to play in the World Series of Golf; and the first black golfer to make the United States Ryder Cup team.

Lee Elder was born in Dallas, Texas, in 1935. He began playing golf as a caddy. When his family moved to Los Angeles, Elder came under the tutelage of Ted Rhodes. When he was only sixteen, he played and beat Joe Louis for the title in the United Golfers Association finals in 1950. Elder moved to Washington, D.C., in the early 1960s and practiced at the practically all-black Langston Public Golf Course. When he played on the course of the University of Maryland, he was tutored by golf coach Frank Cronin.

In 1968, Elder had the distinction of finishing second to golf's folk hero, Jack Nicklaus, in the American Golf Classic at Akron, Ohio, and won $12,750. This was very good money for a golf "hustler."

Elder's career continued to move upward professionally and financially. In 1978, when he won the Westchester Classic and $60,000 in prize money; his total year's earnings were $152,000.

Elder feels the reason many blacks have not entered or succeeded in the field of golf relates to the fact most of the public links require players to be at least twelve years old, whereas many white youngsters have access to private clubs and instruction at an earlier age.

In a 1979 New York *Times* interview, Elder said:

> It [golf] should be a big family, but it still hasn't changed enough. I still overlook a lot of the racial things I should be more forward about. I'm just trying to break it down in my own quiet way.
>
> You usually don't get the racial thing in team sports because the other guys will step in and tell troublemakers to back off. But golf's an individual thing and we go our own separate ways. . . ."

Calvin Peete sinking a birdie putt at the 1979 Milwaukee Open. He started playing golf at the age of twenty-three and joined the tour in 1975. Despite an impaired left arm, he has become a leader of the PGA circuit in driving accuracy. On March 31, 1985, he won the Twelfth Annual Tournament Players Championship by three strokes to take the second-largest purse ($162,000) in PGA history. It was Peete's tenth victory in his pro career and ninth since January 1982, giving him more victories in that period than any other pro. His career earnings have topped the $1.5 million mark.

ICE HOCKEY

Ice hockey developed from field hockey, which has been played since antiquity. A primitive form of field hockey was played by the ancient Persians, the Greeks readily adapted it, and Rome in its days of conquest took it from the Greeks. But then the Aztec Indians also played a rudimentary form of field hockey, while other North American Indian tribes had played a rough stick game for thousands of years, as evidenced by artifacts.

In the eighteenth century, the game developed from field hockey to the early phases of ice hockey. The purpose of the game was to drive the ball into the opponent's goal. Using hooked or bent sticks, often branches, to hit the ball, the teams crudely sought their goals playing on any frozen surface.

The game reached its peak in Canada. The longer winter and iced parks and streams provided more playing time and made Canada a more natural place for the development of the game than the United States. The sport flourished among the French settlers in Quebec, as well as among the English, Irish, and Scot colonists in other parts of Canada. At first, the game was played according to local rules, but as its popularity grew, it became necessary to draw up a general code for the competitive continuance of the sport.

In 1855, ice hockey was recorded as a sports activity in Kingston, Ontario, and played by the Royal Canadian Rifles (an Imperial Army unit). The students at McGill University, Montreal, established the first rules of the game. By 1885, the first hockey league was organized in Kingston.

In 1893, two Yale tennis stars, Malcolm G. Chace and Arthur Foote, were participating in a Canadian tennis tournament; naturally, during that sojourn they saw hockey games and they brought the sport back to their campus. Around this same time, C. Shearer, a Canadian student at Johns Hopkins University, formed an ice hockey team and persuaded a Quebec team to visit Baltimore and display its skills.

With enthusiastic though fledgling interest, the first United States hockey league was organized in New York in November 1896 with four teams.

Ice hockey was to further develop and spread in areas where the winters were long and cold. The location of black colleges and universities in the South made playing the game impossible. Only in the northern white colleges and universities could the game gain a foothold. Since we can find no successful black players in the growth of ice hockey, it can only be concluded that few—if any—of those blacks attending white schools participated.

But Canada must have had some early black ice hockey players. Canada was the end of the line on the underground railroad for slaves seeking freedom. Also, in later years there may have been black West Indians who moved to British-colonized areas of Canada who might have played. Did the intermingling of the races void the obvious racial distinctions of black? Or did the black man in Canada receive similar status of the free black man in America—a life of servitude, one certainly devoid of a sport in which expensive equipment was required? Overall, the reason for the paucity of blacks as well as Jews in professional hockey is because they are few in number in Canada. However, with the expansion of hockey with additional franchises throughout the United States, this might change.

In 1945, the Montreal Royals baseball team (a Triple A farm team under the aegis of Branch Rickey and the Brooklyn Dodgers) broke the unwritten law by signing Jackie Robinson, a black man. Robinson proved to be one of the most popular players on the Royals and ended up by winning the International League batting title. Following the Robinson experiment, the Montreal Alouettes football team signed Herb Trawyck and John Moody, both black, who were the most outstanding men on the team. Blacks were now acceptable sport professionals.

Manny McIntyre

(From left to right) *Manny McIntyre, Herbie Carnegie, and his brother, Ossie.*

A tall, 185-pound black youth of twenty-six years Manny McIntyre joined with Herbie Carnegie and his brother, Ossie, in 1946, to comprise the starting forward line of the Sherbrooke, St.-Francois team in the Quebec Provincial Hockey League in 1946. They were the only all-black line ever signed by an organized nonblack hockey club in Canada. McIntyre played left wing, Herb Carnegie, center, and Ossie Carnegie, right wing.

McIntyre's skating and hockey days began in Fredericton, New Brunswick, where he was born and went to school. In 1942, he was already showing great promise as a hockey player when he went to Timmins, Ontario, where he played for the Buffalo Anchorites. In 1944, the Carnegie brothers and McIntyre signed with the Cataracts, senior team of Shawinigan Falls, Quebec. Then in 1945, the line moved as a unit to the Sherbrooke team.

McIntyre was also an outstanding baseball player and became the sixth black to enter organized baseball when he was signed by Sherbrooke, Quebec, a St. Louis Cardinal farm club in the Border League.

Willie O'Ree

Willie O'Ree

It was not until 1950 that a black hockey player emerged to play in the United States. He was Arthur Dorrington, a Canadian who was signed with the Atlantic City Seagulls of the Eastern Amateur League. The National Hockey League (NHL) waited until 1957. At that time, the Boston Bruins called up left wing Willie O'Ree from its farm club, the Quebec Aces.

Willie O'Ree:
I was born in Fredericton, New Brunswick, Canada, where I began skating at age two and started playing peewee hockey at about age four or five. I was the youngest in my family and one of my older brothers, Richard, used to play in an industrial league. He was very instrumental in my entering the pro ranks. He used to tell me that you have to learn how to take some hits, but always be ready to give one back.

There were only about two black families within the city limits. In my high school, I can only remember about a dozen kids. Our family lived on Charlotte Street in the middle of the city, since my dad was a city engineer. Most of the blacks in the area lived on the outskirts of town. In retrospect, I think my living around whites made me feel I could play in the pros. I always knew I was as good or better than they were.

I played junior hockey before turning pro in 1956. I had made up my mind by then that this was going to be my career. I made $3,500 for six months of hockey and then had a job in town in the other six. I got a $500 bonus for signing, which was pretty good for 1956.

At that time, there were only about four or five blacks in all of pro hockey, a couple I remember were playing in western Canada. I played with another black player, Stan Maxwell, for many years. We were together with the Montreal farm team, the Quebec Aces, and then in the early 1960s with the Los Angeles Blades. The Aces, by the way, had a history of having black players. Before my time, they had an all-black line with the Carnegie brothers, Herbie and Ossie, and Manny McIntyre. They all played with the great Montreal center iceman, Jean Beliveau.

I was a natural right wing, but played out of position for most of my career. When I was a junior at Kitchener, Ontario, I was hit in the right eye by the puck and missed eight weeks. Being a left wing, my right eye was closest to the puck and I found myself having difficulty stickhandling. So I switched to the right side and felt very comfortable there. I had to take most passes on my backhand, but it didn't bother me. This way I had a better angle on the net.

From 1958 to 1959, I was with the Quebec Aces, a Montreal farm team. However, I was under contract to the Boston Bruins. It was during this period, 1957–1958, that I first played in the National Hockey League.

I was having a so-so year and really hadn't played that much. Apparently, Boston needed a left wing at that time, so manager Lynn Patrick and coach Milt Schmidt called me up. At that time, Boston wasn't very strong, although goalie Bruce Gamble and defensemen Leo Bovin and Alan Stanley were good players.

I was there for two games, a Saturday night contest in Montreal and a Sunday game in Boston against Montreal. I received a standing ovation from the fans in Boston that night.

My second stay with Boston lasted forty-three games in the 1960–61 season and I scored 4 goals and had 14 assists. I was treated well by the fans and players around the league. I never had any other problems while I was in the NHL. I do remember, when I was with New Haven of the American Hockey League, I was with a group of players in Baltimore and was refused entrance to a restaurant. Otherwise, I never had to face serious discrimination.

At the end of the 1960–1961 season, Lynn Patrick told me that I'd be reporting to the Bruins training camp. It looked as if I had a good shot at making the team again. But four weeks later, I was told my contract had been sold to the Montreal Canadiens. Considering the talent they had then, I knew I had no chance at making their squads. So, I wasn't surprised when I was assigned to their Hull-Ottawa minor league affiliate. I never did get any information from Patrick on why the move was made.

In November of 1961 Hull-Ottawa sold my contract to the Los Angeles Blades. The Blades weren't affiliated to any NHL franchise and played in the Western League. At that point, I was about twenty-six or twenty-seven and figured my hopes for making the NHL again were small.

But I still loved to play and you could make a good living at it, so I continued. I was with that franchise for six years. When the NHL expanded in 1967, the club moved to San Diego and I played there another seven years. I retired then to work as a sales representative.

Still I played semipro hockey during this period and then prior to the 1978–79 season, I joined the San Diego Hawks of the Pacific League. I felt I was in good shape. At age forty-three I had a good year, 21 goals and 32 assists, and missed only six games.

I had a lot of memorable moments in my career—hat tricks and other big nights. But the moment I'll never forget was in 1960 when I scored the winning goal against the Montreal Canadiens at Boston Garden. I had just received a pass from Leo Bovin and was sweeping around the Montreal defensemen. One of them was Tom Johnson, who went on to coach the Bruins. I took a low shot, keeping the puck along the ice, and it slid into the corner. It was at the fourteen-minute mark of the third period. It's so clear, it was like it happened yesterday. We won 3 to 2 and the crowd just roared.

Alton White

Alton White

The second black hockey player to perform for an American major league hockey team was Alton White. He was signed by the New York Raiders of the new World Hockey Association (WHA) in 1972.

White was born in Amherst, Nova Scotia. His family moved to Winnipeg when he was eight. His father was able to get a job as a porter with the Canadian National Railways. The people of Winnipeg were very generous in supplying children—black and white—with equipment and places to play, thus beginning White's lifelong romance with ice hockey.

White worked his way through the ranks and broke in with Winnipeg in 1962–63, playing as a right wing and occasional center. White's small stature—five feet, eight and a half inches, 175 pounds—was the major reason he had not been able to make it to the National Hockey League. However, he was an established American Hockey League player with Providence for a number of years.

When the World Hockey Association was formed (1972), it had twelve teams. The National Hockey League had sixteen. On the twenty-eight teams comprising 520 players, White was the only black. The press proclaimed him a latter-day Jackie Robinson, to which White replied, "Please don't regard me as a trailblazer. Robinson's case was much tougher than mine. He had to undergo all kinds of hardships. . . . But I must say in all my years playing hockey I have not been treated too badly."

Mike Marson

Mike Marson

When the 1974–75 NHL season opened, there was a most unusual player in the new Washington Capitals expansion team. Out on left wing was a swift skater from Toronto named Mike Marson. His appearance on the ice was the first in the NHL by a black since Willie O'Ree's stay with Boston.

Marson was Washington's number-two pick in the 1974 amateur draft. He had 94 points one year before in the Canadian junior hockey league. He proved a creditable rookie with Washington—16 goals, 12 assists. Despite that excellent start, his career floundered between the NHL and the minors. He had been a $105,000 a year bonus baby, but the pressures of living up to all that money in his late teens affected his play. Racism, however, was never a problem for him.

In 1978–79, Marson saw more ice time in Washington than he had in several years. His scoring was still not up to expectations, but in the corners he was becoming increasingly aggressive.

On June 11, 1979, Marson was traded by Washington to Los Angeles. He finished the 1979–80 season with Binghamton of the American Hockey League. Marson is still only in his twenties and may yet live up to his potential.

Bill Riley

Bill Riley

In the 1977 campaign, the Washington Capitals added another black hockey player to its roster—twenty-seven-year-old Bill Riley.

In 1969, this Nova Scotia native was working as a welder in an aluminum smelting plant in Kitimat, British Columbia. On weekends, he played hockey on a local industrial team. Like so many other Canadian players, he dreamed of playing in the NHL, but with a wife and three children it seemed highly unlikely. Then in 1974, when an opportunity came to try out for the Dayton Gems of the International League—a farm team that was being reorganized by the Capitals—Riley's dream came true. "I guess they were real desperate for bodies," he recalled.

With the encouragement of his wife, Riley gave up his solid $15,000 a year job, sold everything except his stereo and TV, and headed for Dayton, Ohio. The Dayton coach and later the Capitals coach, Tom McVie, fell in love with the rugged right winger. Unfortunately, many fans did not share the enthusiasm of the coaches. Riley had watermelons thrown at him and the organist played "Short'nin' Bread" whenever he hit the ice; he was further abused by the fans screaming "shoeshine boy" and worse at him.

Nonetheless, he scored very well for Dayton, but his totals of 279 and 301 penalty minutes in two International League seasons indicate that his chief value was as an enforcer. His years in the factory had given Riley a hard, uncompromising attitude when it came to fighting. He handles himself well in a battle and is known for helping his younger teammates out against the "bad men" on other clubs.

These were the qualities the Washington Capitals badly needed when they brought him up on New Year's Day, 1977. In forty-three games, he garnered 27 points (13 goals, 14 assists). Twenty-eight percent of his shots went into the net, setting a Capitals club record. His 124 penalty minutes indicate that he was a tough man.

On June 13, 1979, Riley was claimed by the Winnipeg Jets from Washington in the expansion draft. After a brief stay with the Jets, he played with three American Hockey League teams in succession: Nova Scotia; New Brunswick (1980–82); and Moncton (1982–83).

Tony McKegney

Tony McKegney

A winger, formerly with the Buffalo Sabres of the NHL, Tony McKegney was that team's first black player.

He was born on February 15, 1958, in Montreal, Canada. Orphaned as a baby, he was adopted by an affluent chemist, Lowell McKegney, and he was raised in the McKegney family, which included black and white children.

As a player in the Ontario Major Junior League, he scored 44 goals and 49 assists. He was rated that team's fastest skater. Standing six feet one, and 198 pounds, with extremely powerful wrists, he was very attractive to both the Buffalo Sabres and the now-defunct Birmingham Bulls of the WHA. He was the subject of an intense bidding war and received a contract comparable to that of Marson at Washington.

Buffalo picked McKegney in the second round of the 1978 amateur draft. The only reason McKegney was still available was that he had signed a contract with the Birmingham Bulls of the World Hockey Association.

When the Sabres learned that John Bassett, owner of the Bulls, was in deep financial trouble, they easily persuaded him to let McKegney out of his contract. Bassett recalled that after signing McKegney, he received dozens of calls from season ticket holders canceling their orders because McKegney was going to play for Birmingham.

McKegney was not disturbed by the few racial slurs from the fans; he had gotten used to it, but what really amazed him was the press. The usual questions asked about new players were about their junior careers; however, the press only seemed interested in asking McKegney, "How does it feel to be a black man in pro hockey?"

In McKegney's first season training camp, he was put on line with Gil Perreault because he was a big, strong, fast skater. He led the club in scoring in preseason games. He scored a goal in his first NHL regular season game against the New York Islanders.

However, after that things did not go so well. His opponents easily exploited his weakness. He was sent down to Buffalo's Hershey farm club. After playing 24 games with Hershey, he was recalled.

In 1980, McKegney became the first black to score a goal in a Stanley Cup competition when he tallied against the New York Islanders. On June 8, 1983, McKegney was traded to the Quebec Nordiques, along with Andre Savard and J. F. Sauve. The 1984–85 season saw McKegney scoring consistently for the Minnesota North Stars.

Grant Fuhr

Grant Fuhr

Born on September 28, 1962, in Spruce Grove, Alberta, rookie goaltender Grant Fuhr started his first game as a professional against the Winnipeg Jets on October 14, 1981. The Edmonton Oilers lost the game 4–2. No one realized at the time that it would be Grant's only defeat for over three months. From that time, he went twenty-three contests without a setback and it wasn't until January 16, 1982, in Toronto that he took his second defeat. Goaltending with a club that stressed an explosive offense, Grant had a 3.31 goals-against average. He made the midseason All-Star team and was second-team All-Star at the end of the 1982 campaign. In his initial season in the National Hockey League, Fuhr was named a star of the game in no fewer than fifteen of his forty-eight starts, and assisted on Wayne Gretzky's record-shattering fiftieth goal in thirty-nine games.

Ray Neufeld

Ray Neufeld

Ray Neufeld, the big and strong right winger, flip-flopped the past four seasons between Hartford of the NHL and Binghamton of the AHL. In the first seven games of the 1982 American Hockey League Calder Cup playoffs, Neufeld, playing with Binghamton, had 14 points, including 8 goals. He led all Binghamton scorers in postseason play with a total of 17 points and his 9 goals were the most scored by any AHL player. Neufeld participated in twenty-six games with the 1982–83 Whalers.

There were four black hockey stars playing in the National Hockey League in the 1984–85 season: Tony McKegney and Dirk Graham with the Minnesota North Stars, Ray Neufeld of the Hartford Whalers, and Grant Fuhr of the Edmonton Oilers.

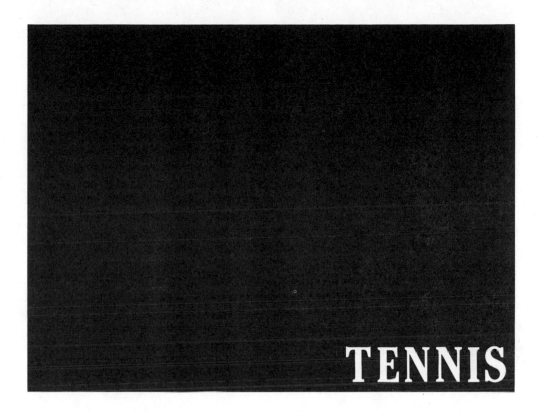

TENNIS

The origin of tennis is obscure. One historian's theory is that the name came from an ancient city on the Nile Delta in Egypt. The Greeks called the city Tanis and the Arabs called it Tinnis. This city was famous for its manufacturing of fine linens. The early balls used for tennis were made of this light fabric and a game using this ball and a crude racket was played in that ancient city.

Other historians point out that Homer mentions that Nausicaa, daughter of King Alcinous of Phacacia, and her handmaidens played a game of handball from which tennis was derived.

Whatever its origins, tennis was a game that was very popular in the royal courts of France and England. The game was played by men and women in all kinds of weather, indoors and out.

In 1874, Major Walter C. Wingfield, an Englishman, devised and patented a new and improved portable court for playing the game. The name of the game was changed to lawn tennis and in June 1877, the first championship tournament, Wimbledon, was held.

Miss Mary E. Outerbridge, an American, spent the winter of 1874 in Bermuda. She saw the game of tennis as it was played by some British officers stationed there. So impressed was she by the game that when she returned to America, she brought with her a lawn tennis net and some rackets and balls. With the help of her brother A. Emilius Outerbridge, she laid out a court on the grounds of the Staten Island Cricket and Baseball Club. Then Dr. James Dwight of Boston laid out a court at Nahant, a seaside resort on Boston Harbor. The popularity of the game spread and on August 31, 1881, the first official championship of the United States, playing under English rules and using English balls, was held in Newport, Rhode Island.

Tennis was considered strictly a game for the elite—a sport for ladies and gentlemen to be played in exclusive clubs and on private courts. In the early days, the game was often called "royal tennis."

In 1881, the United States Lawn Tennis Association was formed and the thought of blacks participating was an idea never even remotely entertained. The Civil War was over, but the status of blacks remained shaky.

Blacks began to play tennis in the 1890s when the game became popular in some of the black colleges. By 1899, black tournaments had begun. A few of the pioneering black champions were Emmett J. Scott, S. E. Courtney, Warren Loggan, and E. T. Atvell, all out of Tuskegee; Charles Cook, Howard University; Thomas Jefferson, Lincoln University; the Reverend W. W. Walker of the Chautauqua Tennis Club; and Edward G. Brown who, with his flair, added another dimension to the game. These men helped to popularize the game among blacks and tennis courts for blacks were established all over the United States.

Since blacks were barred from competition with white players, they organized their own American Tennis Association in 1916. The first black national tournament was held in Baltimore at Druid Hill Park in 1917 and the first black national champion was Talley Holmes. He was victorious again in 1918, 1921, and 1924. Another outstanding black player was Reginald Weir, captain of the City College of New York's tennis team and singles champion in 1931, 1932, 1933, 1937, and 1942.

Reginald Weir

Talley Holmes (left) *and Reginald Weir*

(Left to right) *Nat and Frank Jackson, Gerald L. Norman, Jr., and Reginald Weir, circa 1937.*

Reginald Weir and Gerald L. Norman, Jr., captain of the Flushing High School team, sought entry into an indoor tournament sponsored by the United States Lawn Tennis Association in 1929. They were rejected by the Executive Committee. The National Association for the Advancement of Colored People sent a letter of protest:

December 24, 1929

Mr. Edward B. Moss, Executive Secretary
United States Lawn Tennis Association
120 Broadway
New York City

Dear Sir:

The National Association for the Advancement of Colored People is informed that the United States Lawn Tennis Association has barred from the National Junior Indoor Tennis Tournament two young men, Reginald Weir, of the City College Tennis team, and Gerald L. Norman, Jr., captain of the Flushing High School team, and that school's sole representative in the tournament.

The barring of these young men, we are informed, took place after they had paid their fees and after receipt of their payment had been acknowledged, on the ground that they are colored. Gerald Norman, father of the Flushing High School tennis captain, informs the National Association for the Advancement of Colored People that you explicitly did not permit colored players to participate in national tennis tournaments.

The irony of the present situation will become the more pointed when it is known that Mr. Norman is himself tennis coach at the Bryant High School and that some of the white boys he has coached have been admitted and will play in the tournament.

If the facts are as stated, and we are told the two colored boys' names were omitted from the draw published in the Sunday newspapers, the action of the United States Lawn Tennis Association constitutes an action unfair, unsportsmanlike, and calculated to degrade the sport you profess to cultivate and against which we as well as many other Americans, white and colored, wish to protest in the strongest terms.

Patrons of sport in this country do not relish the administration of public contests by a spirit of caste and snobbery and we are sure that the public, when informed of the methods used by the United States Lawn Tennis Association, will be quick to characterize these methods in the way they deserve. We are, therefore, giving copies of this letter to the press in order that the question of the color and race bar in a sport supposed to draw from the best the country can afford in youth and clean endeavor may be made a matter of open and public discussion.

Very truly yours,
(signed) *Robert W. Bagnall*
Associated Secretary
National Association for the
Advancement of Colored People

RWB/RR

UNITED STATES LAWN TENNIS ASSOCIATION
120 Broadway, New York City
Edward B. Moss, Executive Secretary

Telephone: Rector 3547

December 26, 1929

Mr. Robert W. Bagnall, Associate Secretary
National Association for the Advancement of
Colored People
69 Fifth Avenue
New York, N.Y.

Dear Sir:

Answering your letter of December 24, the policy of the United States Lawn
Tennis Association has been to decline the entry of colored players in our Championships.

In pursuing this policy, we make no reflection upon the colored race, but we
believe that as a practical matter, the present method of separate Associations for
the administration of the affairs and Championships of colored and white players
should be continued.

Yours sincerely,
(signed) *E. B. Moss*
Executive Secretary

EBM/S

December 26, 1929

Mr. Edward B. Moss, Executive Secretary
U.S. Lawn Tennis Association
120 Broadway
New York, N.Y.

Dear Sir:

I have just received information that Gerald F. Norman, Jr., and Reginald
Weir, both members of Clubs associated with the organization of which I have
the honor to be president, have been refused the privilege of competing in the
15th Annual National Junior Indoor championships, to be held at the 7th Regi-
ment Armory in New York City.

As president of the New York Tennis Association, I most sincerely add my
protest to that of the National Association for the Advancement of Colored
People to the action of the tournament committee in rejecting their entries and
the apparent acquiescence in that action by your organization.

The barring of these two young players shows a high degree of inconsistency
on the part of your association that astounds fair-minded tennis fans of the
country and the tennis world at large.

Possessed of all the requisite qualifications that would entitle them to creditably compete in the tournament, there can be no other reason advanced by the tournament committee or the United States Lawn Tennis Association for the rejection of their entries than that they are Negroes.

This reason is un-American, unsportsmanlike, narrow-minded, and short-sighted and will bring down a just and long-continued protest from the fair-minded tennis fans of the country and the world, a protest that will not enhance the standing of your organization as leaders of the game in this country.

Young Weir is a member of the team of the College of the City of New York and has competed creditably for his college in all its matches against other colleges of the past season, with a record of winning all of his matches. He also represented De Witt Clinton High School during his high school days and doubt-less played against some of the juniors that are entered in the present tournament.

He is a former New York state junior champion and 1928 national junior champion of the American Tennis Association, the organization who controls the sport among Negroes in this country. He recently entered and went down to the finals in the tournament of the Hamilton Tennis Club on their courts at Inwood, N.Y., where he met Edward Tarangeoli, former captain of the New York University tennis team, in a memorable and thrilling four-set match that required three hours for a decision. Last summer his parents took him to France to witness the Davis Cup matches and while there he played daily with the coach of the French Davis Cup team, who was delighted with his game, also with all the leading junior players of France.

Young Norman is captain of the Flushing High School tennis team and 1929 junior champion of New York state, among our race. He recently competed in the Queens high school tennis championship and went down to the finals in that event, playing against all the outstanding junior players of Queens County.

Both these boys are from very good families, highly cultured, intelligent, are a credit to their schools and their race, and compare favorably with any lad entered in your tournament.

All these qualifications must have been known to your committee, and if not, were easily obtainable, therefore there is no other conclusion to arrive at than that they were barred because of their color.

Your association and its committee should keep in mind that the accomplishment and valor of Negroes are indelibly written in the history of progress and greatness of the United States and the records prove that the Negro has contributed his share in almost every endeavor that meant advancement and has also represented the United States in international competition with credit to his country.

We are now making strenuous efforts to regain the historic Davis Cup and I am sure that the American public will not shed a tear if a Negro was partly responsible for its being brought back to this country.

Mr. Allan Behr, who coaches young Weir, thinks he has Davis Cup potentialities. So does the French Davis Cup team coach. If they were not barred on account of their color, then may I ask if they were barred because there was a possibility of one of them winning the event? And if one of them did win, are they not Americans? As good Americans, should you not feel equally proud of them as such?

I am, and the country is shocked at your recent action in barring these two young Negro players, and can only say to you, in the words of the late Booker T. Washington, "The only way to keep the Negro down is to stay down with him."

Yours very truly,
Arthur E. Francis
President
New York Tennis Association

THE BOARD OF CHRISTIAN SOCIAL SERVICE
Diocese of Long Island

176 Remsen Street
Brooklyn, N.Y.
December 26, 1929

United States Lawn Tennis Association
New York City

Gentlemen:

I am very much surprised to learn that you have barred the captain of the Flushing High School tennis team from your junior indoor tournament. While Gerald Norman did not officially represent his school in this tournament, he did represent it in the mind of the public and to bar him from competition for the reason given by the Association is an affront to Flushing High School, as well as to Norman himself. As an alumnus of Flushing, I want you to know that I object.

Moreover, inasmuch as you have made a racial issue of the matter, it seems to me manifestly unfair to the white boys who have entered the tournament. It indicates that they are afraid of colored competition and must be shielded if they are to win, whereas in reality the majority of white tennis players are very good sports and do not want the sort of victory that is even in part decided before the tournament starts by the elimination of good players.

Very sincerely yours,
Spear Knebel
Secretary
Board of Christian
Social Service

Reginald Weir waited twenty years until 1948 before he was allowed to compete in a USLTA tournament. At that time and well past his prime, he defeated Thomas Lewyn of Scarsdale 6–4, 6–2, but in the second round he was defeated by Bill Trabert.

On the college level during the late twenties and early thirties, several excellent black players came out of predominately white schools: Richard Hudlin of Chicago was the first black captain of a college team in the Big 10 Universities; Douglas Turner, from the University of Illinois, was a runnerup for the Big 10 title in 1929. James McDaniel became national champion of the American Tennis Association in 1940, 1941, and 1942.

Reginald Weir (foreground) *and Douglas Turner in a match at Tuskegee in the early thirties.*

There were a number of prominent black women champions in the ATA. Lucy Slowe won the title in women's singles in 1917, to be followed by Isadora Chamels and Flora Lomax; these women won the championships several times. Ora Washington of the Germantown YWCA, Philadelphia, was a particularly remarkable woman. For twelve years, she played without being defeated and won 201 trophies. She won eight titles in nine years.

The black tennis world had to wait until the early 1950s for the arrival of the first black to compete at Wimbledon and Forest Hills. The first black was a woman—Althea Gibson.

Althea Gibson

*Althea Gibson at
Forest Hills, 1950*

I thought I had seen everything in women's tennis until Miss Gibson came along
to demonstrate the power and ease with which a smash ought to be hit. To be
sure, she flubs plenty of them because she takes liberties with the ball, asking, as
Bill Tilden says, "too much of the little white pill," but there has never been
anything like that overhand in the distaff department of tennis.

Tennis players are not necessarily natural athletes, as Margaret duPont, and Doris Hart are, as well as Lili D'Alvarez, the lovely Spanish player of years ago. I think Althea has more natural facilities than any of the abovementioned. She has complete freedom of muscle and motion, even enough to be a handicap (as well I know) if she relies on it too much instead of learning fundamentals.

—Alice Marble

Althea Gibson was born on August 25, 1927, to Daniel and Annie Gibson in a small town in South Carolina called Silver. Althea's father and uncle had five acres in a poor farm area. There just was never enough money to make ends meet. Daniel Gibson decided to move to New York to see if he could improve his family's condition. Little Althea was only three years old when she went to live with her Aunt Sally in Harlem. When she was seven or eight, she went to Philadelphia to live with her Aunt Daisy. Meanwhile, her mother, her brothers, and three sisters had settled in Harlem with relatives. Finally, in 1943 when the Gibson family secured their own apartment on West 143rd Street, Althea was reluctant to join them. She had enjoyed moving from place to place and being the "only child."

From the very beginning, school was an anathema. She played hooky every chance she could, preferring to stay around the playgrounds where she could do what she liked best—stickball, basketball, baseball, football, and paddle tennis. Somehow she managed to graduate from junior high school in 1941. Althea says, "They simply made up their minds to pass me on to the next school and let *them* worry about me." She was a tough, streetwise, arrogant teenager who could fight. Her father, at one time, recognizing her athletic abilities, started training her to be a woman boxer. She was always running away from home to play in streets or go to the Apollo Theater on 125th Street or play pool. It became difficult for her when she wanted to return home because she was soundly beaten by her father. She worked in her teenage years as a messenger in a button factory, a dress factory, and department store; ran an elevator; cleaned chickens; and was a mail clerk. None of the jobs lasted more than a few weeks.

At this point, the Department of Welfare picked her up and gave her a choice: reform school or stay with a family of their choosing. Naturally, she accepted the latter. The department gave her an allowance to provide her with money to look for a job and told her to report her progress once a week. To Althea, it was the ideal situation. She promptly forgot about seeking a job and spent all her time playing in the streets and parks or going to the movies.

The Police Athletic League turned 143rd Street, where her parents lived, into a play street and closed it to traffic. Althea became paddle tennis champion of the block. Competing with youngsters from other Harlem play streets, she won a number of medals.

There was a young man named Buddy Walker who was assigned city play leader for 143rd Street. By rights, Walker was a musician, but in the slack summer months he worked for the PAL. He was impressed with what he saw in Althea. He had the idea that she might be able to play regular tennis just as well. Walker bought the young girl two secondhand tennis rackets and started her out hitting balls against the wall on the handball courts at Mt. Morris Park. She did exceedingly well. Then he took her to the Harlem River Tennis Courts at 150th Street and Seventh Avenue to play a few sets with his friends. Despite her inexperience with the game, she did fantastically well.

Another man, Juan Serrell, saw her and offered to try to work out a way for her to play at the Cosmopolitan Tennis Club on 149th Street and Convent Avenue. The Cosmopolitan was on Sugar Hill, the area where Manhattan's affluent blacks lived in those days.

Althea looked like a good prospect, so the Cosmopolitan Tennis Club underwrote her membership and provided lessons from Fred Johnson, a one-armed professional. He taught her the basics of footwork and game strategy and tried to instill in this rough diamond of a girl the polite manners that accompany the playing of the game.

The most impressive event at the Cosmopolitan Club was the day Alice Marble played an exhibition match there. Alice Marble, from Beverly Hills, California, won the women's singles championship at Wimbledon in 1939, beating out Helen Jacobs of Berkeley. In 1938, 1939, and 1940, Marble was the United States women's singles champion. Watching Alice Marble play the game, Althea gained insights she had never imagined. Marble's power and aggressiveness and the effortlessness she seemingly portrayed inspired Althea.

The American Tennis Association was organizing a New York State Open Championship at the Cosmopolitan Tennis Club in 1942. Althea entered the girls' singles and won. During the summer of 1942, the Cosmopolitan took up a collection and entered Althea in the ATA national girls' championship at Lincoln University in Pennsylvania, which she lost in the finals.

World War II precluded the game in 1943, but in 1944 and 1945 Althea won the ATA's national girls' singles championship. Althea was now eighteen and no longer a minor under the supervision of the Department of Welfare. She got a job as a waitress during the day and in the winter months played with a basketball team called the Mysterious Five with a girlfriend of hers. Through her friend, she met Edna Mae and Sugar Ray Robinson. They were both very kind to Althea; they even bought her a saxophone, which she wanted to learn to play.

Now she was out of the girls' class and the ATA paid her expenses to play at Wilberforce College in Ohio in the women's singles. She got to the finals, but was beaten by Roumania Peters. Although she had not won, there were two tennis playing black doctors who saw her possibilities. Unknown to her, these doctors thought they saw the raw material which, along with special training, could break the color barrier in tennis. They talked with the young tennis player, advising her to seek a college scholarship and hone up her game. When she advised them she hadn't attended high school, another plan was devised. Althea was to live with Dr. Eaton and his family in Wilmington, go to high school there, and practice with him in his private tennis court. In the summer, she would live with Dr. Johnson in Lynchburg and travel the tournament circuit. A little fearful of the move, Sugar Ray Robinson insisted she go, advising her that she would need an education to attain her goals in life.

A new world opened for Althea Gibson. She was welcomed with warmth by the Eatons. They were a wealthy black family with a chauffeured limousine and a full-time housekeeper. Althea had her own room and received an allowance, just as Dr. Eaton's children did. For the first time in her life, she really wanted to succeed in school and studied hard; she practiced tennis regularly with Dr. Eaton. She joined the Williston Industrial High School band and played her saxophone.

In the summer months, she worked with Dr. Johnson and a Tom Stowe Stroke Developer—a machine that shot tennis balls across the net. That first summer, she played in nine tournaments and won the singles championship in every one of them. She and Dr. Johnson won eight mixed doubles tournaments. Gibson felt that her greatest achievement was winning the ATA national women's singles. (She was to win that title for ten consecutive years and she was proclaimed the best woman player in black tennis. She stopped entering to afford others the opportunities she had had.) The three years quickly passed. Gibson was graduated from high school, tenth in her class, and she was twenty years old.

Before she even graduated, Dr. William Gray, president of Florida A & M at Tallahassee offered her a tennis scholarship upon the advice of Walter Austin, the tennis coach. The scholarship took care of all her immediate needs and she was able to secure a job as an assistant in the women's physical education department for $40 a month to take care of extra expenses.

In 1950, she was invited to play in the National Indoors—the first black woman to be invited. She got all the way to finals before she was knocked out by Nancy Chafee. Although she lost, this was an achievement for blacks to even reach the National Indoors. Gibson reasoned that since she had done so well she would be invited to play in the summer grass court tournaments. If she was not permitted to play on grass all summer, she would automatically not be allowed to play Forest Hills in September. The USLTA made no offer and, as far as they were seemingly concerned, Gibson did not exist. Some newspapers, though, began to question the obvious discriminatory practices of the USLTA, but still the organization didn't budge.

And then, like a bolt out of the blue, Alice Marble, formerly one of the world's greatest tennis players, wrote an editorial in the July 1950 issue of the *American Lawn Tennis* magazine:

Alice Marble, 1931

On my current lecture tours . . . there are [those] who want to know if Althea Gibson will be permitted to play in the Nationals this year. Not being privy to the sentiments of the USLTA committee, I couldn't answer their questions, but I came back to New York determined to find out. When I directed the question at a committee member of long standing, his answer, tacitly given, was in the negative. Unless something within the realm of the supernatural occurs, Miss Gibson will not be permitted to play in the Nationals.

He said nothing of the sort, of course. The attitude of the committee will be that Miss Gibson has not sufficiently proven herself. True enough, she was a finalist in the National Indoors, the gentleman admitted—but didn't I think the field was awfully poor? I did not. It is my opinion that Miss Gibson performed beautifully under the circumstances. Considering how little play she has had in top competition, her win over a seasoned veteran like Midge Buck seems to me a real triumph.

Nevertheless, the committee, according to this member, insists that in order to qualify for the Nationals, Miss Gibson must also make a strong showing in the major Eastern tournaments to be played now and the date set for the big do at Forest Hills. Most of these major tournaments—Orange, East Hampton, Essex, etc. are invitational, of course. If she is not invited to participate in them, as my committee member freely predicted, then she obviously will be unable to prove anything at all, and it will be the reluctant duty of the committee to reject her entry at Forest Hills. Miss Gibson is over a very cunningly wrought barrel, and I can only hope to loosen a few of its staves with one lone opinion.

I think it's time we faced a few facts. If tennis is a game for ladies and gentlemen, it's also time we acted a little more like gentle people and less like sanctimonious hypocrites. . . . She might be soundly beaten for a while—but she has a much better chance on the courts than in the inner sanctum of the committee, where a different kind of game is played.

If the field of sports has got to pave the way for all of civilization, let's do it. At this moment, tennis is privileged to take its place among the pioneers for a true democracy, if it will accept that privilege. If it declines to do so, the honor will fall on the next generation, perhaps—but someone will break the ground. The entrance of Negroes into national tennis is as inevitable as it has proven to be in baseball, in football, or in boxing; there is no denying so much talent. The committee at Forest Hills has the power to stifle the efforts of one Althea Gibson, who may or may not be the stuff of which champions are made, but eventually she will be succeeded by others of her race who have equal or superior ability. They will knock at the door as she has done. Eventually, the tennis world will rise up en masse to protest the injustices perpetrated by our policy makers. Eventually— why not now?

Then one of the major clubs on the Eastern circuit, the Orange Lawn Tennis Club of South Orange, New Jersey, accepted Gibson's entry for the Eastern Grass Court Championship. Although displeased with her performance, Gibson beat Virginia Rice Johnson in the first round, but she lost to Helen Pastale Perez in the second.

Next, she played in the National Clay Courts Championships at Chicago. Gibson got to the quarterfinals before being beaten by Doris Hart, 6–2, 6–3. It was then that

Gibson quietly received word from one of the officials of USLTA that an application for entrance into the Nationals at Forest Hills would be accepted.

The day she was to play in the Nationals is beautifully depicted in her autobiography, *I Always Wanted to Be Somebody,*

> Mrs. Smith and I got up early and ate a good breakfast, bacon and eggs and toast and milk, and then I got my things ready. I packed a small kit bag with a pair of tailored, white flannel shorts, a flannel skirt, sweatsocks, tennis shoes, and a white knitted sweater that one of the ATA ladies had made for me. I was ready. Rhoda and I walked to the Sixth Avenue subway station, carrying my bag in one hand and two tennis rackets in the other. We took a D train to 50th Street and Sixth Avenue, then changed to an F train, the express to Forest Hills, and got off at 71st Street and Continental Avenue. It was only a short walk, about three long blocks, to the entrance of the West Side Tennis Club. I couldn't help but think that it had taken me a long time to make the trip.

She won the first match with Barbara Knapp of England, 6–2, 6–2.

On the next day, her opponent was Louise Brough, Wimbledon champion and former champion of the United States. The first set was won by Brough, 6–1. Gibson took second set, 6–3. She had a 7–6 lead in the third set. Victory was nearly within Althea's grasp when a sudden storm erupted and the match had to be suspended until the next day. Gibson lost her edge and was defeated when Brough won three straight games. But Gibson won the battle—she was the first black woman to play in the Nationals at Forest Hills. Undaunted, Gibson made plans to play at Wimbledon in the spring of 1951.

Under the auspices of the USLTA, Gibson went out to Hamtromck, Michigan (a suburb of Detroit), for more tennis instruction with Jean Hoxie, a famed tennis teacher. When Gibson arrived in Detroit, Joe Louis gave her the use of his suite at Gotham Hotel. The black people in Detroit put on benefit shows to raise money for her expenses in England and Joe Louis paid for her round-trip ticket. Gibson did not win at Wimbledon.

The years 1951, 1952, and 1953 were disappointing ones in Gibson's career. In the USLTA competition, she was ranked number nine in 1952, number seven in 1953, and number thirteen in 1954. By this time, she had been teaching in the physical education department of Lincoln University in Jefferson, Missouri. She had become very dissatisfied and discouraged about her attempts to continue a tennis career. Feeling that she was a disappointment to the many people and institutions who had helped her almost all of her life, she toyed with the idea of getting married and putting tennis behind her. When that idea did not work out, she actively sought to join the Army's Women's Auxiliary Corp (WAC). What saved her was an invitation from the State Department to make a tour of Southeast Asia with a tennis team. It is interesting to note that the tour was conceived shortly after Emmett Till, a black northern youth visiting the South, allegedly "eyed" a white woman and was murdered. This event reached international proportions in the press. Gibson was "prepped" by the State Department about some questions that might be asked and to remember that she was representing her country. The Asians were very receptive and seemingly proud of her.

The tour was over in January 1956 and Gibson went on to play tournaments in

Stockholm, Germany, and Egypt. By this time, she had won sixteen out of eighteen tournaments and should have been a cinch to win at Wimbledon. Before Wimbledon, though, Gibson became the first black to win the French Open title. With that triumph under her belt, she arrived in London. She lost to Shirley Fry at Wimbledon and lost again to Fry at Forest Hills. Some newspapers were starting to call her a "has been."

But Althea Gibson didn't give up; she continued with international tours and in 1957 the USLTA paid her way to Wimbledon. Everything began to fit into place. Gibson won the Wimbledon title, beating Darlene Hard of San Diego—and she became the first black international champion tennis had ever seen. After winning the women's singles for that tennis crown, she teamed up with Darlene Hard and won the women's doubles at Wimbledon. The next year, 1958, Gibson returned to Wimbledon and won the women's singles and, teaming up with Maria Bueno of Brazil, she won the women's doubles. Upon returning to America in September, she won the women's singles final at Forest Hills, beating her old adversary, Louise Brough, in straight sets.

The paddle tennis queen of 143rd Street in Harlem, U.S.A., was presented with the Wimbledon cup by the Queen of England. In the United States, then-Vice-President Richard M. Nixon shook her hand and presented her with flowers; President Dwight D. Eisenhower wrote his congratulations.

Althea Gibson went on to become a women's golf champion and a member of the New Jersey Boxing Commission. She is now director of a large recreational park and camp in New Jersey. Althea Gibson was inducted into the International Tennis Hall of Fame in 1971. She more than lived up to the dreams that were expected of her.

Darlene Hard congratulates Althea Gibson on her 1957 Wimbledon victory.

Arthur Ashe

Arthur Ashe is without doubt the most promising player in the world and the biggest single threat to our Davis Cup supremacy. —Harry Hopman, coach of the Australian Davis Cup Team

I don't see how he can miss. He has the speed, the power, the agility, and the relaxed attitude about the game necessary to go all the way. He has the strokes and is not the nervous type. —Vic Seixas

Arthur Ashe

Arthur Ashe was born in Richmond, Virginia, on July 10, 1943. When he was six years old, his mother died and his father, a city parks department employee, raised Arthur and his brother by himself. At age seven, with a borrowed racket, Ashe began to play tennis and it became the consuming interest in his life. Unable to play on the well-manicured public lawns for "whites only," he was shunted off to the less favorable public courts for blacks which were a long distance from his home. When he was about ten, he became a member of a local black tennis club, the Richmond Racquet Club.

It was while playing at the club that he was "discovered" by Dr. R. W. Johnson, the Lynchburg, Virginia, physician who had undertaken the early training of Althea Gibson. Dr. Johnson placed Ashe in a group of young hopefuls he coached and trained. The first thing he did was to replace Ashe's racket with one more in keeping with his size. Dr. Johnson noted that the lad learned quickly and he saw a championship future ahead. Ashe went to the semifinals in the under-fifteen division in 1958. He won the Junior Indoors singles title in 1960 and 1961.

Richard Hudlin, former captain of the tennis team of the University of Chicago and at the time of his meeting with Ashe a tennis official in St. Louis, was so impressed by Ashe's prowess that he invited him to live with him and play tennis in St. Louis during his senior year. Since Althea Gibson's breakthrough, desegregation in tennis tournaments had taken place, allowing Ashe to pit his skills against some of the best-trained players in the nation. By the time he was eighteen, the USLTA ranked him number twenty-eight.

Among the many tennis scholarships he was offered, Ashe accepted the one from UCLA. The warm California climate would allow him year-round playing time under the excellent coaching of J. D. Morgan and, very importantly to Ashe, he was far removed from the still seething and simmering racial tensions in Richmond. His idol, Poncho Gonzales, a former champion, also lived nearby. Under J. D. Morgan's direction, Ashe moved up in USLTA's rankings from twenty-eight to eighteen, from eighteen to six, then from six to two.

In his long climb to the top, Ashe's first victory was in the United States Amateur Championship tournament at the Longwood Cricket Club in Brookline, Massachusetts. He won the United States Amateur title. In 1963, while a student at UCLA, he was the first American black to be named to the Davis Cup team.

Then it was on to the United States Open at Forest Hills. It was now 1968 and this was the first time that first-year tennis amateurs and pros were permitted to play in the same tournaments. Ashe, a shy, quiet, introspective, young man, didn't feel he had enough to win. And, fooling even himself, he won by defeating Tom Okker of the Netherlands. Ashe became the first American male to win the United States National title since 1955 and the first black man ever.

By the end of 1968, he had won a total of thirty matches in a row and was rated the top tennis player in the country.

When Ashe requested a South African visa to compete in the South African Open tournament, that country, devoted to the segregation principles of apartheid, denied Ashe's request. South Africa was punished for its outrageous racial policies by being barred from participation in the 1970 Davis Cup competition. Ashe won the Australian Open title that same year.

Ashe's biggest victory was in 1975, when he defeated Jimmy Connors in four sets for the Wimbledon men's singles title. He was the first black man to win that esteemed crown.

Arthur Ashe retired from competition in 1979 after undergoing quadruple bypass surgery after a massive heart attack. On September 7, 1980, he was named captain of the United States Davis Cup team and, as a result, has reached the highest administrative position in international tennis. Ashe says, "When I was a kid, three entities in tennis meant a lot to me: Forest Hills, Poncho Gonzalez, and the Davis Cup. I always wanted to be captain, but I never canvassed for the job. . . ." His priority as team

Arthur Ashe celebrating his 1975 Wimbledon triumph.

captain is "to field the best teams that represent the United States. I'll talk to everyone I consider bona fide contenders for the team."

This is an extraordinary breakthrough for blacks in the field of tennis. Perhaps the impact will affect blacks in other sports fields on the administrative level.

To the black youth of America, Ashe has put forth a provocative and perhaps controversial statement:

We have been on the same roads—sports and entertainment—too long. We need to pull over, fill up at the library, and speed away to Congress and the Supreme Court, the unions and the business world.   —New York *Times,* 1979

Index

Italicized page numbers refer to photographs